T0335139

THE FIFTY YEARS
THAT CHANGED
CHINESE RELIGION

1898–1948

Cover illustration: "Buddhist Monks Expel the Demon of Superstition". Translation of the text on the image: "The combined force of the knife of discipline and the stick of meditation." Source: *Feng Zikai manhua quanji* 豐子愷漫畫全集 (Beijing: Jinghua chubanshe, 1999), p. 681.

The Fifty Years
That Changed
Chinese Religion

1898–1948

Paul R. Katz and

Vincent Goossaert

Asia Past & Present

Published by the Association for Asian Studies.
Asia Past & Present: New Research from AAS, Number 15

The Association for Asian Studies (AAS)

Formed in 1941, the Association for Asian Studies (AAS)—the largest society of its kind, with over 6,500 members worldwide—is a scholarly, non-political, non-profit professional association open to all persons interested in Asia. For further information, please visit www.asianstudies.org.

©2021 by the Association for Asian Studies, Inc.

All Rights Reserved. Written permission must be secured to use or reproduce any part of this book.

Published by Association for Asian Studies, Inc.
825 Victors Way, Suite 310, Ann Arbor, MI 48108 USA

Library of Congress Cataloging-in-Publication Data

Names: Katz, Paul R., 1961– author. | Goossaert, Vincent, author.
Title: The fifty years that changed Chinese religion, 1898–1948 / Paul R. Katz and Vincent Goossaert.
Description: Ann Arbor, MI : Association for Asian Studies, [2021] | Series: Asia past & present ; number 15 | Includes bibliographical references. | Summary: "In recent years, both scholars and the general public have become increasingly fascinated by the role of religion in modern Chinese life. However, the bulk of attention has been devoted to changes caused by the repression of the Maoist era and subsequent religious revival. The Fifty Years That Changed Chinese Religion breaks new ground by systematically demonstrating that equally important transformative processes occurred during the period covering the last decade of the Qing dynasty and the entire Republican period. Focusing on Shanghai and Zhejiang, this book delves in depth into the real-life workings of social structures, religious practices and personal commitments as they evolved during this period of wrenching changes. At the same time, it goes further than the existing literature in terms of theoretical models and comparative perspectives, notably with other Asian countries such as Korea and Japan"— Provided by publisher.
Identifiers: LCCN 2020053985 | ISBN 9780924304965 (paperback)
Subjects: LCSH: China—Religion—19th century. | China—Religion—20th century. | Shanghai Region (China)--Religion--19th century. | Shanghai Region (China)—Religion—20th century. | Zhejiang Sheng (China)—Religion—19th century. | Zhejiang Sheng (China)—Religion—20th century.
Classification: LCC BL1801 .K38 2021 | DDC 200.951/09041—dc23
LC record available at https://lccn.loc.gov/2020053985

CONTENTS

Acknowledgments

We are very grateful to Academia Sinica for funding the international Thematic Research Project "1898–1948: 50 Years that Changed Chinese Religions" in 2011–2013 (AS-100-TP-C03), of which this book is a synthesis.

Introduction

The main goal of this book is to assess processes of change that shaped the fate of Chinese religions during the last decade of the Qing and the entire Republican era. We frame this time of change between two highly symbolic dates separated by fifty years: 1898, when the Hundred Days Reform movement first launched, among many other things, the appropriation of countless Chinese temples;[1] and 1948, the eve of the establishment of the Communist regime. Historians of literature, arts, political thought, and other areas of Chinese culture have vividly shown how creative this period was in shaping Chinese modernity and creating the society in which we now live,[2] and scholars of religion are rapidly following suit. In this book, we endeavor to place religion at the core of understanding modern Chinese history by assessing three forms of change: (1) mutations of communal structures of religion, (2) the innovative production of religious knowledge, and (3) new types of elite religiosity. The first of these analytical frameworks is macrosocial and looks at the entirety of Chinese communal life in both rural and urban areas. The second focuses on smaller institutions, in this case religious publishing houses and the associations that supported them, while the third deals with individuals. These three frameworks are united by a common research agenda, which is to trace the ways in which the vast religious resources (texts, expertise, symbolical capital, material wealth, etc.) that circulated throughout Chinese society during the late imperial period were reconfigured in ways that led to new social formations during the modern era.

State of the Field

Religion was long completely absent from the historiography of modern China, particularly from the story of its chaotic transformations from the last decades of the empire to 1949. This has dramatically changed around 2000 for a variety of reasons, including an interest in religion in the contemporary Chinese world, spurred by a spectacular revival that elicited questions as to its historical roots, as well as a massive increase in the available documentation due to large projects that are reprinting primary sources and providing better accessibility to archival collections.

Several important publications stand out in this new historiographic trend, all of which have served as a foundation for our own work.[3] Some books focus specifically on the social and political dynamics of the Republican period and how they affected religious practices. Particularly noteworthy are Rebecca Nedostup's work on the Nanjing regime's religious policies and their impact in the Nanjing and surrounding areas and Poon Shuk-wah's work on the transformation of religion in Guangzhou.[4] In addition, several larger surveys have attempted to build a broader narrative of continued transformations throughout the period. David A. Palmer and Vincent Goossaert's *The Religious Question in Modern China* devoted about half its story to the first half of the twentieth century, arguing that while it witnessed great destruction and anti-superstition movements on an unprecedented scale it also saw equally impressive religious creativity and new developments.[5] The 2015 two-volume *Modern Chinese Religion*, which includes many essays by the above-mentioned authors, started with the mid-nineteenth century and attempted to place religion and other value systems (the economy, art, science, and politics) in a common framework to see how they shaped the Chinese culture and society we see today.[6]

Two types of religious organization have attracted the lion's share of scholarly attention in this recent surge of interest in religion during the first half of the twentieth century: Buddhism and redemptive societies (*jiushi tuanti* 救世團體). The interest in Buddhism came earlier, notably with the landmark 1968 work by Holmes Welch, *The Buddhist Revival in China*, which showed that, far from the conventional narrative of decline, Chinese Buddhism was bursting with vitality and innovation throughout this period.[7] A new wave of young scholars has been reopening the trail, reading through the enormous production of Buddhist journals, books, and essays and exploring the trajectories and social impact of Buddhist figures beyond the iconic but hardly representative reformer Taixu 太虛 (1890–1947).[8]

Interest in, and indeed awareness of "redemptive societies" came later, initially triggered by Prasenjit Duara, who coined the term in 2003.[9] Since then a group of scholars in Taiwan, Hong Kong, Europe, and North America has shown both their numerical importance and their intellectual and political impact throughout the Republican period and beyond. As recent research has begun to show, redemptive societies helped contribute to a reconfiguration of Chinese religious life during the Republican era.[10] Research by David Ownby and other scholars reveals that during this period of flux and instability these groups attracted large numbers of adherents due to their ability to voice lay salvationist ideals that had flourished in China for centuries in the so-called sectarian traditions that operated independently of more established religious movements like Buddhism and Daoism. In addition, redemptive societies gained notoriety for their emphasis on proper moral conduct, acceptance of all major world religions, engagement in philanthropic activities, and the practice of spirit-writing rituals (generally referred to as *fuji* 扶乩, *fuluan* 扶鸞, or *feiluan* 飛鸞).[11] Scholars are now only beginning to appreciate the extent to which these movements challenged conventional dichotomies, such as elite/popular or institutionalized/diffused, due to their national organization, hierarchical structure, systematized doctrine, and canon formation. Redemptive societies also call into question the traditional/modern dichotomy due to their commitment to a "new civilizational discourse" embracing Asian solutions to the problems of the modern world, as well as their attempts to define self-cultivation practices (including meditation, the martial arts, and healing) as fitting the categories of both "religion" and "science."[12] Some of the largest and best organized of these societies gained legitimacy by being allowed to register with the state from 1912 to 1949, including the Society of the Way (Daoyuan 道院), the Fellowship of Goodness (Tongshanshe 同善社), the Universal Morality Society (Wanguo daodehui 萬國道德會), the Teachings of the Abiding Principle (Zailijiao 在理教), and the Way of Pervading Unity (Yiguandao 一貫道). We will see all these traditions at work throughout our book while we consistently attempt to place them in the larger picture of complex and fluid religious arenas.

Based on this understanding of the field, we organized a Thematic Project, funded by an Academia Sinica grant from 2011 to 2013, which aimed to develop a deeper understanding of the religious transformations at work during that crucial period.[13] The members of this project worked on various aspects of the three dimensions outlined above, and the results were published in an edited volume.[14] This provided a wealth of data and insights that have fed our analysis and informed an important part of this book.

Thus, while it is based on recent scholarship, this book aims to break new ground in three ways. First, it focuses on one region: Shanghai 上海 and the neighboring central-coastal areas, comprising Jiangnan 江南 plus Wenzhou 溫州 to its south. This regional focus allows for a more fine-grained and contextualized description of the changes at work, as we see to what extent a shared political framework played out differently in very different local religious cultures and social ecologies throughout the Chinese world. Second, there is a more sustained comparison with other countries such as Japan or Korea. Third, a more systematic analytical framework makes the Chinese trajectory of religious modernization more open to cross-cultural comparison and discussion on terms that are not simply copied and pasted from scholarship on the West.

At this point, a couple of caveats are in order having to do with place and time. In terms of place, Jiangnan's was just one of many regional religious systems, and, while a preponderance of previous research has focused on Jiangnan and the Southeast, increasing amounts of data are being collected for other regions. For the North China Plain (Hebei, Henan, Shandong, Shanxi), as well as Shaanxi, Gansu, and Manchuria, new research suggests that sometimes anti-superstition campaigns had a greater impact there (although variations at the local level were as important as those between regions), including on temple cults and the mammoth pilgrimages and festivals of Taishan 泰山 and Bixia yuanjun 碧霞元君. At the same time, however, redemptive societies and other devotional groups played increasingly important roles in local religious life, often taking the place of temples and their festivals. Buddhist and Daoist specialists participated actively in ritual events, albeit in ways that differed from their counterparts in Jiangnan and the Southeast. In addition, the significance of spirit-mediums and their rituals is gaining increasing attention, as is the place of non-Han (Mongol and Manchu) religious traditions. There seems to have been some resemblance to Jiangnan as well, particularly in terms of cities like Beijing serving as key nodes of religious publishing and urban elites taking part in a wide range of religious activities.[15] In Southwest China, and especially in areas that were home to non-Han peoples, temple destruction campaigns seem to have been far less effective, while policies aimed at reforming religious life tended to enjoy only limited success, and then mainly in cities. With the exception of major urban centers like Chengdu 成都 and Chongqing 重慶, this region seems to have been less active in religious publishing. As for southwestern religious elites, we know relatively little about their lives, although some founded redemptive societies and spirit-writing groups.[16]

Concepts and Methods

In imperial times, a wide range of religious groups (Buddhist, Daoist, Confucian, so-called sectarian movements, temple cults, etc.) interacted and competed with each other while also facing occasional suppression campaigns by the Chinese state. In contrast, the modern era witnessed graver challenges due to the unprecedented impact of modern western values and organizational modes, especially those linked to Christianity; this impact went far beyond the mere number of converts (which by the Republican period was not very high). While traditional elites (particularly the rural gentry) had tended to be hostile toward Christianity during the late imperial era, this was not the case with much of modern China's elite, which was largely composed of civil and military officials, as well as merchants and urban professionals.[17] As a result, Christianity exerted a profound influence on many facets of Chinese social life. One of the most obvious impacts was in education, with almost half of Republican China's institutions of higher learning being run by Christian organizations, the leaders of which viewed traditional temple cults as one of the leading obstacles to their efforts. In addition, Christian elites launched new forms of religious publishing while also using the mass media to support their proselytizing enterprises, and their efforts were emulated by non-Christian elites in part inspired by their late imperial predecessors, who had printed large numbers of morality books and other religious texts. Finally, Christian groups regularly founded hospitals and initiated other forms of modern philanthropy. As in the case of religious publishing, non-Christian elites quickly learned to copy such efforts while also drawing on indigenous forms of these practices.[18]

One of Christianity's most significant influences on modern China was in the conceptual realm. During the latter half of the nineteenth century, western and Christian ideas of modern religion, and even the term *religion* itself (*zongjiao* 宗教), spread to China from Japan as part of the gradual adoption of modern social science categories.[19] China's own field of religious studies (*zongjiaoxue* 宗教學) was in large part molded by the Christian impact.[20] As a result, by the end of the Qing dynasty many Chinese elites began to adopt western definitions of religion as part and parcel of their vision of a modern Chinese nation while also viewing indigenous religious traditions as "superstition" (*mixin* 迷信) and one of the main factors underlying China's decline. Many of these elites were also influenced by western ideas of secularization (which eventually came to be called *shisuhua* 世俗化).[21] There are legitimate reasons for caution about applying the concept of secularization to China, especially because many definitions treat secularization as a historical process of the modern West by which the religious system loses its dominance over communal life. Such a conceptualization may not be fully applicable in the case of Chinese history, however, since religion has continuously interacted with a range of other subsystems from ancient times to the present day, including commercial, philanthropic, and political ones. As we will see, some modern Chinese elites strove to rid China of religion altogether, while others advocated relagating religion to its own unique sphere, which would be severed from yet also closely regulated by the state. In the end, however, Chinese religious culture did not "secularize" in the same way it did in the West (even if some of China's modern elites wished for this to happen), with religion continuing to have potential legal and political importance in ways that are rarely seen in the West, both during the Republican period and up to the present day.[22]

For the reasons discussed above, this volume does not inscribe itself within a paradigm of secularization, although it does observe that various processes of secularization (often partial, sometimes reversible) were at work during the period under study. Theoreticians of secularization often propose to distinguish three levels: macro (religions and politics), meso (religion in social groups), and micro (religion in individual lives).[23] At the macrolevel, while the Republican state's secular policies did provoke a deep reconfiguration of state-religion relationships, the two realms of religion and politics did not become separated, as the government continued to be closely involved in the management of clerical institutions and the definition of orthodox versus superstitious practices and organizations. At the mesolevel, certain social groups began to differentiate between their religious and secular identities and activities, but there again it was often a matter of appearance as much as substance. Consider, for instance, the charities that registered with the authorities in purely nonreligious terms but continued to work for their core members as vibrant devotional communities or the guilds that confined their cultic activities to grassroots branches while at a higher level acting as purely secular chambers of commerce and professional associations. Last but not least, at the microlevel, our chapters on elite religiosity show that, for at least some members of the commercial, cultural, and political elites, religious worldviews continued to be at the core of their vision of how China should modernize. For all these reasons, we confine the concept of secularization to the description of discrete, specific mutations, in those cases where it appears relevant, without using it as part of a larger analytical framework.

The other dominant paradigm in the social-scientific analysis of religion in the modern world, and China in particular, is the rational choice theory of religious markets.[24] We have not found it useful in the present volume, even though we fully admit that in some sectors of Republican period China markets for religious goods were fully developed.[25] Prior to the early twentieth century, access to religious services was intensively regulated precisely so as to limit competition, and this is especially well documented in the east-central part of China on which this volume focuses.[26] While it is true that the secular policies of the Republican state encouraged and developed competition in markets, choices by groups and individuals tended to continue to follow, to an important extent, the logic of a division of religious labor. Many religious choices continued to be collective rather than individual. Accordingly, market theories can only go so far in explaining the nature of the religious changes we see at work during the 1898–1948 period.

Of far greater interest is what Peter Van der Veer calls the religion-spirituality-secularity triangle in which, under the impact of the encounter with the West but in very different ways in different societies, local traditions were reconfigured, thereby inventing religions and spiritual traditions as well as secularity.[27] Among other virtues, this approach allows us to see how the same global situation (that of "imperial encounters" with the West) led to very different outcomes in different Asian (and other) countries. Van der Veer's focus is on comparing China and India, but in such an endeavor other East Asian countries, notably Japan, Korea, and Vietnam, should also be brought into the picture, and we have attempted such a comparison at various junctures in this volume. Let us just note here that concepts (including, religion, superstition, and secularization), legal models for managing religion, and institutional forms for reviving religion circulated intensively between these countries and between colonial regimes and sovereign countries throughout the period considered. And yet very different choices were made: the Japanese model of separating a civil religion (state Shinto 神道) from congregational religions was considered but rejected in China while religious aspects of a national identity invented in counterreaction to colonial rule in Korea and Vietnam had no equivalent in China.

Van der Veer's analytical framework of the religion-spirituality-secularity triangle also meshes with what Robert P. Weller describes as "religionization," namely, "the development of religion as an institutionally and ideologically independent formation."[28] (Goossaert and Palmer refer to this as the "Christian-secular normative model.")[29] As noted above, modern Chinese elites whose worldviews had been molded by Christian views of religious life strove to construct a new religious landscape that conformed to western and especially Protestant mores. The result of these processes was that Chinese religious movements wishing to be deemed worthy of state support, or at least tolerance, came to be conceived of as voluntary associations possessing shared scriptural and other textual traditions that were led by trained specialists who had received at least a modicum of modern education. Accordingly, while religion could be allowed to exist, the actual freedom to practice religion would only be extended to groups that could rebrand themselves according to the criteria deemed necessary for China to become a modern secular society. Those groups that did not adhere to such criteria were to be labeled "superstition" (also a western neologism) and subject to state suppression.[30] In short, the modern Chinese state's mission of governing based on western ideas of secularization impelled Chinese religious groups to redefine themselves in ways that the authorities could accept and attempt to regulate due to the fact that any separation of "church and state" could only prove viable if "religion" was accepted as a legitimate category distinct from other political and social entities. As Weller aptly puts it, "Secularization as a state project thus requires religionization."[31]

In the face of these challenges, if not outright threats, Chinese religious organizations could hardly afford to be idle, and many did take the initiative in responding. One example of these processes was attempts by indigenous groups to copy the Christians by forming their own national associations, which would work to counter state suppression while also promoting religious publishing and philanthropic projects, with the Buddhists proving the most successful.[32] It is these processes of response combined with innovation that are the subject of this book.

Structure of the Book

This book draws on a wide range of sources (local gazetteers, archives, newspaper accounts, religious literature, etc.) in order to trace the evolution, both quantitative and qualitative, of Chinese religious life. It is organized in three parts that correspond to the three dimensions of religious change we have identified: communal organization, religious knowledge, and individual religiosity. Each part is made up of a chapter outlining the larger issues and a case study.

Part 1—"Communal Organization"—explores how numerous Chinese temples and their extravagant festival cultures ended up being gradually (though with considerable local variations) reduced to ruins while also considering following qualitative questions. What changes occurred in temples and their ritual functions? What was lost and what was preserved and why? Who were the key actors in these processes of historical transformation? Chapter 1 retraces the main stages of the policies that marked the increasingly brutal state intervention in temples, notably the appropriation of buildings, endowments, and other temple property and their diversion to other uses. While the history of these laws and policies has been elucidated by earlier scholars, our aim here is to quantify their effects and determine how they played out, both along the 1898–1948 chronological arc and in the geographic continuum from large cities to suburban areas, small towns, and the countryside. This sheds new light on the social response to top-down policies according to local factors, based on detailed sets of data, in Shanghai and the Wenzhou region. Chapter 2 looks precisely at the mammoth festivals and processions (*saihui* 賽會) that local temples organized either on their own or within higher-order alliances throughout the Jiangnan region. These festivals were a key part of the local constructions of territory and thus came into conflict with the expanding local state. We argue that the religious policies deployed during the period extending from the late Qing to the 1930s affected different kinds of festivals in diverging ways, with pilgrimages not much impacted but territorial festivals declining rapidly, especially in the larger cities.

Part 2—"Religious Knowledge"—reveals that even as communal religious life was coming under extreme duress, and in a novel development related to this process, urban religious centers recycled the religious cultures of the temples that were being destroyed and transformed them into new forms of knowledge, most notably in the form of new books and periodicals, as well as other forms of mass media. Indeed, recent reprints of vast collections, as well as Republican era catalogs, afford us a hitherto unknown mass of tens of thousands of religious books and journals published during our fifty-year period. To gain a better view of the whole field of religious publishing (rather than focusing on one religion), chapter 3 deals with one major (indeed, the dominant) publication center: Shanghai. This chapter centers on the following questions. Who wrote, edited, or reprinted these works? Which texts did they choose and why? What prices did these works sell for, and who were their intended and actual audiences? What networks of production and distribution facilitated their transmission, and what innovations in content and/or form characterized them? Chapter 4 focuses on one important genre of religious publication that cuts across many denominational barriers: morality books (*shanshu* 善書). Numerous Shanghai presses published thousands of such books, some from the imperial era and others newly composed to propose religious worldviews and ethics adapted to the changing conditions of modern China. Indeed, we find a stark contrast among them, from bleak warnings that postimperial, westernized China was in its final moral decline and would soon be annihilated by angry gods to utopian visions of progress that provided religious justifications for Nationalist social projects. And yet, rather than opposing these visions as belonging to different worlds, we see them mixed in the same series and collections, showing the complex interplay of religious ideas old and new in cosmopolitan and yet still enchanted cities such as Shanghai.

The first two parts of this book look at the macrolevel where people participated in communal forms of religion and took part in religious culture through reading and writing. In contrast, Part 3—"Individual Religiosity"—focuses on a narrower but crucial category of people: urban elites (defined as all those who held an elected or meaningful political or military position or a directorship of a large civil body) who, through positions of power in urban city governments or influence through charities, educational boards, and chambers of commerce, called the shots in urban management right up to Communist takeover and the creation of the People's Republic of China (PRC). Traditional scholarship has held that these people were modernist and therefore secularist. Modernist they may have been, but the case studies in this book show that they engaged in spirit-writing, converted to a wide range of religions (including the newly emerging redemptive societies), engaged in self-cultivation regimens, and so forth. For many of these people, creating a modern urban China could entail curtailing and otherwise regulating local communal devotion, but certainly did not mean ushering in a totally soulless culture. One particularly important question is when, why, and to what extent local elites shifted from participation in local communal religious institutions (mostly temple committees) to other types of religious engagement such as running charities, organizing religious publishing enterprises, and participating in new forms of religious self-cultivation. Chapter 5 starts from the religious lives of late Qing elites to develop a new analytical model that allows us to think about their engagements and practices in more fruitful ways than using concepts such as "belief." It identifies two key factors, level of commitment and knowledge of religion (as practiced by others), and then charts them on a graph that allows us to place individuals and group them in coherent types. This graph, when used to chart Republican period elites, shows an evolution not of less commitment to religion but rather of less understanding (and thus tolerance) of nonelite forms of religion. Finally, chapter 6 applies this model to some selected individuals, notably Shanghai-based elites such as the famous businessman, philanthropist, and artist

Wang Yiting 王一亭 (1867–1938), to show how much religion was present in their lives but in ways that differed from the patterns that had characterized previous generations.

Taken as a whole, this book qualifies as a regional study of modernization, but, more innovatively, it is a regional study of *religious* modernization. It attempts to map the transformation of the Chinese religious landscape in Jiangnan and Wenzhou from the late Qing through the Republican era, in terms of both discourse and practice. As we shall see, the reformation of Chinese religious life did not result in an inexorable march toward modernity. Despite the fact that the state and those elites who supported its mission aggressively promoted secularist projects, Chinese communities were never fully secularized.[33]

PART 1

COMMUNAL
ORGANIZATION

CHAPTER 1

THE TRANSFORMATION
OF TEMPLE CULTS

This chapter examines temple destruction campaigns in China from 1898 to 1948, including the tearing down of temple buildings or their conversion into schools or other nonreligious edifices, the confiscation of temple lands, and the criminalization of their ritual activities and the specialists who participated in them.[1] It is divided into three sections. The first provides a critical overview of the different campaigns that targeted temples and other forms of traditional religious life. These included the "build schools with temple property" (*miaochan xingxue* 廟產興學), "eradicating superstitions" (*pochu mixin* 破除迷信), and "rectifying customs" (*fengsu gailiang* 風俗改良) campaigns, which lasted during the entire time period covered by this book (albeit varying significantly by region). There are also some data on related undertakings such as the New Culture Movement (Xin wenhua yundong 新文化運動) of the 1910s and 1920s and the New Life Movement (Xin shenghuo yundong 新生活運動), which lasted from 1934 to 1949 in China and was revived in Taiwan in the 1960s. The second part of the chapter considers the roles played by different actors who supported or opposed these campaigns, as well as the outbreaks of resistance their efforts could provoke. The third assesses the effects of these campaigns in the Jiangnan region. We know that during this period China's central, regional, and local governments frequently labeled temples and their rituals (especially festivals) as forms of "superstition" and launched campaigns to both seize their property and assert the state's authority over communal society. Some of these temple cults have reemerged since the 1980s, yet the extent to which these facets of communal religion were destroyed during the fifty years covered by this book makes a vital difference in explaining their revival or lack thereof. In this chapter, we utilize archival data, newspaper articles, and other primary sources to assess the ways in which China's temple cults strove to adapt to the challenges of this era. We look more specifically at festivals in chapter 2.[2]

As Thomas David DuBois notes in his recent study of temple cults, Chinese religion is essentially a "religion of place," with rituals performed as means of both representing and constructing family and/or communal identities.[3] For China's modern era, one particularly striking phenomenon is how changes in communal religious life could vary by location. Accordingly, our research has endeavored to reassess the relationship between processes of modernization and urbanization, on the one hand, and religious transformations on the other. This attention to human geography and its rapid evolution allows us to avoid the pitfall of the schematic urban versus rural dichotomy, which works as a trope in many source texts but in reality dissolves into a more complex continuum linking villages to market towns and county seats all the way up to the major metropolises (chief of which in this study is Shanghai). The data on modern communal religion presented below reveal how temple destruction and the curtailing of festivals occurred later and to a lesser degree the farther one went down this scale. At the same time, however, enhanced means of transportations allowed people to travel increasingly easily between these levels. This was also the case for religious knowledge, with change at one level affecting the others (see chapters 3 and 4), while the locations where elites resided might also influence their religious lives (chapters 5 and 6).

The question of spatial differences is of critical importance to research on this topic because the "eradicating superstitions" and "rectifying customs" campaigns appear to have been centered on cities and large market towns while the "build schools with temple property" movement was undertaken throughout China, including in cities, towns, and villages. At this point, the largest amounts of primary source data about temple destruction campaigns (especially archives and newspapers reports) have been collected for major metropolises such as Beijing, Nanjing, Shanghai, and Hangzhou 杭州.[4] Should one choose to look beyond such cities, however, a very different picture emerges. One of the most thought-provoking investigations of these issues has been undertaken by Poon Shuk-wah 潘淑華 in her recent article on the ancestral temple (*zumiao* 祖廟) of the Dragon Mother (Longmu 龍母), located in the market town of Yuecheng 悅城 (Deqing 德慶 County, Guangdong 廣東). Despite the fact that this cult and its festival were subjected to constant and vehement attacks by modern intellectuals in Guangzhou 廣州 (often being derided as a "vulgar custom" or *louxi* 陋習), the town's officials and local elites had far more ambiguous feelings, as they were torn between the pressures of political correctness and the need for economic development. Moreover, the anti-superstition drives organized by Guangzhou's officials and elites did not spell the end of religious life for urban dwellers, as many citizens took advantage of new transportation networks to visit sacred sites in nearby towns and villages.[5] While the representativeness of Poon's case study has yet to be fully ascertained, the data she collected suggest that, while the rural-urban divide seems quite vivid in much elite discourse, religious activities provided one important link between cities and the countryside. Urban dwellers may not have wished to trade in their modern material culture for a rustic one, but the numerous temples that survived in towns and rural areas remained integral components of their spiritual lives.

Overview

Before the waning years of the Qing dynasty (1644–1911), the Chinese imperial state endeavored to control local society and culture through a combination of coercive and persuasive policies that were essentially a utopian project intended to enforce a top-down cosmic moral order.[6] The court possessed a strong commitment to ritual practice, with the emperor's authority deriving in large part from sacrifices to imperial ancestors and nature spirits that only he and his officials could worship. In theory at least, commoners' sacrifices could only be made to their ancestors, the local territorial god, the unruly dead, and the stove god, with exceptions to be made for the worthy.[7] The state also attempted to regulate Buddhist and Daoist clergies,[8] while launching suppression campaigns against so-called sectarian religions and brotherhood associations, particularly groups that openly espoused millenarian ideologies possessing the potential to overthrow the established order.[9] Such campaigns were eventually directed at Christians as well, including a blanket ban during the mid-Qing (ca. 1723–1840), with occasional repression of unlicensed churches continuing into the twentieth century and up to the present day.[10] As for communal religious traditions, while the state had the authority to label unsanctioned temple cults as "illegitimate/illegal sacrifices" (yinsi 淫祀),[11] it could also co-opt popular deities and include them in official registers of sacrifice (sidian 祀典), which meant annual offerings and occasionally state-funded temples. Temple cults that the state chose to support were generally perceived as adhering to "orthodox" or "Confucian" ideals and practices (including making meat offerings to the gods) that the state promoted in order to "standardize" local religion and "superscribe" its agendas onto local society.[12] The state generally followed a five-part strategy in dealing with temple cults, which encompassed absorption, patronage, acceptance, tolerance, and suppression, with the success or failure of these efforts varying depending on their strength in a particular region at a certain point in time.[13]

These policies and procedures underwent a dramatic shift during the Republican era in large part due to the adoption of the western distinction between "religion" and "superstition." As a result, the authorities proved willing to recognize the legitimacy of groups conforming to the western/Christian category of "religion," especially those possessing elites able to found organizations that could negotiate with the state, while also doing their utmost to eliminate religious phenomena belonging to the "superstition" category.[14] This meant that many cults venerating deities that had originally been approved or simply tolerated were now targeted for state suppression.[15] The resulting temple destruction campaigns, led by officials like Minister of the Interior Xue Dubi 薛篤弼 (1890–1973) and educators like Tai Shuangqiu 邰爽秋 (1896–1976), were undergirded by a wide range of laws, including the "Regulations for Registering Temples" (*Simiao dengji tiaoli* 寺廟登記條例, 1928), "Regulations for Managing Temples" (*Simiao guanli tiaoli* 寺廟管理條例, 1929, which replaced the "Regulations for Overseeing Temples" (*Jiandu simiao tiaoli* 監督寺廟條例, enacted earlier in 1929).[16] Perhaps the most influential of all was the "Standards to Determine Temples to Be Destroyed and Maintained" (*Shenci cunfei biaozhun* 神祠存廢標準, enacted in November 1928), which divided temples into four categories. The first two types of temples, dedicated to "former sages" (*xianzhe* 先哲) and deities of the five state-recognized religions (Buddhism, Daoism, Catholicism, Protestantism, and Islam), were to be preserved. The latter two, namely, temples for the worship of "ancient deities" (*gushen* 古神) and those placed in the traditional category of "illicit/improper shrines" (*yinci* 淫祠), were to be eradicated.[17] Regulations were also enacted to eliminate divination and geomancy (e.g., the *Feichu bushi xingxiang wuxi kanyu banfa* 廢除卜筮星相巫覡堪輿辦法, 1928), as well as the manufacture and sale of ritual items deemed "superstitious" (*Qudi jingying mixin wupin banfa* 取締經營迷信物品辦法, 1929). While actual enforcement of these rules varied considerably by place and time, they nonetheless exerted immense pressure on many forms of Chinese religious life.[18]

At the same time, the Nationalist regime also launched an active and widespread program to reform local customs. According to a lengthy manifesto entitled "The Significance of and Methods for Destroying Superstitions," published in 1929, temple destruction campaigns had links to policies such as the adoption of the western calendar (also one form of "rectifying customs"), promoting literacy, and launching propaganda campaigns with catchy slogans to attract popular attention.[19] Some of these efforts ranged from the sublime to the ridiculous. For example, one set of regulations about door gods (*menshen* 門神) enacted by the Fujian provincial authorities in 1935 strongly objected to the use of the term *deity* (*shen* 神) but proved willing to allow its continued use as long as the paintings of door gods were limited to historical exemplars such as Yue Fei 岳飛 (1103–42), Wen Tianxiang 文天祥 (1236–83), and Qi Jiguang 戚繼光 (1528–88), all of which was meant to achieve the goals not only of eradicating superstition but also of "cultivating nationalist consciousness" (*peiyang minzu yishi* 培養民族意識).[20]

In addition, considerable among between these movements occurred. Research by Zheng Guo 鄭國 reveals that activists promoting "eradicating superstitions" campaigns also viewed one of their goals as "rectifying customs," while those in favor of the latter campaign classified "build schools with temple property" as a form of "rectifying temples" (*miaoyu gailiang* 廟宇改良).[21] Tai Shuangqiu and those officials and activists who supported his cause also viewed the eradication of all superstitions as an integral component of the "build schools with temple property" campaign. Such forms of overlap should not cause us to overlook qualitative differences in all three campaigns, however. In general, "build schools with temple property" campaigns tended to be largely peaceful regardless of whether they were undertaken in urban or rural areas. Anti-superstition campaigns often proved to be more violent and largely urban in nature, in part because they attracted the support of a younger generation of students inspired by revolutionary ideology. As for customs reform movements, these covered the broadest range of social and cultural phenomena (etiquette, marital and mortuary rites, geomancy, etc.), meaning that religion was only one of many goals they espoused and one not always at the top of their list of priorities. However, it is essential to recognize that the one common denominator linking all three of these movements was the vital importance of temples as both material and symbolic resources.[22]

The fact that these policies were enacted with particular energy in the 1920s and 1930s may be due in part to the urgency China's leadership felt in the face of numerous threats, be they immediate or impending, real or imagined.[23] Such threats included warlord armies, peasant uprisings, criminal elements, Communist guerrillas, and especially Japanese imperialist encroachments. There were also long-term quests for cultural reform dating back to the May Fourth Movement (Wusi yundong 五四運動) of 1919, most notably the above-mentioned New Culture Movement, which, in addition to advocating the adoption of western models of democracy and science (the so-called Mr. Democracy [De xiansheng 德先生] and Mr. Science [Sai xiansheng 賽先生]) also emphasized the rejection of superstition as one of its core values. Some intellectuals called for the widespread adoption of western culture, arguing that traditional culture was an obstacle preventing China's successful modernization. Such views were highly prevalent but by no means universal or unchallenged. Other intellectuals advocated the study of Chinese history and traditional culture, while others undertook research on Chinese folklore.[24] For its part, the Kuomintang (KMT) state attempted to find a middle ground between these two positions while also promoting policies such as the New Life Movement, which attempted to use traditional "Confucian" values and the "Three Principles of the People" (Sanmin zhuyi 三民主義) as a way to maintain social stability and unify popular support. These ideals had a strong impact on the temple destruction policies of the Republican era, especially those linked to the "eradicating superstitions" and "rectifying customs" campaigns, including the "Standards to Determine Temples to Be Destroyed and Maintained."[25]

In general, while some campaigns proved effective in and around China's larger cities, the enforcement of the regulations described above appears to have been largely irregular and inconsistent.[26] Even in major urban centers like Guangzhou, some schools still contained altars or shrines for the worship of deities taken from the temples they had occupied or with which they shared space.[27] As we will see below and in our book's next chapter, the situation proved to be highly dynamic in the Jiangnan region. In Shanghai, for example, some temples and their festivals were able not only to survive but even to flourish amid the heat of some of the most strident campaigns.[28] Other regulations, such as those governing "superstitious" items, were put on hold in Jiangsu and Zhejiang due to fears about the impact they would have on religious businesses.[29] Official reluctance to follow through on temple destruction campaigns was compounded in the face of organized and at times impassioned outbreaks of resistance.

Change and Continuity

Underlying the temple destruction campaigns described in this chapter were discursive changes that can be traced back to the waning years of the Qing dynasty. They continued throughout the Republican era, particularly with the advent of new labels for religious phenomena based on western (and Christian) categorizations such as "religion" and "superstition." Such concepts, as well as legal and institutional models for managing religion and innovative attempts at religious reform, circulated extensively among Asian nations during the modern era, thereby constituting a promising variable for cross-cultural comparisons. Of particular interest is Peter Van der Veer's work on the ways in which one global phenomenon ("imperial encounters" with the West) led to very different outcomes throughout the region as political leaders attempted to reconfigure their traditions and invent new forms of religious life alongside the processes of inventing secularity.[30] While a sustained comparative analysis is outside the ambit of this volume, we would note here that many Asian forms of nationalism drew extensively on indigenous religious traditions. One well-known example is Japan's establishment of state Shinto 神道 as a civil religion.[31] Islam attained a similar status in postcolonial nations such as Indonesia and Malaysia.[32] In contrast, large numbers of Chinese elites engaged in the wholesale rejection of their religious heritage, one result being that the public face of Chinese nationalism was largely devoid of such elements. For example, the Japanese model of establishing a civil religion was considered but rejected in early Republican China.[33] While religious elements of a national identity invented as a counterreaction to colonial rule flourished throughout the region (one notable example being Vietnam),[34] few such equivalents can be found in China. The case of Korea seems somewhat similar to that of China. During the late nineteenth and early twentieth centuries, many progressive elites there also converted to Christianity. Viewing traditional religious beliefs and practices as leading factors in the nation's decline, they organized their own "anti-superstition" campaigns in order to extirpate them.[35]

This new terminology helped inspire the first "build schools with temple property" campaign, which was initiated by leading elites like Zhang Zhidong 張之洞 (1837–1909) and Zhang Taiyan 章太炎 (1869–1936), and, in a different spirit, pushed into policy in 1898 by reformers like Kang Youwei 康有為 (1858–1927), who once complained, "Foreigners come in our temples, take photographs of the idols, show these photographs to each other, and laugh."[36] However, data culled from newspapers like *Shenbao* 申報 suggest that many new terms, including superstition and reform (*gailiang* 改良), did not become widespread until the Republican era.[37] One work of Christian authorship, the *Comprehensive Writings for Eradicating Superstition* (*Pochu mixin quanshu* 破除迷信全書, 1929), employs this new term "superstition" to cover a veritable catch-all of religious phenomena, namely, a combination of traditional and modern categories such as geomancy (*fengshui* 風水), divination (*bushi* 卜筮), physiognomy (*kanxiang* 看相), attaining Buddhahood (*chengfo* 成佛) or immortality (*chengxian* 成仙), and so on. The most striking of these categories may be "heterodox movements and practices" (*zuodao* 左道), which covers not only sectarian movements but also festivals (*yingshen saihui* 迎神賽會), pilgrimages (*chaoshan lifo* 朝山禮佛), and exorcistic Nuo rituals (*xiangren Nuo* 鄉人儺).[38]

Be that as it may, however, not all the concepts adopted in modern discourses about religion had a negative impact on temples and temple cults. Some elite authors, including such notables as Gu Jiegang 顧頡剛 (1893–1980), viewed religion as a form of "folklore" (*minsu* 民俗) meriting both study and protection.[39] Other elites argued in favor of designating China's most venerable temples as historical monuments (*guji* 古蹟, a traditional term in its own right), with their statues and other ritual artifacts meriting protection as cultural artifacts (*wenwu baohu* 文物保護; the term *wenwu* 文物 is a traditional one as well).[40] Republican era archives are full of regulations about both monuments and artifacts,[41] while even those officials and elites who most stridently advocated temple destruction campaigns conceded that some temples and their ritual items deserved to be preserved.[42] Such terminology, along with its underlying agendas, seems strikingly similar to that used in current campaigns to protect religion as a form of intangible cultural heritage (*feiwuzhi wenhua yichan* 非物質文化遺產).

Finally, it is essential to note that the temple destruction campaigns of the late Qing and Republican eras exhibited considerable historical continuity in terms of both discourse and practice. This is because these campaigns can be analyzed as one phase of a centuries-long contest over the control of religious authority and resources, one that has extended into the present day. As for terms like superstition, while they represented neologisms taken from the West via Japan, they could also be used alongside traditional labels applied to religious traditions deemed unacceptable, most notably "illicit cults."[43] The work of Sarah Schneewind is especially instructive in this regard. One common slogan during the late imperial era was "destroying illicit shrines in order to erect community schools" (*hui yinci li shexue* 毀淫祠立社學), and such campaigns resembled those of the Republican era in featuring attacks on sacred sites. In just one example, one district magistrate of Kunshan 崑(昆)山 named Yang Ziqi 楊子奇 (1458–1513) earned praise for turning 110 Buddhist and Daoist monasteries into schools, yet such campaigns also sparked numerous acts of both passive and violent resistance.[44] Even the "Standards to Determine Temples to Be Destroyed and Maintained" featured its own mix of tradition and modernity, on the one hand advocating a new manifestation of Chinese religious life inspired by the West and on the other citing historical figures like Ximen Bao 西門豹 (fl. 446–396 BCE) and Tang Bin 湯斌 (1607–87) as paradigms of reformist officials who were effective in eradicating temple cults. Moreover, the editors of the "Standards" retained the traditional term illicit shrines while attempting to broaden its scope to encompass all manner of temple cults that did not fit the modern category of "religion," including those that had once belonged to the imperially approved register of sacrifices.[45]

Some facets of these campaigns seem unique to the modern age, however. Apart from the realm of terminology, as seen in the form of new labels like "religion" and "superstition," significant changes may be found in the nature of those individuals and organizations that took part in the campaigns, with many new actors appearing on the scene. As Vincent Goossaert's research has shown, the late Qing and Republican eras witnessed a shift from a model in which Buddhist and Daoist officials helped the state manage the local religious scene to one in which new administrative organs (especially the Ministry of Education, local civil affairs bureaus, and the police) were placed in charge, with the members of such organizations having less knowledge of religious affairs than their predecessors did.[46] To make matters even more complicated, during the first half of the twentieth century China was ruled by a combination of governments, including not only the Beiyang and KMT but also the Chinese Communist Party (CCP) and the Japanese.

Of equal if not even greater significance was the advent of the party-state. While government agencies such as the Ministry of the Interior (Neizhengbu 內政部) and social affairs bureaus (Shehuiju 社會局) took charge of formulating many of the policies discussed in this chapter,[47] their actual implementation was often done hand in hand with KMT party cadres and other activists, especially at the local level.[48] Much of the best data on this phenomenon come from the KMT power base of Jiangsu province, where the capital city of Nanjing was located.[49] Relations among party cadres, local officials, and nonparty elites were not always harmonious, however, and could spark tensions or even acts of violence when the latter groups opposed temple destruction policies (see below). Such instances of resistance, which clearly merit consideration in the larger context of the links between state and society,[50] occurred sporadically during the late Qing and Republican eras and ranged in nature from editorials and other critical writings to lawsuits and even violent actions such as tearing down new schools and thrashing the officials and activists who had helped build them.[51]

Another change involved the age of those individuals who proposed and attempted to carry out temple destruction policies, many of whom students or recent graduates of modern western schools.[52] Their ranks included some highly educated Buddhist monks and nuns, as well as lay Buddhists, who, while strongly opposing attempts to expropriate or destroy Buddhist monasteries, were far less sympathetic to local temple cults.[53] Students (and at times their mentors) were at the vanguard of many of the most violent temple destruction efforts, including one 1929 campaign in Xiaoshan 蕭山 County (northern Zhejiang near Hangzhou) that targeted its City God temples.[54]

Christianity and especially Christian activists also played key roles in these campaigns. The wholesale destruction of communal religious traditions embraced by Sun Yat-sen 孫逸仙 (Sun Zhongshan 孫中山, 1866–1925) appears to have been rooted in Chinese Christian iconoclastic movements,[55] while the Christian warlord Feng Yuxiang 馮玉祥 (1882–1948, also a patron of Xue Dubi) gained considerable renown for his efforts to extirpate "superstition" during the 1920s and 1930s.[56] Many ideals underlying modern China's temple destruction campaigns found expression in Christian periodicals such as *Xinghua* 興華,[57] while the preface of the 1929 *Pochu mixin quanshu,* mentioned above, edited and compiled by two leading Methodists named Li Ganchen 李幹忱 and Luo Yunyan 羅運炎 (1890–1938?), also expressed clear Christian agendas.[58]

A final group of actors whose roles have only recently begun to be fully appreciated consisted of women practitioners. A number of documents from 1929 preserved in the Buddhist periodical *Sound of the Tide* (*Haichaoyin* 海潮音) expressed the state's profound uneasiness over religious activities undertaken by Buddhist nuns and laywomen.[59] Such concerns dated back to imperial times, with Goossaert's recent research on the *Shenbao* and other late Qing sources vividly documenting all manner of bans (or at least attempted bans) on women practicing at temples (especially nunneries) and taking part in religious processions as penitents (sometimes in the nude). It is also quite striking that many of the Shanghai and Hangzhou temples that were turned into schools during the late Qing were in fact Buddhist nunneries.[60] Many religious women refused to go quietly into the night, however, and did not hesitate to take part in or even lead resistance efforts against temple destruction campaigns.[61]

While state and sympathetic elites could work together in their efforts to extirpate temple cults,[62] the fact that so many different actors were competing for control over their plentiful economic and symbolic resources resulted in interactions among national officials, local officials, and party activists that were often marked by friction and in some cases even outright violence. Such tensions were often most intense outside the big cities, usually in county seats and market towns where elites tended to maintain closer ties to traditional religious activities. He Zhiming's 何志明 study of the 1928 "eradicating superstition" campaigns in Yancheng 鹽城 County (Jiangsu) reveals that they were marked by an uneasy alliance between provincial government officials from the Department of Civil Affairs (Minzhengting 民政廳) and cadres from the county party offices (Xiandangbu 縣黨部).[63] Another example took place in Gaoyou 高郵 County (also in Jiangsu), where anti-superstition campaigns during the 1930s were wracked with discord between party and local officials.[64] In other instances, including the Yancheng campaign mentioned above, the local citizenry would wreak its wrath on KMT party offices, new schools that had once been temples, and/or government offices.[65]

Some of the best organized and most effective yet highly selective acts of resistance to temple destruction campaigns were led by renowned Buddhist elites such as Wang Yiting 王一亭 (1867–1938; see chapter 6), who during the late 1920s and early 1930s successfully persuaded Chiang Kai-shek 蔣介石 (Jiang Zhongzheng 蔣中正, 1887–1975) to not implement many of the harshest regulations in Buddhist institutions.[66] In September 1931, Wang and other members of the Buddhist elite composed a powerful rebuttal against intellectuals who supported temple destruction campaigns. Their arguments involved a harsh critique of that era's national crisis, which they blamed on a flawed educational system that placed too much emphasis on western values like materialism and utilitarianism while "abandoning traditional morals" (*biqi jiuyou daode* 鄙棄舊有道德). The solution to this crisis, they maintained, lay in the adoption by China's educational system of Buddhist doctrine, which was viewed as "a limitless and beneficial medicine (*wushang liangyao* 無上良藥) and the supreme means of cultivating morality."[67] Wang and his fellow Buddhist elites often proved able to persuade the state to accept their arguments, as can be seen in a number of decisions by the Ministry of the Interior and other government organizations to delay the implementation of laws advocating the destruction or expropriation of temples while also protecting their artifacts.[68] These elites also took the lead in filing petitions and/or lawsuits, which happened in 1929 when workers seized control of the Iron Mountain Monastery in Beijing. After a three-year lawsuit, the courts ruled in the temple's favor, and its properties were restored.[69]

Other key elites were those who led redemptive societies. While they may not necessarily have been directly impacted by the temple destruction campaigns described in this chapter, their writings expressed profound concern about how the state's attempts to regulate temples and festivals might influence the future of Chinese religious life as a whole.[70] One recent study by Yau Chi-on 游子安 reveals that, in contrast to the general decline of communal temples, sacred sites belonging to voluntary religious groups found ways to survive and even flourish during these trying times, developing in new settings such as large cities and overseas. His analysis of the Daoyuan 道院 (one of the most successful redemptive societies of the 1920s and 1930s) shows that its branches in Hong Kong and Singapore enjoyed a period of rapid expansion in large part due to the "conversion" of a preexisting and active network of spirit-writing halls, itself typical of the Daoist-oriented elite groups that flourished in the Cantonese world (and other places) during the late Qing and beyond. Yau's work also suggests that while redemptive societies are often understood to be a new phenomenon of the Republican period their links to sacred sites need to be analyzed in the context of the long-term continuity and adaptation of elite religious groups and the temples they patronized.[71] One example is discussed in chapter 6, which describes how an association led by Wang Yiting helped restore a Daoist temple in Nanjing.

Assessing the Impact of Temple Destruction Campaigns

The differing and at times conflicting agendas embraced by different actors in modern China's temple destruction campaigns lie at the heart of another key issue, namely, the extent to which these campaigns were actually enforced. When considering the impact of temple destruction movements, one needs to distinguish between campaigns aimed at utilizing a portion of temple properties for other uses and those that resulted in a temple's utter destruction. The original goal of the "build schools with temple property" movement, as articulated by Zhang Zhidong in his "Essay Advocating [the Construction of] Schools" (*Quanxue pian* 勸學篇), stipulated that at most 70 percent of a temple's assets were to be used for this purpose with the rest left in the hands of those specialists who owned or resided at the temple. Other campaigns focused on extracting revenue from temples via taxes and fees.[72] Such nuances are also reflected in a second slogan used in the course of such movements, namely, "destroy temples and found schools" (*huimiao banxue* 毀廟辦學). The distinction between "build schools with temple property" and "destroy temples and found schools" was hardly a rigid one, and they could be used interchangeably in some contexts, yet many people did distinguish between the two. Even activist educators like Tai Shuangqiu and the officials who promulgated such laws as the "Regulations for Overseeing Temples" tended to favor using temples and their resources for education without utterly demolishing them. Moreover, they were not always able to successfully expropriate resources from Buddhist temples, especially those backed by patrons who were members of the elite with the will and means to resist these campaigns. Thus, despite the fact that in 1930 the Shanghai city government recommended that all temple properties under its jurisdiction be confiscated for educational uses, such policies were never effectively implemented.[73]

There were also differences in the targets of various temple destruction campaigns. For example, movements aimed at turning temples into schools had to focus on those religious establishments possessing sufficient resources for such a purpose, especially the monastic centers and large communal temples.[74] By the Republican era, temples that had once been state cult sites were also being transformed into schools, since many had ample resources on a par with (or even exceeding) those belonging to other temples, but local residents rarely worshipped on their premises and were thus much less likely to intercede on their behalf.[75] In addition, wealthy Buddhist monasteries and nunneries were often leading targets of these campaigns, but once Buddhism proved able to successfully define itself as a "religion" meriting state protection, activists tended to turn their attention to local temple cults.[76] In contrast, many sacred sites that were targeted during anti-superstition campaigns tended to be smaller shrines with little property and far fewer backers.[77] It is also necessary to differentiate between destroying temples and their statues and banning festivals, which is discussed in chapter 2.

Another key issue that has yet to be adequately addressed is how temple destruction campaigns influenced the lives and careers of religious specialists. These men and women were certainly targets of discourses aimed at reforming or eradicating aspects of Chinese religious life, with texts like "The Significance of and Methods for Destroying Superstitions" criticizing both specialists and the rituals they performed.[78] In general, it seems that religious specialists tended to come out on the losing side of struggles against the state.[79] In one example from 1930s Guangzhou, the local authorities engaged in vigorous efforts to outlaw the practices of ritual specialists known as "at-home Daoist masters" (*huoju daoshi* 火居道士) due to the fact that they were viewed as "superstitious." The local Daoist association (managed by celibate, monastic Daoists) offered no support, prompting the Daoist masters to form their own ad hoc association and petition the government to recognize them as real Daoists, citing as evidence the fact that they had been licensed by the Heavenly Master at the leading Daoist sacred site in the city, the Xuanmiao Guan 玄妙觀. Regrettably, this temple had been converted into a school after 1912, meaning that one of these Daoists' main forms of legitimacy and protection had disappeared.[80]

Scholars are now starting to examine the actual impact of temple destruction campaigns in modern China, but the limited amounts of data collected to date make it difficult to advance any definitive conclusions. However, at present it does appear that such policies tended to be more strictly enforced in areas near centers of political authority, where the state had more authority to wield its will over religious life. For example, in Dingxian 定縣 (central Hebei 河北) the number of active temples belonging to a cluster of 62 villages dropped from 432 in 1900 to just 116 in 1915. In Changli 昌黎 County (northern Hebei), 34 of 42 temples possessing landed endowments had these assets expropriated by 1933, with 17 becoming the property of the village government and 17 being converted to schools. Whether these temples were completely destroyed or simply forced to share some of their space and funding has yet to be determined. In Liangxiang 良鄉 County (near Beijing), most temples were turned into schools and all their lands confiscated by village assemblies by 1923.[81] Research by Liu Xun 劉迅 and Mei Li 梅莉 reveals that in Nanyang 南陽 (Henan) the Xuanmiao Guan 玄妙觀 and its affiliated temples had accumulated approximately 77 *qing* 頃 of farmland prior to 1911 (1 *qing* = 6.7 hectares). However, during the first year following the birth of the Republic this temple suffered the loss of nearly half its lands, much of which was utilized as part of an endowment for new educational agencies and schools. By 1949, its remaining land holdings had shrunk to barely 20 *mu* 畝 (1 *mu* = 1/15 of a hectare or 1/6 of an acre) due to state expropriation, private takeovers, illicit pawning, and overall mismanagement.[82] This hardly means that temple cults had disappeared from the scene, however. Temple surveys undertaken in 1941–48 by Willem A. Grootaers (1911–99) and a Fu-jen University research team that included Li Shih-yu 李世瑜 and Wang Fu-shih 王輔世 revealed an average of between 4.2 and 6.5 temples per village in Xuanhua 宣化 and Wanquan 萬全, while the surveys of Sidney D. Gamble (1890–1968) in the early 1930s found a total of 38 temples in 6 Hebei "sample villages," with 15 in one village alone.[83]

Temple destruction campaigns seem to have been less effective in other areas, especially those on the edge of the state's span of control or where power resided in the hands of lineage organizations and ascriptive temple cults.[84] One example is the treaty port of Wenzhou, with Lo Shih-chieh 羅士傑's doctoral dissertation convincingly demonstrating that these policies caused considerable disruption to local cults and festivals but ended up doing little to change the ways in which Wenzhou natives worshipped their deities.[85] As was the case in much of China, the campaigns began in earnest during the early 1900s, with reformist officials attempting to turn local temples into schools and even imposing new taxes (such as one on oranges) in order to help pay for them, all of which only served to augment tensions between the Qing state and local society.[86] One of Wenzhou's first temple destruction campaigns took place just south of Wenzhou City, where the local magistrate, assisted by sympathetic or at least sycophantic local elites, transformed four local temples from the official register of sacrifices into the first new-style schools in the county.[87] One of these elites, who also provided support for subsequent anti-superstition campaigns, was none other than the prestigious late Qing literatus Sun Yirang 孫詒讓 (1848–1908), who also inspired a younger generation of western-educated students to commit themselves to the causes of reform and modernization.[88] Other activists attempted to ban official worship of state cult deities such as Confucius, Guandi 關帝, and Yue Fei 岳飛 while also transforming state temples dedicated to Confucius (the Wenmiao 文廟) into Sun Yat-sen memorial shrines.[89]

Qi Gang 祁剛's research provides an invaluable view of what happened to temples in Wenzhou during the late Qing, a period that marked the first phase of the destruction process. Based on his detailed database of schools and temples, built using both published and archival materials, Qi shows that for the period covering 1896–1908 a wide variety of edifices could be turned into modern schools. In Wenzhou Prefecture, of the 126 buildings that were converted into new-style schools, just over one-third (47 or 37.3 percent) were temples and a larger number (52 or 41.2 percent) were lineage halls (zongci 宗祠). Another 11 (8.7 percent) were old-style schools (shuyuan 書院, xueshu 學塾) while the remainder consisted of yamen offices and private residences. In contrast, the neighboring prefecture of Chuzhou 處州 had the following rates for new schools: 38 temples (46.9 percent), 20 lineage halls (24.6 percent), 15 old-style schools (18.6 percent), and 8 yamens/private residences (9.8 percent). The diverse fates of temples are even more striking when one considers data at the county level. In Ruian 瑞安 and Pingyang 平陽, for example, the figures for temples converted into schools are 14 (56 percent) and 18 (58 percent), much higher than for lineage halls, at 9 (36 percent) and 11 (35.4 percent). A very different picture emerges for Yongjia 永嘉 and Yueqing 樂清, with only 7 (19.4 percent) and 8 (29.6 percent) temples turned into schools, as opposed to the 17 (47.2 percent) and 15 (55.5 percent) lineage halls that suffered such a fate. Qi's analysis suggests that temples were more likely to survive in places where they enjoyed strong elite support, where lineages lacked the ability to turn their halls into schools, and where state funding proved insufficient to effectively undertake temple destruction campaigns.[90] In addition, Lo Shih-chieh shows that Nationalist efforts to clamp down on City God temples were less than successful, with ideas of good governance incarnated in the City God thriving despite criticism by Republican officials.[91] In one instance, despite the fact that the Wenzhou City God's statue was destroyed in 1928, the temple's festival was held as planned.[92]

Wenzhou resembled other areas of China in that students took the lead in attempting to reform communal religious traditions, often with the assistance of KMT party leaders. One example took place in Yueqing County in 1928, where a local Nationalist cadre named Chou Yuesan 仇約三 led a group of students to express their commitment to the creation of a new modern culture by organizing a "deity-demolishing troupe" (daoshen tuan 搗神團) with the express goal of smashing temples and the statues of deities housed within. In one instance, this troupe even took one temple's statues of horses back to their school to rebuild as athletic equipment while using the bell from a local Buddhist monastery for their school's clock.[93] And again, as had happened in other parts of China, such campaigns sparked an array of resistance tactics, including posting anonymous poems accusing officials and/or party members of corruption, telling stories about those who had taken part in the campaigns dying sudden and horrible deaths, bribing the police to look the other way, insisting on holding festivals even when the relevant temples and/or statues had been destroyed, and tearing down the new schools that had been built in place of temples.[94]

Temple destruction campaigns also proved largely ineffective in Southwest China. For example, Xu Yao's 徐躍 study of late Qing Sichuan 四川 reveals that, while as many as three-quarters of the province's new schools may have been established in temples, their income rarely exceeded 50 percent of the worth of these temples' properties, meaning that coexistence rather than destruction was the norm.[95] Hundreds of Guangxi 廣西 temples survived into the twentieth century despite the devastation of years of warfare. In Guixian 貴縣, many temples may have continued to survive, as only 11 of this county's 42 new schools were built in temples from 1917 to 1932.[96] Such trends continued into the 1940s in provinces like Hubei, with Fu Haiyan's 付海晏 research on Luotian 羅田 County in eastern Hubei indicating that 207 of its 286 temples survived from 1936 to 1949.[97]

The limits of temple destruction campaigns are particularly noteworthy in parts of the Southwest that were widely populated by non-Han groups. In the Miao 苗 and Tujia 土家 areas of Western Hunan (Xiangxi 湘西), for example, only 3 out of 125 temples were destroyed in Baojing 保靖 County during the period covered by this study. In the case of Fenghuang 鳳凰 County, local temple cults continued to thrive, due in large part to the support of elites who actively invested in sacred sites due to religious devotion and the desire to accumulate symbolic capital. The first Republican era campaign against temples in Fenghuang did not take place until 1945, when the state attempted to expropriate leading sacred sites in order to build a new school (the Tuojiangzhen zhongxin xuexiao 沱江鎮中心學校). During the winter of that year, the authorities detained the abbot of one Buddhist monastery for three days and forced him to cede large portions of the temple's lands. Some were returned to the temple after an appeal to the provincial authorities, but the number of monks residing at the temple soon fell from 45 to 5, while higher prices and reduced income from fewer landholdings forced them to roam the streets asking for contributions (muhua 募化). Similar events impacted other Buddhist sites as well. Daoist temples, as well as shrines that had formerly belonged to the state cult, appear to have had less land, and in the end most of that was also returned to these temples. Many temples dedicated to local deities did not have any land at all, with resident specialists supporting themselves via textile manufacturing, fees from performing rituals, and contributions. All in all, while the 1945 campaign did have an impact on temple income and the livelihoods of its specialists, no attempt seems to have been made to utterly destroy religious structures or use all their resources for other purposes. In addition, from 1946 to 1948 the Nationalist government launched a series of campaigns to further regulate Western Hunan's temples, festivals, and specialists, but archival sources suggest that, while they proved relatively successful in urban areas, their impact in rural ones was negligible.[98]

Another striking case study may be found in early colonial Taiwan, where the Japanese appropriated 226 (12 percent) of the island's registered temples between 1895 and 1902. Of these the highest rates of appropriation involved temples being used as military barracks (69 temples or 4 percent of the total) or police stations (63 or 3 percent). Only 27 temples (just over 1 percent) were converted into schools. Moreover, many temples were returned to their ritual communities once the colonial state had consolidated its rule over Taiwan. During the Kōminka 皇民化 (Japanization) campaigns of the late 1930s and 1940s, large numbers of temples were destroyed, but these efforts varied greatly by area and were gradually discontinued as the Pacific War raged.[99]

The main exceptions to the patterns described above centered on large urban areas. Detailed information from Jiangnan is presented below, but one relevant example comes from Minhou 閩侯 County in Fuzhou 福州. Its Republican era county gazetteer lists a total of 95 temple reconstruction projects, but not one was undertaken between 1911 and 1933, which suggests that Fuzhou temples had either been expropriated or were falling into disrepair.[100] In one other instance, city government officials in Kunming 昆明 took control more than 61 temples, justifying their actions by quoting from the "Standards" as to why each seized temple (including Buddhist and Daoist ones) had not been deemed sufficiently "religious".[101] Even in major metropolises, however, temple destruction campaigns were not uniformly enforced. In Beijing, for example, while many temples were torn down, this was largely due to urban planning, not attempts to root out "superstition" (this was also the case in Hangzhou [see below]).[102] In the case of Guangzhou, while some sacred sites were confiscated (including the Huang Daxian 黃大仙 (Wong Tai Sin) temple, which was converted first into a school for girls and subsequently into an orphanage), many schools shared space with temples while preserving altars or shrines for the worship of their deities. Even when the city government confiscated temples and sold them as a means of raising revenue, the purchasers of these properties were often members of neighborhood religious communities.[103] In nearby Hong Kong, despite the fact that the colonial government passed its own set of regulations in 1928 (the *Huaren miaoyu tiaoli* 華人廟宇條例) and required 200 sacred sites to register with the authorities, only 28 temples were destroyed.[104] This suggests that foreign officials may have espoused more lenient attitudes toward Chinese temples, a phenomenon that seems to have shaped temple destruction campaigns in Shanghai as well (see below).

Despite the patterns delineated above, the number of temples throughout China did continue to decline during the Republican era. Temple destruction campaigns appear to have become more widespread and thoroughly enforced during the 1930s,[105] as was also the case for policies against festivals and other ritual activities deemed to be "superstitious."[106] Be that as it may, other factors apart from government policies appear to have contributed to this decline. The first was warfare, most notably the War of Resistance against Japan. On the one hand, devastating destruction ravaged many rural areas that had previously escaped temple destruction campaigns unscathed. At the same time, wartime needs prompted the state (and especially local governments) to be much more proactive in seizing temples and their assets, at times even going beyond the scope of central government regulations.[107] Policies enacted immediately after the war also had harsh consequences for some temples, especially those whose leaders and/or specialists stood accused of collaborationist activities.[108]

The second factor had to do with economic decline. As numerous scholars have noted, temples lay at the heart of many local economies, including various forms of gift exchange, local investment, and marketing networks.[109] Festivals and other ritual activities were also highly commercialized and could help spark economic growth.[110] On the one hand, these factors made temples and their festivals attractive targets of state expropriation and taxation policies;[111] on the other hand, temples and festivals were also highly sensitive to economic downturns. The severe deterioration of the Chinese economy during the 1930s and 1940s had a major impact on both temple cults and the elites that supported them. As remains the case today, bad years resulted in lower incomes for temples, which in turn meant delayed reconstruction projects and much smaller festivals.[112]

The Jiangnan Region

The Jiangnan region lay at the heart of the Nationalist government's sphere of control and was also a major publishing center (including religious publishing). Accordingly, this region is home to a wealth of data about local temple destruction campaigns, some of which have already been discussed. Jiangnan boasted its share of thriving temple cults, as well as mammoth festivals, but many of these had been devastated during the Taiping Civil War, while the decimation of this region's population and destruction of both private and communal property caused many cults and festivals to wither away without any form of state intervention.[113] The temple destruction campaigns enacted during the time period covered by this chapter put further pressure on communal religious life, especially in large cities.

As one would expect, some of the best (yet also highly problematic) statistical data come from the Shanghai area. The data collected to date show concentrations of sacred sites located in the northeast corner of the walled city, outside the Old Western Gate (Lao Ximen 老西門), in the Xuhui District 徐匯區 outside the

French Concession, and in the Hongkou District 虹口區. Many of these areas were not only home to large numbers of Chinese but also functioned as Shanghai's commercial centers and residential areas for urban elites. As a result, temples located in these areas might have had an easier time attracting support, but it might also have been easier for the state to monitor them during various temple destruction campaigns. The areas mentioned above were also leading destinations for people who migrated to the city, especially from Guangdong. Leading temples founded by Guangdong migrants included the Huang Daxian Guan 黃大仙觀 (located in Hongkou), the Cihang Xianguan 慈航仙觀 (also dedicated to Huang Daxian but located in Zhabei 閘北), and the Baode Lüyuan 報德律院 (also in Zhabei but a Buddhist temple built by Guangdong merchants as a place where their daughters could practice self-cultivation).[114] Some of these temples were built in the aftermath of the Taiping Civil War, although the devastation tended to impact temples outside the city walls (the Taipings did not reach the city itself and Small Swords Society [Xiaodaohui 小刀會] members do not appear to have been as iconoclastic). However, we have yet to fully determine the exact locations of Shanghai temples newly built or rebuilt after the Taiping Civil War, as well as the percentage of those that were destroyed during the fighting.[115]

Another topic with great potential for future research involves those temples located in Shanghai's foreign settlements (the French Concession and the International Settlement). In general, there appear to have been less dense concentrations of temples in these areas, and those that did exist tended to be located closer to the old city where large numbers of Chinese resided. These included the Xiafei District 霞飛區, as well as the New North Gate (Xinbeimen 新北門) and West Gate (Ximen 西門) areas of the French Concession, plus the central and western sections of Sima Road 四馬路 (also known as Fuzhou Road 福州路) and Wuma Road 五馬路 (Guangdong Road 廣東路) situated to the south of Nanjing Road 南京路. While extensive research has been done on social and cultural aspects of life in the foreign settlements, the religious lives of their residents have been largely overlooked. One particularly striking phenomenon involves the fact that, while the managers of Shanghai's foreign settlements could and did regulate temples as part of zoning policies, for example, forbidding the construction of new temples in residential areas, they largely hesitated to intervene in the affairs of Chinese temples under their jurisdiction and were not zealous about implementing the temple destruction campaigns that were being undertaken by Shanghai's Chinese elites. The relatively lax attitudes that Western officials in Shanghai exhibited toward Chinese temples merits comparison with Hong Kong, especially since temple destruction campaigns there also do not appear to have been rigorously enforced.[116]

An immense amount of data has been compiled in the *Comprehensive Overview of Shanghai Religion* (*Shanghai zongjiao tonglan* 上海宗教通覽). This work draws on archival data to show that prior to 1949 Shanghai city and its suburbs remained home to a total of 2,186 temples of various types and sizes, ranging from Buddhist and Daoist institutions to small shrines.[117] The *Overview* also contains detailed tables documenting the historical development of 1,952 temples, including 1,135 labeled "Buddhist" (*fosi* 佛寺) and 817 labeled "Daoist" (*daoguan* 道觀). These categories are utterly arbitrary, however, based mainly on the identity of each temple's principal deity. As the editors of the *Overview* noted themselves, only a few temples were formal Buddhist institutions. The deities worshipped in many so-called Buddhist temples could have been Daoist or communal gods, while the specialists who resided in them or performed rites on their premises were not necessarily members of the Buddhist monastic order (*sangha*).[118] Similar problems can be found for the "Daoist" temples, many of which were also communal temples or spirit-writing centers and some of which were probably managed by redemptive societies. Regardless of how they were labeled by the state, a sizable percentage of these sacred sites were in fact communal temples (or sacred sites that had once been part of the state cult), including 20 dedicated to the City God (Chenghuang 城隍), 16 to Guandi, and 6 to Tianhou 天后 (Mazu 媽祖).[119]

Data on these 1,952 Shanghai temples in the *Overview* indicate that of the above-mentioned temples a total of 339 (17.3 percent) were turned into schools, with the majority (277 or 82 percent) of these being used as elementary schools (see Figure 1.1).[120] An additional 74 temples (3.7 percent) were utilized for other purposes, including 27 turned into township government offices (*xianggongsuo* 鄉公所), 4 into hospitals, 5 into clinics, and 5 into shelters for war refugees. Only 46 temples (2.3 percent) were destroyed during wartime, far fewer than the 97 that suffered the same fate during the Taiping Civil War, while 112 others (5.7 percent) were listed using terms such as abandoned (*fei* 廢), ceased to function (*ting* 停), or occupied (*zhan* 佔). In all, 571 temples (29.2 percent of the total) suffered some form of destruction and/or appropriation during the late Qing and Republican eras.

The statistical evidence in the *Overview* merely provides a rough sketch of the destruction campaigns, however, as the processes of attempting to wipe out urban sacred sites could be both highly complex and tied to intricate networks of power. This was the case with the Abbey of Sagely Longevity (Shousheng An 壽聖庵), a highly popular Buddhist sacred site founded in 1861 and patronized by Huzhou 湖州 elites, including members of an organization they founded known as the Huzhou Society (Hushe 湖社). In 1928, following the successful completion of a reconstruction project, the abbey's resident monk, Disong 諦松, asked Yang Kuihou 楊奎侯 (the Huzhou banker in charge of managing the temple) for all the contracts and other legal documents necessary to register the abbey with the authorities, only to learn that Yang had transferred control of the temple to the Huzhou Society. After repeated attempts to get the documents back,

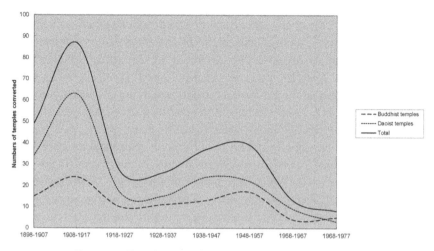

Figure 1.1. Temples turned into schools in greater Shanghai

Disong took his case to court. Legal wrangling dragged on for more than three years, accompanied by frequent accusations of corruption and other forms of malfeasance. The city and even national authorities attempted to intervene, but to no avail, and the entire incident was the subject of frequent reports in *Shenbao*. In the end the monks lost their case, and the Abbey remained in the control of Huzhou's elites until it was shut down for good in 1954.[121]

The *Overview* also tends to overlook the existence of smaller shrines built during the late Qing and Republican eras. Some of these sacred sites are listed in the "Table of Investigations on Illicit Shrines and Heterodox Sacrifices in Shanghai City" (*Shanghaishi yinci xiesi diaochabiao* 上海市淫祠邪祀調查表), compiled in 1930 during one of the city's anti-superstition campaigns. Of the 52 shrines listed in this table, a total of 38 were built during the Republican era, while 6 others date back to the reign of the Guangxu 光緒 emperor (1875–1908). None of these shrines possessed any property, and the vast majority were altars (*tan* 壇) dedicated to Lü Dongbin 呂洞賓 and Huang Daxian 黃大仙. These deities tended to be worshipped by members of spirit-writing (*fuji* 扶乩) groups, and it is possible that some of these shrines had links to redemptive societies.[122]

Shanghai was also a major center of "rectifying customs" (*fengsu gailiang* 風俗改良) campaigns, some of which focused on temples and their festivals.[123] In 1929, for example, the Shanghai city government, at the urging of the Buddhist elite Qin Xitian 秦錫田 (1861–1940), launched a campaign to forbid City God festivals. However, such rituals and the festivals that often accompanied them persisted into the 1930s, as can be seen in bans enacted as part of the New Life Movement. There were also attempts to abolish activities of specialists deemed to be "superstitious," most notably spirit-mediums, generally referred to as *shiwu* 師巫 or *taibao* 太保, albeit accompanied by a three-month grace period in order to allow these specialists sufficient time to find new lines of work.[124] The effectiveness of such policies has yet to be determined.

Temple destruction campaigns were also carried out with great alacrity in some urban areas of Zhejiang, which put the provincial government in a somewhat awkward position. On the one hand, it made numerous attempts to limit the construction of new temples or the repair of old ones. On the other, it had to respond to frequent complaints from members of the elite, especially Buddhist practitioners, about overzealous acts of destruction by young intellectuals and party activists.[125] The provincial capital of Hangzhou was the site of many temple destruction campaigns, including those conducted as part of anti-superstition or customs rectification movements. At the same time, many temples were also torn down or taxed out of existence in order to make way for major urban planning projects.[126] Temples in the market towns surrounding Hangzhou suffered grievously as well. In Tangqi 塘棲 (just north of Hangzhou), for example, twenty-five out of twenty-nine temples were slated for destruction, with only nine surviving by the 1940s.[127]

The impact of temple destruction campaigns varied significantly in other parts of Zhejiang. In 1929 officials and party activists in Shaoxing 紹興 went so far as to organize their own Committee for Building Schools with Temple Property (Miaochan xingxue weiyuanhui 廟產興學委員會), but the fruits of their efforts are as yet unclear.[128] As in Shanghai, temple destruction movements often sparked complex conflicts of interest. This was the case in Huzhou, when, during one "build schools with temple property" campaign in 1922, a local nunnery known as the Abbey of Blessings in this Lifetime (Fuchen An 福塵庵, popularly referred to as the "little temple" or *xiaomiao* 小廟) was converted into a public school and the nuns sent home. However, much of nunnery's property was not used for the school but rented out for profit. The nuns filed a complaint, and some residents petitioned the county government to have the nunnery preserved as a historical monument (*guji* 古蹟). Their petition was rejected, but the authorities did decide to evict all the illegal tenants.[129]

Some of the most controversial temple destruction campaigns, which also sparked frequent clashes, took place in and around the venerable port of Ningbo 寧波. Efforts to destroy these sacred sites commenced in 1929, when party activists, police officers, and soldiers in Ningbo, Yuyao 餘姚, and Cixi 慈谿 announced special dates for destroying deity statues and organized troupes of students to attack local temples, starting with the Palace of the Eastern Peak (Dongyuegong 東嶽宮). The participants in this onslaught, which included KMT party members, students, and members of the local chapter of the Boy Scouts (Tongzijun 童子軍), gathered in Ningbo's Sun Yat-sen Park (Zhongshan gonguan 中山公園), where they were issued small flags inscribed with the slogans "eradicate superstition" (*pochu mixin* 破除迷信) and "overthrow the idols" (*dadao ouxiang* 打倒偶像). After listening to speeches by the county magistrate, mayor, and other officials, they marched to the Palace of the Eastern Peak, where, after considerable efforts, they smashed its statues to smithereens.[130] The abuses that resulted from these campaigns, as well as the conflicts that ensued, prompted state attempts to reconcile the interested parties, but to no avail.[131] By 1931 elites concerned about the extent to which the situation had deteriorated began to publish articles pointing to the positive aspects of religious values and criticizing the wanton destruction of temples without providing viable spiritual and psychological alternatives.[132]

Four years later one of Zhejiang's most dedicated educational officials, Huang Shiling 黃式陵 (1911–51, a Hunan native who helped edit and frequently published in the *Zhejiang jiaoyu yuekan* 浙江教育月刊), wrote a five-page article describing the violence that regularly accompanied local temple destruction campaigns while also analyzing its causes and possible solutions. In this article, Huang conceded that educators had misjudged the situation and overlooked the need to work with local elites and the networks of power that undergirded their authority. He also wrote that he appreciated the need to recognize local concerns, as well as realities on the ground such as poverty and slow economic development, not to mention thorny issues such as what to do about ritual specialists who stood to lose their livelihoods. He concluded by pointing out that the entire anti-superstition movement was both a cultural and a social issue and that officials responsible for undertaking such campaigns should at least partially adapt to local conditions.[133]

Despite the fury they aroused, these campaigns seem to have enjoyed only limited success. According to the highly detailed records of temples in Yin County preserved in the Republican era edition of the *Yinxian tongzhi* 鄞縣通志, of the 517 communal temples that had existed there prior to the twentieth century only 57 had been turned into schools by 1935, with an additional 57 being used for government offices. Apart from 2 that had fallen into ruin and 6 that had been converted into private facilities such as guild halls, the remaining 391 temples (more than 75 percent of the total) had survived.[134] This indicates that, despite strenuous efforts to implement temple destruction campaigns in its political heartland of Jiangnan, the KMT had trouble effectively enforcing such policies on a long-term basis. In other parts of China, especially those located far from urban centers, temple destruction campaigns appear to have had even less impact. It many such areas, the devastation of years of warfare combined with economic deterioration proved more decisive, and CCP campaigns after 1949 often finished off what was left of local religious life.

The evidence presented here vividly indicates that the temple destruction campaigns of the late Qing and Republican eras marked a major watershed in the modern history of Chinese religions. This era witnessed new discourses used to describe temple cults, new policies of varying effectiveness designed to regulate or extirpate them, and new actors committed to achieving these goals. State cult temples, as well as large Buddhist, Daoist, and local sacred sites possessing extensive amounts of property, often bore the brunt of campaigns to turn temples into schools, while smaller shrines featuring spirit-mediums and/or spirit-writing cults were frequently targeted during temple destruction campaigns. In the face of these potentially devastating challenges, the elites, ritual specialists, and worshippers who supported temple cults chose a wide range of responses, as well as innovations, some of which proved more successful than others. Moreover, the impact of these campaigns on Chinese religious life varied significantly from one region to another and also in terms of whether temples were located major cities, county seats, market towns, or villages. In general, temple destruction campaigns tended to be more successful in large cities, but they could lead to sharp conflicts between different elite groups in county seats and proved far more difficult to enforce in market towns and villages. As a result, the Nationalist state does not seem to have been much more effective than the Qing in terms of asserting its authority over local religious life, especially when the temples and/or festivals targeted for destruction enjoyed the support of that area's political and economic elites.

CHAPTER 2

FESTIVALS IN JIANGNAN DURING THE LATE QING AND REPUBLICAN PERIODS

As the previous chapter has shown, state management of local society and religion had begun to change by the early twentieth century. Historians have noted that a late imperial model of local officials engaging with and attempting to reform local cults and customs gave way to a new model of eradicating "superstition," appropriating temples, creating a separate and controlled realm for "religions," and enforcing a top-down program of scientific progress. Yet we still know very little about how this played out in terms of communal life and how politics mixed with other factors (including socioeconomic change and urbanization) to stimulate a complex evolution in local society—a process that is still going on today.[1] One way to help clarify this evolving scenario is to examine data on large-scale temple festivals over time at specific sites.[2]

Based on a wide range of sources, and especially the very rich (and now digitized) descriptions of local festivals in newspaper reports, this chapter traces the modern history of festivals in Jiangnan. Our primary focus is on the cities of Hangzhou, Suzhou, and Shanghai, but we occasionally draw on data concerning other sites in Jiangnan by way of comparison, and we pay particular attention to the City God cult. We first provide an overview of festivals in the mid-nineteenth century based on three types of patronage: territorial cults, voluntary associations, and pilgrimage groups. After setting the scene, so to speak, we turn to a discussion of press reports pertaining to policies of the late Qing officials who tried to reshape festivals in the wake of this area's reconstruction after the widespread devastation caused by the Taiping Civil War (1851–64). We then take up policy changes that emerged following the 1898 movement to confiscate temples and the Republican period anti-superstition campaigns. All the while, we consider how local society adapted to these evolving policies while trying to maintain its communal festivals. Whereas the appropriation of temples began suddenly in 1898, the policies related to festivals evolved throughout the modern period, and for this reason this chapter discusses the late imperial situation at more length than the previous chapter did.

We use "festival" as an umbrella category here and define three specific types (territorial festivals, *saihui* 賽會 processions, and pilgrimages) based on emic, not etic, standards. The chapter concentrates on one particular type: festivals featuring processions of the gods and rituals in open spaces, which drew large crowds on the streets, not only from local communities but from distant sites as well. The most common term used in modern sources to denote such festivals in Jiangnan is *saihui* (other terms include *shenghui* 盛會, *chuhui* 出會, and *shenhui* 神會), and we generically call them *saihui* here. We pay much less attention to the Lunar New Year and Lantern Festival (which was to a much larger extent a family-based event) and the seventh-month Ghost Festival (which deserves a separate study, being in some cases less closely linked to temple cults than the three types of festivals introduced above), even though they were also crucial to local social life.[3]

The *saihui* are discussed in local gazetteers (*difangzhi* 地方志), anecdotes (*biji* 筆記), and works on local customs. Such sources have been used by historians from a historical-anthropological perspective to understand the place and role of festivals in local society.[4] For our present purposes, one particularly important source is *Hangsu yifeng* 杭俗遺風 (Traces of Hangzhou Customs),[5] a loving description of the city published during the Taiping Civil War against the backdrop of massive destruction caused by the fighting, as the city was taken by Taiping armies in December 1861 after a horrific three-month siege and was not retaken until March 1864, resulting in hundreds of thousands of deaths. This work provides a very detailed description of various aspects of Hangzhou culture, with its entire first section devoted to festivals. It was further annotated during the 1920s by Hong Yueru 洪岳如, who noted which aspects of the city's life had endured from the 1850s to the 1920s and which had declined or disappeared altogether.

While it provides an overall view of the city's festivals, *Hangsu yifeng*, like similar accounts of local customs, does not allow us to understand how they changed other than in the long term. Understanding short-term change requires us to look at other sources, notably newspaper reports. The *Shenbao* newspaper (1872–1949) in particular offers the advantage of continuous reporting over a period comprising the last four decades of the Qing (starting eight years after the end of the Taiping Civil War) and the entire Republican period. So far we have identified and read more than a 1,000 articles on Jiangnan's religious life, including some 350 on Hangzhou festivals. *Shenbao* articles are anonymous, but we know that during the late Qing journalists tended to be lower degree holders among whom a variety of views on religion could be found.[6] They were often hostile to exuberant popular religious practices but nonetheless evinced traditional elite forms of religiosity (on which see chapter 5), at least until the turn of the century.

Indeed, the nature of *Shenbao*'s reporting changes to a considerable extent over time. The late Qing *Shenbao*, even though it is often (but not systematically) extremely critical of local religious life, provides numerous and detailed descriptions of both festivals and their management by local officials. By contrast, after 1900 temples and festivals largely disappear from its pages, only discussed when major conflicts between local religious activists and officials broke out or major incidents occurred. On the other hand, many more newspapers of various places and religious or political persuasions offer reporting on festivals during the Republican period; we have only begun to use them here, but they provide a basis for future research. We hope the data presented below can help sketch the trajectory of festivals in the complex world of late Qing and Republican local politics in the Jiangnan area.

We argue that, due to political and social changes, certain types of festivals, notably pilgrimages (largely but not exclusively associated with Buddhism) continued to thrive while territorial processions and communal Daoist rituals sharply declined. The massive *saihui* festivals that had been a mainstay of Jiangnan local religion were targeted by large-scale efforts at repression during the last years of the Qing and the whole Republican period as part of anti-superstition policies. Based on a synthesis of what we know of *saihui* festivals during the late Qing, and on evidence from the Republican period, including newspaper reports, this chapter attempts to trace the impact of such repressive policies on the organization and ritual practices of these festivals. It identifies key aspects of the changes that festival organizers had to adopt in order to maintain these events, when they could. Such aspects included the urban or rural location of the festival and procession routes, the connection between central temples and local territorial communities, and the role of various types of religious specialists. Tracing the history of festivals thus sheds light on larger changes in the religious structure of local society as a whole. While we unfortunately do not have as yet any full-fledged case study of a Jiangnan festival and its history through the modern period, we hope this study can suggest larger trends at the macrolevel.

Festivals in Late Qing Jiangnan

In this section, we first offer a typology of this region's festivals by distinguishing the higher-order *saihui* from territorial temple festivals and pilgrimages. We then look at late Qing policies related to *saihui*, explaining the rationales behind the frequent but often ineffective bans on *saihui* by local officials throughout the region. We argue that the dominant mode of policing *saihui* was through negotiations between officials and temple leaders, which often allowed the *saihui* to take place but curbed certain aspects deemed particularly offensive (female participation, nighttime processions, etc.).

Based on descriptions found in sources such as newspapers (notably *Shenbao*) and local gazetteers, as well as other sources, we have classified Jiangnan festivals during the late Qing under three broad types as follows.[7]

Territorial Cults

Festivals of territorial (village or neighborhood) temples clearly formed the bedrock of Jiangnan social and festive life. References to territorial communities (literally all those under the authority of a given *shexia* 社下 [Earth God]), as well as their well-delimited territories (called *miaojie* 廟界, especially in the Suzhou area),[8] abound in *Shenbao* descriptions of urban life in Jiangnan cities, and always in connection with temple activities. Most temples clearly had a well-defined territory and were supported by levies on all inhabitants. The religious organization of modern Jiangnan society was characterized by a very close integration of the territorial dimension of local society and Daoist ritual.[9] For that reason, festivals of neighborhood territorial gods involved not only theater, music, banquets, and sacrifices within the temple, as well as a procession around its territory, but also a visit to higher divine authorities, either at a central Daoist temple (a City God temple, Eastern Peak temple, or the equivalent) or in an open-air space where the god engaged in a ritual of audience to Heaven, *chaoque* 朝闕 with a human impersonating the god holding an audience tablet and performing the *sangui jiukou* 三跪九叩 prosternation rite, a practice particularly well attested in Hangzhou. A journalist noted in 1896 that this was *never* forbidden by officials.[10] The close integration of territorial cults and their festivals with imperial and Daoist bureaucracy is repeatedly evidenced in reports. For instance, in 1890, when the Zhejiang governor had secured state canonization for a Hangzhou local god known as Jinhua jiangjun 金華將軍, the temple leaders went in procession to a Daoist temple to thank the Jade Emperor 玉皇大帝 and then to the Wanshougong 萬壽宮 to thank the Qing emperor before touring the temple's territory.[11]

Linked to these ritual hierarchies, local territorial gods (and their communities) had to pay homage and taxes to their superiors. One occasion when this was most visible was the famed *sanxunhui* 三巡會, the thrice-yearly festivals mandated by the state in all counties (Qingming 清明, occurring during the 3rd lunar month, the 15th day of the 7th lunar month, and the 1st day of the 10th lunar month),[12] when the City Gods traveled to the altar for vengeful spirits (*litan* 厲壇) to preside over official sacrifices intended to placate them. In Suzhou, for instance, all the city's Earth Gods came first to the City God temple and then followed the Suzhou prefectural and the three county City Gods (all based in Daoist-managed temples) to the *litan* situated near Tiger Hill (Huqiu 虎丘) and back. This is already documented for the late Ming up to the late nineteenth century; before the Taiping Civil War, more than thirty different neighborhood gods joined the procession.[13] Similar practices were common throughout Jiangnan.

Moreover, every year in the area extending broadly between Shanghai and Nanjing each local community (village and neighborhood) collected spirit-money from each household in the name of the local Earth God as a tax to Heaven (i.e., the Jade Emperor) and then brought this "tax," together with the statue of the Earth God, in procession to the local central temple (managed by Daoists and usually dedicated to the City God, the Emperor of the Eastern Peak, or the Jade Emperor) to burn the spirit-money. This ritual is called "dispatching Heavenly taxes" (*jie tianxiang* 解天餉, *jie qianliang* 解錢糧, or *jie huangqian* 解皇錢).[14] In some places, the City God went in turn to his superior (the Eastern Peak or Jade Emperor) to pay homage and remit the tax. Heavenly taxes seem to have appeared around the beginning of the seventeenth century in the area between Shanghai to the south and the Yangzi River to the north, with descriptions becoming commonplace between the eighteenth and twentieth centuries. This practice is documented by numerous anecdotes, poems, accounts in local gazetteers, and reports in the press.

The collection of Heavenly taxes was the occasion for local communities to organize one of their major festivals, complete with processions, operas, and so on. In quite a few cases the performance of large Daoist community offerings (*jiao* 醮) was organized jointly by various tax-paying communities. For instance, in Suzhou a newspaper article dated 1879 describes how all families paid to organize a citywide *jiao*, during which all participating Earth Gods came to "remit the tax" at Suzhou's central temple, the Xuanmiaoguan 玄妙觀.[15] The numerous descriptions of territorial temple festivals in the Suzhou area in the late Qing and early Republican periods show that participants first paraded around the city (be it the city center, a suburban neighborhood, or one of its townships), then went to Qionglongshan 穹窿山 (a major Daoist center on the western outskirts of Suzhou) to pay the taxes, and then returned home at night.[16] While the idea of local temples having a Daoist *jiao* offering once a year (or at less frequent intervals) to renew the alliance with the rest of the heavenly pantheon is very common throughout Jiangnan and the rest of the Chinese world, what is particularly noteworthy in the case of Suzhou is that communities traveled to a Daoist central temple for this purpose rather than inviting Daoists to their temple, thus emphasizing embedded hierarchies.

Voluntary Associations

Our second type of festival is the citywide *saihui* organized by voluntary associations. These associations operated supralocal networks, often integrating territories and other groups in higher-order structures. The festivals of the territorial cults discussed above were often also called *saihui* (because they included a procession), but we focus here on higher-order *saihui*. In many Jiangnan cities, the City God temple and its *sanxunhui* were a major locus of these associations and citywide processions. We have already mentioned the importance of these processions in Suzhou, but they are documented throughout Jiangnan and beyond. Whereas the City God temples themselves were mostly managed by officials, Daoists, and gentry organizations (such as charitable halls [*shantang* 善堂] and guilds), the processions were in the hands of yamen staff and voluntary devotional associations (which members joined with a view toward obtaining personal salvation) in coordination with territorial communities. Some Jiangnan City God temple gazetteers even provide detailed discussions of these voluntary associations.[17]

In Hangzhou, two major temple festivals built on citywide associational networks attracted the lion's share of reporting throughout the period covered here: the festivals of the Old Eastern Peak Temple (Laodongyuemiao 老東嶽廟) in a suburban neighborhood west of Hangzhou and processions featuring the deity Marshal Wen (Wen Yuanshuai 溫元帥, aka Wen Qiong 溫瓊). The first is being studied in great detail by Fang Ling.[18] The largest of several Eastern Peak temples in Hangzhou, the Laodongyuemiao organized a procession for the divine emperor's birthday (28th day of the 3rd lunar month) and an even larger festival, called "audience and judgment" (*chaoshen* 朝審) held between the 1st and 15th days of the 7th lunar month, during which hundreds of thousands of devotees came from all over Jiangnan. These devotees were all formally registered as servants of the divine emperor and were organized in a bureaucratic way to fulfill all the roles and functions of the emperor's divine administration.

The Marshal Wen cult has been explored in great detail by Paul R. Katz, who has traced its history and described celebrations in both Wenzhou and Hangzhou, showing that the god's primary role was plague fighting by controlling and expelling the demons of pestilence.[19] The two cults were very intimately connected, as Marshal Wen was a divine general under the orders of the Emperor of the Eastern Peak, and his temples were considered subordinate (*xiayuan* 下院) to Eastern Peak temples.[20] In Hangzhou, Marshal Wen's birthday was celebrated on the 18th day of the 5th lunar month, and a mammoth procession traversed the city on the 16th day of that month, with all its territorial temples (more than eighty in all) sending delegations.[21] Daoists do not feature prominently at all in descriptions of the Marshal Wen Festival, yet it clear that they managed his temple and that the cult was often embedded in a Daoist liturgical framework.

Mentioned alongside the Eastern Peak and Marshal Wen festivals, another major festive occasion in Hangzhou was the birthday of Zhenwu 真武 (Xuantian shangdi 玄天上帝, another deity at the top levels of the Daoist pantheon). This was celebrated on the 3rd day of the 3rd lunar month at his temple at Xiaoheshan

小和山, also in the western suburbs farther from downtown than the Old Eastern Peak. Apparently guilds played a prominent role in organizing the associations (*xianghui* 香會) that went to Xiaoheshan.[22]

Comparable situations could be observed in many other Jiangnan cities. For instance, in Yangzhou and other urban centers, a citywide festival honoring the Marshal [Who Patrols] All of Heaven (Dutian yuanshuai 都天元帥, the title of Zhang Xun 張巡, who was, like Marshal Wen, a local god under the authority and in close connection with the Emperor of the Eastern Peak) was the largest event of the annual ritual calendar.[23] This festival, referred to as the Dutianhui 都天會 or Dushenhui 都神會, drew under its umbrella numerous voluntary associations and territorial communities.

The social basis of these higher-order festivals was voluntary groups, of which we can distinguish two types. The first, performing groups, featuring music, theater, stilt walking, martial arts, portable floats (*taige* 台閣), and penitents,[24] generically known as "ancillary associations' (*zhuhui* 助會), were formed to participate in processions, and some joined several distinct festivals. The second group was composed of registered servants of a god (runners, ushers, secretaries, attendants, etc.) called *banhu* 班戶 (especially in Hangzhou). Those of the Old Eastern Peak temple were particularly numerous and famous, but the City God temple in Hangzhou and many other Jiangnan cities also had some.[25] Typically, a festival was organized by the *banhu,* who formed the core of the procession, followed by the ancillary associations, which added spectacle and excitement. The festivals of the Eastern Peak and Marshal Wen were so widely admired that they served as models for other such events, which imitated their elaborate bureaucratic organization and rituals.[26]

Yet another type of festival organized by voluntary groups was the nine-day prayers to Doulu 斗姥, the Mother of the Dipper, between the 1st and 9th days of the 9th lunar month (often called the Nine Emperors 九皇 Festival in honor of Doulu's nine sons, who are in charge of the seven visible stars of the Dipper 北斗 plus two other stars). Regular associations, apparently led by members of the Hangzhou upper class (rich merchants) set up altars (*doutan* 斗壇) in temples or other open spaces every year, invited Daoists to perform rituals (including a passing-the-destiny-gates [*guoguan* 過關] on the 7th day of the 9th lunar month), which attracted huge crowds. There apparently were up to thirty such celebrations in various parts of Hangzhou, with Wushan 吳山 (the hill within the walled city) being the number-one spot.[27] The Dipper associations could also organize ad hoc rituals, notably *jiao* 醮 offerings in times of fire or epidemics; in one such case, in 1895, a Dipper association put together a large-scale ritual to ward off an epidemic combined with daily Marshal Wen processions, culminating in a boat-burning rite to expel the demons of pestilence.[28]

Pilgrimages

In contrast to the neighborhood or citywide festivals, pilgrim groups coming to sacred sites traveled long distances (there were associations from far away participating in festivals such as the Laodongyue festival in Hangzhou, but they joined forces with locals). In Hangzhou, the major pilgrimage seasons (*xiangshi* 香市, around the New Year, for the first of the three Guanyin birthdays on the 19th day of the 2nd lunar month, and in the sixth month) mostly drew out-of-towners,[29] people from both the surrounding countryside and more distant cities, such as Shanghai and Suzhou, whose leaders (*xiangtou* 香頭) chartered pilgrimage boats (*xiangchuan* 香船). This is still the case today (buses having replaced the boats), with pilgrim groups touring the eight major Hangzhou temples during the New Year period (between the 1st and 15th of the 1st lunar month) being mostly comprised of villagers. Such groups tend to visit several temples (including the Quanzhen Daoist Fuxingguan 福星觀 atop Yuhuangshan 玉皇山, which emerged as a major temple during the 1870s), but the major cult was that of Guanyin centered on her temples, notably the Upper Tianzhusi 上天竺寺 (also called Faxisi 法喜寺) and the nearby Lingyinsi 靈隱寺 (both in the hills to the northwest of West Lake). A historical and anthropological study of this pilgrimage has been conducted by Yü Chün-fang.[30] Here we would like to point out that, whereas Buddhist monasteries thrived on the Jiangnan-wide pilgrimages (and were richer than Daoist and local temples), the city's own religious fabric and festive life remained closely linked to Daoist ritual.

Not all pilgrimages were predominantly Buddhist though: the other prominent pilgrimage in the Jiangnan area was centered at Maoshan 茅山 (south of Nanjing) and devoted to the cult of the San Mao *zhenjun* 三茅真君, three brothers turned immortals, whose cult has been continuously present on Maoshan since the late Han period.[31] Maoshan had been a major clerical Daoist center since medieval times, and just as the Guanyin pilgrimage in Hangzhou was based on interactions between the Buddhist monasteries and pilgrim associations, the one at Maoshan was negotiated between Daoist lineages on the mountain and local village communities, their spirit-mediums, and *baojuan* 寶卷 vernacular scriptures performers. Many localities in southern Jiangsu had their own local San Mao shrine and festival, and sent a delegation to the sacred mountain once a year during the pilgrimage season (held between the 24th of the 12th lunar month and the 18th of the 3rd lunar month). These delegations were led by *xiangtou* 香頭 who had contracts with Daoists. The term *xiangtou* refers to their role as organizers, but they could often be spirit-mediums as well. We have heard that nowadays spirit-mediums who organize pilgrimage groups are called *daxiangtou* 大香頭 and those who just do the organizing are called *xiaoxiangtou* 小香頭. Buddhist and Daoist clerics (in Maoshan, Hangzhou, and indeed the whole of Jiangnan) were organized in lineages (*fang* 房, *yuan* 院). A monastery was comprised of an alliance among several such lineages, and each lineage had accommodations for pilgrims and maintained long-term relationships with specific pilgrim associations, villages, and *xiangtou* 香頭. The major cities also hosted pilgrims, and indeed as late as 1937 Shanghai residents went in large numbers to Hangzhou, Maoshan, and a many smaller (though still very significant) pilgrimage sites.

The Politics of Festivals in the Post-Taiping Context

The politics of festivals in Jiangnan took a new turn during the post-Taiping period.[32] First, temple destruction during the war, a subsequent population decline, and the loss of corporate property by both temples and associations caused many festivals to be discontinued independent of any government intervention. Many temples took fifteen to twenty years to be properly rebuilt, and some had to wait until the late 1880s; most festivals could not resume until the temple was at least partially rebuilt. An 1876 report about a Hangzhou neighborhood temple tells us that its formerly famous festival did not take place between 1861 and 1876, when it was restored on a huge scale.[33] Key actors in the revival of festivals were the guilds, which controlled vast resources. One of the major festivals in Hangzhou, the Zhushenghui 助聖會 (organized by the Zhushengmiao 助聖廟, the main deity of which was the Tang period official Chu Suiliang 褚遂良 [596–658]), was sponsored by the powerful textile guild, which added its weight in 1887 in order to transform a lackluster festival into a major one.[34] In effect, to some extent officials tried to prevent festivals from resuming while the city's economic elites did the very opposite. Similar reports abound from other parts of Jiangnan, where guilds also proved instrumental in reviving large festivals during the late 1870s.[35]

The post-Taiping regime and high-ranking officials in Jiangnan in particular engaged in a policy of reforming local society and bringing festivals and other aspects of religious life under much tighter control than had been the case before the 1860s. The reasons for this policy were many, ranging from fear of disorder to religious condemnation of practices deemed sacrilegious. Rationales listed in the proclamations, edicts, and other official decisions banning festivals included pragmatic concerns about social order (with large vagrant populations and demobilized soldiers, as well as anti-Christian mobs, sometimes creating trouble). Beyond the mere crowd management aspects, since processions not infrequently resulted in cases of theft or accidents (horses, an important feature of the processions, sometimes panicked and hurt spectators), officials were aware that festivals could turn into large-scale protests or even riots in times of social tension. Wu Jen-shu has documented urban riots of all kinds (protests against corrupt officials, rent riots, etc.) that occurred from the sixteenth to eighteenth centuries, often during festivals, especially those dedicated to judicial deities such as the City

God and Eastern Peak.[36] In such cases, protesters considered their actions to be a just uprising against oppression and made appeals to gods that administered justice and supervised officials. Issues of public morality loomed large as well, with festivals often described by their opponents as occasions for gambing and the improper mixing of men and women. Economic issues were also mentioned, with the huge costs of festivals draining scarce resources for wasteful and useless activities and local leaders (described by officials as ruffians) forcibly collecting money in order to enrich themselves. Last but not least, officials enacting bans were also driven by religious aspirations to improve moral standards and atone for the collective sins that (in the view of many members of the elite) had brought heavenly punishments, notably in the form of the Taiping Civil War.

Of course, in theory *saihui* festivals had always been banned,[37] but in actual practice outright bans on local festivals were quite rare. Officials mostly tried to negotiate with local temple leaders by focusing on specific issues while using the threat of violence to get their way.[38] Officials and journalists alike often reminded their readers that whereas *saihui* were banned by the Qing Code, this did not apply to "spring and autumn prayers to the Earth God" (*chunqi qiubao* 春祈秋報, meaning village and neighborhood temple festivals); how to draw the line between the two was anyone's guess. An 1867 imperial edict had banned the rebuilding of nonofficial temples destroyed during the war, except the territorial temples (*shemiao* 社廟).[39] In Hangzhou, local people routinely gave the names of neighborhoods and wards to their ritual associations in order to be recognized as lower-order territorial groups celebrating their own Earth God (such groups were exempt from the law banning *saihui*) and thus bypass the bans on festivals.[40]

Furthermore, most of the major *saihui* in Jiangnan took place in and around temples that were on the official register of sacrifices (*sidian* 祀典), including the contentious Jingdeguan 旌德觀, which organized the Marshal Wen procession in Hangzhou,[41] thus blurring the distinction between "popular" and "official" religion. One prominent case was that of the City God festivals and processions,[42] but there were others as well. The mammoth rituals for the salvation of the victims of the Taiping Civil War were among the largest in 1870s, 1880s, and 1890s Hangzhou, with tens of different Buddhist and Daoist clerical troupes performing at the same time. They took place at officially sponsored shrines such as the Zhongyici 忠義祠 and with full-fledged participation by officials, yet they also featured the collection of spirit-money among the entire Hangzhou populace, which was heaped in huge piles around the temple and torched through the night—exactly the kind of practice to which officials objected.

In some cases, officials tried to ban processions outright, but pressure from local elites often forced them to reconsider and permit their staging, albeit with limitations.[43] Indeed, in most cases, officials focused on limiting certain aspects of processions rather than trying to ban an entire festival. In particular, they tried to have the opera and processions end at dusk, to curtail the participation of women (and female penitents in particular),[44] to ban gambling dens, and to limit the collection of informal taxes on all inhabitants.[45] Such negotiations on what could be recognized by all parties as an acceptable festival had one model: the City God *sanxunhui* procession, the thrice-yearly processions of the god from his temple to the *litan* and back. For instance, a Ningbo prefect banning the procession of a local god in 1884 wrote in his public proclamation that should an epidemic break out he might allow it again, but "only on a limited scale, like that allowed for the City God."[46]

City God processions have a great deal in common with processions for other gods, but in terms of regulation they were unique. Since these processions, and most notably the *sanxunhui*, were associated with an official ritual (the sacrifice at the *litan*), they could not be banned altogether. Whereas other large-scale processions in Jiangnan cities during the late Qing (such as the Marshal Wen processions in Wenzhou and Hangzhou or the Dutian 都天 processions in Yangzhou) had sometimes been suppressed (never for very long, but at least that made the threat of outright suppression credible), this was not the case for the City God. The one exception we know of is Beijing, which was much more heavily policed than other cities, and where processions were less common; an 1888 report describes a grand City God procession there organized for the first time in twenty years.[47]

So, outside of Beijing, the most extreme measures taken were to curtail the procession to the god in his sedan chair, insignia bearers, and nothing else. For instance, in 1877 the Ningbo prefect, fearing trouble because of the large numbers of demobilized troops present in the city, curtailed the third yearly procession of the two City Gods (of the prefecture and county) to this bare minimum.[48] Allowing such minimal City God processions was largely considered to be an emergency measure only. Only exceptionally committed officials attempted to curtail City God processions in the long term; in his highly confrontational tenure as Jiangsu's governor (1879-80, 1881, 1885), Tan Junpei 譚鈞培 (1828–1894), banned the Suzhou City Gods' procession from aggregating all the neighborhoods' Earth Gods, which used to accompany the deity in a massive display of local religious hierarchies and networks.[49] Thus, in spite of all the specific processional practices that they tried to fight, officials still held the City God procession as a model of acceptable popular religion—if properly managed and patrolled.

Since City God processions were linked to the state cult, late Qing local officials regulated them in much greater detail than other processions, which they often simply ignored or tried to curtail. Willingly or not, they had to come to terms with the *sanxunhui*. They did so according to their own religious interests and convictions: some let be and just performed their own prescribed part; others tried to fully reform popular practices and preside over the whole procedure. The latter efforts, echoing Ming dynasty utopian projects by local officials who attempted to take control of the entirety of local popular religion, are occasionally attested during the Qing. Lu Longqi 陸隴其 (1630–93) organized in person the City God birthday (this was not an official sacrifice) by banning operas, while requiring the local population to attend the sacrifice and subsequent reading of the Sacred Edicts.[50] But less authoritarian approaches were more common. Commenting on the Suzhou City God procession, one mid-nineteenth-century author remarked that "officials consider that this is part of the education of the masses through the gods 神道教俗, and therefore let it be done; they do not try to ban it."[51] But they did enact countless interdictions banning the aspects they found most objectionable. *Shenbao*, for instance, rarely failed to mention before each City God procession that the Shanghai magistrate had banned a number of specific practices.[52] The most frequent elements on the list were (1) female penitents, (2) self-mutilators, (3) Heavenly tax collectors, (4) people dressed up as runners for the underworld bureaucracy, and (5) various itinerant musical troupes (the reason for banning them is not explicit, but it might be related to the fact that these performers often resorted to begging or mild extortion to earn their keep). On less frequent occasions, officials insisted that the procession return to the temple and end by nightfall.[53]

One well-documented aspect of this micromanagement of processions was the 1870s and 1880s attempts by Shanghai local officials (the Shanghai magistrate, Daotai, and others) to ban female penitents from City God celebrations. Although the ban was systematically announced before each procession, there seem to have been women at each event, though sometimes so few as to suggest partial success in enforcement.[54] Officials sometimes arrested women, but they eventually released them, so the dissuasion effect was quite limited.[55]

Behind the bans on various practices in processions, such as penitents, was the question of the legality of the devotional associations that organized the processions and other celebrations. In Qing times, festivals and associations formed a large part of the gray zone of underregulated, negotiated toleration of local religious practices. According to the Qing Code, forming an association distinct from territorial or kin structures was illegal, but in practice most associations were actually tolerated. Local officials who wanted to clarify and enforce distinctions between officially tolerated associations and actively repressed ones had to resort to devices not found in law, such as recognizing and allowing "old associations 老會" in contrast to new ad hoc groups.

Reports on policies intended to curb Jiangnan festivals that appeared in *Shenbao* rarely mention local territorial temples, elite groups such as the Dipper associations, or Guanyin pilgrims. Jiangsu governor Tan Junpei strove to ban pilgrimages in 1880 and 1881, blocking the canals so that pilgrim boats from Jiangsu could not go to Hangzhou or Maoshan,[56] but this was an exceptional measure and we have not seen any evidence of sustained policies against pilgrims adopted by other officials. Before 1911, Hangzhou-based officials actually went to the Tianzhusi on Guanyin birthday celebrations, thus participating in the pilgrimage.[57]

The prime target of the policy to curb festivals in Hangzhou, as applied by a succession of Zhejiang governors, was the Marshal Wen Festival, which was banned on and off for more than three decades.[58] The story of the Marshal Wen Festival in Hangzhou fits into a more general late Qing pattern in which bans on local celebrations were usually relaxed after some time. Bans were accepted within local society as emergency measures under special circumstances but not over the long term. For instance, around 1875, Governor Yang Changjun banned all theater performances in temple festivals (following a brawl during a performance at a temple), a ban that apparently had some effect for about two years before one gentry group invited a troupe to perform in a temple, then another, and everybody quickly followed suit.[59] A common response to a ban on *saihui* was to organize them but reduce the scale.[60] Self-regulation was the rule; procession organizers themselves occasionally banned certain types of processional shows in order to avoid incidents.[61]

To sum up, late Qing officials tried to curtail the largest citywide festivals and processions but with limited success. In spite of the fiery rhetoric of some journalists opposed to any form of popular religion, one gets from the press reports the impression that large numbers of Jiangnan merchants and gentry were behind the festivals,[62] and under such conditions it was extremely difficult for officials to maintain a ban. Repeated pleas to lift bans are documented in numerous Jiangnan cities: the case of the Marshal Wen Festival in Hangzhou compares well with those of the mammoth Eastern Peak procession and festival (also called Yongchanghui 永昌會) in Ningbo and the Dushenhui festival in Yangzhou, which evolved through a similar trajectory.[63] We do not know to what extent significant (albeit certainly not unanimous) gentry support for festivals during this period was a continuation of an earlier practice or whether it reflected the specific post-Taiping context (since we do not have press reports or archival material for these earlier periods).

In any case, the common pattern during the last decades of the Qing was negotiation; in instances when a major festival coincided with a public service examination (when crowds of students were in town), a crisis (including military threats and the Boxer uprising), or a national celebration (such as mourning for a member of the imperial family), temple leaders and officials often negotiated a new date for the festival. And, during the disastrous North China famine of 1876–

79, and again in 1896–97, when calls were made to seize temple and association funds and direct them toward famine relief, many festival organizers voluntarily made donations to charities and scaled down the celebrations.

Negotiation was based on the idea that the vast majority of these festivals were legitimate; officials allowed activities within the temple (sacrifices, banquets, maybe music and theater, and rituals performed by Buddhists and Daoists, which were rarely questioned) and possibly small-scale processions with limited numbers of participants and no "ancillary associations."[64] For instance, as mentioned above, Jiangsu governor Tan Junpei could not ban the City God processions (they were part of official liturgy) but did forbid other gods to take part. On this basis, parties haggled over interpretation, margins of tolerance, and benign ignorance or over specific limits. Officials sent their runners to control festivals, but these runners typically were part of the festival organization and thus were clearly not bent on enforcing any ban. Constables under the authority of the gentry-run Baojia bureaus 保甲局 were somewhat more reliable, but not until the creation of the post-1901 new police forces was law enforcement solidly on the side of antifestival policies. Before that, officials fully determined to enforce a ban had to resort to using soldiers (themselves often organizers of their own festivals),[65] with the agreement of military officials (who were not under the direct command of same-level civil officials), and they did not do this very often.[66]

The Post-1898 Politics of Festivals

The politics of local religion changed dramatically beginning in 1898, which marked the beginning of the temple confiscation movement, and changes further accelerated after the fall of the imperial regime—as shown in the previous chapter. Festival and ritual culture in Jiangnan was affected by a whole range of anti-superstition and other policies. The history of festivals during this period has not been explored in detail, but from the scattered available evidence the overall decline of festivals (and processions in particular) is quite clear, as is the strong gradient of this decline along the rural-urban continuum.

The Xinzheng 新政 period (1901–11) introduced a number of important changes. First, at the same time as temples were beginning to be appropriated for secular uses, the assets of the devotional associations that organized the festivals were being confiscated and allocated to education and other purposes.[67] Crucially, guilds were being progressively turned into (or coming under the control of) chambers of commerce (*shanghui* 商會) and professional associations (*tonghanghui* 同行會),[68] and the portions of their income allocated to festivals (be it endowments, taxes, or levies on members) redirected toward education.[69] This is certainly the one aspect of the whole history of modern festivals that comes closest to the concept of secularization, even though serious archival work would be needed to assess the process of ritual disengagement within guilds. The issue of funding festivals was certainly debated, as we find merchant leaders on both sides (for and against festivals) as early as the 1870s and as late as the 1920s. This indeed was a gradual process, as we still see some guilds maintaining their temples in the 1920s.[70]

Another development during this crucial transition was that a growing number of local elite organizations turned against festivals and lobbied officials (and after 1909 local assemblies) to act decisively against them. We hear during these years of local activists sending telegrams all around when they witnessed *saihui* preparations under way. Not all local elites were so disposed however: for instance, when the 1909 spring festival season was opening in Wuxi and temples were organizing their "paying Heavenly taxes" rituals, educational activists mobilized against the festival while merchants rallied to defend it.[71] In any case, officials (wary of the riots that occasionally occurred when local people were prevented from organizing their festivals) were often more compromising than local reformist gentry activists; this continued to be the case during the early Republican and Nationalist periods, with anti-superstition KMT activists sometimes opposing the more tolerant (or indifferent) attitudes of local officials, who also sometimes allowed festivals so as to boost local trade.

These trends continued after 1912. The two policies that were most crucial and warrant discussion here are, first, outright bans on festivals and processions and, second, the end of official status and in many cases partial or total confiscation of the central temples that organized the higher-order *saihui*. Based on detailed descriptions of specific bans found mostly in newspaper reports, we argue that the difference between the late Qing bans on *saihui* and the Republican period bans hinged on (1) less willingness on the part of local authorities to negotiate and find a compromise that would allow some sort of *saihui* to take place and (2) a much more intense use of coercion, with armed police ready to use force to stop processions at all costs, leading to shootings and casualties. One reason for this is that such bans were not only issued by local magistrates but also by local assemblies and police authorities, who tended to be more radical in their visions of social reform. As a result, such bans, even though they carried some of the motivations and rhetoric of late Qing bans, were less detailed in what was allowed and what was not and instead of arguing about the morality of a practice rejected all processions as superstitious.

The case of the City God temples is central, as they were the locus of some of the largest processions in late Qing Jiangnan cities and figured among the key targets of anti-superstition campaigns.[72] Even though gentry organizations (such as charities and post-Taiping reconstruction bureaus or Shanhouju 善後局) increased their control over some City God temples in the post-Taiping period, thereby changing cults and practices to a significant extent, the major festivals, notably the thrice-yearly *sanxunhui*, continued much as before, mainly because they were largely organized and funded by independent groups (mostly territorial units and devotional associations, as well as guilds). The political changes that began in 1898 and accelerated with the 1911 revolution dealt a much harsher blow to these temples and their festivals. First, in some places local officials, who had hitherto been the guarantors of City God temples, even though they often delegated their management to Daoists or gentry associations, now turned against them. No longer part of the "register of sacrifices," City God temples were sometimes designated as the first targets of anti-superstition campaigns, and some local officials went to destroy the statues in person and oversee the transformation of such temples into secular institutions as early as the spring of 1912.[73] The 1926–28 Northern Campaign led to a second moment of massive vandalism, with City God temples very often a prime target.[74] This was only logical, as City God temples served as key foci for the traditional socioreligious organization of urban communal life and were thereby viewed as prime obstacles to the creation of a new society.[75] Moreover, territorial communities and their temples, which in imperial times were the bedrock of officially recognized religion, found themselves (and their festivals) without legal protection overnight.

Even in cases in which the City God temples were not destroyed, local officials withdrew their patronage and participation (even though in smaller county seats county officials sometimes maintained a minimal role),[76] as did local yamen employees. The seizure of temple lands and the decline of territorial and devotional groups (whose property was also often seized) affected the ability to organize festivals. The transfer of City God temples to local elite bureaus in a way continued the post-Taiping trend of taking over such sacred sites but took it much further thanks to the new regime's removal of the remaining checks and balances provided by their pre-1911 status as official temples. City God temple life and festivals thus fell entirely into the hands of local power holders (guilds, lineages), and, while some managed to continue staging festivals and processions up to the Japanese invasion, this was but a shadow of the more multifaceted, pluralist religious world of the mid-nineteenth century.

The giant processions of the City Gods thus stopped in many cities where these temples were expropriated. In Shanghai, where the politically powerful City God temple management committee supported festivals to some extent, the thrice-yearly procession was nonetheless discontinued from 1912 to 1919, from 1927 to 1934, and after 1937,[77] even though during that period the devotional associations' leaders managed to have a ritual performed at a cemetery with Daoists officiating in lieu of the full procession and sacrifice to wandering ghosts.[78] We unfortunately do not have information on the Hangzhou City God festival during that period (the temple itself remained open until 1949); in Suzhou the City God temples were not destroyed, but processions stopped shortly after 1911.

Other processions were affected as well. Outright police bans were often ignored by temple leaders; for instance, Ai Ping's and Yu Zhejun's studies of processions in Republican period Shanghai suggest that, in spite of political leaders' stern determination to abolish all processions, police forces were too few to effectively enforce such bans and when they tried the resulting shootings and casualties led all parties find compromises.[79] During some campaigns, these tensions erupted into outright violence, including police shooting at Pudong 浦東 residents when they insisted on staging a local festival in April 1919 and defied all efforts to shut it down. Four worshippers were injured, one critically, but all recovered and the festival proceeded as planned. Mediation by local elders resulted in a settlement satisfactory to both sides, which then dropped the lawsuits they were filing. And, while there were special efforts at enforcement in 1912–15 and 1927–31, they were followed by periods when the police were mostly resigned to leaving processions alone in spite of any bans. Policemen were locals with loyalties to their communities, and we occasionally see them participating in festivals themselves,[80] although this was still very different from the late imperial period, when yamen staff frequently played a major role in organizing such events. The effect of state building in villages and townships also increased the possibility of enforcing bans. Under the KMT regime village heads (now salaried with public funds) were dismissed if they failed to prevent festivals from taking place, whereas late Qing or early Republican officials merely summoned and hectored local leaders in similar circumstances.

The case of Suzhou is most revealing. In that city many processions had ceased in 1912, if not a few years earlier, including those of the four City Gods (for Suzhou Prefecture and the three counties based in the city), which were famous throughout Jiangnan for their magnificence (yet often said in the *Shenbao* to have never recovered their pre-Taiping splendor). A 1928 book on Suzhou customs claims that "the *saihui* since the establishment of the Republic have largely been discontinued" (*Minguo lai, ci feng shao zhi* 民國來, 此風少止).[81] By contrast, the festivals in the townships were affected later, and in the villages around Suzhou processions continued through 1937. This pattern is similar to that analyzed by Poon Shuk-wah in an article on a festival near Guangzhou and shows that less social control outside the large cities created space for religious developments there.[82] That space began to close during the 1930s, one example being KMT activists disrupting the massive processions of village temples to the Qionglongshan Daoist central temples in townships around Suzhou,[83] yet in the end such policies were not thoroughly enforced, and the failure of state-sponsored efforts to catch locusts (*buhuang* 捕蝗), one of the purposes of this festival, only further contributed to popular sentiments to perpetuate it.

A severe drought in July 1934 created a whole new situation, and local governments, wary of igniting riots, let people organize rain-making rituals (*qiuyu* 求雨) and processions on an ever-increasing scale until it actually rained, plus a few days afterward when processions took place all over the city to thank the gods. Many processions that had not been held for twenty years resumed and most of the time included a visit to the Suzhou central temple, the Xuanmiaoguan. The four City Gods processions also resumed, led by the Daoist in charge of one of their temples, followed by the neighborhoods' Earth Gods.[84]

At the same time, factors other than brute force played against the *saihui*. To return to Hangzhou, even townships around the city proper had mostly stopped their largest *saihui* by the 1930s both because of political pressure, with KMT activists present at every festival propagandizing and threatening local leaders, and because the traditional elites who depended for their livelihoods on the silk industry, which supported these festivals, had been largely ruined by a severe downturn in the rural economy and silk exports (as well as a lack of new industries in the city).[85] We have seen that the economic climate was key to festival organization in the late Qing, and most certainly earlier periods (bad years for trade led to much reduced festivals), and that guilds proved critically important in their funding; this proved to be a major factor behind the Republican period decline. Although details are lacking, the Marshal Wen Festival seems to have been permanently discontinued by the 1910s. The Old Eastern Peak temple, which drew devotees from throughout the region, maintained itself better, but it was affected by a series of bans, especially from 1927 on. Some local festivals continued; as He Shanmeng has shown on the basis of archival data, the police forces banned *saihui*, but some festivals could be authorized if they requested permission under the category of "ordinary worship" (*putong shaoxiang* 普通燒香).[86] In contrast, pilgrimages to the Hangzhou Buddhist monasteries or Maoshan (which were much less dependant on corporate property than processions) continued to take place on a major scale through 1937,[87] after 1945, and again today.

Hong Yueru, commenting on the *Hangsu yifeng* during the 1920s, had very interesting things to say about such changes in Hangzhou. While he nowhere notes a decline in family religious practices, he does mention the dwindling of certain types of large-scale rituals. He observed that pilgrimages to Buddhist (and a few Daoist) temples thrived (for even when some temples were destroyed, others replaced them in the pilgrimage circuits),[88] while community rituals, including the Marshal Wen processions and the Dipper altars of the ninth month, had all but vanished. He also lamented the demise of the festivals of the Fire God and Thunder God (on the 23rd and 24th days of the sixth lunar month respectively). The former, in particular, which used to be celebrated in each neighborhood, was the victim of, among other factors, a strict ban on theater performances in the city's public spaces.[89] In some cases, the decline of a festival was linked to the destruction of a temple (such as the Jingdeguan) but not always. The Dipper altars were organized in open-air ad hoc spaces, and their demise seems to have been more closely linked to the decline of the urban classes (silk merchants, yamen staff, etc.) that sponsored them.

Republican Period Changes in Local Religious Life

Based on the examples discussed in the previous section, we would like to identify broader trends in changes in local religious life caused by evolving policies toward festivals, as well as larger social, economic, and political mutations. First, pilgrimages and festivals based in either rural/mountainous areas or suburban temples (e.g., Maoshan, the Hangzhou Tianzhusi 天竺寺, etc.) actually thrived during the Republican period and up to 1937, while many sacred sites in city centers (including City God temples) had to stop their *saihui*, sometimes as early as 1911. The effect of anti-*saihui* measures affected large cities as early as the Xinzheng period, starting with Hangzhou, Suzhou, Nanjing, and Shanghai, followed by county seats and townships, while villages were less affected before 1937. Nonetheless, festivals had long served to connect all these levels (as shown, e.g., in the "Heavenly taxes" rituals in which low-level temple gods visited high-level urban temples), and disruption at one level had an immediate effect on the others.

Indeed, during that period, the embedded networks and hierarchies that managed festivals in late imperial society tended to dissolve, with their elements becoming looser and more independent. Different groups (yamen staff, guilds, neighborhood associations, devotional groups, etc.) that cooperated in late imperial times now tended to organize festivals (when feasible) on their own; for instance, we read about City God festivals entirely organized by guilds, without (as far as the record can tell) other groups playing a significant role. The high-order processions and festivals often lost their ability to integrate all wards and neighborhoods into integrated organizations, even though such encompassing networks occasionally resurfaced. On the other hand, many neighborhood *saihui* continued, even though their links to central temples were more or less severed; what we see here is less a loss of the territorial dimension, which remained strong at the grassroots level, than of its nested hierarchies.[90] Furthermore, a number of new entrepreneurial temples actually developed their own festivals during that period, albeit on the margins of the established socioreligious order.

The *saihui*, where they could continue to operate, were marked by a reconfiguration of their social basis. Certain groups (professional guilds) either disappeared or disengaged, and so did local government staff members, who were key actors in late imperial festivals. On the other hand, new actors tended to take a more visible place, most notably women, who benefited from new social policies. Imperial bans on their participation in festivals had come to an end, and when processions did take place women were routinely reported as having been important participants. New religious groups (lay Buddhist organizations, redemptive societies) also appeared on the scene, organizing their own public rituals on a voluntary basis.

The Republican period also witnessed new modes of regulation of local social and religious life, with less devolution to local actors (gentry organizations, clerical elites, etc.) and more direct intervention by administrative and police forces. As the latter were less cognizant of and involved with local religious actors, they were much less effective at licensing and control, and this led not only to dislocations but also to a certain amount of deregulation, which favored entrepreneurial actors over the long-established territorial and clerical structures. For instance, spirit-mediums, who were extremely important actors in local festivals, continued to be banned during the Republican period, but they actually thrived. Xiao Tian 小田, who has studied the fate of Jiangnan female mediums during the modern period, found numerous prohibitions of all kinds but less than impressive effects on actual social practice.[91] Indeed, during the late Qing these mediums lived under a sort of local licensing and control system that disappeared with the Republican regime and mostly left them under the radar of state intervention.[92] One noteworthy case was the possession cult of the Wutong 五通, long banned, but never successfully, and still very common in Shanghai and southern Jiangsu. Since the early Ming at the latest, this cult had been based at Shangfangshan 上方山, a hill close to central Suzhou.[93] While the territorial festivals of the Suzhou area encountered times of trouble, the small-scale but omnipresent domestic rituals of the Wutong and the visits of families and small groups to Shangfangshan continued apace; indeed, spirits worshipped nowadays at Shangfangshan feature successful medium cults dating back to the Republican period.

Fieldwork shows that while some worshippers come to Shangfangshan on their own, many are brought there by their local spirit-medium. Apparently there were a significant number of mediums who claimed connections with the deities of Shangfangshan yet lived in Shanghai during the 1930s.[94] While many of these mediums must have moved to the city from the rural areas around Suzhou, they also attracted city folks to both the cult and Shangfangshan, including many who might otherwise never have gone there. Clearly mediums took advantage of the rapid urbanization to spread their cults; this phenomenon is still observable, as a good number of present-day worshippers at Shangfangshan come from greater Shanghai. Wutong mediums in Republican period Shanghai had a rather high profile; while many may have started with a modest domestic altar, some soon were able to develop full-fledged shrines with names such as Shangfangshan xianlaoye tang 上方山仙老爺堂.[95] Such shrines were most often housed in rented shops or street-level apartments and were colloquially known as "Buddha shops" (*fodian* 佛店). Such largely unlicensed entrepreneurial shrines were found all over the city, sometimes run by migrant Daoists or Buddhists but most often by spirit-mediums. They were constantly criticized by some elites and banned by the authorities (the concessions' authorities, being very lenient, proved utterly uninterested in the issue), but nonetheless they remained a key feature of the urban landscape from the late Qing to 1949. Newspaper reports discussing the Shangfangshan mediums and their shrines in Shanghai mostly mention their healing services,[96] even though this is no proof that it was the only defining feature of the cult. One Wutong temple in Kunshan (between Shanghai and Suzhou) run by female mediums was known for its cures during epidemics.[97] One man who was healed by the Shangfangshan second brother in 1927 expressed his gratitude by paying to publish a note of thanks to the god in *Shenbao*.[98] It is also noteworthy that, in some cases, such Shanghai shrines associated the Shangfangshan gods with more "respectable" ones, such as one home shrine combining them with Guanyin, Lüzu 呂祖 and Jigong 濟公 (the two latter being the leading deities in modern Jiangnan spirit-writing cults).[99]

The Shangfangshan festival, held on the 18th day of the 8th month, remained popular in the 1930s and continued to attract countless local mediums, both male and female, with some engaging in self-mortification and other physical feats, including running the *tiao mapi* 跳馬匹 (running in trance).[100] For example, the article "Stone Lake on the eighteenth day of the eighth moon" (*Ba yue shiba ri zhi Shihu* 八月十八日之石湖) in the series of ethnographic notes entitled *Fengtu xiaozhi* 風土小誌 (1935) mentions numerous pilgrims, as well as mediums performing all over the hill on that date.[101] Pilgrimages on the day of the temple festival naturally declined during the Japanese invasion and especially after the antireligious campaigns in the 1950s.

Shangfangshan was vandalized at least twice during the first half of the twentieth century: newspaper reports tell of one member of the local gentry, a provincial laureate (*juren* 舉人), who on his own initiative went there on the 18th day of 4th lunar month in 1905 and found the local constable (*dibao* 地保) and worshippers in a dispute over petty profits from the site. Perhaps taking advantage of the confusion, the *juren* destroyed the statues while hectoring the worshippers to stop making offerings to "immoral" gods. However, the report ends on a sobering note, for when the *juren* returned two days later a new statue was already in place.[102] Furthermore, the township head (*zhendong* 鎮董) was furious and had the *juren*'s porters beaten, showing that the cult enjoyed the active support of large segments of the local elite.[103] More seriously, the 1927 Northern Campaign and its immediate aftermath were occasions for widespread vandalism at religious sites wherever the KMT armies went, and Shangfangshan was no exception. We read that in late 1928, the magistrate of Wuxian ordered that the statues be thrown into the lake during a campaign that also targeted another possession cult near Suzhou, that of Muhuajing 木化精.[104] Be that as it may, descriptions of the Shangfangshan pilgrimage in subsequent years clearly show that such destruction was quickly followed by reconstruction.

Given the intensity of the anti-superstition campaigns in the Suzhou area from the 1900s onward, and especially during the KMT period, it would be quite surprising to find that a site such as Shangfangshan, notorious, highly visible, and easily reached from downtown Suzhou on tramways as early as the 1920s, plus having high iconic value as a site of state campaigns against local religion, continued to thrive throughout the period—all while the great procession of the Suzhou City Gods, which had been state supported until 1910, had been discontinued. Yet, it did. The *Shenbao* reports tell us about crowds of worshippers more or less regularly from the 1870s through 1948. Even at the height of the KMT anti-superstition campaigns we read that police patrolled the pilgrimage but did not prevent it. It was banned in 1927 but took place all the same.[105]

Another reason the Shangfangshan cult survived is that its key actors, the spirit-mediums, were able to continue practicing throughout the period. We hear of specific bans on spirit-mediums at Shangfangshan but with very limited success.[106] One aspect of Republican policies that influenced spirit-mediums was the increased focus on public health through campaigns to outlaw faith healing and divine consultations. For instance, in 1947 the Shanghai police raided a number of prominent spirit-medium shrines offering cures and arrested five mediums, one of whom was channeling the Shangfangshan gods.[107]

To sum up, not only did the Shangfangshan site not suffer significant destruction during the first half of the twentieth century, but it actively played a role in the development of local spirit-medium traditions. One way it fulfilled this mission was by enshrining dead spirit-mediums. Jiangnan religious culture, though certainly not unique in this regard, does favor the divinization of spirit-mediums as local deities. Long Feijun, who has worked on a temple in the rural Pudong area of Shanghai, has documented that local temples' side shrines have statues or tablets of numerous deceased spirit-mediums, now worshipped as intermediaries.[108] In this area, another related practice was the enshrinement of dead young women as spouses or concubines of local gods. This practice was long decried and fought against by local elites, and also became a target of anti-superstition campaigns during the Republican period.[109] Yet it is also possible to take a more anthropological view of such reports and consider that such enshrinement gave a positive, even desirable posthumous destiny to young women (and sometimes men) who had otherwise no prospects but to be forgotten. Rather than seeing the gods as killing and abducting young people (as late imperial literati did), we can alternatively see them as offering a solution to the issue of untimely death.

Two fascinating reports published in *Shenbao* relate such cases. One, dated 1909, tells of a young man from a village near Suzhou who died shortly after marrying. A local female medium revealed he had been hired in the service of one of the Shangfangshan gods; the groom's family built a statue of him and placed it in a new a shrine at Shangfangshan, where the female medium operated a successful healing cult until the local magistrate arrested her and burned the statue.[110] A later report, from 1946, discusses a rich merchant from Shanghai whose beloved young daughter had just died. When he went to Shangfangshan to have salvation rites performed for her, a medium told him that the daughter had married one of the five Wutong brothers. The merchant then not only erected a statue but built a whole nuptial chamber for her within the Shangfangshan temple, complete with a bed, toilet stands, and so on.[111] Such a nuptial chamber can be seen today at Shangfangshan, and locals explain that it was built for a young woman from Shanghai. Whether or not this is the same woman reported in *Shenbao* is moot, but the point is that the practice of enshrining young people and spirit-mediums at Shangfangshan is continuing.

Among the many reasons explaining the different trajectories of various types of festivals during the late Qing and Republican periods, two seem to stand out. First, pilgrimages fared much better because they were organized by small, voluntary, ad hoc groups based in the countryside and brought outside business to the city; by contrast, the urban networks of ascriptive territorial temples were much more deeply impacted by anti-superstition policies and urban modernization, with displacement caused by urban development and migration and the local state taking over neighborhood corporate resources (land, endowments). The anti-superstition campaigns clearly focused on territorial festivals rather than voluntary pilgrimages. Second, festivals and other religious activities were much better tolerated in the suburbs and townships than in urban centers, and the link between neighborhoods and downtown central temples were distended if not altogether broken.

We see similar phenomena of thriving pilgrimages and declining territorial *saihui* in other Jiangnan cities.[112] In Hangzhou, the walls that encircled the Qing city were dismantled soon after 1912, and the former Manchu garrison was flattened to make room for a new business and leisure district, Xinshichang 新市場, which caused the sharp decline of Wushan as a center for ritual and entertainment and the rise of a tourist industry on the lakeshore.[113] As in other places, the local government focused its efforts to foster social and urban modernization on the city centers, relegating "superstition" to the outskirts. Somewhat paradoxically, then, the dismantling of the city walls did not reduce the gap between city center and suburbs. Tellingly, Hong Yueru explains that after the demise of the Marshal Wen Festival, local religious activists tried to develop new processions to take its place;

one featured Zhang Daxian 張大仙, a local Daoist saint (who had actually lived there as a successful healer during the Guangxu period).[114] Zhang's procession on the 18th day of the 7th lunar month toured the neighborhood of his temple at Gongchengqiao 拱宸橋, in the northern suburbs, but, he adds, it was not allowed to enter the town.[115] The Guanyin pilgrimage in the hill monasteries flourished while the urban procession declined.

Thus, the Republican period saw a growing divide between city center and suburbs and countryside in terms of public religious life; however, memories of the place of *saihui* and Daoist ritual in urban life were still very vivid by the 1930s and 1940s. Large-scale celebrations uniting local temples and neighborhoods around the City God or other central temples could be, on a few occasions, revived as soon as circumstances allowed it, such as in Suzhou during the 1934 drought. Yet they had ceased to be the norm, organized every year in each city with the full support of officialdom, as they were before 1911. As these citywide celebrations waned, the significance of the City God and other central temples in local life, and the motivations for controlling or investing in them, changed. Furthermore, as Poon Shuk-wah shows,[116] urbanites often chose to travel to countryside festivals, so these worlds were by no means separate. In Republican Jiangnan, thriving train and bus services carried urbanites to festivals in suburban or more remote areas.

The politics of festivals during the late Qing and Republican periods are marked by both continuities and ruptures. In terms of continuities, officials manifested a long-standing aversion to very large processions and constantly feared threats to public order, yet they could relax the bans in times of disaster (epidemics, droughts); they also attempted to channel resources spent on festivals to other uses. However, Republican period officials differed from their late Qing predecessors in a number of significant ways. First they did not focus only on the largest festivals (such as the Marshal Wen procession in Hangzhou) but also took aim at local neighborhood festivals, thus destroying the bedrock of local festive life. Second, unlike Qing officials, they had little interest in negotiating by drawing a line between licit and illicit rituals but instead tried to ban all forms of temple celebrations. By tolerating pilgrimages but clamping down on processions, they dramatically altered local social and ritual life.

Such processes, based on both modern secular politics and urbanization processes, are clearly not unique to China. Modern states do pay very close attention to the use of public spaces, and in this perspective processions and other large-scale rituals outside temples are a favorite target, especially since they come into competition with the state's own civic rituals,[117] while regulators also wish to confine popular entertainment (include opera and other performances that feature so prominently in festivals) to specific locations such as public theaters.[118] In Hong Kong, processions became subject to very constraining police regulations, with those now allowed limited to very small circuits.[119] In France (and other mainly Catholic countries), the separation of Church and state was accompanied (and sometimes preceded) by very strict regulations on processions around cities on holy days.[120] Such processions were extremely common up to the early twentieth century, but in a decade or two (around 1905 in the case of France) they became exceptional.

A particularly illuminating point of comparison is Japan. While Japan never had the equivalent of the sweeping anti-superstition campaigns that modern China has experienced, and while the role of festivals in reaffirming local political order was not denied, in sharp contrast to China, the modern (post-1868) state there also managed temples, rituals, and festivals with a heavy hand, with effects that in certain ways are comparable to those described in our discussion of Jiangnan.[121] The 1868 separation of Buddhism and Shinto (which mandated separate temples and shrines in the place of hitherto syncretic places) had an immediate and radical effect on celebrations, as this law commanded the reinvention of separate Buddhist and Shinto rituals at almost all sites. This also entailed inventing "pure" Shinto rites, purging Buddhist festivals of their Shinto elements, and more generally radically transforming all festivals that used to combine elements from both traditions. A generation later the merger campaign (1906–14) reduced the number of Shinto shrines from more than 200,000 to some 120,000; the aim was to have just one officially recognized shrine per village, to dispense with others, and more generally to eradicate small, underfunded shrines. The state-paid Shinto clergy participated in the process (albeit sometimes reluctantly), one result being a standardization of ritual practices. The official clergy was instructed to apply standard norms and liturgy that dramatically reduced local festival practices, especially when they were considered vulgar or licentious (including explicit sexual plays, spectacular spirit-possessions, etc.). One of the motivations for this campaign, indeed, was to "reduce the numbers of local festivals that . . . took people from their jobs and diverted much money to amusements and entertainments."[122] After the merger, local communities were supposed join the festival of their consolidated shrine, but that could be in a distant place, and they were not necessary welcome. Thus people were deprived of their holidays (meaning fun, special foods, and a different social atmosphere) and their ability to appropriate their own space.[123] This is an interesting reversal of the situation in Jiangnan; in Japan, local shrines were suppressed and only central shrines remained, while in Jiangnan to a large extent it was the other way around. In both cases, a whole ecology of local socioreligious life was deeply altered.

Meanwhile, in Japan, too, pilgrimages to holy mountains, whether classified as Buddhist or Shinto, flourished throughout the period,[124] while the urban festivals and processions (*matsuri* 祭) came under ever closer control and restrictions. The former, situated largely outside the urban system and supported by associations, were conceived as separate religious spaces, whereas the urban *matsuri*, very much like the Jiangnan *saihui*, were directly targeted by the modern state striving to take direct and close control over urban populations and public space. In Japan, too, as in China, Korea, and indeed many parts of the world, festivals had to wait until the late twentieth century to see tourist interest revive attention to processions and their local varieties.

PART 2

RELIGIOUS
KNOWLEDGE

CHAPTER 3

STORES OF KNOWLEDGE:
NEW FORMS OF PROSELYTIZING

The previous two chapters have shown that many temple cults and their festivals were teetering on the edge of elimination during the fifty-year period covered by this study. In contrast, the very same era witnessed an astounding transformation in the way religious knowledge was transmitted, including the publication of books and periodicals plus the use of audio media such as radio broadcasts and phonograph records plus visual media like advertisements and cartoons. Previous scholarship on the history of modern Chinese mass media has tended to neglect its impact on indigenous Chinese religious movements.[1] In fact, however, one key aspect of Chinese religion during the Republican era was its dynamically public nature. Inspired by the example of using the printed word in Christian proselytizing, yet also drawing on indigenous Chinese traditions of publicizing morality and philanthropy, numerous religious groups devoted themselves to using mass media for the transmission of Chinese religious traditions.[2] This chapter focuses on the ways in which they strove to publicize their beliefs and practices, the types of texts they chose to utilize, the messages contained in these media, and their intended and actual audiences. We will also consider the overall historical significance of these phenomena, including late imperial precedents. The ways in which they continue to shape Chinese religious life today are discussed in the Conclusion.

While handwritten manuscripts, oral instruction, and the use of artworks have consistently proven essential means of transmitting religious knowledge,[3] the printing of scriptures and other doctrinal or ritual texts became a core activity for Chinese religious groups as early as the Tang dynasty (618–907). The earliest Chinese printed book for which we have a clear date is a Buddhist scripture, and the various editions of the Buddhist Canon were among the most mammoth publication projects in early modern history.[4] Printed texts continued to shape the development of Chinese religions during the late imperial era,[5] including among sectarian movements. Some sources describe such groups printing hundreds of morality books (*shanshu* 善書) and precious scrolls (*baojuan* 寶卷),[6] while state crackdowns resulted in the confiscation of numerous texts.[7] Be that as it may, during the late imperial era commercial printers played only a minor role in religious publishing, choosing instead to publish texts that possessed inherent market value such as novels (many of which had significant religious meaning), textbooks, manuals for examination candidates, and so on. Even when commercial printers did take on religious projects, they tended to do so on a commission basis, not as a regular activity. The lack of commercial incentives did not necessarily inhibit the printing of religious texts, however, due to the wide range of motives underlying such activities, including transmitting doctrine, displaying erudition, attempting to standardize beliefs and practices, establishing or reinforcing networks of power, and, perhaps most important of all, accumulating merit.[8]

All this changed during the modern era, when religious publishing was transformed into a major commercial activity. During the late Qing and early Republican eras, the adoption of western printing techniques such as movable metal type made it possible to print high-quality texts on a much greater scale yet lower cost, all of which had been impossible using xylographic systems. Chinese religious publishing also benefited from the introduction of stone-based lithographic printing and especially the cylinder printing machine, brought to China in 1847 by western missionaries. Improved speed of production, quality of products, and economies of scale were further augmented by the implementation of a modern postal system, which allowed publishers in urban centers such as Beijing and Shanghai to exert their influence on a broad range of regional markets. These innovations had a profound impact on the history of modern Chinese religions by sparking the growth of new forms of religious print culture involving mass-produced books and periodicals. Such works were produced by new organizations, namely, modern religious publishing houses that depended on lay support and established wide-ranging distribution networks to market their products, including via a modern postal system. By the Republican era, nearly all major religious organizations and their leaders were involved in publishing enterprises. As Gregory Adam Scott and Philip Clart note in the recent introduction to their edited volume on the subject, religious publishers proved to be "keenly adept at navigating the new conditions generated by modern print culture; In embracing new print technologies and practices, they helped change religious publishing in modern China. Yet in doing so, they were often transformed themselves, adopting new religious ideas and practices as a result of their engagement with print."[9]

The development of religious publishing in modern China was in large part due to the influence of Christian missionaries. Mindful of the impact that printing had made on the Reformation in Europe, missionaries such as Robert Morrison (1782–1834) of the London Missionary Society took the lead in promoting modern forms of religious publishing in China. One of the first Christian periodicals was the *Eastern Western Monthly Magazine*, published by Karl Friedrich August Gutzlaff (1803–51) in Canton from 1833 to 1838, followed by the *China Serial* in Hong Kong from 1853 to 1856. Beginning in the late 1850s, however, Shanghai became host to more than 50 percent of Chinese religious publishing, starting with periodicals such as the *Shanghai Serial* (1857–58). Numerous other Christian magazines came into being during the 1860s and 1870s, the most important of which was the *Chinese Scientific Magazine* (founded in 1876). Of all these publications, however, by far the most influential was the *Church News*, founded by Young J. Allen (1836–1907) in 1868 and renamed the *Chinese Globe Magazine* in 1876.[10] This periodical, published continuously until Allen's death, helped shape the lives of many modern Chinese elites. Printer-missionaries such as Walter Henry Medhurst (1796–1857), Samuel Dyer (1804–43), and William Gamble (1830–86) used modern publishing techniques to further the efforts of the London Missionary Society Press and American Presbyterian Mission Press, organizations that quickly gained the attention of many Chinese urban elites.[11] These men and the organizations they helped found had a profound impact on Chinese religious publishing, and their achievements were actively emulated by non-Christian elites who also continued to adhere to the ideals and values expressed by late imperial publishers.[12] A number of other religions also pursued publishing enterprises in China, including Islam and Judaism, but their endeavors are not discussed here.[13] One other topic that merits exploration and comparative research in the future is the impact of new technologies on religious organizations in other Asian nations.[14] This included not only printed works but also the innovative use of new media (including large-scale exhibitions, photographs, and documentary/narrative movies) to promote their mission.[15]

Means of Communication, Old and New

The fifty years covered by this study were marked by the publication of astounding numbers of religious books and periodicals. Pioneering research on this topic by Wu Yakui 吳亞魁 indicates that nearly 6,000 religious works (5,983) were published during this era by a total of twenty-eight publishing houses. Moreover, since reasonably complete records exist for only nine of these publishers, the actual number of works is likely very much higher.[16] In the case of Buddhism, Gregory Adam Scott's "Digital Bibliography of Modern Chinese Buddhism" now lists a total of 2,328 works published between 1860 and 1949, with nearly half (1,019) published in Shanghai (the figures for Nanjing and Beijing are 462 and 37 respectively).[17] These texts were produced by numerous Buddhist publishing houses sponsored by lay elites, most notably the Society for Propagating the

Dharma (Honghuashe 弘化社, founded in 1930) and Shanghai Buddhist Books (Shanghai Foxue shuju 上海佛學書局, literally "Shanghai Buddhist Bookstore"). The latter organization, established in 1929 by leading lay Buddhists such as Wang Yiting, was divided into four departments that managed its operations: Circulation (Liutongbu 流通部), Printing (Chubanbu 出版部), Reproduction (Fanyinbu 翻印部), and Management (Daibanbu 代辦部). By 1934, it had expanded to encompass eight branch offices and more than a hundred resellers.[18]

At the same time, Buddhist publishers soon came to realize that new types of texts were needed to meet the needs of lay readers, which can be seen in the production of increasing numbers of texts in the vernacular (*baihua* 白話) accompanied by annotations (*zhu* 註) and/or illustrations (*tu* 圖). There were also extensive efforts to produce dictionaries (*cidian* 辭典), primers (*rumen* 入門), and guides (*zhinan* 指南) that endeavored to simplify Buddhist subjects for a mass audience.[19] As Philip Clart has observed, such works, which tended to follow a (Japanese-mediated) late-nineteenth-century western model of representing religious traditions, "opened whole intellectual worlds that had been buried in scholastic traditions barely accessible to lay people."[20] One example involves the lay Buddhist polymath Ding Fubao 丁福保 (Ding Zhongyou 丁仲祐, 1874–1952), who devoted five years (1918–22) to producing a series of books entitled *Buddhist Studies Collectanea* (*Foxue congshu* 佛學叢書). This series was especially noteworthy for including annotated scriptures that explained complex doctrinal concepts, as well as reference tools for lay readers such as dictionaries of Buddhist terminology. The series became highly popular and was regularly reprinted during the Republican era. In addition, other religious publishers imitated Ding's effort by producing their own primers and other reference works, some of which can still be found in today's Buddhist seminaries (Foxueyuan 佛學院).[21] Other Buddhist groups, and especially lay ones, also practiced spirit-writing, and they did not hesitate to publish the results of their efforts.[22]

Buddhist publishers also devoted extensive efforts to producing periodicals, with scholars estimating that between 150 and 300 such works were published during the Republican era, especially in Shanghai.[23] Leading Buddhist monastics such as the Venerable Monk Xuyun (Xuyun laoheshang 虛雲老和尚, 1864?–1959) and Dharma Master Yinguang (Yinguang fashi 印光法師, 1861–1940), as well as their lay followers, relied extensively on periodicals to spread their teachings.[24] Many periodicals were specifically aimed at nonspecialist readers, a point made explicitly in the "Editorials" section of the *Buddhist Studies Magazine* (*Foxue congkan* 佛學叢刊, published in 1912–14): "For the sake of those who are unlearned in Buddhist studies . . . [we] thus establish a standard of plain and simple writing. In composition seek only clarity; don't use deep principles or abstruse language."[25] Buddhist periodicals also attracted readers because they were printed using a newspaper format and included local reports from Buddhists around the country, personal accounts of miraculous events, and question-and-answer dialogues (*dawen* 答問) between authors and readers. Such trends continued up to the CCP's rule in China in 1949, with organizations such as the Deer Park Buddhist Study Society (Luyuan Foxuehui 鹿苑佛學會) buying space to advertise in Shanghai's major newspapers in 1946–47 in order to publicize Buddhist teachings and try to convert readers directly. There was much discussion of this method in contemporary Buddhist periodicals, with leaders claiming that advertisements were especially effective among youths.[26]

Buddhist proselytizing was hardly limited to the printed word, however, and included broadcasts of Buddhist programming and the circulation of Buddhist phonograph records. Research on these means of spreading the dharma is in its early stages, but we do have some data for Shanghai. The first radio station there was founded in 1923, and by the 1930s and 1940s at least twenty more were broadcasting Buddhist programs, including some founded by Buddhists themselves. One instance took place in late 1933, when members of the Pure Karma Society (Jingyeshe 淨業社, located in the Jueyuan 覺園 or Enlightenment Garden) began to raise funds for a radio station of their own, which went on the air in January 1934 under the name Foyin (Sound of the Buddha) Broadcasting Station (Foyin guangbo diantai 佛音廣播電台). A list of this station's programs in July 1937 shows a wide range of items, including not only scripture chanting (*songjing* 誦經) but also information about western medicine, as well as popular stories and dramas. For its part, beginning in March 1933, Shanghai Buddhist Books arranged for the chanting of Buddhist sutras on the Shanghai Yongsheng Broadcasting Station (Shanghai Yongsheng diantai 上海永生電台). One year later it set up a committee to arrange for Buddhist programs to be broadcast on a wide range of non-Buddhist stations and in 1936 established its own Buddhist radio station, the Shanghai Huaguang Broadcasting Station (Shanghai Huaguang diantai 上海華光電台). Apart from scripture-chanting, programming for this radio station featured lectures on Buddhist doctrine by such eminent monks as Dharma Master Taixu (Taixu fashi 太虛法師, 1890–1947) and lay Buddhists such as Fan Gunong 范古農 (1881–1951). A third Buddhist radio station was founded in 1940 by Luo Jialing 羅迦陵 (1864–1941), a devout lay Buddhist who was married to a renowned Jewish merchant from Great Britain, Sir Silas Hardoon (1851–1931; see chapter 6).[27] Originally the Guangming Broadcasting Station (Guangming diantai 光明電台), its name was subsequently changed to the Miaoyin Broadcasting Station (Miaoyin diantai 妙音電台), and it continued to operate up to the late 1940s. One account of this radio station states that the venerable monk Baisheng (Baisheng laoheshang 白聖老和尚, 1904–89) was ordered to broadcast Japanese propaganda by the occupation authorities but chose to sabotage the station's equipment instead.[28]

As for phonographic recordings of Buddhist chants, some were produced by the Desheng Company (Desheng gongsi 得勝公司), selling at 1.8 dollars (*dayang* 大洋) each or 8.5 dollars for a set of five. In addition, Shanghai Buddhist Books produced a set of five phonograph records in 1935 plus a second set of six in 1936. These contained recordings of Buddhist chants, including "In Praise of Amitabha" (*Mituozan* 彌陀讚), "The Dhāraṇī of Great Compassion" (*Dabeizhou* 大悲咒), and "The Heart Sūtra" (*Xinjing* 心經), and the chanters included leading lay Buddhists such as Guan Jiongzhi 關絅之 (also written as Guan Jiongzhi 關炯之, 1879–1942). These records were meant to be distributed to Buddhist temples and lay groups, although their actual circulation has yet to be determined.[29]

Another method Buddhists used to spread the dharma that has yet to be fully studied involved music.[30] Admittedly, music occupied a problematic position in traditional Buddhism, often being viewed as a distraction to proper self-cultivation, and the only musical forms allowed in most monasteries were traditional liturgical chants (*fanbai* 梵唄). All this changed during the modern era with the advent of new devotional songs (Fojiao/Fohua gequ 佛教/佛化歌曲) generally intended not for monastic rituals but for lay congregational gatherings. Such works differed from earlier *Foqu* 佛曲 sung by lay groups in that many were based on school songs (*xuetang yuege* 學堂樂歌) that combined western tunes and Chinese texts, and more than a few were borrowed from Japan (there was also some Christian influence, as seen in some Buddhist schools that maintained their own choirs).[31] New devotional songs were especially popular in urban centers like Shanghai, and works by both monastic and lay composers were published in anthologies such as the *Qingliang geji* 清涼歌集 (1936), *Miaoyinji* 妙音集 (1943), and *Haichaoyin geji* 海潮音歌集 (1950s). Some of these works resembled Christian hymnbooks, with a few titles even using the same term (*shenggeji* 聖歌集).

One of the Republican era's most esteemed Buddhist composers was none other than Great Dharma Master Hongyi (Hongyi dashi 弘一大師, 1880–1942, lay name Li Shutong 李叔同).[32] Hongyi had extensive experience with music and the mass media, studying piano in Japan and composing or playing a role in the composition of some seventy types of songs, including patriotic songs (*aiguo gequ* 愛國歌曲), school songs, and Buddhist songs. His earliest collection, entitled *Songs for National Schools* (*Guoxue changgeji* 國學唱歌集) and published in 1905 while he lived in Japan, belonged to the first category. Hongyi also founded the first Chinese magazine devoted to music in 1906, the *Little Music Journal* (*Yinyue xiao zazhi* 音樂小雜誌), and when he returned to China from Japan in 1910 he supported himself as a (western) music teacher at some of China's new modern schools, including the Chengdong Women's School (Chengdong nüxue 城東女學) in Shanghai and the Zhejiang First Teachers College (Zhejiang shengli Diyi shifan xuexiao 浙江省立第一師範學校) in Hangzhou. While at these schools, and later as a lecturer at some Buddhist seminaries, Hongyi composed songs that borrowed melodies from American popular tunes (albeit via Japanese works that used these melodies). Hongyi was also personally inspired by Beethoven because he was a brilliant composer despite severe personal setbacks. He appears to have viewed Beethoven's experiences as a metaphor for modern China, believing in both the power of the human will to triumph over all manner of adversity and the power of religion and aesthetics to change China.[33]

These experiences helped shape Hongyi's Buddhist songs, which belonged to the new devotional category. One example is the "The Song of the Triple Gems" (Sanbaoge 三寶歌, composed with Taixu in 1930), which was intended for congregational singing at lay Buddhist gatherings. Here is a portion of that song, the melody of which was typical of school songs, with the lyrics suggesting Christian missionary influence.

In the long everlasting night of the sentient world
And the darkness of the universe
Who can be the one to show us the direction of a luminous future?
To the human life within the house in blaze
And all its sufferings
Who may be the one to bring the comfort and solution?
Of the great compassion
The immense wisdom
And the unsurpassed heroic power
Is the Buddha![34]

In addition, Feng Zikai 豐子愷 (1898–1975), who enjoyed a particularly close relationship with Hongyi (becoming his disciple in 1927 on the occasion of his twenty-ninth birthday), edited and published a collection of Hongyi's songs (*Li Shutong gequji* 李叔同歌曲集) through the Kaiming Bookstore (Kaiming shudian 開明書店), where he was one of its editors (see also the discussion of Buddhist cartoons below).[35]

Another influential promoter of Buddhist music was Hongyi's disciple Chen Hailiang 陳海量 (1909–82), a lay composer whose *Essentials for Studying Buddhism in the Home* (*Zaijia xueFo yaodian* 在家學佛要典, first published in 1943) made extensive use of songs (some accompanied by Feng Zikai's illustrations) while also encouraging Buddhists to use dramatic performances as well as newspaper and magazine advertisements for proselytizing.[36] Chen and his peers relied on songs to disseminate Buddhist ideas and promote social reform, and they did not hesitate to copy songs that were used in social movements and wartime mobilization. Songs written in the vernacular, such as "The March of Great Hero's Disciples" (Daxiong Fenxuntuan jinxingqu 大雄奮迅團進行曲), composed by

Chen Hailiang, and "March On" (Jingjin 精進), by Lin Shiyuan 林師遠, borrowed tunes from and closely imitated popular works like the "March of the Volunteers" (Yiyongjun jinxingqu 義勇軍進行曲). Chen also made use of themes from the New Life Movement in songs such as "Practice Buddhist New Life" (Shixing Fohua xinshenghuo 實行佛化新生活), "Early Rising" (Zaoqi 早起), and so on.[37] Apart from Chen, Hongyi was also close to the lay Buddhist composer Liu Zhiping 劉質平 (1884–1978), one recipient of some of his death poems.

Apart from audio forms of proselytizing, visual ones could prove significant, most notably cartoon drawings (*manhua* 漫畫). Such cartoons were highly popular during the Republican era as a form of social commentary and mobilization, especially during wartime.[38] By the 1920s and 1930s, lay Buddhist elites had also begun to use cartoon drawings, most likely copying their use by Christian groups, including organizations like the YMCA.[39] One notable example of Buddhist cartoons is the series of volumes by Feng Zikai and Hongyi known as the *Collection of Paintings for Protecting Life* (*Husheng huaji* 護生畫集), which vividly promoted the need for kindness to all sentient beings (see figure 3.1). The first set of fifty cartoons (drawings by Feng with poetry in Hongyi's calligraphy) was published by the Kaiming Bookstore in 1929 in honor of Hongyi's fiftieth birthday. A second series, this time consisting of sixty works by Feng and Hongyi, appeared in 1940 on the occasion of Hongyi's turning sixty. In 1950 the Dafalun Bookstore (Dafalun shuju 大法輪書局) published seventy more illustrations by Feng, this time with poems and calligraphy provided by Ye Gongchuo 葉恭綽 (1881–1968) (Hongyi having left this world in 1942). Fifth and sixth sets were published in Singapore in 1965 and 1979, respectively, and complete sets of all the works appeared in 1981 and 1993. This work continues to be widely distributed to the present day, including versions in Japanese and English (the latter, entitled *Protection for Living Beings*, was published for free distribution by Taiwanese Buddhists in 2003).[40]

Relatively less work has been done on the mass media's role among non-Buddhist groups during this time period. In the case of Daoism, Liu Xun 劉迅's work on Chen Yingning 陳攖寧 (1880–1969) and lay Daoist circles in Shanghai reveals that, as in the case of Buddhism, both books and journals proved highly important for Daoist publishers. Renowned enterprises like the Yihuatang 翼化堂 (literally "Hall of Assisting in Transformations," established in the 1840s) and the DanDao kejinghui 丹道刻經會 (Association for Carving Daoist and Alchemic Scripture) printed works that contributed to the formation and maintenance of connections among Daoist monastic communities and lay Daoist practitioners and even the spread of nationalist discourse in the face of Japanese aggression. Different types of texts were produced that featured a range of intended audiences and strategies for reaching them. In just one example, in early 1935 the Yihuatang published four series of books that treated Daoist learning and

Figure 3.1 "Pleading for Its Life," a cartoon by Feng Zikai.
(*Feng Zikai manhua quanji* 豐子愷漫畫全集, p. 17)

inner alchemy (*neidan* 內丹). The first, entitled *The Little Daoist Learning Series* (*Daoxue xiaocongshu* 道學小叢書), featured five titles that had been transformed into primers for all interested readers due to extensive editing and annotation by Chen Yingning and other Daoist elites. While the second set of books (*The Daoist Learning Series* or *Daoxue congshu* 道學叢書) centered on two rare inner alchemy texts produced for more skilled adepts, the third (*Little Daoist Learning for Women,* or *Nüzi Daoxue xiaocongshu* 女子道學小叢書) was aimed exclusively at female practitioners and featured extensive annotation. The final series, entitled *The Collection of the Immortals' Way* (*Xiandao congshu* 仙道叢書), consisted of two works by Chen that treated the historical, doctrinal, and technical facets of Daoist inner alchemy. Liu Xun's research is especially important for noting the tension between public and private in Daoist publishing, with works like the series described above both promoting Daoism to the general public and stressing the value of intimate personal experience for individual practitioners.[41]

Journals also played an important role in the new Daoist movements, especially the *Immortals' Way Monthly* (*Xiandao yuebao* 仙道月報) and the *Biweekly to Promote the Good* (*Yangshan banyuekan* 揚善半月刊). Liu Xun's research reveals that Daoist elites like Chen Yingning and his colleagues resembled their Buddhist peers in viewing journals as vital means of attracting popular support, and they made every effort to improve communication between themselves and their readers by making their journals more palatable to a general readership, including the introduction of new columns and letters to the editor. Their success can be seen in the fact that thousands of copies of these journals circulated throughout Chinese communities, including some as far away as Manila, distributed in large part by means of mail order subscriptions, with subscribers allowing family and friends to borrow copies for their own use, which further enhanced these texts' impact. New forms of mass media, such as journals, thus proved essential for publicizing self-cultivation techniques that originally belonged to the private realm and for doing so in ways that could attract new converts, solidify bonds between practitioners, and overcome gender barriers.[42]

A few scholars, most notably Philip Clart, Fan Chun-wu 范純武, Wang Chien-ch'uan 王見川, and Yau Chi-on 游子安, have also begun to assess the mass media's impact on redemptive societies and other voluntary religious associations.[43] Some groups utilized modern printing and marketing techniques to distribute the morality books they produced, while others made use of newspapers and periodicals to publicize their religious ideals and philanthropic deeds, the best known being *Morality Magazine* (*Daode zazhi* 道德雜誌) and *Morality Monthly* (*Daode yuekan* 道德月刊).[44] In addition, some redemptive societies operated their own publishing enterprises, one notable example being the Illuminating Goodness Bookstore (Mingshan shuju 明善書局), founded by the Fellowship of Goodness in Shanghai in 1931. This bookstore utilized both woodblock and lithographic formats to produce venerable scriptures written in classical Chinese, as well as illustrated works in the vernacular (the latter were said to be especially worthwhile due to their appeal to less educated readers). Moreover, apart from marketing books and periodicals, publishers like the Illuminating Goodness Bookstore also sold religious goods (statues, paintings, etc.) and recordings of scriptural/liturgical texts (this was also the case for other enterprises, including Shanghai Buddhist Books). The bookstore's 1932 catalog contains a price list for such items,[45] while nearly half of its 1935 catalog is devoted to advertisements for statues, paintings, calligraphy, and other religious artifacts.[46]

Another fascinating facet of redemptive societies and similar associations is their embrace of spirit-photography (*linghunzhao* 靈魂照). It is fascinating in part because this type of photography, as well as parapsychology, represented forms of western knowledge that appealed to Chinese religious elites.[47] The pioneering study by Huang Ko-wu 黃克武 of the Shanghai Spiritualism Society (Shanghai Lingxuehui 上海靈學會), founded by Yan Fu 嚴復 (1854–1921), Ding Fubao, and other urban elites in 1917, reveals that the study of spiritualism (influenced by western and Japanese forms of psychic research, mesmerism, mentalism, etc.) spread rapidly in urban China during the early twentieth century. The mass media played a vital role in transmitting such knowledge by means of newspaper articles and advertisements, including those published in the *Journal of Spiritualism* (*Lingxue congzhi* 靈學叢誌) from 1918 to 1920.[48] Photos said to be of spiritual beings proved to be an integral part of this movement, with some religious elites employing modern photographic technology to display what they claimed were images of deities, demons, and the dead. One case involved the publisher and lay Buddhist Di Baoxian 狄葆賢 (1872–1941), who was a passionate recorder of people's spiritual experiences. Di also had an interest in spirit photography, and emphasized its use in psychic research.[49] In addition, modern image printing technology allowed groups to mass-produce photographs of their living saints. For example, members of the Moral Studies Society (Daode xuezhe 道德學社) treasured photos of its founder, Duan Zhengyuan 段正元 (1864–1940), as objects of worship that could also facilitate self-cultivation practices. As a result, the society established its own photography studio (the Datong sheyingshe 大同攝影社), which was assigned the task of recording, printing, and disseminating Duan's images.[50]

Highly useful information on the overall state of religion and the mass media during the Republican era may be found in Rudolf Löwenthal's *The Religious Periodical Press in China*, compiled in 1940 for the Synodal Commission in China.[51] Based on a series of articles written in the course of undertaking fieldwork, surveys, and questionnaires during the 1920s and 1930s, this work provides valuable insights into the state of religious periodical publishing in Republican China. Overall, *The Religious Periodical Press* identified 400 religious periodicals that were circulating in 1939 (211 Protestant, 74 Catholic, 61 Buddhist, 39 Islamic, 17 Daoist, and 2 Confucian), distributed throughout 21 provinces and 103 cities. In terms of Buddhist journals, Löwenthal's survey identified a total of 155 works, of which only 61 were still being published by 1939. Prices for these journals ranged from 1 to 45 cents per copy or 50 cents to 4 dollars per year, with circulation figures averaging 1,000 to 3,000 copies per issue, with the exception of publications like *Sound of the Tide* (*Haichaoyin* 海潮音, published in China from 1920 to 1949 before moving operations to Taiwan), which totaled about 20,000 copies per month. Approximately 2.5 million copies of these Buddhist periodicals were published on an annual basis, with each copy read by an estimated five to ten individuals (some subscribed to more than one journal, while others shared journals with friends and fellow worshippers).

Periodicals identified as "Daoist" tended to be published by the new religious movements currently referred to as redemptive societies. *The Religious Periodical Press* lists forty-one such publications, of which only eighteen still existed, the oldest being the *Journal of Moral Learning* (*Daode xuezhi* 道德學誌, 1917–18) and the [*Red*] *Swastika Daily News* (*Wanzi riri xinwen* 卍字日日新聞, 1926–37). These periodicals cost between 1.5 and 15 cents per copy or 30 cents to 5 yuan per year, with their circulation largely limited to initiated elites. While print runs for more popular periodicals could reach 2,000 copies per issue, most totaled only a few hundred, for an overall circulation of between 5,000 and 10,000 copies. Actual Daoist publications included those published by Chen Yingning (see above), as well as the *Daoism Quarterly* (*Daojiao jikan* 道教季刊, founded in 1932) and the *Daoism Monthly* (*Daojiao yuekan* 道教月刊, founded in Shanghai in 1936).

The Religious Periodical Press also provides data for a total of twenty-one "Confucian" periodicals founded between 1913 and 1936. Most were published by associations dedicated to the worship of Confucius, and all were defunct by the time Löwenthal's book was compiled. These works proved to be more expensive (10 to 35 cents per copy or 1.8 to 5 dollars per year, with prohibitive advertising rates of 15 to 100 dollars per page) and enjoyed limited circulation (mostly to educated elites, approximately 200 to 500 copies per issue at most). In addition, a total of thirty-six Jewish and one hundred Islamic periodicals were published during the time period covered by the Löwenthal survey.

Despite the prevalence of religious periodicals in Republican China, Löwenthal's survey also noted that many had only a limited impact due to that era's poor literacy rates, unreliable communications networks, and low purchasing power of the populace. Furthermore, the very existence of many publications depended on the efforts of individual elites. If one key figure were to die or move away, the periodical could well be at risk. Other publishing enterprises had to cope with labor disputes, while the outbreak of the Sino-Japanese War and subsequent disruptions of postal networks severely hindered journals' circulation. Only a few Chinese religious publications were able to survive in Japanese-controlled territories, especially those that were at least partially owned by Japanese.[52]

Business Models and Circulation Strategies

When it came to publishing religious books and periodicals, religious publishers faced a number of challenges in attempting to establish viable business models, the main one being how to generate sufficient revenue to cover the costs of publishing religious texts. Such costs could be substantial. In one instance noted in

The Religious Periodical Press, the 1916 initiation of publishing operations for the above-mentioned *Journal of Moral Learning* required the Morality Society to invest $4,705 for printing machinery, $3,800 for paper, and $2,030 for printing costs. Funds came from advertisements ($12 per page), subscriptions (2.5 cents per issue; 75 cents per year) and especially from membership fees and donations.[53] Such challenges were further exacerbated by the fact that most religious publishers were reluctant to charge exorbitant rates for their works. In the case of the Yihuatang, for example, managers only charged a minimal price or subsidy (*jintie* 津貼) to cover the printing and labor costs (postage often cost extra). These works could then be purchased wholesale by philanthropists throughout China, who usually distributed them free of charge. Such strategies help explain why the Yihuatang was able to produce more than 850 titles before it ceased operations in 1946.[54] Religious publishers could also choose to sell their works for a relatively high price but use most of the proceeds for charitable enterprises. In one such instance, in 1921 the Jinan 濟南 (Shandong) branch of the Society of the Way (Daoyuan 道院) marketed ten thousand copies of a religious text entitled *True Scripture of the Shanghai Rescuing Life Association* (*Shanghai Jishenghui zhenjing* 上海濟生會真經) for $2 per copy. Apart from 20 cents to cover printing costs and 40 cents for society-related expenses (*yuanfei* 院費), the rest of the revenue raised from selling this text was to be used in disaster relief efforts.[55]

Buddhist publishers were often quite adept at raising the necessary funds. For example, Brooks Jessup's research on Shanghai Buddhist Books shows that its leaders raised ten thousand dollars from the sale of a thousand shares of stock while also establishing a board of directors. However, they encountered difficulties attracting investors after the level of capitalization stabilized at fifty thousand dollars, which prompted them to collect donations for an endowment fund that generated interest. Buddhist publishers also successfully challenged conventional wisdom about distributing religious works for free as an act of merit by selling their books to the reading public, maintaining that this strategy made more sense commercially and also reached people who were truly interested in their contents. Shanghai Buddhist Books even took the initiative of founding a book club (reading association) for morality books (*zengyue shanshuhui* 贈閱善書會), the members of which signed up to pay for the regular delivery of its various publications. And, in a precursor to electronic databases such as CBETA today, Buddhist publishers came up with the idea of selling religious works to research libraries. This trend began with the publication of the Buddhist Canon (Tripiṭaka, *Dazangjing* 大藏經) during the 1920s, which was copied by publishers of the Daoist Canon (*Daozang* 道藏) from 1923 to 1926. This reveals a combination of commerce and philanthropy, with some Buddhist elites advancing the traditional argument that investments in religious publishing helped one accumulate merit.[56]

Buddhist publishers utilized similar marketing strategies for their periodicals, with Shanghai Buddhist Books distributing three leading journals of the Republican era. Apart from the renowned monthly magazine *Sound of the Tide,* mentioned above, it also published 43 seasonal issues of the *World Buddhist Householder Grove Magazine* (*Shijie Fojiao jushilin linkan* 世界佛教居士林林刊) from 1923 to 1937, while also founding its own periodical entitled *Buddhist Studies Bi-Monthly* (*Foxue banyuekan* 佛學半月刊) in 1930, which ran 313 issues up to 1944. By 1937 it was printing well over three thousand Buddhist books and periodicals on an annual basis and had branch offices throughout China, as well as in Hong Kong, Singapore, and even Rangoon. Shanghai Buddhist Books also took the initiative in pursuing even more diversified investments, including sponsoring radio programs and eventually launching its own radio station (see above).[57]

Other religious publishers also strove to commercialize their operations while finding the proper balance between accumulating merit and staying economically viable. Rostislav Berezkin's research reveals that throughout the imperial era, as well as in the present day, many religious groups consistently favored the free distribution of their works, with the covers of such texts containing expressions like "this is not a commercial item" (*feimaipin* 非賣品), "reprints are welcome" (*huanying fanyin* 歡迎翻印), and even "we welcome the printing and free distribution [of this text as] it brings immeasurable merit" (*huanying yinsong, gongde wuliang* 歡迎印送，功德無量).[58] However, some modern religious publishers that specialized in lithographic editions of texts such as morality books and especially *baojuan* adopted a different approach, distributing commercial catalogs with price lists and embracing the western concept of copyright, adding notes to that effect (*banquan suo you* 版權所有) in the works they offered for sale.[59]

Once production and marketing obstacles had been overcome, religious publishers also had to deal with the problem of how to arrange for these texts to reach their intended audiences. While some works could be read by individual worshippers, many others were meant to be chanted or otherwise performed for mass audiences, including scriptures, liturgies, and *baojuan.* Accordingly, the expression "to be used exclusively for chanting and recitation" (*zhuanggong songdu* 專供誦讀) appears after many titles. Recent research by Berezkin clearly demonstrates the presence of a wide range of reading practices during the Republican era (and perhaps earlier time periods as well), including silent reading by educated individuals and different types of amateur and professional performances (*nianjuan* 念卷).[60] Despite the fact that some authors of religious texts assumed that people could read such works, most publishers were well aware of the importance of recitation and simple language. This was especially the case for women, often one of the main intended audiences of many such works, which generally reached them through group recitation rather than individual reading. Elite families had their share of literate women,[61] and their numbers rose steadily during the late Qing and Republican eras with the founding of ever more public schools for girls.[62] Evidence of such trends may be found in the writings of intellectuals such as Zhou Zuoren 周作人 (1885-1967), who in a 1936 essay described how one girl was forced to abandon her education after elementary school but continued to read novels and *baojuan* at home, probably having been first exposed to the latter during performances she attended with her mother.[63] Moreover, an autobiographical essay by Hu Shih (who helped lead the charge against traditional Chinese religions) tells the story of the mother-in-law of one of his elder brothers, who was not only literate and liked to read morality books but would also recite their contents for other women or to use them to tell stories to younger generations.[64] Women writers also attested to the importance of such practices, one example being Pan Xizhen 潘希珍 (pseudonym Qijun 琦君, 1917–2006), of Yongjia 永嘉 County in Wenzhou, who in an autobiographical story entitled "Mom's Hands" (*Mama de shou* 媽媽的手) movingly recounted how her mother would, after finally finishing all the household chores, soak her hands in a basin of hot water before devoting herself to reading *baojuan*. According to Pan, that was the most relaxing time of her mother's long day.[65] All this suggests that religious works could find their way into the hands of their intended readers and audiences, including women, but the overall success of such efforts remains to be determined.

Another problem involved the ways in which religious texts were distributed. In his survey of Republican era religious periodicals, Löwenthal maintained that the dissemination of free or low-cost religious publications "[did] not necessarily reflect the real interest of the population but rather the financial strength and ability to organize on the part of the distributing agency."[66] This cautionary point clearly has merit in terms of assessing the impact of religious publishers, but it is also essential to consider that these publishers could often rely on sophisticated distribution networks in order to achieve their goals. Many works published in Shanghai were meant to reach their intended readers via distribution outlets that ranged from nearby Zhejiang and Fujian provinces all the way north to Liaoning 遼寧, Jilin 吉林, and Inner Mongolia, as well as westward to Sichuan 四川 and Yunnan 雲南. Of these, the distribution center for morality books (Shanshu liutongchu 善書流通處) in Quanzhou 泉州 was especially important for the religious history of modern Taiwan, with leading publishers such as the Ruicheng Bookstore (Ruicheng shuju 瑞成書局), Lanji Bookstore (Lanji shuju 蘭記書局), and Yuzhen Bookstore (Yuzhen shuju 玉珍書局) relying on its services while also reprinting Shanghai works and including them in their own catalogs.

One example of how Cross-Strait interaction shaped the transmission of religious knowledge in Japanese colonial Taiwan may be found in the case of Taiwan's oldest religious publishing enterprise, the Ruicheng Bookstore, founded in the city of Taizhong 台中 in 1912 by Xu Kesui 許克綏 (1892–1983). Born into a poor peasant family in Xianxi 線西 Township in today's Zhanghua 彰化 County, Xu was a fifth-generation descendant of migrants who had come to Taiwan from Quanzhou. His family's financial circumstances prohibited Xu from receiving a formal education, but he tried to learn as much as he could by attending local schools (*xueshu* 學塾) when the opportunity presented itself. Xu married at age eighteen and then moved to Taizhong, where in 1912 he opened a shop selling seeds and other agricultural products. His commitment to studying Chinese language and culture persisted unabated, however, so later that year he expanded his store to include a space for selling books, journeying to Shanghai and Amoy on a regular basis to collect not only works of fiction and drama but especially Buddhist and Daoist scriptures, as well as morality books. After many long years of hard work, Xu was finally able to rent a separate storefront for use as an independent bookshop in 1928 and set up his own printing press in 1932. Such progress came at a high price, however, including regular inspections by the colonial authorities (who were concerned about his promotion of Chinese culture) and the tragic death of his son, who passed away while Xu was on a business trip to Shanghai. Contact with Chinese publishers came to an abrupt end with the outbreak of the War of Resistance against Japan in 1937, but Xu continued to use his printing press to publish the religious texts he had acquired, and his descendents manage the Ruicheng Bookstore to this day.[67]

Cross-Strait religious ties also shaped the growth of the Lanji Bookstore, which was established in 1925 by a member of the Jiayi 嘉義 elite named Huang Maosheng 黃茂盛 (1901–78). Huang was deeply committed to both preserving traditional Chinese culture and transmitting moral values, not only inviting Chinese elites to take part in literary contests but also setting up his own distribution center for morality books. Huang took regular journeys to religious publishing centers like Shanghai, where he collected, brought back to Taiwan, and reprinted a wide variety of religious works and periodicals in order to distribute them free of charge.[68] Huang's efforts attracted the support of Chinese religious elites, including the renowned Shanghai businessman, philanthropist, and religious practitioner Wang Yiting. Huang met Wang during one of his trips to China and became a member of a charitable-religious organization that Wang had helped found known as the Association of Conscience for Upholding Goodness (Zhongguo liangxin chongshan hui 中國良心崇善會). One result of this friendship was that Wang composed a preface for a morality book entitled *Record of the Spirit* (*Jingshenlu* 精神錄) compiled by the renowned East Haven (Donggang 東港) physician and philanthropist Chen Jiangshan 陳江山 (1899–1976), which was published by the Lanji Bookstore in 1929. Wang also composed a calligraphic couplet for this work, which read, "Do nothing that is evil; practice all forms of philanthropy" (*zhu'e mozuo, zhongshan fengxing* 諸惡莫作，眾善奉行). The *Record*, which also includes a preface by Huang, subsequently spread back across the Strait to Shanghai, and five editions totaling 6,700 copies were published in both Taiwan and China prior to the outbreak of the Second World War.[69] One final example involves Chen Yuzhen 陳玉珍 (1897–1972), the founder of the Yuzhen Bookstore (also located in Jiayi), who dedicated himself to publishing all manner of Chinese works when he opened for business in 1926.[70]

Conclusion

The evidence presented in this chapter, while admittedly limited in both scope and depth, may help shed some light on the importance of the mass media in shaping the course of religion in modern Chinese history. This is a relatively new area of research, so much work remains to be done. In particular, it will be essential for scholars to transcend the limitations of focusing on a single religious tradition since such parameters clearly had little impact on religious publishing itself. In just one example, Shanghai Buddhist Books produced not just Buddhist texts but the works of other religious traditions,[71] which is hardly surprising when one considers the fact some redemptive society leaders actively supported Buddhist organizations.[72] Contrariwise, publishers like the Illuminating Goodness Bookstore printed numerous Buddhist and Daoist works in addition to redemptive society texts.[73] In addition, where the source materials allow, it will also be necessary for scholars to expand the scope of their endeavors to audio and visual works. This body of data should help us better understand that religious groups in China during the fifty years covered by this project were not passive respondents to state policies and social changes but actively strove to create new spaces for their activities, including in the mass media.

CHAPTER 4

MORALITY BOOKS IN
THE MODERN AGE

The previous chapter discussed the economy and materiality of new forms of religious knowledge production. Here we would like to explore innovations and continuities in the content of such production, particularly as seen in morality books. At issue are the connections and disjunctions between technical modernity and intellectual change: some of the more challenging new religious ideas were published by small wood-carving presses, while the modern mass-printing technologies were used to a significant extent to reproduce earlier books, in some cases without any new materials. And yet, as Jan Kiely has noted, the very fact that religious books could now, thanks to the mechanical press, be distributed in identical form and within a short period of time throughout the country also changed their meaning, as they suddenly became available for mass use in institutions such as schools, the military, and prisons.[1]

Important work has been done on Buddhist and Daoist texts during the Republican period, but morality books were at least as important in volume, impact, and intellectual innovation; and yet they have heretofore been relatively neglected by scholarship, with a few exceptions, Yau Chi-on having long been a pioneer.[2] Many definitions have been offered for the genre of morality books; it suffices here to describe them as nonconfessional works (i.e., not linked to any religious institution, inclusive, and typically encompassing Daoist, Buddhist, and Confucian references) that prescribe proper behavior and describe its consequences for human destiny in this world and the next. Although essays, stories, and commentaries by identified living humans represent an important part of the genre, spirit-written revelations from gods are its driving force and lend it its particular authority. By the beginning of the twentieth century, when our enquiry begins, the genre had been a major one for many centuries in terms of numbers of titles, print runs, and impact. One Protestant missionary writing in the early twentieth century lamented that the archclassic of the genre, the twelfth-century *Taishang ganyingpian* 太上感應篇, had more copies in circulation than the Bible.[3] Throughout the 1898–1948 period, countless presses both reprinted earlier morality books and printed newly composed ones.

Indeed, the circulation of morality books during the first half of the twentieth century originated from all corners. Certain presses, the so-called *shanshuju* 善書局, which had thrived since the mid-nineteenth century, specialized in them, mostly on a local or at best regional basis. The new large-scale Shanghai presses also generously featured morality books in their catalogs. This was obviously the case for those affiliated with redemptive societies, such as the Fellowship of Goodness's Mingshan shuju or Tianhuaguan 天華館, but we should also note that bona fide Buddhist presses also published morality books, beginning with the Foxue shuju, which listed over a hundred such titles in one of its catalogs.

Innovations during the Republican period

A number of innovative features found in the Republican period morality books have attracted the attention of scholars. The first change involved language, especially the rapid growth of books written in *baihua*, even though simple classical language remained just as accessible to audiences with low- to mid-level literacy and was thus extremely common until the 1930s. Illustrations were also more common and elaborate than before thanks to the possibilities offered by the mechanical press, even though illustrated woodblock-printed morality books had been common for centuries. In terms of content, morality books composed between 1898 and 1948 not only commented on current events and social change, as they had always done, but sometimes became politicized in new ways. This was especially the case with books produced in connection with the KMT propaganda apparatus, most obviously at the time of the New Life Movement (launched in 1934).[4] Partly overlapping such developments, we also see the rise and success of elementary ethical guides claiming universal value, which quote classical and late imperial Chinese authorities (a favorite being the general who put down the Taipings, Zeng Guofan 曾國藩 [1811–72]) but also western philosophers and Christian texts.

Yet another change is that morality books, old and new, became choice material for the outreach activities of new types of institutions or individuals who came to dominate the Republican religious landscape: redemptive societies, lay Buddhist organizations, and industrial age philanthropists-cum-politicians. We described in chapter 3 the role of presses and newspapers linked to, or directly operated by, redemptive societies such as the Mingshan shuju. Buddhists were equally active in this regard. A key figure in the world of morality book publishing during the Republican period was Yinguang, arguably the most widely revered and read Buddhist leader of this period.[5] As an ardent promoter of Pure Land practices, Yinguang was naturally close to the world of morality book writers and publishers. His interest was far from unprecedented: consider, for instance, the involvement of the late Ming monk Zhuhong 袾宏 (1535–1615) in the practice of ledgers of merits and demerits (*gongguoge* 功過格), or the lay Buddhist Zhou Mengyan's 周夢顏 (1656–1739) oeuvre, *Anshi quanshu* 安士全書, which combined commentaries on the classic morality book *Wenchang dijun Yinzhiwen* 文昌帝君陰騭文 with his own essays on Pure Land practices. Yinguang himself, indeed, prefaced and sponsored the reprinting of these works.

Yet this overlap was not without problems. Many of the morality books (including the *Wenchang dijun Yinzhiwen*) were spirit-written, and Buddhist clerics had issues with granting authority to such forms of direct communication with non-Buddhist deities. In mainstream Buddhist theology, such gods can exert no doctrinal authority; the laity should follow the teachings of the Buddha, as explained by monks, rather than the instructions of unenlightened gods. Indeed, some clerics were adamant in their rejection of spirit-writing. Yinguang was more careful, granting that doctrinal issues were outside such gods' remit but that their moral admonitions were entirely sound and worth following.[6] In his own letters to lay disciples, many of whom (like Wang Yiting) were spirit-writing practitioners, Yinguang attempts to bridge the two worlds. Let us note in passing that this question is still unfolding, as many charismatic monks who trace their filiation to Yinguang, notably Jingkong 淨空 (1927-), are major actors in the twenty-first-century landscape of morality book production and distribution.[7] The huge numbers of morality books printed or posted online by the organizations around Jingkong often exhibit the editorial hand of Yinguang.

The involvement of Yinguang with morality books took several forms.[8] He encouraged his lay followers and sometimes himself supervised the publication of morality books with the Buddhist presses that were developing at that time, as seen in chapter 3. Yet his role was also intellectual: in his many prefaces to morality books thus reprinted, Yinguang attempts to Buddhicize or give a Buddhist interpretation of books that had hitherto circulated mostly in milieus that qualified as Daoist or Confucian and used very little specific Buddhist vocabulary. To give but one example, in 1922 Yinguang published a version of the *Bukelu* 不可錄, a short treatise on sexual morality first published in 1856 during the Taiping Civil War that was devoted to sexual restraint for laypeople. In his preface, Yinguang explains how Buddhist ascetic and monastic self-control techniques are relevant to modern family life and advises his readers to apply ancient techniques of visualizing all women they meet outside home as their own mothers or, alternatively, as corpses.

This type of approach was taken up by lay Buddhists, such as Chen Hailiang, discussed in chapter 3, and down to the present day, where Buddhist manuals on family life are widely circulated.

Buddhist monks were not alone in reshaping the world of morality book publishing. Jan Kiely has identified a type of "public moralist"–cum–modern entrepreneur through a case study of textile magnate Nie Qijie 聶其傑 (1880–1953). Nie was a complex figure. Zeng Guofan's grandson, he was baptized in 1915 but went on a retreat with Yinguang in 1925. He published in 1924 the *Ganying leichao* 感應類鈔, a collection of commentaries and stories based on the *Taishang ganyingpian* (expanding on his father's own edition of that work in 1906 [the *Ganying leichao* was originally composed in 1670]), which went through several revisions and reprints, often with the support of Yinguang's organization, the Honghuashe 弘化社. He also published his own essays during the KMT decade and into the Japanese occupation period. Nie was an industrialist whose grand plans to reform society certainly took root in attempts to provide moral discipline for workers. His vision combined deep-seated conservatism with scientism; as Kiely shows, his own version of eschatology, which lent urgency to his calls for moral reform, was couched in terms of nationalist social Darwinism.[9] This discourse thus introduced new ideas of moral education (*jiaohua* 教化), the natural duty of elites that sometimes intersected and sometimes diverged from their Buddhist or redemptive society counterparts.

Modern Canons

The sheer number and variety of morality book titles published during the Republican period, coupled with the fact that this literature is scattered in numerous libraries, hardly studied at all, and often not reprinted, make it nearly impossible to provide an overview of these works and thus identify major trends. One way to get closer to such trends is by looking at compilations and canons, that is, by relying on the lists of what people involved in the morality books milieu of the time selected as worthy of being anthologized and thus somehow representative and important. Of course, such canons were not everyday reading material; most people chose to read short volumes. Thus, we see the importance of canons less in terms of their influence in molding readers' worldviews and more in terms of the way they both reflected and shaped the authority of certain texts or textual traditions selected for inclusion. Canon formation processes have been at work throughout Chinese religious and intellectual history, and the twentieth century proved to be no exception. Such processes are highly interesting for several reasons, including the fact that they allow us to look beyond specific works of supposed representativeness or importance, focusing instead on how authorities organize an entire field of circulating literature.

The late imperial period was marked by specific stages of canonization in the realm of religious literature and morality books in particular. The accelerating production of spirit-writing texts between the mid-eighteenth and mid-nineteenth centuries led to a rapid succession of canons, most often called *quanshu* 全書, devoted to specific deities. Notably, three gods came to dominate this field: Patriarch Lü (Lüzu 呂祖), Wenchang 文昌, and Guandi 關帝. The first two had their first *quanshu* canons by 1744; the last would have to wait half a century longer. By the late 1850s, each of these three deities had a dozen different versions of a *quanshu* canon to his name, and several other deities had acquired their own. Such works played a major role in defining the most authoritative scriptures and key ideas in a burgeoning field where new texts were revealed on an almost daily basis.[10] They also continued to circulate and be reprinted during the Republican period: to give but one example, the 1744 *Lüzu quanshu* 呂祖全書 was reprinted lithographically in 1917 by the Qianqingtang 千頃堂 in Shanghai (and reprinted again in 1920 and 1930); this edition still circulates widely in temples across the Chinese world today.

At the other end of the spectrum between traditional and modern we find from the 1910s onward collections of books marketed by modern presses entitled "series" (*congshu* 叢書) rather than "canons" (and thus not using terms such as *zang* 藏 or *quanshu* 全書) but nonetheless aimed at providing comprehensive sets of authoritative texts. One of the most prominent figures in the world of both religious and scientific publishing of the time, Ding Fubao, as noted in chapter 3, not only edited a series of books on Buddhism inspired by modern text editions and criticism,[11] but also series on Daoism (the hundred-title *Daozang jinghualu* 道藏精華錄, published in 1922), medicine, literature, and morality. His series on morality, *Jinde congshu* 進德叢書, never got very far and, as far as we can reconstitute it, comprised several ethical essays by Ding himself plus earlier work by late imperial moralists.

Maybe just as interesting as the "traditional" *quanshu* canons and "modern" *congshu* collections are a number of textual compendia produced and marketed by modern presses in Shanghai that aimed to provide comprehensive sets of texts encapsulating the essence of traditional wisdom. It is to what might be the finest of these oeuvres that we now turn.

The Last Canon before Wartime: Fushou baozang 福壽寶藏

Like Nie Qijie, Wang Yiting, now familiar to our readers, was a prominent industrialist-cum-philanthropist who published morality books as part of his self-perceived duty to society. He differed from Nie, however, by devising and compiling a canon rather than republishing one extant work or his own tracts.[12] Wang's canon-making effort allows us to probe further into the variety of morality books in circulation during the Republican era, the tensions involved in selecting specific works, and the way such tensions were resolved by the team around Wang Yiting, which compiled a list of works that granted authority to certain texts or types of texts.

The *Fushou baozang*, or "Precious Canon on Blessings and Longevity" is both a large and remarkable product of Republican period religious innovations, and an utterly neglected collection.[13] The reason for this neglect is most certainly that it was printed in Shanghai in 1936, just before the outbreak of the war, and was thus not well distributed. Indeed, there is no contemporary reprint (as yet), and we have only been able to locate one complete set, held at the Shanghai Library. Therefore, the *Fushou baozang* is interesting less as an influential formulation of new religious ideas than as one large and articulated synthesis of the current state of what was being read, a remarkable snapshot of the state of the religious knowledge and religious worldviews of Shanghai elites on the eve of the 1937 war. It documents intellectual trends of the time that were given a prominent place in the canon and that we thus must consider as significant elements in the intellectual and religious landscapes of 1930s urban elites.

The *Fushou baozang* presents itself as a set of 92 volumes containing 140 individual titles; some titles extend over several volumes, but most are short books gathered in one volume (one volume could include as many as five titles). It is unclear whether the volumes could be sold separately; each volume carries on its cover the name of the collection, the press that published it, and the distributor: 珍本善書福壽寶藏，樂善社列印，上海大眾書局發行. The press, Leshanshe, is not well known. Certainly, Wang Yiting used his wide business connections to have the *Fushou baozang* distributed by one of the largest general publishers in Shanghai, Dazhong shuju (interestingly rather than one of the Buddhist presses he was closely associated with). It is a beautiful thread-bound edition; the layout (fonts, numbers of columns, and characters per column) varies by text, but all texts are punctuated.

The collection does not provide much information about itself: it opens with a series of portraits and short biographies, presumably of those project leaders, without clearly distinguishing those who financed it and those who engaged in the actual editorial work. These portraits are first of Wang Yiting, Ju Diancheng 居殿丞, Lin Weiying 林偉英, Wen Deming 文德銘, and Lü Zhengyuan 呂正元.[14] Ju was a doctor from Gaoyou (south of Nanjing) who apparently was a donor to the project. Ms. Lin was the spouse of Hu Zhongming 胡仲鳴, a lay Buddhist disciple of (among other luminaries) Taixu. Wen was a journalist and poet, and Lü is described, in a fascinating late invention of tradition, as a forty-seventh-generation descendant of Patriarch Lü (an interesting claim for an ancestor both legendary and reputedly celibate). Further calligraphies grace this prefatory material, including one by Wang Jianhu 汪鑑湖, one of the top-ranking Daoist officials running the administration of the Heavenly Master.[15]

The first volume provides the table of contents, which is arranged under twelve categories of unequal size.

1. Moral transformation (*Huadaolei* 化導類, 24 titles in 21 vols.)
2. Sagely words (*Geyanlei* 格言類, 34 titles in 25 vols.)
3. Eight Virtues (*Badelei* 八德類, 4 titles in 2 vols.)
4. Admonitions for filial piety (*Quanxiaolie* 勸孝類, 7 titles in 5 vols.)
5. Sexual morality (*Jieyinlei* 戒淫類, 5 titles in 2 vols.)
6. Inspiration for women and children (*Qidilei* 啟迪類, 20 titles in 8 vols.)
7. Ledgers of merit & demerit (*Gongguogelei* 功過格類, 6 titles in 3 vols.)
8. Karmic retribution (*Yinguolei* 因果類, 10 titles in 11 vols.)
9. Loving all sentient beings (*Boailei* 博愛類, 4 titles in 3 vols.)
10. Nourishing life (*Yangshenglei* 養生類, 6 titles in 2 vols.)
11. Buddhist scriptures (*Fojinglei* 佛經類, 15 titles in 8 vols.)
12. Daoist cultivation (*Xiuzhenlei* 修真類, 5 titles in 2 vols.)

The very classificatory scheme is interesting, as it resembles those used during the same period by many morality book presses, which also arranged old and new morality books in categories mixing classical and modern vocabulary.[16] In our case, this hybridity is further enhanced by the fact that the *Fushou baozang* includes both morality books, on the one hand, and scriptures and self-cultivation essays on the other, while giving clear precedence to the former, hence the quantitatively shorter final three sections.[17] Also noteworthy is that the canon combines well-known classical texts that were circulating in other editions with much rarer ones. Indeed, for several texts we have not been able to locate any other extant copy.

Rather than going through the table of contents, we would like to point out several general features regarding the choices made by Wang Yiting and his associates. First, the chosen texts were not parochial or limited to the groups with which Wang was most closely associated. Wang was a disciple of Yinguang, but the latter only appears only marginally as the author of prefaces to a few of the selected texts. Hardly any key works of Wang's favorite lay Buddhist group (the Jishenghui 濟生會) and lay Daoist group (the Jin'gaishan 金蓋山 spirit-writing network) were included.[18]

Second, the *Fushou baozang* was decidedly a canon of its time, with several of the innovative features outlined above well represented. "Political" texts appear within the category of Eight Virtues (number 3).[19] Admittedly, this is the shortest of the twelve categories, with only four texts and two volumes, but it is nonetheless highly visible within the canon. One of these four texts, *Bade yanyi* 八德衍義, carries a KMT flag plus the text of Sun Yat-sen's *Three Principles of the People*. Modern hygiene and proto-*qigong* body cultivation are also well represented in category 10: texts such as the 1934 *Yangsheng xuzhi* 養生須知 deal with scientific hygiene and western medicine, as well as ways to stay healthy in the midst of hectic urban life.[20] Western wisdom is presented in *Zhongwai mingren geyan* 中外名人格言.[21] Modern in both format (cartoon drawing) and inspiration is Feng Zikai's famed drawings on the subject of protecting animals, *Husheng huaji* 護生畫集 (see figure 3.1 in chapter 3), which appears alongside three Qing period texts in section 9, devoted to caring for life. None of this is surprising: we know that Wang Yiting was interested in these issues (sports and hygiene, animal life, KMT politics), and it makes sense that he should have found a place for renowned friends such as Feng Zikai in his canon.

That said, we should keep in mind that these modern elements are but a minority of the canon. The bulk of *Fushou baozang* is made up of late imperial and especially nineteenth-century material. Nonetheless, it is also significant that this canon does not attempt to foreground ancient, foundational texts. Category 11, on Buddhist scriptures, is an exception; other categories do not open with the earliest texts or texts widely considered to be the most sacred. Many late imperial canonical collections of morality books open with the "three classics" of the genre (the twelfth-century *Taishang ganyingpian*, the *Wenchang dijun yinzhiwen*, and Guandi's *Jueshi zhenjing* 覺世真經). By contrast, *Fushou baozang* opens (vols. 1–2) with the *Taishang baofa* 太上寶筏, a 1755 commentary and elaboration on the *Taishang ganyingpian*.[22] This is true of the canon as a whole: among the 140 titles, 107 are clearly dated. Among these, 25 date from the Republican period, as opposed to 36 from the 1800–1911 period (many undated texts probably also date from this time); only 23 are from the 1644-1800 period; and 23 are from pre-1644 times (even though, of course, we have large numbers of pre-1644 texts anthologized or commented on in later texts).

The longest book in the *Fushou baozang*, also widely reprinted during the Republican period, is a work very representative of nineteenth-century moral writing: the *Quanjielu* 勸戒錄 by Liang Gongchen 梁恭辰 (b. 1814).[23] Liang was a scholar from Fuzhou who published moral anecdotes through his life (between 1842 and 1882) under different titles. This edition was a Republican period selection and thematically reordered version of his anecdotes (*Quanjielu leibian* 勸戒類編), first published in 1921: its twenty-four categories cover the entirety of morality book discourse, starting with (1) proving the existence of souls (*zhengming yougui* 證明有鬼), going through the retribution for various sins, to (21) exhortations based on proofs that good humans become gods (*mohou wiehen zhi quanjie* 歿後為神之勸戒);[24] (22) exhortations based on proofs that disasters are preordained (*jiezhu zhi quanjie* 劫數之勸戒); and (23) converting to Buddhism (*guiyi Fojiao* 皈依佛教, a focus not so apparent in Liang's original work). It is quite remarkable that, in an age noteworthy for producing reams of contemporary stories on retribution,[25] the largest body of such works was chosen (though rearranged) from the writings of a Qing literatus.

More precisely still, while all periods in the nineteenth century are well represented in our canon, including the last decades, we cannot fail to notice the relative importance of the Taiping Civil War. Between 1851 and 1864, huge numbers of elite loyalist activists produced tracts through spirit-writing, presenting the war as an apocalyptic punishment visited on sinful humanity and promising salvation to those who would repent and embrace strict moral ways.[26] Large numbers of these texts were then reprinted during the postwar decades and continuously into the 1930s. Indeed, some documents in the *Fushou baozang* provide detailed accounts of wartime events.[27]

In short, then, our canon reflects to an important extent the textual productions, ideas, and preoccupations of nineteenth-century religious activists. As a result, several of the themes that were prominent among these activists are extensively documented. While at first sight one may be surprised that the reflections on war, chaos, and political and moral decline that informed 1850s and 1860s religious production should be bundled with the utopian modernist visions of the Republican elites, the two actually converge on a number of points, most crucially issues of moral regeneration of the Chinese people in times of rapid change and external challenges.

We would like to discuss three themes inherited from the mid-nineteenth century that are prevalent in our corpus: eschatology, sexual morality, and animal life. First, as Vincent Goossaert has shown elsewhere, eschatological themes have been continuously present in Chinese religious texts since medieval times but became heightened in spirit-written texts from the early Qing onward.[28] While opposing popular messianism and its dangerous political implications, late imperial elites developed their own strand of apocalyptical eschatology whereby the high gods were ready to unleash the final apocalypse on sinful humanity, but savior gods and their elite devotees could still prevent its occurrence by spearheading a movement of moral reform in which morality books played a central role. This scenario developed countless variations and is found repeatedly in the texts collected in the *Fushou baozang*.

Importantly, while eschatological themes abound in the nineteenth-century texts included in the *Fushou baozang*, and notably those composed during the Taiping Civil War, which was widely understood to be the final apocalypse, they are also quite prominent in the Republican period texts. The inclusion of such contemporary apocalyptic texts shows that, for Wang Yiting and his associates, the possibility of an impending apocalypse was very much a pressing concern rather than an abstract inherited idea. One of the longest texts included in the canon is the *Dongmingji* 洞冥記 (sometimes *Dongming baoji* 洞冥寶記), a spirit-written tour of the underworld and heavens written in the form of a novel.[29] This lengthy work was revealed between 1920 and 1921 at a spirit-writing altar in Eryuan 洱源, Yunnan Province (an area with a mixed ethnic heritage also famous for its Pu'er 普洱 tea). This altar was connected to one of the most important redemptive societies of the time, the Fellowship of Goodness, which we have already seen was a leading entrepreneur of religious publishing.[30]

The major deity at this altar is Guandi, who has been portrayed as the new Jade Emperor or savior of endtimes since the year 1900.[31] Indeed, the subtitle of the *Dongmingji* is "a novel to awaken the world and bring humanity back to its origins and save everyone, at the time of the apocalypse at the end of the third age" (*Sanqi mojie pudu shouyuan xingshi xiaoshuo* 三期末劫普度收圓醒世小說). This is a direct continuation of a theme that emerged and thrived during the Taiping Civil War, whereby the Jade Emperor had decided to bring on the final apocalypse but Guandi (assisted by other gods) had pleaded and obtained a reprieve during which he would use spirit-writing to persuade as many humans as possible to repent their sins. In most versions of the story, this period had begun in 1840. In later developments, a sixty-year cycle later, Guandi had now succeeded to the position of Jade Emperor and was further intensifying his campaigns to avert the apocalypse by preaching to humans. Indeed, large parts of this eschatological literature develop narratives that portray the horrors of the Taiping Civil War as an early warning of the gods, to be now followed by even worse disasters since humans have failed to repent and return to moral lives.

When the *Dongmingji* was finally edited and published in 1924, it came with prefaces by various deities, such as Guandi, Wenchang, Lüzu, or Guanyin, all of whom insist that this text is a remedy for the rampant westernization of Chinese culture and the related loss of all moral values, best summarized in a phrase that appears repeatedly: "equality, freedom, and negation of father and lord" (*pingdeng ziyou wufu wujun* 平等自由無父無君). It aims to remind readers of the harsh divine laws that dictate punishments for human sins in direct and explicit continuity with two earlier (both nineteenth-century) such codes, which are both included in the *Fushou baozang*: the renowned *Yuli baochao* 玉歷寶鈔;[32] and the *Yuding jinke jiyao* 玉定金科輯要 (Compilation of the Golden Rules on the order of the Jade Emperor), revealed in 1856–59 in the very midst (chronologically and geographically) of the Taiping Civil War.[33] The latter is an excruciatingly detailed law code describing how humans will perish in the current apocalyptic war due to their various sins. It was also adopted by the Fellowship of Goodness as a major scripture and was widely reprinted by their presses during the 1920s.

We must note that the *Dongmingji* was not included incidentally or for its entertainment value: several other texts produced by the same sprit-writing groups in early 1920s Eryuan were also selected for inclusion in the *Fushou baozang*, including the *Xunnü baozhen* 訓女寶箴, also revealed there in 1921 by He Xiangu 何仙姑.[34] Thus, there was a conscious choice on the part of the *Fushou baozang* editors to include not only texts that represented the KMT values of the time but also texts that very explicitly deplored the end of the imperial system and berated western ideas of individual freedom. To what extent this was as much a patent contradiction for people like Wang Yiting as it is for us remains unclear. Yet one should not consider the *Dongmingji* as entirely nostalgic and anachronistic as the text also adopts notions such as Sun Yat-sen's theory of the Five Races forming the Chinese nation or the idea that humanity consists of countries of equal status (rather than one central civilized empire surrounded by barbarians) that a universal faith (such as the Fellowship of Goodness) should convert. Jan Kiely has described the cognitive dissonance found in morality books published by Nie Qijie as "combinations of language and ideas that can appear as jarring and unsystematic as the mixing of ghosts and spirits with trains and telegraphs, but this does not mean that they necessarily were incongruous or lacked coherence."[35] Here we also seem to have contradictory visions of morality and collective human destiny somehow reconciled, on the surface, by their inclusion in the same canon.

The inclusion of texts such as the *Dongmingji* also shows the porous nature of boundaries between the realms of "Buddhism," "Daoism," "Confucianism," "redemptive societies," and "sectarian religions." The few historians who have looked into the issue suggest that the convergence of "sectarian traditions" that carry a millenarian, messianic message (notably the Xiantiandao 先天道) and elite spirit-writing cults (which typically had a nonmessianic form of eschatology) started in the mid-nineteenth century.[36] Wang Chien-ch'uan has made the important point that during the same period (the second half of the nineteenth century) morality book presses started to distribute "sectarian" texts and thereby contributed to making them mainstream and acceptable.[37] By the Republican period, this merging had coalesced into redemptive societies that had a largely elite and self-declared Confucian following and at the same time developed the three ages type of apocalyptic teachings; it also, even more greatly, resulted in the wide acceptance of such teachings among all sorts of elite groups. This is one reason why we see people like Wang Yiting, well known among the top ranks of the KMT and international business elites of Shanghai, printing and disseminating apocalyptical texts of the "popular" messianic type.

While eschatological discourses are found throughout the *Fushou baozang* canon, our second key theme, sexual morality, is the subject of one whole category (number 5) and is also well represented in the next category, which deals with the education of women and children. Obviously, issues of gender relationships and sexual practices were present from the onset of morality books. The importance of this theme grew, however, from the "puritan turn" of the eighteenth century onward, to elevate sexuality to a dominant theme to which countless specialized morality books were devoted. Nineteenth-century eschatological writings give sexuality pride of place among the sins that will usher in the final apocalypse.[38] At the same time, this discourse was more complex than pure and simple patriarchal condemnation of female sexuality and autonomy, as it is often described. Like English Puritans, late Qing Chinese moralists upheld all women's rights to their honor; passionately fought the idea of the sexual availability of female servants, nurses, and tenants; and tended to describe women as victims in asymmetrical relationships with powerful men (such as landowners, officials, or senior lineage members). Codes such as the *Yuding jinke jiyao,* discussed above, certainly castigated promiscuous women, but most of all condemned abusive men; so do anecdotes on sexual misbehavior (in anthologies such as the *Quanjielu*), which typically stage situations in which a powerful man abuses a subservient woman. Obviously, this rang bells with people like Wang Yiting or Nie Qijie who made fortunes (with which they printed the morality books we read) employing cheap female labor in their textile, tobacco, and other factories.

Sexual morality was still a hotly debated topic in a context in which the Republican regime had ushered in drastic changes in gender roles, in terms of both law (the civil code of 1931 introduced marriage as a free choice of individuals) and social attitudes.[39] The liberation of women from both "Confucian" patriarchal society and "superstition" was a major theme of revolutionaries and reformists of all stripes.[40] As a result, morality books tended to portray westernization as corrupting women and to defend "traditional" ideas of gender segregation, female submissiveness, and chastity, but they did not do so by rejecting all forms of social change. Philip Clart has looked at Republican and contemporary morality books discussing women and finds accommodations with social change in more recent texts; late-twentieth-century morality books quietly acknowledge female labor outside the home, as well as love marriage.[41] He contrasts this with one text contained in our canon (the above-mentioned 1921 *Xunnü baozhen*), in which, he writes, Republican China is described as "the end of civilization."[42] But we also find in the *Fushou baozang* texts on female morality and sexuality that appear quite "progressive" compared to late Qing ones.

The third and last theme we would like to highlight here, animal life, is also the topic of one specific category within the *Fushou baozang* (number 9, *Boailei* 博愛類). Again, we see a close-knit conjunction of late imperial and Republican concerns and motivations. Of the four texts anthologized in this category, two are from the eighteenth century, one was compiled during the Taiping Civil War, and the last one is the above-mentioned album of cartoons by Feng Zikai.[43] The Taiping Civil War was, for rather obvious reasons, a time of heightened anxiety about life, with many books on animal life (and infanticide) compiled at the time claiming that the massive slaughter of humans caused by the war actually was just desserts for humanity's wanton slaughter of animals during previous generations.[44] This is, for instance, a claim made in one Taiping period collection of spirit-written revelations included in the *Fushou baozang*, the "Boat to Save Lives," *Jiushengchuan* 救生船.[45] Even though the 1930s groups that mobilized for animal rights, in which Wang Yiting and Feng Zikai were prominent figures,[46] were also inspired by less apocalyptic, western concerns for animal rights, the eschatological concern for human life as one aspect of fragile animal life remained very vivid.

By contrast, it is also interesting to note that certain themes that are well represented in the morality book tradition in general are not particularly common in our canon, even though, naturally, they can be found here and there within books that cover the whole range of moral issues (e.g., the *Quanjielu leibian* has a whole section on debt). Particularly noteworthy, perhaps, is the theme of business morality, which might seem counterintuitive for a canon edited by a prominent businessman. There is no single work devoted specifically to issues pertaining to the monetary economy, international trade, labor relations, or other morally sensitive aspects of the new China under KMT rule that people like Wang Yiting were trying to save from its own demons. This should remind us that morality books are not merely reflections of the society that produces them but also products of a long, continuing religious tradition with its own priorities.

Conclusion

The wide range of texts Wang Yiting and his associates selected as they composed the last great religious canon to be published in China before the Japanese invasion reveals the array of ideas and resources available to them. It further evidences their willingness to encompass an amazing variety of ideas, from the most conservative, backward-looking revelations to the most revolutionary, idealistic tracts. As a whole, the *Fushou baozang* evinces a frank embrace of new formats and genres that made the cachet of 1930s publications but at the same time shows deep continuity with the concerns of nineteenth-century elites panicked by the breakdown of social and moral order.

In this regard, the *Fushou baozang* is not an outlier but aptly encapsulates the larger world of religious textual production during the first half of the twentieth century. The presses that published tens of thousands of religious titles also had in their catalogs the same mix, in various proportions, of volumes in innovative formats (lay-oriented handbooks written in colloquial language, cartoons, etc.) plus late imperial tracts glorifying a sociopolitical order that readers knew was gone for good but still found meaningful. It is harder to gauge the content of the other media used by religious groups of that period, such as the musical recordings and radio broadcasts discussed in chapter 3, but again one must not confuse technological and intellectual modernity. The recorded sermons mass-distributed in China from the 1980s on, as well as increasingly common religious TV channels, all show that conservative content and innovative media can go very well together. In that respect, the Republican period reveals many of the trends we now observe in the twenty-first century. All this strongly suggests that the vibrant, almost exuberant creativity of Republican period religious publishing, and that of morality books in particular, should be understood as a new stage in a long history rather than a revolution that started anew from a clean slate.

PART 3

INDIVIDUAL
RELIGIOSITY

CHAPTER 5

ELITE RELIGIOSITY FROM LATE IMPERIAL TIMES TO THE REPUBLIC

The 1898 reforms launched the revolutions of modern China in matters religious as in every other aspect of social and intellectual life.[1] From this point on, a growing estrangement seems to have taken place between elites and popular culture, in particular with regard to the latter's religious aspects. This estrangement took very different forms, from all-out westernization to a radical reinvention of Chinese identity that excluded whole realms of culture; it resulted in violent propaganda against "superstition" and repressive policies that caused the destruction of many temples, bans on festivals and other rituals, and paved the way for the post-1949 attempted eradication of most aspects of lived religion (see chapters 1-2).

Certain historians assert that these conflicts find their roots in earlier periods. William T. Rowe, analyzing the attitudes of eighteenth-century elite officials, writes of the "great religious war waged by devout *lixue* 理學 [neo-Confucian] adherents against Buddhist and Daoist beliefs and practice" and their "more persistent assault on popular culture"[2]. Other historians, however, observe that, not unlike their prerevolutionary counterparts in early modern Europe, Qing elites maintained a biculturalism that allowed them to participate in both the culture (religious and otherwise) proper to their milieu and that of the society around them.[3] This biculturalism extended to many realms, including language (local vs. *guanhua* 官話), food and social etiquette, performing arts, and naturally rituals and cults. The ruptures of modernity would then have been accompanied by a decline of such biculturalism and resulted among elites in utter misunderstanding of, and deep aversion to, the religious practices and worldviews of the lower classes— misunderstanding and aversion still in evidence today, albeit obviously highly dependent on variables such as personal life histories and place of residence.

At the same time, estrangement from popular culture did not entail an overall decline in religiosity among modern elites. Far from it, our research indicates that there was a sustained high level of religious commitment among many Republican elites that should be analyzed in terms of both certain continuities with the late imperial era and multifarious forms of reinvention and innovation. In considering the issues of biculturalism and estrangement, our emphasis here is to explore the personal religious worlds of the elites as opposed to their public activities or philosophical pronouncements.

Late Qing Elites

Exploring these issues requires a better understanding of elite religious practices and attitudes, as well as their connections to those of the society around them before 1898, and then gauging the changes that unfolded during the following fifty years. Were elites in the last years of the Qing already so estranged from the religious traditions of the people that they only required a favorable political context to participate in its repression? Or did they continue to maintain connections, not necessarily warm but nonetheless close, natural, and regular, with the temples, cults, and rituals around them? To what extent were elite types (such as urban upper elites and rural-based local gentry) a factor in such differences? How did post-1898 political and social changes affect such connections at both the personal and social levels?

Such questions raise numerous methodological issues. First, the term *elites* suggests a certain cultural homogeneity that on closer examination proves rather elusive. Internal differences are quite notable between upper gentry (the *jinshi* 進士 laureates, almost all of them officials, active or retired), who adhered quite closely to Confucian norms and practices, and the middle to lower gentry plus other elites (especially non–degree holders), whose religious identities were more varied.[4] These various strata of elite society were less differentiated by education than by social role, in particular active officials having to enforce imperial laws that were quite repressive in matters religious—even though in practice tolerance and negotiation were the dominant modes of interaction between state agents and local communities.[5] Members of the gentry not employed by the state were much freer to interpret and enact in diverse ways their roles as educators of the people. Among the latter, one finds not only local notables who played leadership roles within local religious structures but also activists (people who by personal choice devoted themselves to a moral/religious cause and invested large portions of their resources in supporting it) trying to reform local religious practices. Some of these activists were fundamentalists, that is, people who dreamed of returning to the golden age described by the Classics and wanted to abolish all later ritual, practical, and theological accretions not warranted by these works. Others (even though distinctions were never so clear-cut) had a more encompassing approach, often tied to the practice of spirit-writing, the production and diffusion of morality books, and philanthropy. We return in the next chapter to the private use of spirit-writing in elite lives, while we have already seen in the previous chapter their public use for disseminating messages of collective salvation.

Furthermore, economic elites were closely allied to the gentry but could also engage in their own distinct religious activities; in just one example, the leaders of major guilds organized the great festivals (*saihui* 賽會) that so irked officials and fundamentalist activists.[6] To further complicate the picture, the upper strata of the Daoist and Buddhist clergies were full members of the local elite. In a nutshell, late imperial elites had about as much religious plurality as society as a whole.

State bureaucracy and its recruitment shaped the composition of elites, but so did other factors, notably urbanization and its corollary, the gradual dismantling of the rural-based landlord elite families. It is no coincidence that early Republican-period anti-superstition activists were often people cut off from their extended families and country homes (*laojia* 老家) while advocating the "small family" (*xiao jiating* 小家庭).[7] It has been well noted that the process of elite families moving to the cities, and changing their cultural practices in the process, had begun long before the late Qing, but city-based politics gave this trend a sharp acceleration. As cities became the windows and front lines of modernity, small families became a norm. Ideas of public and private lives also evolved as a consequence. Why this matters is amply demonstrated by the case study of Yu Yue 俞樾 (1821–1906) evoked below. Back in the 1890s, Yu could claim to be a sophisticated literatus removed from the peasant's lack of culture, sitting in his studio on an island at West Lake in Hangzhou, the very Mecca of literati refinement, and at the same time be very well informed indeed about what spirit-mediums were doing in his native villages through discussions with his servants, daughters-in-law, poorer kin, and other relatives who traveled there. Similar cases become much harder to find from the 1920s onward.

There was thus considerable strain between urban intellectuals and more rural elites. Relatively few modern Chinese elites chose to promote religion as a form of national identity, a phenomenon markedly different from what occurred in many other Asian countries. Numerous western-educated urban elites, including Hu Shih 胡適 (1891–1962) and Chen Duxiu 陳獨秀 (1879–1942), felt a profound sense of crisis about China's future and became especially concerned about "superstition" in the aftermath of the Boxer uprising. Their support of temple destruction and other anti-superstition campaigns contrasts sharply with elites in more rural areas, as well as market towns. While some (especially those not holding formal office) may have supported temple destruction campaigns in order to side with what they perceived to be the winning power of the state, many others steadfastly defended their local religious traditions.[8] Both sides proved adept at using the mass media (what Nedostup aptly refers to as a "toolbox of modernity") to their advantage.[9]

The historiography of elite religion so far has largely focused on state policies toward religion and their impact rather than the convictions and worldviews that informed such policies and officials' pronouncements. Various theoretical and methodological tools have been applied, or at least proposed, toward such a task. Among such tools, normal religious affiliations are not really relevant here, as elites were defined ex officio as "Confucian" (ru 儒) while they also followed the state in recognizing (to various extents) the validity of Buddhist and Daoist teachings. Similarly, "faith" or "belief" is hardly useful as a category, as sources rarely addressed religious involvement in such terms. The notion of piety is more useful; it allows us to focus our attention on the sensibility, style, aesthetics, and concrete ways in which one engages in or with religion, including in informal settings. The aesthetic dimension is crucial to understanding this concept and sheds light on how elites self-identified with practices (meditation, moral self-improvement, liturgy, etc.) characterized by self-control, solemnity, and restraint, in explicit contrast to what was described as the exuberant style (excess of colors, sounds, expenses, etc.) of "popular" practices.

Another, related concept, "modalities," also cuts across confessional religious identities (Confucian, Buddhist, Daoist, etc). Adam Y. Chau distinguishes between five modalities of "doing" religion within Chinese (and other) societies: discursive (text-based); relational/organizational (organizing festivals, running temples), personal (self-cultivation, body techniques), liturgical, and immediate/practical.[10] The practices of modern Chinese elites certainly conform to several of these modalities. Some elites devoted themselves to a discursive, exegetical mode, as they read and commented on large numbers of religious texts while declining as much as possible to take part in public religious activities while others favored the organizational modality through moral activism (distributing morality books, public teaching and preaching, charitable activities).

Useful as they are, these two concepts mostly allow us to apprehend the conceptions and practices of the most religiously involved elites: the activists. Yet, in modern China as elsewhere, the degree of interest and involvement in things religious was highly variable: some people observed sustained personal practice and were active in religious organizations, while others had limited interest in such things, participating when they had to with little personal commitment. The notion of religious knowledge seems useful to bring into the analysis the large numbers of elites who had little visible religious involvement.[11] By religious knowledge we mean what actors knew and understood about religion and the vocabulary they used to discuss it; this includes conceptions and practices that are not those of the actors themselves but the ones they see and understand (or not) among the people around them. Focusing on religious knowledge also allows us to ask the question of what elites ignored or misunderstood, as well as the limits of their capacity to comprehend the society around them, thereby probing the issue of the modern distance between popular and official cultures.

We propose for our present purposes to define *religiosity* as the sum of the three concepts briefly outlined above—religious knowledge, piety, and modalities of doing religion—in other words, what individuals knew, felt, and did. Defined thus, this notion opens new windows on differences between various members of the elites, differences that are linked not only to context (historical, local, familial) but also to individual choices and preferences. Understanding any person's religiosity involves distinguishing between different spheres, spanning the spectrum from official to public and familial to intimate. One must be careful when discussing public and private in the late imperial context, as these could be markedly different from what we know from our own experience. Furthermore, late imperial culture was imbued with a strong age-old conviction that one's public actions reflect the quality of one's private moral cultivation. Yet a number of practices were compartmentalized; an official could engage at ease in Buddhist or Daoist self-cultivation as long as he did not discuss it in his capacity as an official.

Religiosity in public life concerns mandatory practices and observances, imposed by either law, custom, or etiquette. Late imperial officials had to attend a very large number of sacrifices all year long and visit temples on a regular basis; for instance, they went to the City God temple twice a month. Students had to participate twice a month in rituals at the Confucius temple. Besides this, officials and many other members of the elite were invited to all major local festivals and could hardly decline them all. Even when in temporary residence at the capital, they had to participate in the ritual activities of their *huiguan* 會館 (guilds and native-place associations), as well as attending family and lineage rituals of their kin and other social networks. Very often they were invited to take an active role in such celebrations, being invited, for instance, to perform the consecration of the tablet of the deceased (*dianzhu* 點主). More generally, literati who had passed the first degree of the examinations, and were thus part of the gentry, were qualified to act as Confucian ritual performers (*lisheng* 禮生). Some poor scholars, or those from families that specialized in Confucian ritual, made a living from their liturgical expertise; many more did it occasionally.

Browsing through the diaries (*riji* 日記) of late Qing scholars, one realizes the pervasiveness of this form of social religious life.[12] Arguably, in many if not most cases, participating in such rituals was routine and did not imply a deep emotional or spiritual involvement on the part of the participants, who were waiting for the end of the ritual so they could chat with their kin, friends, or colleagues during the banquet that followed. Yet one cannot deny that these rituals could induce meaningful religious experiences and that they informed, possibly passively and unconsciously, the habitus and worldviews of those who had to attend them so often. At the very least, they nourished the literati's liturgical culture.

Another type of participation in local religious life concerns the roles of elites in community religious institutions, notably the management of the large temples. Historians tend to assume that elites gradually retreated from this role at the end of the imperial period, but no study has yet documented in detail the chronology, causes, and scope of this phenomenon.[13] Merchants remained deeply involved in the management of urban temples into the first decades of the twentieth century, showing a case of partial continuity across revolutionary transformations. Even when they were not active in the management of temples, elites continued to be called on to write inscriptions for temples and monasteries (a form of literary patronage), which required some knowledge of the cults and traditions involved; similarly, many literati were involved in the compilation of local gazetteers and other essays about local history, which necessarily dealt with local cults and ritual culture.[14] Furthermore, elite activists managed their own religious associations, which organized Confucian, Daoist, and Buddhist rituals; let us just mention here the Wenchanghui 文昌會 (for the worship of Wenchang) and charitable halls (shantang 善堂).

Apart from these forms of social religious life, literati had, to a highly variable degree, a private religious life, chosen and characterized by more intense spiritual involvement. Some were lay Buddhists. Maybe the best known in the existing scholarly literature is Peng Shaosheng 彭紹升 (1740–96), a jinshi and member of the extremely prestigious Suzhou Pengs, who left many influential works on both the Classics and Buddhism.[15] Other elites immersed themselves in Daoist self-cultivation techniques, notably inner alchemy, taking an active part in the writing, editing, and distribution of manuals and teaching a few select disciples.[16] Such Daoist self-cultivators were by no means recluses. Consider the case of the famous Daoist-cum-businessman-cum-reformist intellectual Zheng Guanying 鄭觀應 (1842–1921).[17] Buddhist meditation and Daoist inner alchemy were part of a larger set of spiritual techniques that appear (usually only in a very allusive manner) in the writings of the literati, whereby they controlled their minds and bodies and dealt with dangers, the presence of spirits, and illnesses. Other techniques included the recitation of incantations (zhou 咒), visualization, divination, devotional rites, penance, and meditation (jingzuo 靜坐).[18]

One of the most widespread and influential of these techniques was spirit-writing, which lay at the core of the religious lives of many late imperial elites.[19] As we saw in the previous chapter, morality books revealed by spirit-writing constitute the largest part of the production of religious texts by elites; these books carried a vision of educational, charitable, and moral reform, but they also had a strong devotional dimension built around savior deities. Some of these productions defined religious practices explicitly linked to the literati, such as the cult of written characters (*xizi* 惜字).

Indeed, far from exposing a "secular" ethics, the omnipresent spirit-writing cults and attendant moral reform movements developed a vibrant eschatology whereby literati were entrusted with saving the world from the impending apocalypse. Movements of religious and cultural revitalization that emerged during the tumultuous second decade of the nineteenth century continued through the twentieth, such as those centering on the Eight Virtues (Bade 八德); they constituted a major case of continuity between late imperial and Republican elite religious worldviews.[20] Linked to these eschatological scenarios was a deeply held aspiration for self-divinization. Late imperial elites, quite independent of being transformed into ancestors by their kin, hoped to become gods as members of the divine bureaucracy and were confident that their good deeds would result in their nomination as a City God or other such office.[21]

Post-1898 Chinese elites had decidedly mixed attitudes toward spirit-writing. On the one hand, there are scathing critiques of the practice and records of attempts to suppress it during anti-superstition campaigns, with the authorities especially incensed by the fact that many spirit-writing groups issued medicinal prescriptions to worshippers (a practice also common in modern Taiwan until it was banned).[22] At the same time, however, an equal (if not greater) number of elites described spirit-writing in a neutral or even positive light, recounting these practices in a matter-of-fact manner.[23] Some authors debated the extent to which spirit-writing rituals could be considered "science" (*kexue* 科學),[24] in large part due to a worldwide interest in paranormal psychology among intellectuals in Europe, the United States, and Japan, with Chinese students becoming exposed to these practices while pursuing their studies abroad. Prominent warlords, including figures such as Wu Peifu 吳佩孚 (1874–1939), appear to have had a great interest in spirit-writing, particularly when it came to asking the gods about strategic matters.[25] One tongue-in-cheek account describes Chen Jitang 陳濟棠 (1890–1954) deciding to lead his forces into battle against Chiang Kai-shek after receiving a poem written by Lü Dongbin 呂洞賓 during a spirit-writing session, only to suffer a devastating defeat because he had misconstrued its contents.[26]

Studies of activist milieus such as those for managing spirit-writing cults and publishing their revelations are obviously crucial to our understanding of the religious world of late imperial elites, but they should not finesse questions about other members of the elite. What proportion of elites participated in spirit-writing séances and was actively involved in the other activities of the groups that held them? What portion read spirit-written revelations and morality books? We know of some elite activists through their publications (spirit-written texts and their paratexts: prefaces, notes, appended records), but other elites left traces of their individual religious worldviews in their private writings. In an innovative work, Liu Xun studied the artistic and poetic productions of the literati in an aristocratic Manchu family, the Wanyan 完顏, which gave the Qing state successive generations of officials until the late nineteenth century. These literati-officials embraced a Daoist vision of the world expressed in poems that helped them make sense of the vicissitudes of their careers and found an outlet in the worship of Lü Dongbin.[27] Another major textual resource, already mentioned above, is diaries and autobiographies. Henrietta Harrison's study of the diary of Liu Dapeng 劉大鵬 (1857–1942), a poor provincial laureate (*juren*) from Shanxi, is particularly enlightening. This scholar, as he represented himself in his daily notes, saw the moral retribution of actions at work in every turn of events and felt certain every time he encountered a setback that Heaven was punishing him for his sins. Considered by the local population to be an exemplary Confucian, Liu was also highly pious, regularly visiting local temples and even encountering Confucius in dreams.[28] This shows to what extent literati training and religious habitus were closely interwoven.

Whereas personal texts such as poetry and diaries express an intimate religious world, chosen and nonconfrontational, other genres allow the literati to pass judgment on the religious culture of others. The Chinese press, following its appearance in the 1870s, played an active role in pronouncing such judgments, notably the best known of the daily newspapers, *Shenbao*, published in the Shanghai concessions from 1872 to 1949. Apart from a very large number of reports describing local religious life in Shanghai and other major cities (including spirit-writing activities) plus anecdotes on the extraordinary (healings, exorcisms, miracles, strange apparitions), the pages of *Shenbao* also expressed a highly developed polemical discourse, often anticlerical and occasionally hostile toward large community rituals.[29] Such polemics are important not only in prefiguring elite attacks on popular religion as they unfolded from 1898 onward but also in revealing diverse levels of understanding of and familiarity with the religious ideas and practices under attack.

One more genre opening a window onto the religious worlds of late imperial elites is anecdotes (*biji* 筆記), most notably those devoted to "records of the strange" (*zhiguai* 志怪). This genre is far from being hermetically separated from those mentioned above; very similar accounts can be found in anecdotes, the press, and the narrative sections of morality books. In a separate publication, Vincent Goossaert has developed a case study of one very prominent late Qing intellectual, Yu Yue, to explore his religious knowledge based on his large collection of *zhiguai*, the *Youtai xianguan biji* 右台仙館筆記.[30] Yu is interesting because he was not an activist, and he stated quite clearly that his private religious life was less intense than that of many of his peers, friends and relatives. He did author commentaries on the *Jin'gang jing* 金剛經 and *Taishang ganying pian* 太上感應篇, but these are minor parts of his abundant oeuvre. Yet in the *Youtai xianguan biji* Yu documents his sustained interest in local religious culture, which he was able to grasp in large part due to his female relatives (mother, wives, daughters, daughters-in-law, servants) who themselves were active participants in local religious life. Yu could be critical of vernacular rites and specialists, but not systemically, as he also embraced a nuanced discourse on spirit-mediums. He readily admitted that the world he lived in was saturated with ghosts and spirits, yet he also felt that proper moral practice was superior because right was destined to triumph over evil (*xie bu sheng zheng* 邪不勝正). Yu was also interested in the multifarious spiritual techniques practiced by his friends and students; he did not himself engage in spirit-writing, but many people around him did. Like so many other authors, Yu dismissed *some* cases as fraud but not on principle. Last but not least, Yu accepted as a matter of fact that scholars could become gods; most of his deceased kin and friends had been granted postings in the other world.

Because he was anchored in a rural domestic universe, Yu had some familiarity, albeit not always sympathetic, with the religious world of the common people; he thus considered the beliefs and practices unfolding around him to be comprehensible. As a member of the elite, he took very seriously his role as a moral authority, but he mostly comes across as a benevolent observer rather than a fiery reformer of "popular" practices. One generation later many scholars would view the same world of popular cults, rites, and specialists as altogether absurd and alien. Yet we should not overvalue rupture over continuity. Yu did not participate in local religious life beyond domestic activities, apparently hardly ever going to temples and festivals. He did not chronicle cults and festivals as folklorists do, and he does not appear to have considered them particularly important aspects of culture worth preserving. Yu thus can be viewed as a link between classical culture and the early-twentieth-century redemptive societies that would strive to reformulate and revitalize the Chinese spiritual heritage and in which several of Yu's students were active.[31] His religious vision was in line with the "popular Confucianism" described by Philip Clart, based on a social strata of educated people aspiring to become gods and bring moral order back to the world. Yu shares with them a conception of holiness based on self-discipline and moral self-cultivation, as well as a steadfast conviction of the scholar's spiritual superiority.

A Model of Elite Religiosity

Based on these considerations, we would like to propose a simple model of Chinese religiosity, valid across time, which would chart members of the elite according to two key parameters that seem most heuristically important: commitment and knowledge.

Commitment means the degree to which a given individual devotes an important part of his or her time, energy, and resources (both material and symbolic) to religious activities and endeavors. Obviously, it has been remarked repeatedly that in pre-1911 China (and even after that) any distinction between religious and nonreligious institutions and activities can be moot. Still, humans have by character and training widely varying appetites for rituals, cults, and other religious activities, and among modern Chinese elites there is a clear gradient between people who seem to have, or indeed admit to having, little patience with performing sacrifices, listening to sermons, and meditating and those who confess and profess a strong attraction to such activities. Keeping in mind that commitment varies according to modality (intense meditators can eschew participation in temple management), we give high marks to those individuals who devote time and money to such activities as founding religious associations or temples, organizing rituals, and writing, editing, or publishing religious books.

The second parameter is knowledge of religious culture, which we define here, as discussed above, as an interest in things religious and an expressed understanding of the role of religion in social life, whether the individual in question participates or not.

If we set these two parameters as the axes on a chart and place individuals on it (admittedly a subjective exercise), patterns and clusters begin to appear that we can theorize as ideal types (see figure 5.1). One benefit of such an exercise is that it allows for the clustering of people who may have lived different lives and practiced rather different types of religion but who nonetheless exhibit rather similar attitudes toward the religious.

Let us look at the clusters that form in the four quadrants of our chart, remembering that most people tended to be located somewhere in the middle, as in any such chart. At the top left are people with a high level of commitment but a low level of knowledge. We call them "fundamentalists," people intensively engaged with their own particular tradition but willfully ignorant, and usually rather dismissive, of other traditions and forms of religious practice.

At the top right are people both engaged and cultured. We deem them "activists," as many such elites tend to have broad interest and participate in groups (such as spirit-writing cults) that encompass a wide spectrum of religious convictions. Consider, for instance, Yu Zhi 余治 (1809–74), an extremely engaged Jiangnan scholar who wrote, printed, and disseminated religious texts in many genres (theater, *baojuan* 寶卷, tracts in classical Chinese) and was famous for his charitable activities. During the Taiping Civil War, Yu lived as a refugee collecting funds for loyalist armies and militia, organizing anti-Taiping propaganda, and relentlessly preaching in public that people must repent and engage in moral

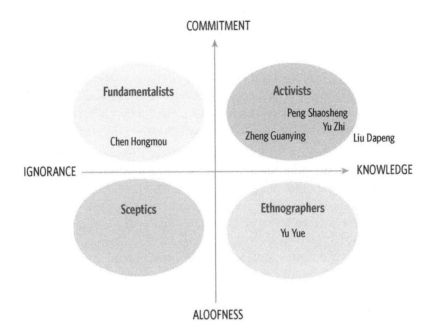

Figure 5.1. Types of elite religiosity among selected late Qing individuals

reform so the gods would be appeased and peace could return to China.[32] Peng Shaosheng, mentioned above, is another good example.

At the bottom right are people interested in and knowledgeable about religion but with a low level of personal participation. We call them "ethnographers," and we take Yu Yue as a good example. Yu wrote about beliefs, local gods, and rituals at length, yet he told us that he had little belief in these things. In a different perspective, academics like Gu Jiegang continued in the Republican period to document religion from a non-committal standpoint.

Finally, at the bottom left are people both ignorant of and aloof from religion: the "sceptics." This is likely the category that experienced the most growth as Chinese society moved from the late imperial to the Republican period.

Changes among Republican Elites

Before we move on to using our chart to look at the religiosity of Republican elites, a few words about the elites themselves are in order. The social and political dynamics that created elite classes changed dramatically between the imperial and Republican eras. Think, for instance, of the first Chinese parliament, elected (albeit indirectly) through assemblies of local elites between December 1912 and January

1913; 60 out of 274 members were Christians who would have been viewed as outlaws just two generations earlier.[33] With the end of the civil service examinations in 1905, the criteria for official recruitment changed to favor graduates of modern schools, both civil (many of which were Christian run) and military. Yet the social and cultural makeup of the Chinese elite did not change overnight. Many of those educated under the imperial regime, who held values inculcated at that time, enjoyed honorable careers under the Republic, most importantly (but not uniquely) among the military warlord-oriented elites.

Indeed, many Beiyang 北洋 grandees swelled the ranks of the new voluntary religious associations (generally referred to as "redemptive societies," see above), which called, among other things, for a restoration of at least some traditional values. Such elites argued in favor of carefully distinguishing between legitimate religious practices (especially self-cultivation) and indiscriminate worship of deities for personal gain (which even they considered to be a form of "superstition"). Adopting forms of discourse at times strikingly similar to those espoused by the state, they nonetheless used writings published in their own religious periodicals to warn the authorities against recklessly implementing anti-superstition policies. One example may be found in a spirit-writing text attributed to the Song dynasty Buddhist monk Jigong 濟公, which appeared in 1922 in the *Morality Magazine* (*Daode zazhi* 道德雜誌) published by the Society of the Way (Daoyuan 道院, also known by the name of its philanthropic branch, the World Red Swastika Society or Shijie hongwanzihui 世界紅卍字會 (for more on religious periodicals, see chapter 3).

> [Jigong:] Sit down and listen. What you refer to as superstition is not those beliefs and practices to which we devote ourselves. Those people who our elders (*fuzi* 夫子) refer to as superstitious include both ignorant men and women (*yufu yufu* 愚夫愚婦) who engage in idolatry (*bai ouxiang* 拜偶像) and those who claim to believe in gods and buddhas but fail to live by their teachings. Today we adhere to the true principles (*zhenli* 真理) of the sages, immortals, and buddhas. We incorporate the Five Teachings (*wujiao* 五教) [Buddhism, Daoism, Catholicism, Protestantism, and Islam] as one great way (*dadao* 大道), practicing internal and external cultivation, saving ourselves while also providing salvation for others. As such, we hardly compare to those who blindly engage in various practices. What do you have to say to that?[34]

The success of redemptive societies in being recognized as legitimate religious groups was in part due to the fact that they boasted among their membership some of the leading military figures of that age. Among the many Beiyang politicians supporting the Fellowship of Goodness (Tongshanshe 同善社) were Yan Xishan

閻錫山 (1883–1960), Lu Yongxiang 盧永祥 (1867–1933), Cao Kun 曹錕 (1862–1938, who is said to have bribed his way into the presidency of the Republic in 1923), and most notably Duan Qirui 段祺瑞 (1865–1936, who served as the nation's chief executive from 1924 to 1926).[35] Many KMT leaders were also active members, including former premier Xiong Xiling 熊希齡 (1870–1937), who presided over the Red Swastika Society. As a result, some modern Chinese leaders proved willing to condone a wide range of religious activities, including spirit-writing, which could avoid the "superstition" label if associated with religious organizations that had gained the sanction of the authorities. In the case of redemptive societies, state approval was facilitated by the fact that many such groups registered with the authorities as philanthropic associations or organizations devoted to the practice of self-cultivation. At the same time, however, while the state often embraced such groups for their charitable actions or adherence to traditional Chinese culture, it could also end up denouncing them as heterodox manifestations of superstition.

Arguably the most important factor that affected changes in elite religiosity during the 1898–1948 period was education. Traditional education in private *sishu* 私塾, official temple schools, and prestigious academies (*shuyuan* 書院) was in large part devoted to Confucian liturgy, as well as its underlying cosmology and theology. Let us not forget that all familial and communal events (weddings, funerals, sacrifices to ancestors or local gods) required the intervention of a Confucian ritual specialist (*lisheng* 禮生), for which all laureates of the first degree of the civil service examinations were qualified. After civil service examinations were abolished in 1905, it was gradually accepted that being a college graduate was the equivalent in rank (albeit not in terms of the content of the training received), but not all such graduates accepted invitations to serve as *lisheng* and officiate.[36]

Indeed, the modern school education that replaced the temple schools and academies (and, at the grassroots level, albeit much more gradually, the *sishu*) dispensed with such ritual education altogether. The issue of teaching the Classics was much debated, with the Four Books removed and put back in the curriculum countless times, yet beyond the philological and philosophical reading of the Classics, all training in liturgy had gone for good. This of course, was even more the case in the Christian schools that rapidly came to play a central role in the training of the new Chinese elites.[37] Such schools instructing the scions of the modern Chinese elites, whether in China or abroad, had a rather poor record of converting them into baptized Christians, yet they were more successful in instilling rather hostile views toward the traditional cosmology that formed the foundation of late imperial religiosity. Education did not necessarily mean distancing oneself from Chinese religion though; consider the case of Zhang Taiyan 章太炎 (1869–1936), one of Yu Yue's most famous students, who was trained in Japan and converted to Buddhism there.

As important as education was urbanization. The trend toward urban life and small families was of course both real and also a foil. Reading from the likes of Lu Xun 鲁迅 (1881–1936) and other progressive writers, moving from the country to the big city was a liberation from the shackles of superstition. But in actual life Shanghai, Beijing, and Guangzhou were special cases (and, indeed, very different from each other), and many people lived in regional capitals, county seats, and market towns, which were urbanized but where local socioreligious structures survived better and longer and where ties to the countryside were stronger. Furthermore, urbanization went hand in hand with fast-developing modern transportation, and by the 1920s trains and buses conveniently took urbanites on day trips to the festivals and temples in the suburbs and farther away (such excursions were actively marketed by transport companies). Space became more differentiated as people moved ever more easily (at least until 1949) between spaces.[38]

As a result of a general (albeit variegated) trend toward urbanization, elites found themselves less and less engaged in ascriptive forms of religious communities (kinship, territory, and profession). While they maintained connections with lineage organizations, they often lived in large cities where the ascriptive neighborhood temples (which all resident families had to register with and contribute to) were losing their power to dictate communal life. The guilds and native-place associations (*huiguan* 會館) also tended to marginalize their ritual and devotional dimensions (even though this process was not completed before the 1950s). In Jiangnan, many elites maintained their distance or even denounced the system of contractual registration that each family had with a number of religious specialists (including *lisheng*, Buddhists, Daoists, ritual workers, and performers).[39] Yet some communal temples retained strong elite support. For instance, Liu Wenxing has explored in depth the connections between the community of Huzhou businesspeople in Shanghai and one temple that their main association (the Hushe 湖社) collectively owned and maintained. While this temple, like so many others during the Republican period, was embroiled in a property dispute, many of these businesspeople were committed to keeping it active and operating at the same time that they were engaged in charitable and spirit-writing activities.[40]

In contrast to the relative decline of the ascriptive dimension of elites' public religious lives, the voluntary, associational dimension (which had always existed) became far more dominant. Many were active in voluntary elite groups such as spirit-writing halls and philanthropic associations (the two often being one and the same).

Another major correlate of the social evolution spurred by education and urbanization is the increased participation of women in mixed-gender religious activities such as spirit-writing, publishing, and lecturing. Late imperial elite women had a wide range of religious practices at their disposal, including devotional and self-cultivational forms at home, and some became religious virtuosi who instructed their male kin,[41] but their participation in collective religious activities outside the family sphere was always contentious. By the Republican period, the discourse on the "new woman" was claiming, on the one hand, to liberate women from the shackles of superstition but on the other was actually giving them more freedom to participate in spirit-writing groups (where they often became very numerous), scripture study groups, mixed-gender sutra recitation groups, and other types of public religious organizations.[42] Many women also published in the religious press and maintained published correspondence with religious leaders.[43]

It is difficult to measure and document systematically such broad and inchoate historical evolution. A few types of sources seem to capture it though. The language one uses to discuss religion is a key criterion, and some works that straddle the late imperial–Republican divide tell the tale. Local gazetteers are a case in point, and the treatment of local religion in these texts (compiled and edited by local officials and scholars) evinces an important shift between late Qing and Republican period editions, which were evolving toward a more distanced, scientific view of what religions are, although, of course, there was no sudden shift and many gazetteers proposed hybrid and mixed discourses. Whereas late Qing gazetteers discussed religion in various sections (most notably local customs, official sacrifices, Buddhist and Daoist monasteries, and biographies of famous Buddhists and Daoists), Republican ones gradually tended to gather that material in a separate section on "religion" organized by confessional identity: Christianity, Islam, Buddhism, and Daoism.[44]

As a result of these various, mutually reinforcing factors, we see evolution unfolding that can be traced on the chart in figure 5.2. To sum up our most basic findings, many members of the Republican elites seemed to lose knowledge of religious culture rather than disengaging from it: they moved leftward rather than downward on our chart. Naturally, the chart, which includes some of the persons we have mentioned, has far too few names to be representative while placement along the two axes itself is necessarily subjective. Yet it seems to us that many elites we have surveyed maintained high levels of commitment (running institutions, devoting time and money to organizing ceremonies, raising funds, etc.) but were more focused on a specific type of religious endeavor. Even Wang Yiting, who, as we will see shortly, was an epitome of religious commitment, seems to have had very little connection to or interest in a whole facet of Chinese religion: local cults and communal rituals.

This, we hasten to add, is a very general trend that tells us nothing about many types of individuals. Moreover, all four ideal types were still to be found

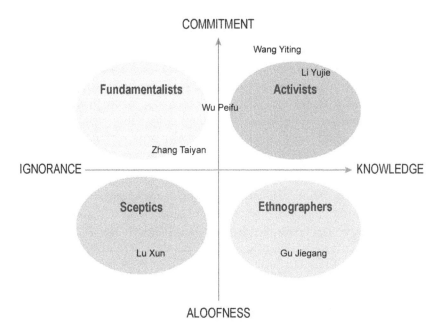

Figure 5.2. Types of elite religiosity among
selected Republican period individuals

throughout our period. There were countless religious activists in Republican China. Consider people like Wang Yiting, discussed in chapter 6, who canvassed for support to organize and fund countless religious organizations, rituals, and projects, from the most orthodox monastic Buddhism to a wide assortment of spirit-writing cults and redemptive societies. As we will see in more detail below, Wang and his many friends carried forth the spirit of the engaged layperson. Educated noncommitted people were also around. Local intellectuals in Wenzhou who into the early Communist period recorded local customs while finding ways around the strictures of atheist orthodoxy to paint them in the best possible light are fine exemplars of this type.[45]

Yet there is no doubt that the ranks of both fundamentalists and skeptics grew throughout the fifty years covered by this study. Many Christians, who wanted to rid China of its superstitions, swelled the ranks of its fundamentalists. So did adepts of reformed Buddhism, and we find representatives of both categories among the KMT politicians and activists who devised and implemented anti-superstition policies. Indeed, many elites who rejected traditional Chinese religious culture were not atheists but Christians. Christians were overall a small minority in China—reasonable estimates put the numbers at three million

Catholics and one million Protestants by 1949—but they were a significant part of the new elites trained in modern schools who filled the ranks of the liberal professions (doctors, lawyers, engineers). To a significant extent, their religiosity was comparable to that of other elites, with a focus on strict self-discipline and moral self-examination. Consider, for instance, the case of Chiang Kai-shek, who studied neo-Confucianism and learned of Buddhism from his mother but then chose to convert to Methodism in order to marry Soong May-ling 宋美齡 (1898-2003) in December 1927 (he was not baptized until October 1930). We know that Chiang regularly read the Bible, and that his faith provided him with much-needed strength during the difficult days of the Xi'an Incident (Xi'an shibian 西安事變).[46] Apart from the Bible, another important source of inspiration was a collection of Christian testaments entitled *Streams in the Desert* (*Huangmo ganquan* 荒漠甘泉), which stressed unwavering faith in the face of failure. Chiang is known to have devotedly jotted down his thoughts beside its daily inspirational messages.[47]

Further evidence for the importance of Christianity in Chiang's life may be found in his diary, the recent publication of which has shed new light on his hopes and fears, his self-doubts and desire to repent his failings, and his daily regimen of self-cultivation and self-discipline, which included calisthenics, Bible study, meditation, and prayer.[48] Chiang's diary, as well as his other writings, reveals that he found Christian morality consistent with the neo-Confucian teachings he had learned as a child, particularly their emphasis on shame, atonement, and perseverance. This is congruent with the very widespread practice of late Qing and Republican era intellectuals to keep daily records and accountings of their thoughts and actions based on the ledgers of merit and demerit (*gongguoge* 功過格).[49]

Just like Christians, the more numerous elite lay Buddhists tended to maintain a high level of commitment to their own cultivation while showing a lesser degree of knowledge about "popular" and local religious traditions. Indeed, they were instrumental in the massive distribution of self-cultivation manuals and morality books during that period (see chapter 4). The standardized classroom teaching of self-cultivation methods introduced by both Buddhist groups and redemptive societies such as the Fellowship of Goodness meant that probably more people engaged in meditation and/or Daoist-inspired self-transformation techniques in the 1920s and 1930s than during any other period before the *qigong* boom of the 1980s. Thus ambient scientism spurred rather than hampered such developments.[50]

All this contributed to the development of urban, modern styles of piety, reflected not only in religious textbooks and other literature couched in "scientific" language but also in religious tastes and aesthetics. As Brooks Jessup showed in the case of the Worldwide Householder Grove (Shijie Fojiao jushilin 世界佛教居士林), organized by Shanghai's lay Buddhists, the chosen architecture and style conveyed a strong statement about what kind of religion these officials, intellectuals, and businessmen wanted to be seen engaging in.[51] This sober style was designed in clear contradistinction to the "hot and noisy" atmosphere of local temples. Such a dichotomy, which was basically a new iteration in a very long history of elite rationalization of Chinese popular religious culture, ran, like its predecessors, into major practical difficulties. Jan Kiely has shown how the same Shanghai lay Buddhist elites successfully adopted and promoted a charismatic monk, Yinguang, but were eventually overwhelmed by his popular appeal, so that they had to find ways to prevent him from living among the people and accepting their invitations.[52]

On the other hand, factors of continuity were also numerous and important. As chapters 3 and 4 have shown, religious knowledge of the late imperial era continued to circulate on a massive scale, reprinted and further disseminated by the new religious presses. Equally important was the continued popularity of spirit-writing.[53] In spite of the continued opposition of Buddhist leaders, not to mention skeptics, many members of the political, economic, and cultural elites continued to engage in this practice, thereby exposing themselves to the soteriological discourses that circulated in such milieus. Redemptive societies became a major venue for such discourses, and even if their political ideologies and organizations were in clear contrast to their pre-1912 forerunners, one must realize that their moral and soteriological discourses (apocalyptic eschatology, need for moral reform, hope for divinization) remained in direct continuity with those of the late imperial period. If one compares, for instance, the participation of warlords and politicians in redemptive societies (such as Wu Peifu) with that of the Taiping Civil War loyalist generals, we can discern such patterns of the past.

These trends of deep continuity certainly explain the acceptability of religious commitment, including in very messianic terms, of members of modern China's political elite. One need only think of the young KMT activist and official Li Yujie 李玉階 (1901–94), who became around 1934 one of the divine lords charged with universal salvation while keeping his government position with no apparent problems.[54] On another register, the publicly professed Christian faith of certain leaders, beginning with Sun Yat-sen and Chiang Kai-shek, was certainly considered acceptable in part because it was comparable to the sense of moral mission that drove members of the redemptive societies. The religious options available to Chinese elites, already quite diverse by the late imperial period, had further increased in number, but the idea that one should have strong moral values and a firm commitment to self-discipline and self-cultivation did not change. Indeed, it continued beyond the Republican period to inform Communist ethics and worldviews.[55]

CHAPTER 6

THE RELIGIOUS LIFE
OF WANG YITING

While current scholarship has delineated the overall development of modern Chinese religions, relatively little research has been done on individual elites.[1] This chapter complements the previous one's analysis of elite religiosity via a case study of Wang Yiting, a renowned businessman, artist, and philanthropist who actively participated in a plethora of religious groups, including several devoted to Buddhism, Daoism, and spirit-writing. One reason may be that, despite his many accomplishments, Wang also experienced his share of tragedy, including the loss of his first wife less than one year into their marriage, the death of his third daughter in infancy, and witnessing the brutal assassination of his comrade-in-arms Song Jiaoren 宋教仁 (1882–1913). These incidents seem to have attuned Wang to the suffering of others, prompting him not only to serve in leadership positions in philanthropic organizations but also to make paintings of the victims of natural disasters, which were then sold at auctions to raise money for relief efforts. Many such deeds were linked to Wang's Buddhist faith, as he served on the Charity Committee (Cishan weiyuanhui 慈善委員會) of the Chinese Buddhist Association (Zhongguo Fojiaohui 中國佛教會, founded in Shanghai in 1929). Wang also participated in the philanthropic activities of other religious movements, serving as founder and head of the China Rescuing Life Association (Zhongguo jishenghui 中國濟生會), a charitable organization whose members practiced spirit-writing rituals (see below). In short, his beliefs and practices both reflect and helped shape his life experiences.

Wang's Life and Career

Some of the most detailed information about Wang may be found in works composed by his contemporaries. For example, the *Wang Yiting jushi shilue* 王

一亭居士事略 features a necrology for Wang entitled "Brief Account of the Deeds [Performed by] Householder Wang Yiting" (Wuxing Wangjun shilue 吳興王君事略) written by Qin Xitian 秦錫田 (1861–1940), who like Wang was an avid philanthropist. This necrology documents the influence Wang's mother had on his life, including on his devotion to Buddhism and philanthropy.[2] Additional information on Wang's deeds in the realms of politics, commerce, and philanthropy may be found in Tang Wenzhi's 唐文治 (1865–1954) "Zhejiang Wang Yiting xiansheng gongde jinianbei" 浙江王一亭先生功德紀念碑, which regrettably has nothing to say about Wang's religious life.[3] Further data may be found in Wang Zhongxiu 王中秀's chronological biography,[4] as well as a number of scholarly studies.[5]

Wang's family came from Wuxing 吳興 in Huzhou 湖州, namely Shuiqiao 水橋 village near White Dragon Mountain (Bailongshan 白龍山) in the town of Yangjiapu 楊家埠,[6] but Wang was born in Shanghai because his father had fled their home during the 1860s (most likely as a result of the Taiping Civil War). However, in a pattern discussed in the previous chapter, Wang did return to his native place on important occasions, especially mortuary rituals for family members. In 1898, for example, Wang brought his father's body home for burial, also doing the same for his mother, two wives, and his maternal grandmother between 1914 and 1924. It would also seem reasonable to assume that Wang would have adhered to the standard filial practice of at least occasionally returning to his native place for the Tomb Sweeping Festival (Qingming jie 清明節) and the Ghost Festival (Zhongyuan jie 中元節), especially since transportation between Shanghai and Huzhou was relatively convenient. Wang also maintained close ties to Huzhou elites living in Shanghai, including the renowned artist Wu Changshuo 吳昌碩 (1844–1927), the revolutionary activist Chen Qimei 陳其美 (Chen Yingshi 陳英士, 1878–1915), and the literatus and Buddhist elite Dai Jitao 戴季陶 (1891–1949), who was born in Sichuan but from a Huzhou family).[7]

Wang's father died when he was a boy, and he was raised in relative poverty by his mother (née Jiang 蔣) and maternal grandmother. His sense of filial duty may have prompted his appreciation of the *Classic of Filial Piety* (*Xiaojing* 孝經), the illustrations of which are said to have inspired his early painting and calligraphy (some accounts also state that his love of painting began with his maternal grandmother).[8] In 1872 one of Wang's uncles noticed his aptitude for art and book learning and helped subsidize his education in a private school where he was also a tutor. Eight years later Wang was apprenticed at a famous picture-mounting shop known as the Yichun Tang 怡春堂, where he met and studied under renowned modern artists such as Ren Bonian 任伯年 (1840–96) and Li Ruiqing 李瑞清 (1867–1920).[9] During the early 1880s Wang also became acquainted with the renowned Ningbo merchant and collector Li Weizhuang 李薇莊 (1873–1913),[10]

who helped him find a job at a local banking house, which Weizhuang managed along with his brother, Li Yunshu 李雲書 (1867–?), who was a lay Buddhist. In addition to working at the banking house, Wang began to devote his evenings to learning English and Japanese at Shanghai's School for the Diffusion of Languages (Guang fangyanguan 廣方言館), founded by Li Hongzhang 李鴻章 (1823–1901).[11]

During the remaining decades of the nineteenth century and first years of the twentieth, Wang devoted his efforts to making his fortune and starting a family. He made his first trip to Japan (Yokohama 橫濱) in 1886, and in the same year married his first wife (née Xi 奚). She died of consumption less than one year later, and in 1888 Wang married his second wife (née Cao 曹). Their first child, a daughter, was born in 1889, followed two years later by a son, Mengnan 孟南. Additional children entered the world at regular two-year intervals, although, as noted above, the couple's third daughter (born in 1897) died young. In 1902, Wang drew on his skill in Japanese to start working as comprador (*maiban* 買辦) for the Osaka Shipping Corporation, earning considerable income due to his hard work and knowledge of Shanghai's commercial realm. His rising status may be seen in the fact that in 1904 he was chosen as one of the directors (*dongshi* 董事) of the Shanghai General Chamber of Commerce (Shanghai shangwu zonghui 上海商務總會). His experiences as a self-made man instilled in Wang a strong sense of the value of thrift, which he attempted to transmit to his offspring in a set of family instructions (*jiaxun* 家訓) published in 1931.[12]

In 1906 Wang spent a year living at White Dragon Mountain near the family home in Wuxing, which is also when he started to use the style name (*hao* 號) Bailong shanren 白龍山人. Just one year later, however, he took a position at the Nisshin Steamship Corporation, and by 1910 he was earning more than one hundred thousand dollars in commissions a year while working at Mitsubishi. Wang was also active in Shanghai's artistic community, helping to establish the Yu Garden Calligraphy and Painting Charitable Society (Yuyuan shuhua shanhui 豫園書畫善會) in 1909 and the Shanghai Association for Research on Painting and Calligraphy (Shanghai shuhua yanjiuhui 上海書畫研究會) in 1910. His friendship with Wu Changshuo dates from this time. He was also involved in the Celestial Horse Association (Tianma hui 天馬會), which encouraged interactions between Chinese and western art, and in 1927 he helped found the Shanghai Girls Aesthetic School (Shanghai nüzi meishu xuexiao 上海女子美術學校).[13]

In a more tranquil era, Wang might have spent the rest of his life as a prosperous and contented businessman, artist, and family patriarch, but he found himself unable to stay aloof from the tumultuous events of the early twentieth century. Thus, he joined the Chinese Revolutionary Alliance (Zhongguo tongmenghui 中國同盟會), supported Chen Qimei during the 1911 Xinhai 辛

亥 Revolution, and even helped lead a suicide squad (*gansi dui* 敢死隊) during an attack on the Jiangnan Arsenal (Jiangnan zhizaoju 江南製造局) along with his eldest son Mengnan.[14] Chiang Kai-shek is also said to have fought in this attack, and Wang's connections with Chiang proved invaluable when he was working to support the cause of Chinese Buddhism (see below). In 1912 Wang was elected to the A Roll of Shanghai City Assembly, and he also served the new Republican government as minister of communications and later minister of commerce, helping to underwrite the revolution by borrowing 350,000 dollars and buying 400,000 dollars' worth of government bonds. Wang's concern with philanthropy also appears to have begun during this time, as he is listed as one of the founders of the Chinese Society for the Rescue of Women and Children (Zhongguo jiuji furu zonghui 中國救濟婦孺總會), which was formed in 1912.[15]

After 1913 Wang abandoned the world of revolutionary politics and began to devote himself to philanthropy, painting, and self-cultivation, eventually converting to Buddhism. He did not take part in the May Fourth Movement but remained an active member of Shanghai elite society. He hosted Albert Einstein and his wife for dinner at his home on November 13, 1922,[16] and was elected director of the Shanghai General Chamber of Commerce (Shanghai zongshanghui 上海總商會). However, his greatest concern appears to have been providing assistance to others less fortunate than himself, perhaps in the pattern of late imperial elites.[17] For example, he served as one of the managers of the Shanghai Orphanage (Shanghai gu'eryuan 上海孤兒院), which he had helped found in 1906.[18] In 1917 he helped to found a hospital for the practice of Chinese medicine (Shanghai guangyi zhongyiyuan 上海廣益中醫院) and in 1919 helped establish an institute for the handicapped (Shanghai canfeiyuan 上海殘廢院). He was also an active member of the city's leading philanthropic organizations, including the International Relief Association (Huayang yizhenhui 華洋義賑會, founded in 1920) and the Shanghai Union of Charitable Associations (Shanghai cishan tuanti lianhehui 上海慈善團體聯合會, founded in 1919), serving as the latter's first chairperson.[19] One 1924 record of charitable activities organized by Shanghai elitesprovides detailed information about Wang Yiting's leadership role.[20] The same record contains photos of Wang along with leading lay Buddhists such as Guan Jiongzhi 關絅之 (also written as Guan Jiongzhi 關炯之, 1879–1942) and Huang Hanzhi 黃涵之 (Huang Qinglan 黃慶瀾, 1875–1961).[21]

It may be no coincidence that this time period is marked by a change in Wang's artistic style. Wang sold paintings of flora and fauna in order to raise money for charity as early as the spring of 1887,[22] but the year 1916 was marked by his completion of a horizontal scroll entitled *Blind Men's Enjoyment* (Xiaqu tu 瞎趣圖), which bears a long colophon by Wu Changshuo about the need to show compassion toward the disabled. The next year Wang completed a painting about floods entitled *Hongshui hengliu* 洪水橫流, and in 1919 he joined with Wu to paint the plight of refugees (the *Liumin tu* 流民圖).[23] It also seems significant that a painting by Wang exhorting people to provide aid for disaster victims cited the venerable morality book *Wenchang dijun yinzhiwen* 文昌帝君陰騭文 (see chapter 4), which was highly popular among the spirit-writing associations in which Wang and other elites participated (see below).

Another activity Wang engaged in during these years that may have links to his religious life was martial arts (*wushu* 武術). A series of August 1920 newspaper articles list Wang and his former Chinese Revolutionary Alliance comrade Ye Huijun 葉惠鈞 (1862–1932) as cochairmen of Shanghai's Martial Arts Association (Wushu hui 武術會), which, like some of the redemptive societies described below, took as its founding principle the ideal of preserving China's national essence (*baoyou guocui wei zongzhi* 保佑國粹為宗旨).[24] Wang also worked as an "outside instructor" (*chuwai jiaoshou* 出外教授) for the Society of Gentle Fists (Zhirou quanshe 致柔拳社), a Taiji boxing (Taiji quan 太極拳) association that flourished in Shanghai during the late 1920s.[25] Wang's friend and fellow lay Buddhist Guan Jiongzhi was also active in this group, serving as its honorary chairman (*mingyu huizhang* 名譽社長). In a preface written for a work entitled *Taiji Boxing Techniques* (*Taiji quanshu* 太極拳術) in 1925, Guan documents his and Wang's participation in the society and notes that both joined because of the health benefits that could be gained from practicing these techniques.[26] Another work, entitled *Questions and Answers about Taiji* (*Taiji dawen* 太極答問), also emphasizes the links between Taiji boxing and good health (especially for women).[27] Such interest and involvement in self-cultivation (literally "cultivating life" or *yangsheng* 養生) and inner alchemy (*neidan* 內丹) techniques was commonplace among many Shanghai elites.[28]

In recognition of Wang Yiting's long years of service, the Shanghai city government planned to name a street after him in honor of his seventieth birthday, but these designs never came to fruition due to the outbreak of the War of Resistance against Japan. Wang fled to Hong Kong following Japanese attacks on Shanghai, which commenced on August 13, 1937, but he continued to be active in philanthropic efforts on behalf of the many refugees who flocked to the city, helping to found the Shanghai Union of Charitable Associations for Disaster Relief (Shanghai cishan tuanti lianhe jiuzaihui 上海慈善團體聯合救災會). However, he fell seriously ill while in Hong Kong, and decided to return to Shanghai to wait for the end. He arrived in the city he loved on November 12, 1938, and passed away the very next day. His funeral was held on January 22, 1939 at the Huzhou Society. More than 1,800 people attended, including representatives of over 150 organizations, as well as many of Wang's closest Buddhist companions.[29]

Devotion to Buddhism

Wang Yiting's Buddhist faith might best be understood in light of the challenges this religion faced and the innovations it undertook during a time of traumatic transformation. The Republican era was a time of rapid institutional growth for modern Chinese Buddhism, including large-scale Buddhist associations run by the *sangha*.[30] These included the China Association of Buddhism (Zhonghua Fojiao zonghui 中華佛教總會, founded in 1912), the Shanghai Association for the Preservation of Buddhism (Shanghai Fojiao weichihui 上海佛教維持會, founded in 1926), the Chinese Buddhist Association (founded in 1929), the Shanghai City Buddhist Association (Shanghaishi Fojiaohui 上海市佛教會, also founded in 1929), and the Shanghai Branch of the Chinese Association for Buddhist Studies (Zhongguo Foxuehui Shanghaishi fenhui 中國佛學會上海市分會, founded in 1935).[31] With the exception of the China Association of Buddhism, Wang was involved in all these organizations.[32]

The Republican era also witnessed extensive elite support for various forms of lay Buddhism (literally "householder Buddhism" or *jushi Fojiao* 居士佛教). Shanghai was home to numerous lay Buddhist associations, in all of which Wang played a leading role.[33] These included the Shanghai Buddhist Householder Association (Shanghai Fojiao jushilin 上海佛教居士林), which was founded in 1918 and four years later grew into the better-known World Buddhist Householder Association (Shijie Fojiao jushilin 世界佛教居士林), as well as the [Buddhist] Enlightenment Society (Jueshe 覺社, also founded in 1918) and the Shanghai Buddhist Pure Karma Society (Shanghai Fojiao jingyeshe 上海佛教淨業社, founded in 1922). Lay Buddhists were also active in philanthropy and ritual, and the World Buddhist Householder Association was renowned for its sponsorship of philanthropic activities (including preaching the dharma at prisons), while the Shanghai Buddhist Purity Society helped organize a wide range of Buddhist rituals, particularly ceremonies meant to protect the nation and ease calamities (*huguo xizai fahui* 護國息災法會).[34] Wang and other lay Buddhists eagerly took an active part in numerous charities, ranging from establishing institutions for the unfortunate, such as the Shanghai Buddhist Orphanage (Shanghai Fojiao ciyouyuan 上海佛教慈幼院, founded in 1933), to participating in the provision of disaster relief.[35] Another important aspect of modern Chinese Buddhism was its openness to female lay practitioners, such as Lü Bicheng 呂碧城 (1883–1943) and Luo Jialing 羅迦陵 (1864-1941), some of whom interacted extensively with Wang (see, e.g., the discussion of Luo below).[36]

Modern Chinese Buddhism was highly public in nature, with believers using various forms of mass media to transmit their views.[37] Wang and his fellow elites helped sponsor the city's numerous Buddhist publishing houses, including some of those discussed in chapter 3. Their efforts bore considerable fruit, and it hardly seems a coincidence that so many elite accounts of conversion to Buddhism mention the importance of reading the texts these publishing houses distributed. Wang also joined other leading Buddhist figures to sponsor the reprinting of the *Anshi quanshu* 安士全書, whose author, Zhou Anshi 周安士 (Zhou Siren 周思仁, 1656–1739), was a devout lay Buddhist. More than three million copies of this text are said to have been printed during the Republican era, and it attracted the attention of such luminaries as Lu Xun 魯迅 (1881–1936).[38]

This lay Buddhist activism occasionally focused on countering state attempts to limit Buddhism's growth, particularly on the part of leaders who attempted to convert monasteries into schools (see chapter 1). In other instances, however, Buddhist activism was less a response to external pressure than an expression of deeply personal religious devotion. For Wang Yiting, who was also a leading member of modern Shanghai's elite, Buddhist faith involved a complex combination of motivations, including self-cultivation, concern for the welfare of others, and a commitment to helping this religious movement find its place in modern Chinese culture, including resisting temple destruction campaigns.

Wang Yiting's devotion to Buddhism is movingly described in Qin Xitian's "Brief Account of the Deeds [Performed by] Householder Wang Yiting." According to this work, Wang first learned about Buddhism from his mother and maternal grandmother, and set aside a portion of the family garden for the construction of a Buddhist hall (Foge 佛閣) where his mother could practice daily devotions in her old age.[39] Wang is also said to have been visited in a dream by the Bodhisattva Guanyin during a childhood illness.[40] However, Wang's conversion to Buddhism appears to have been directly linked to the tumultuous events of the early twentieth century. Due to Wang's support of revolutionary efforts, his name was placed on a wanted list by then president Yuan Shikai, and he also witnessed the assassination of Song Jiaoren, standing beside Song when he was gunned down and helping to prepare his tombstone.[41] Believing that he had escaped from harm by chanting the name of the Bodhisattva Guanyin, Wang began to undertake an annual pilgrimage to Mount Putuo (Putuo shan 普陀山) beginning that same year, and he also devoted much of his time to painting Buddhist deities, particularly Guanyin and the Amitabha Buddha.[42]

While Wang's devotion to Buddhism appears to have intensified after 1913, he did not formally become a Buddhist (*guiyi* 皈依) until 1916. In March of that year, during his annual pilgrimage to Mount Putuo, he engaged in a series of fervent conversations with the eminent monks Taixu and Yinguang, which resulted in his becoming initiated into the Buddhist religion by taking the vow of the Three Refuges (*sangui* 三皈).[43] Subsequently, Wang began to devote an increasing amount of time to Buddhist causes, working alongside renowned *sangha* such as Taixu, Yinguang, Hongyi, and Yuanying 圓瑛 (1878–1953) and leading lay

Buddhists such as Guan Jiongzhi, Huang Qinglan, Shi Xingzhi, Li Yunshu, Ding Fubao, and Di Baoxian.[44]

One of Wang's first acts in support of Buddhism was joining with Kang Youwei 康有為 (1858–1927) to establish the Huayan Institute (Huayan daxue 華嚴大學), which from 1913 to 1915 was located in Hardoon Gardens (Hatong huayuan 哈同花園/Ailiyuan 愛儷園). Its history clearly reflects the cosmopolitan nature of this city's modern history, having been built in 1909 by Sir Silas Hardoon (1851–1931), a wealthy Jewish merchant from Great Britain. His wife, Luo Jialing, was a devout Buddhist and allowed the Huayan Institute to operate on the garden's grounds. However, following a dispute between Luo and the Buddhists, the institute moved to Hangzhou in 1915. A few years later the Cangsheng mingzhi daxue 倉聖明智大學 was founded in Hardoon Gardens, with renowned elites such as Wang Guowei 王國維 (1877–1927) and Xu Beihong 徐悲鴻 (1895–1953) serving as instructors. The gardens also served as a site for meetings and other charitable events linked to the provision of disaster relief, many of which featured Wang Yiting and his comrades from the China Rescuing Life Association.[45] Sadly, all came to naught following Hardoon's passing in 1931, a fire in the 1930s, and the death of Luo in 1941.[46]

Wang's Buddhist art during this time period appears to have been shaped by his friendship with the eminent monk Hongyi. This can be seen in a set of couplets (*lian* 聯) that Wang wrote in 1925 after reading Hongyi's handwritten copy of the Vinaya text known as the *Brahma Net Sutra* (*Fanwang jing* 梵網經), which extols the virtues of Buddhist meditation.[47] It seems especially significant that Wang and Hongyi shared an interest in this scripture, as its fifty-eight bodhisattva precepts had proven inspirational to such prominent Ming dynasty monks as Zhuhong 袾宏 (1535–1615).[48] Moreover, the *Brahma Net Sutra* is also well known for its emphasis on the ideal of nonkilling (*jiesha* 戒殺), which served as a motivating force underlying the vegetarianism of elites such as Wang Yiting and Feng Zikai and also featured prominently in works described in chapters 3 and 4.[49]

Wang appears to have been especially active in the Enlightenment Society and the World Buddhist Householder Association, serving as deputy head of the latter group in 1924 and as head for three consecutive terms beginning in 1927.[50] One especially instructive episode in Wang Yiting's Buddhist career involves the way he utilized his friendship with Chiang Kai-shek to obtain government approval for the registration (*li'an* 立案) of the Chinese Buddhist Association. While Chinese Buddhism experienced considerable growth during the Republican era, it often proved difficult for Buddhists to gain state approval for their efforts, especially when Buddhism became caught up in temple destruction campaigns. Things came to a head in August and September 1928, when both the Ministry of Education and the Ministry of the Interior were on the verge of imposing strict policies to regulate religious activities, including Buddhist ones. It was at this time that Wang visited Chiang and persuaded him to protect the interests of legitimate Buddhist practitioners and their sacred sites. Chiang responded by stating that he was generally supportive of modern Buddhists' reform efforts as long as they complied with the state's need to maintain social order.[51]

Wang also helped mediate a long-running dispute between Huzhou elites and Buddhist monks at the Abbey of Sagely Longevity (Shousheng An 壽聖庵), a popular sacred site founded in Shanghai in 1861 by leaders of the Huzhou Society.[52] In 1928, following the successful completion of a reconstruction project, the abbey's resident monk, Disong 諦松, asked Yang Kuihou 楊奎侯 (the Huzhou banker in charge of managing the temple) for all contracts and other legal documents necessary to register the abbey with the authorities, only to learn that Yang had transferred control of the temple to the Huzhou Society. After repeated attempts to get the documents back, Disong took his case to court. Legal wrangling dragged on well into 1931, accompanied by frequent accusations of corruption and other forms of malfeasance. The city and even national authorities attempted to intervene, to no avail, and the entire incident was the subject of frequent reports in *Shenbao*. Wang tried to mediate for both sides in the dispute, but it proved impossible to reach a settlement. In the end the monks lost their case, and control of the abbey remained in the control of Huzhou's elites until it was shut down for good in 1954.[53]

Wang's participation in the institutional side of Buddhism declined significantly following his entanglement in a schism between Taixu and Yuanying that also took place in 1931 just as the Abbey of Sagely Longevity dispute was reaching its dénouement. Wang was close to both of these eminent monks, using his connections in Japan to arrange for Taixu to attend the East Asian Buddhist Conference in Tokyo in November 1925,[54] and also working with Yuanying to prevent the confiscation of Buddhist monasteries and their property during the 1920s and 1930s. However, the Buddhist reform movement in modern China had suffered intense differences of opinion since its beginnings in the 1910s, and things came to a head when Taixu and Yuanying each tried to gain control of the Chinese Buddhist Association in 1931. Taixu resigned from its standing committee in April, following which he launched an attack on the association and its record. Shortly afterward Taixu and his allies were elected to association's executive committee but were unable to effectively run the association due to opposition by more conservative Buddhists and their constituencies, leaving Taixu with no alternative but to resign in June. Wang tried to mediate the impasse and offered to help Yuanying manage the association's affairs, but to no avail.[55]

Following this debacle, Wang continued to be involved in some aspects of Buddhist philanthropy, and in 1932 he issued a strongly worded appeal to his fellow Buddhists to become more involved in providing assistance to others.[56]

In general, however, Wang appears to have devoted the remainder of his life to the meditational side of Buddhism,[57] leaving its institutional affairs for others to handle.[58] Wang's Buddhist faith appears to have remained steadfast despite personal suffering and disillusionment with monastic infighting, however, and he took time to help host the Ninth Panchen Lama (Banchan Lama 班禪喇嘛), Thubten Chökyi Nyima (1883–1937), during his visit to Shanghai in 1934.[59] That same year one of Wang's grandsons was married during a vegetarian banquet, an event that attracted a veritable "who's who" of Shanghai notables and also provided a public occasion for extolling the merits of vegetarianism.[60] A later account, in the October 2, 1936 issue of Zhe-Ou ribao 浙甌日報, describes Wang presiding over a Buddhist-style vegetarian wedding ceremony for lay members of this religion.[61] Wang's devotion was also recognized by the leading figures of that era. For example, Taixu's necrology aptly summarizes Wang's religious life with the following couplets (lian 聯): "Saving others through philanthropy, protecting the dharma and the Buddhist faith, his paintings and calligraphy are transmitted through the ages, [his reputation] soars across the oceans" (ciji jiuren, Fomen hufa, shuhua chuanshi, haiguo feisheng 慈善救人，佛門護法，書畫傳世，海國飛聲).

Transnational Religious Activities: The Case of Japan

Buddhism also shaped Wang Yiting's interactions with many Japanese elites who visited Shanghai. Walter B. Davis's research shows that Wang often gave his Japanese guests paintings and calligraphy and hosted banquets at his residence's Catalpa Garden (Ziyuan 梓園) and a restaurant he managed known as the Bodhi Grove (Juelin 覺林). The fare was invariably vegetarian and was said to have been popular among both Japanese and Chinese residents of Shanghai.[62] Wang's friends included not only leading industrialists such as Shibusawa Eiichi 澀澤榮一 (1840–1931) but also the renowned Buddhologist Omura Seigai 大村西崖 (1867–1927), as well as Otani Kozui 大谷光瑞 (1876–1948), who served as abbot of the Nishi Honganji 西本願寺. Another Japanese Buddhist, Shigahara Ryōsai 信々原良哉 (dates unknown), visited the Catalpa Garden in the spring of 1936 and enjoyed a vegetarian meal there, referring glowingly to Wang as "China's foremost Buddhist layman."[63]

Wang's commitment to Buddhist philanthropy blended neatly with his links to Japan. His crowning achievement may have involved the massive relief effort that he helped organize following the Great Kantō Earthquake of September 1, 1923. This disaster and the fires that ensued (most people were cooking their lunch when the earthquake struck at 11:58 a.m.) caused 91,344 deaths, with an additional 13,275 people listed as missing and more than 550,000 homes partially or totally destroyed. Wang sprang into action as soon as he heard the news of this horrible tragedy, helping to form the Buddhist Relief Association for the Japanese Calamity

(Fojiao puji Rizai hui 佛教普濟日災會), as well as raising more than 185,000 Japanese yen by means of front-page announcements in newspapers like *Shenbao* and charitable auctions of artworks, including his own. He then arranged for the purchase of tons of supplies (most notably rice and flour), with the first shipment of relief aid leaving Shanghai on September 8 aboard the steamship Xinminglun 新銘輪 and arriving in the port of Kobe 神戶 on September 12.[64] Wang's efforts involved far more than material aid, however; he was also profoundly concerned for the spiritual condition of survivors and the souls of the loved ones they had lost. Accordingly, he devoted himself to sponsoring Buddhist services to pray for the souls of the dead. These rites, designed to achieve a "transfer of merit" to the earthquake's victims, were held on a massive scale, starting with the forty-nine-day Land and Water Masses (Shuilu puli daochang da fashi 水陸普利道場大法事) held at the four sacred mountains of Chinese Buddhism: Emei 峨嵋, Jiuhua 九華, Wutai 五台, and Putuo 普陀. A second series of rites was held at two of the Buddhist monasteries with which Wang and his fellow Buddhists had the closest links, the Monastery for Attracting Worthies (Zhaoxiansi 招賢寺) at West Lake (Xihu 西湖) in Hangzhou (also a key sacred site for Hongyi) and the Jade Buddha Monastery (Yufosi 玉佛寺) in Shanghai.[65]

Apart from undertaking ritual remedies, Wang drew on his influence as head of the Chinese Buddhist Association to arrange for the casting of a Ghost Bell (Youming zhong 幽冥鐘) to commemorate earthquake victims. On November 7, 1923, Wang contacted Japan's foreign minister, Izyūin Hikokichi 伊集院彦吉 (1864–1924), as well as the United Buddhist Association of Japan (Nihon Bukkyō rengōkokai 日本佛教聯合會), to express his intent to undertake this task. The bell was cast in Hangzhou, completed in 1925, and shipped to Tokyo via Shanghai and Yokohama in 1926. Four years later, in September 1930, it was moved to the newly constructed Tokyo Earthquake Memorial Hall (Tōkyō shinsai kinendō 東京震災紀念堂), which was later renamed Tokyo Hall for the Comfort of Souls (Tōkyōto ireidō 東京都慰靈堂) after it was expanded to commemorate the victims of the Tokyo fire bombings of 1945. A mammoth instrument, the bell weighs 1.56 tons, is 1.69 meters high, and has a diameter of 1.21 meters at its mouth. On its side are carved the words "For the benefit of all who hear the bell's sound, be they dead or living" (*puwen zhongsheng, mingyang liang li* 普聞鐘聲，冥陽兩利) along with the date the earthquake struck (1923) and Wang's name. It is rung every year on the anniversary of the earthquake, a ceremony that Wang's descendents have also attended, including on the ninetieth anniversary of the disaster.[66] In addition, the hall contains four paintings that Wang donated on the occasion of its inauguration, the content of which encompass both Buddhist and Daoist themes. There are also records of the relief efforts he helped organize, his photograph, and a second inscription commemorating his accomplishments.[67]

The grateful Japanese referred to Wang as a bodhisattva (*pusa* 菩薩), and he was granted an audience with the Shōwa 昭和 Emperor. The emperor's third son also visited Wang in Shanghai in 1927. The goodwill generated by Wang's deeds was reciprocated during the 1930s, when Shibusawa Eiichi and other friends of Wang formed the Association of Sympathetic Support for the Republic of China's Flood Calamity (Chūka Mingoku suisai dōjōkai 中華民國水災同情會) to aid the Chinese people when they suffered their own natural disasters.[68] In 1983 the head of the Japan-China Friendship Association (Nitchū yūkō kyōkai 日中友好協會), Utsunomiya Tokuma 宇都宮德馬 (1906–2000) presented China with a stele reading, "Mr. Wang Yiting, your benevolence and righteousness will never be forgotten" (*Wang Yiting xiansheng, en'yi yongyuan bu wangji* 王一亭先生，恩義永遠不忘記). Some Chinese biographers emphasize Wang's patriotism,[69] but there is little evidence that he attempted to blend Buddhism and nationalism.[70]

Spirit-Writing

Wang appears to have become an active participant in spirit-writing groups during the 1910s, roughly the same time that he converted to Buddhism. In doing so, he was hardly alone. As we saw in chapters 4 and 5, many urban elites practiced spirit-writing for a broad range of reasons, including self-cultivation, composing morality books, and contacting the dead.[71] The activities of Zheng Guanying 鄭觀應 (1842–1921) were discussed above.[72] Another well-known example was Chen Yingning 陳攖寧 (1880–1969), who staged such rites with his wife Wu Yizhu 吳彝珠 (1882–1945) and two other women "questioners" (*wenshizhe* 問事者), most likely spirit mediums.[73] Other elites, including such luminaries as Wu Tingfang 伍廷芳 (1842–1922) and Bao Tianxiao 包天笑 (1876–1973), wrote articles exploring the nature of spirit-writing.[74] And then there is the case of Xu Dishan 許地山 (1893–1941), a scholar who may not have believed in the efficacy of spirit-writing and hesitated to do fieldwork on groups that performed it (relying mainly on accounts in the *Gujin tushu jicheng* 古今圖書集成), but tacitly admitted that its importance merited academic research.[75]

Some urbanites performed these rites for seemingly frivolous purposes, causing critics to compare them to the worship of the "plate immortal" (Diexian 碟仙, somewhat similar to the western Ouija board).[76] Others focused on far more serious concerns, inviting revered leaders like former president Sun Yat-sen to comment on current affairs and assess the likelihood that Chiang Kai-shek could unify China.[77] Even China's top political elites were hardly immune to the power of such practices, as can be seen in the case of Yu Jinhe 余晉龢 (1887–1946), who served as mayor of Beiping under both the Nationalist and Wang Jingwei 汪精衛 (1883–1944) regimes. Yu erected an altar in his home and did his utmost to perform charitable deeds and intercede on behalf of the city's populace after receiving inspirational spirit-writing messages from Guandi. However, as the years passed and the political atmosphere became more dire, Yu received a warning from Zhang Fei 張飛 advising him to resign and flee. He hesitated to do so, and after the United States dropped atomic bombs on Nagasaki and Hiroshima in 1945, Yu consulted Zhang Fei once more, only to be told, "When I ordered you to leave, you didn't leave. Now that you wish to leave, you cannot. It is over" (*Ming ni qu, ni buqu, jin xiang qu, buneng qu, wanle wanle* 命你去，你不去，今想去，不能去，完了完了). Resigned to his fate, he continued practicing at home until his arrest and imprisonment.[78]

Some elites practiced spirit-writing for deeply personal reasons. One example involves the renowned boxing instructor Chen Weiming 陳微明 (1881–1958), who utilized spirit-writing to engage in regular exchanges with his deceased son.[79] Chen was hardly the sole elite to turn to spirit-writing as a means of coping with a death in the family. The writer Gao Chuiwan 高吹萬 (1879–1958), for example, attempted to use these rites to contact his teenage daughter following her tragic death just prior to marriage.[80] Another example involves Huang Yanpei 黃炎培 (1878–1965), an educator who helped found the China Democratic League (Zhongguo minzhu tongmeng 中國民主同盟) in 1941. Years later, despite his ostensible commitment to science, Huang developed an interest in spirit-writing after getting to know none other than Xu Dishan. Huang later used these rites as a means of reaching out to not only his deceased daughter and father but also members of the league, including Wen Yiduo 聞一多 (1899–1946), although he was not always happy with the advice they provided.[81]

In contrast to private (including household) spirit-writing altars used by urban elites to fulfill their personal needs, larger sites founded and managed by religious associations served as public arenas in modern China's urban cultural field. One favorite Shanghai spirit-writing center appears have been a Jigong 濟公 altar inside the Great World (Dashijie 大世界) amusement center. Reports in *Shenbao* in the spring of 1926 indicate that this altar had been in existence for many years and attracted the support of more than a thousand worshippers, many of whom claimed to be seeking a quiet space to practice self-cultivation amid the hustle and bustle of Shanghai's "roaring 20s." Membership fees to join the association that sponsored the altar were low and came with a set of five tickets to the amusement center. Spirit-writing rites were gratis, and on some dates the gods would decree that members be granted free admission to the amusement center.[82]

Another of Shanghai's most active spirit-writing associations was the Immortal Altar of Merciful Succor (Ciji xiantan 慈濟仙壇), whose members also practiced philanthropy under the name Society of Universal Affinities (Puyuan she 普緣社). The society was Shanghai's charitable branch of the Teachings of the Principle (Lijiao 理教), a religious movement that arose during the late imperial era in the North China Plain and continued to be active in China during the early

1950s before it was suppressed in the 1960s (it still survives in Taiwan).[83] This organization produced at least two morality books during the Republican era, one of which, *Instructions for the Ignorant and Enlightened* (*Xunmengming* 訓朦明), contains 810 printed pages of data documenting the religious and charitable activities of both the altar and the society. Its compilers were clearly proud of their group's achievements, but they also made no effort to hide the many problems its members had encountered based on the belief that their successes and failures could serve as didactic examples for future generations of worshippers.[84]

For Wang Yiting, spirit-writing readily overlapped with Buddhist practice, and one of the first religious groups he is mentioned as joining in 1916 (and later leading) was the China Rescuing Life Association. Some scholars have assumed that the association was essentially a philanthropic group,[85] but in fact the term *ji* 濟 in its name also stands for Jigong, the leading figure in its spirit-writing rituals. During such rites, Jigong regularly exhorted association members to make ever larger contributions to the welfare of others.[86] Wang Chien-ch'uan has convincingly demonstrated that the China Rescuing Life Association's own history was intimately linked to spirit-writing, having been founded during the late nineteenth century as a spirit-writing altar known as the Gathering Clouds Studio (Jiyunxuan 集雲軒), which joined other such groups in providing famine relief for North China victims of the Boxer uprising.[87] The association developed into the group's charitable branch, with the two groups constituting a sort of dual identity (a religious association combined with a philanthropic society). The association's philanthropic activities included famine and flood relief, providing medicines during outbreaks of epidemics, and constructing hospitals, and branch groups were founded in other urban centers, including Beijing and Tianjin.[88] As for the studio, apart from the worship of Jigong it produced books of Daoist poetry and played an active role in hosting the Panchen Lama during his visit to Shanghai in 1934.[89] The two groups complemented each other, with the association promoting its charitable aspects and serving as a vehicle for registering with the authorities and the studio embodying its religious practices.[90] Similar pairings marked the development of Chinese redemptive societies, one notable example being the Society of the Way (which used the autonym Daoyuan 道院 for religious activities) and Red Swastika Society (Hongwanzihui 紅卍字會 for philanthropy).[91] News of the association and its manifold activities spread to Taiwan as early as 1918, where one newspaper article noted the importance of Buddhist doctrine to its members and stressed their emphasis on keeping male and female worshippers separate.[92]

A number of sources claim that Wang joined the association after undergoing a second conversion to Buddhism via Jigong (*guiyi Jigong huofo* 皈依濟公活佛) and taking the dharma name Jueqi 覺器 while performing a spirit-writing ritual at the studio.[93] Wang proved to be an active participant in both philanthropic and religious activities sponsored by the association, becoming its leader following the death of Chen Runfu 陳潤夫 (Chen Zuolin 陳作霖, 1841–1919) and working to build numerous charitable schools and hospitals. His interest in spirit-writing also continued unabated. One account from the year 1924 describes large numbers of worshippers (including Wang Yiting) taking part in spirit-writing rites held on the premises of the China Rescuing Life Association and is especially significant for indicating the roles played by elite women in this group, as well as the enforced segregation of the sexes, characteristics that were very common among other spirit-writing groups as well.[94] It is also important to note that Buddhist leaders like Taixu openly described Wang's involvement in spirit-writing associations in great detail, which would seem to indicate that few objections were raised to lay Buddhists taking part in such groups.[95] Moreover, Buddhist elites such as Yinguang, Ding Fubao, and Ye Erkai did not hesitate to become involved in the association's religious activities.[96]

Apart from worshipping Jigong at the association, Wang was also an active patron of many of this deity's sacred sites.[97] One example involves the modern history of a famed Jigong temple located at Mount Tiantai (Tiantai shan 天台山) in Zhejiang, the Hall of the Buddha Ji[gong] at the Cave of Auspicious Mists (Ruixiadong Jifoyuan 瑞霞洞濟佛院), which was originally founded on Chicheng shan 赤城山 in 1209. Wang provided financial support for a temple reconstruction project organized by a local spirit-writing group in 1927 and also composed a calligraphic inscription reading "The ancient monument again shines with light" (guji chongguang 古跡重光).[98] In addition, he wrote an article in 1929 using his pen name Master of the Plum Flower Hall (Meihua guanzhu 梅花館主), which described a Shanghai theater that decided to stage a Jigong play following a medium's intervention.[99] Wang's faith in Jigong was vividly expressed in a painting of this deity that he completed in 1926.[100]

Wang also joined a number of redemptive societies that practiced spirit-writing,[101] the most notable of which was the Teaching of Celestial Virtue (Tiande jiao 天德教), founded by Xiao Changming 蕭昌明 (1895–1943).[102] Wang was a prominent donor/guardian (hufa 護法) of this group, having been inaugurated as one of its eighteen Perfected Sovereigns (zhenjun 真君) in 1934.[103] He also participated in the activities of the World Red Swastika Society, and one set of reports about its charitable works in the year 1937 lists him as an honorary chairman (mingyu huizhang 名譽會長).[104] When Wang joined this organization is not clear, but he probably became familiar with its activities in 1923, when it played a major role in organizing relief efforts following the Great Kantō Earthquake. The society also sent a delegation to Japan and subsequently helped found a Japanese branch known as the Great Root Teachings (Ōmoto-kyō 大本教).[105]

Participation in Daoist Groups

Spirit-writing appears to have shaped Wang Yiting's involvement in some of the leading Daoist movements of his era. This phenomenon might best be understood in the context of the history of modern Daoism, as seen in Vincent Goossaert's innovative analysis of the complex interactions and competition among Daoism, spirit-writing groups, and redemptive societies, which contributes immensely to our understanding of the extensive diffusion of Daoist beliefs and practices in modern China. Many Daoist lay organizations were organized around spirit-writing cults, and such groups were widespread throughout China during the late nineteenth and early twentieth centuries. Devout believers could be formally accepted as disciples by the immortal Lü Dongbin 呂洞賓 during spirit-writing rituals, with some also practicing various forms of "cultivating life" (*yangsheng* 養生) and internal alchemy (*neidan* 內丹).[106] Daoist spirit-writing groups were also prominent in Guangdong and Hong Kong, where they contributed to the growth of the Wong Tai Sin (Huang Daxian 黃大仙) cult, which featured elites such as Feng Qizhuo 馮其焯 (?–1953) and Huang Yuntian 黃允畋 (1920–97), as well as sacred sites such as the Puqing Tan 普慶壇 and Sik Sik Yuen 嗇色園.[107]

Daoist spirit-writing associations proved to be extremely popular in the Jiangnan region, where they interacted extensively with Buddhist and sectarian groups. These associations tended to be organized around altars (*tan* 壇) dedicated to the worship of Lü Dongbin, yet they also included deities such as Jigong.[108] Many of these movements appear to have originated at Daoist temples and sacred sites, one being the Venerable Plum Flower Temple (Gu Meihuaguan 古梅花觀), also known as the Hall of Purified Yang (Chunyanggong 純陽宮), located on Mount Jingai (Jin'gaishan 金蓋山) in Wang Yiting's native home of Huzhou. This temple was home to one of the most renowned Qing dynasty figures of the Longmen 龍門 branch of Quanzhen 全真 Daoism, Min Yide 閔一得 (1758–1836), and under the leadership of Min and his disciples branch altars were soon established throughout much of the region, including Shanghai.[109]

The Venerable Plum Flower Temple spawned a network of seventy-two branch altars, the largest of which was Shanghai's Cloud Enlightenment Altar (Jueyun tan 覺雲壇), which was founded in 1888 and had clear links to Longmen Daoism. According to its genealogy, the *Longmen zhengzong Jueyun benzhi daotong xinchuan* 龍門正宗覺雲本支道統薪傳 (published in 1927), Wang had become a member of Shanghai's Cloud Enlightenment Altar in 1920, and his disciples played active roles in other Daoist altars throughout the city.[110] Other branch altars included the Gathering Clouds Studio discussed above. Wang was a leading member of this group, where he assumed the religious name Benzhen 本真.[111] Wang is also listed under the religious name Wanchan 完禪 in another source concerned with these Daoist groups, the *Daotong yuanliuzhi* 道統源流志 (1929),

which lists both his Daoist and Buddhist names (Benzhen and Jueqi) mentions his artistic skills and devotion to a Buddhist vegetarian lifestyle, and concludes that he was one of the most admired senior religious figures in Shanghai.[112] In short, there is little doubt that joining a Daoist altar (as well as initiating one's disciples in others) fit neatly with Wang's Buddhist practice.

The network of Daoist spirit-writing altars in Shanghai and other nearby metropolises constantly evolved during the late nineteenth and early twentieth centuries, with some branch altars blending with groups that worshipped Jigong, leading to instances of both deities featured on the same altar (they still are in some altars that have been revived in contemporary times). In other words, while these networks had different origins, they shared similar modes of practice and many of the same members, often becoming close allies. This meant that people active in both groups (like Wang Yiting) could have both a Daoist name given by Lü Dongbin (in Wang's case Benzhen) and a Buddhist name given by Jigong (in Wang's case Jueqi). Thus, it is hardly surprising that Wang would choose to lead members of the China Rescuing Life Association in the restoration of a prominent Daoist sacred site in Nanjing 南京, the Monastery of the Jade Void (Yuxuguan 玉虛觀) and also compose an inscription to commemorate its completion.[113]

Universalist Perspectives

Wang's commitment to both embracing and transmitting the doctrines and values of the many different religious organizations with which he was affiliated may be seen in his support of publishing houses that printed texts representing a wide range of religious traditions. For example, he was a leading patron of the Illuminating Goodness Bookstore, which, as noted above, was founded in Shanghai by the Fellowship of Goodness. Wang penned the calligraphy adorning the title pages of many bookstore titles, most notably a couplet reading, "While you can use speech to admonish people for one generation, you can admonish them for a hundred generations with the written word" (Yishi quanren yi kou, baishi quanren yi shu 一世勸人以口，百世勸人以書).[114] Wang also worked with Taiwanese elites to distribute morality books on both sides of the Taiwan Strait (see chapter 3).

Wang further put these ideals into practice by publishing his own mammoth collection of morality books in 1936, entitled *Precious Canon on Blessings and Longevity* (Fushou baozang 福壽寶藏, discussed in chapter 4). His preface is notable in that it embraces both science and religion.

> In this age, when people vie with each other in their admiration of new knowledge and engage in the study of science and evolution, the Populace Publishing House (Dazhong shuju 大眾書局) has striven to collect writings that promote goodness (quanshan 勸善), blending them into this huge compilation. Its contents are profound indeed, revealing

that the establishment of the individual self (*lishen zhi ben* 立身之本) derives primarily from mastering oneself and reviving ritual propriety (*keji fuli* 克己復禮). All things have their origins: the tree its roots, the river its source. There are no distinctions between ancient and modern, just as none exist between China and the foreign.[115]

A statement attributed to Wang by one of his biographers expresses sentiments quite similar to the universalist values propagated by the redemptive societies of his era, specifically in that it mentions the Five Teachings (*wujiao* 五教), in this case Buddhism, Daoism, Christianity, Confucianism, and Islam, and their links to preserving moral values.[116] These ideas are also reflected in the fact that the *Jueshe congshu* 覺社叢書, a journal published by the Enlightenment Society, which Wang helped run, expanded its definition of religion to not only encompass Confucianism, Daoism, Christianity, and Islam but also Hinduism (*ru, dao, ye, hui, fan* 儒、道、耶、回、梵).[117] Wang put these ideals into practice by painting images of Jesus Christ.[118]

Wang's open attitude toward all manner of religious traditions was also manifested in his attendance at events hosted by the International Institute of China (Shangxian Tang 尚賢堂), established by the American Presbyterian missionary Gilbert Reid (Li Jiabai 李佳白, 1857–1927). Reid journeyed to China in 1882 and, in order to achieve his goal of preaching the gospel among members of the Chinese elite, founded the International Institute in Beijing in 1894 (it was formally established with state approval in 1897). After the institute was destroyed during the Boxer uprising, Reid moved its operations to Shanghai in 1903, where it became the site of a wide range of cultural and religious events that attracted many members of Shanghai's upper classes, including Wang Yiting. In 1912 Reid also joined forces with the British Baptist missionary Timothy Richard (1845–19) to found the Shanghai Society of World Religions (Shanghai shijie zongjiaohui 上海世界宗教會). Reid also proved willing to take part in some redemptive society activities, including serving as an honorary president of the Universal Morality Society and being involved in the Society of the Way.[119]

Despite the fact that it was ostensibly a Christian organization, the International Institute of China resembled redemptive societies in its use of the term *hall* (*tang* 堂) for sacred space, its emphasis on the ideals of "rescuing the world" (*jishi* 濟世) and "saving the people" (*jiuren* 救人), and especially its universalist goal of encouraging the union of all Chinese and western religions. This ideal was expressed both in words, with slogans like "Confucius plus Jesus" (*Kongzi jia Yesu* 孔子加耶穌) and "Confucianism plus Christianity" (*Kongjiao jia Jidu* 孔教加基督), and in actions, such as inviting eminent Buddhist monks like Taixu, as well as the sixty-second Heavenly Master Zhang Yuanxu 張元旭 (1862–1925), to give lectures.[120] One undated institute publication entitled *Religion and*

Revolution, which is preserved at the Oriental Library (Tōyō bunkō 東洋文庫) in Japan, presents a series of ten Sunday lectures on many of world's major religious traditions, including Confucianism, Daoism, Buddhism, Shinto, Islam, Hinduism, Judaism, and Christianity. A letter dated January 1, 1912 states, "Representatives of every Faith are welcome, that the interchange of ideas between men with widely differing viewpoints may promote tolerance and brotherliness, remove friction, and emphasize the supremacy of the ethical and the spiritual. . . . We ask for the cooperation of the leaders of religious and philanthropic movements among the Chinese."[121] These shared values apparently caused the relationship between Wang and Reid to become quite close, as can be seen in the touching memorial couplet (*wanlian* 輓聯) Wang composed for Reid's funeral. The first line stresses their long friendship, as well as their common concern for universal religious values, while the second expresses Wang's profound sorrow over Reid's untimely departure from this world.[122]

Conclusion

The evidence presented here reveals the vibrant diversity of religious traditions that influenced the lives of China's elites. In this chapter, we have seen that urban elites like Wang Yiting lived in a world that defies easy labeling using current academic categories, a world where "religion" and "science," or for that matter "tradition" and "modernity," coexisted and interacted; where one worked to make a profit yet also donated one's savings to aid others; where one could have dinner with Albert Einstein and his wife one night and receive revelations from Jigong via spirit-writing the next. Wang's life is especially striking in terms of its diversity, including his religious experiences. This man, who has so often been lauded as a modern and secular Chinese elite for his political and commercial activities, also possessed a sense of faith that inspired many of his words and deeds yet did not seem in conflict with his "modern" existence in the eyes of his contemporaries or himself. Thus, the religious life of Wang Yiting might best be understood in terms of what Paul Cohen calls the "lived or experienced past,"[123] a seemingly inextricable knot of information that defies easy exegesis.

Wang was hardly unique. Numerous Chinese urban elites belonged to a closely knit cultural world that featured a wide range of personal and organizational connections. They circulated in and out of each other's networks and were kindred spirits in their emphasis on morality, their pursuit of self-cultivation, and their commitment to philanthropy. These men lived in a new world largely unimaginable by their forefathers, yet they did more than simply respond to or cope with change; they created new organizations and contributed to the well-being of those less fortunate than themselves. Although they lived during an age when many intellectuals viewed religion as one of the main forces obstructing China's modernization, elites like Wang do not seem to have suffered a similar sense of disillusionment. Instead they dedicated themselves to a religious lifestyle, which suggests a need to rethink the very nature of modern Chinese life. Until recently, the religious lives of modern Chinese elites have been largely overlooked due to a bias in the field that has been shaped by western ideas of secularization (see the "Introduction"). Such views have limited our ability to fully describe the complexities of the past, especially when it comes to nonwestern cultures that experienced very different processes of modernization.[124] In fact the data presented above and in previous chapters indicate the clear presence of a "modern" religious culture in urban China that flourished in the form of the diverse religious groups that Wang Yiting and other elites chose to join, including lay Buddhist and Daoist associations, redemptive societies, and spirit-writing groups. The case of Wang Yiting, which illustrates how Chinese elites attempted to negotiate the seeming contradictions between secularization and religion, suggests that urban modernity in China encompassed a wide range of meanings and possibilities. These included not only such standard features as capitalism, consumerism, and scientism but also the beliefs and practices that helped shape elite religious lives.

CONCLUSION

This book has endeavored to more fully comprehend how, during the fifty years covered by this study, Chinese religious traditions and the diverse resources associated with their practice either survived or were reconfigured. In chapters 1 and 2, we considered how communal religious traditions were impacted by a range of campaigns launched against temples and festivals. Chapters 3 and 4 examined how new technologies sparked the growth of religious publishing enterprises and other forms of mass media that contributed to the spread of innovative forms of knowledge, as well as copious amounts of late imperial ideas and practices, while Chapters 5 and 6 portrayed the ways in which religiosity shaped the lives of modern Chinese elites. The data we have collected reveal changes in different types of temple cults and festivals, the appearance of new forms of religious media, a new typology for understanding how elites participated in and wrote about religious beliefs and practices, and so on.

This book, while covering the entire fifty years between 1898 and 1948, has devoted greatest attention to the 1920s and 1930s, when transformations are most in evidence and sources most abundant. As we conclude, then, a few words about the specificities of wartime (1937–45) and its aftermath are in order. This period and its tragic events were lived very differently in various parts of China: from Manchuria, which had become a satellite state of Japan in the early 1930s; to zones of constant warfare; areas occupied by the Japanese army; KMT-controlled provinces; and soviets run by the Red Army. A growing body of scholarship has looked at wartime society,[1] but religion has not featured prominently. Jiangnan, the focus of this book, was under the nominal control of the Wang Jingwei regime, which was itself under the control of the Japanese. This meant that after the initial chaos of invasion, which culminated in the Rape of Nanjing, the region was mostly peaceful but suffering severe constraints on public activities, not to mention economic hardship.

During wartime, religious organizations had to choose between open collaboration, attempts to steer clear of politics as much as possible, and covert resistance. The Japanese authorities tried to organize Chinese religious groups and actively cooperated with several redemptive societies, pursuing a policy that had been developed in Manchukuo.[2] A number of religious leaders chose to collaborate; after the end of the war in 1945, this resulted in purges and extremely bitter conflicts, sometimes played out as public lawsuits but also as more covert settling of scores. On the other hand, some religious leaders built capital as resistance agents and were later promoted to key positions under either the Nationalist or Communist regimes.[3]

In the realm of communal religion, wartime resulted in additional cases of temple destruction due to both actual fighting and military confiscation. At Maoshan, one of the main pilgrimage sites in the Jiangnan area, a Japanese army raid against resistance fighters in August 1939 destroyed most of the temples and killed twenty-four Daoists. Even more importantly, a depressed economy put a damper on religious life while curfews and other laws curtailed festivals and pilgrimages, which could only survive on a much-reduced scale. Similar effects can be observed among the publishing houses and activities of the religious elite. The International and French settlements in Shanghai, which had long provided a free space for religious activities, were occupied by the Japanese army in 1941 and abolished forever in 1943, yet spirit-writing activities and religious publishing continued unabated in spite of it all, partly because the dramatic events unfolding in the country fed earlier apocalyptical discourses that now gained heightened immediacy. The Yiguandao, among other groups producing such discourses, experienced spectacular growth during this period, including in Jiangnan, where it rallied many previously established spirit-writing groups to form a new network/ federation.[4]

The end of the war lifted many restrictions on religious life. In just one example, newspaper reports show a robust revival in pilgrimages during the 1945–49 period. The KMT regime soon made it clear, however, that its programs of religious reform, which had been largely put aside during the war, were back on the agenda, with a new round of temple censuses launched in 1946. Meanwhile, civil war soon engulfed much of the country, even though Jiangnan was among the last regions to be controlled by the Red Army. Then, in 1949, a new story began.

Many of the trends described above continued to shape Chinese religious life after 1948 and down to the present. In this conclusion, we would like to sketch some of these continuities, thus showing how understanding the changes of 1898–1948 can help us understand the contemporary situation. We survey these continuities according to our three aspects of religious change: communal life and political control, knowledge and technology, and elite religiosity.

In the case of political control of religious communities, while the CCP proved willing to establish alliances with a wide range of religious movements during its formative years, in the 1950s many groups were labeled "reactionary secret societies" (*fandong huidaomen* 反動會道門) and persecuted. In contrast, temple cults initially were a lower priority and less actively suppressed during the early 1950s (there was even a minor revival in some areas, with temples being rebuilt).[5] All this changed during the Great Leap Forward and Cultural Revolution, which featured the wholesale destruction of temples combined with the persecution of religious specialists. Throughout most of China, the result was that most religious activity came to an end and temples were reduced to desolate shells of their former glory.[6]

For the Jiangnan region, the main focus of this book, in major metropolises like Shanghai the temple destruction campaigns launched after 1949 caused much more damage than earlier ones had. During the first decades of CCP rule, a total of 738 documented temples (37.8 percent of the city's 1,952 sacred sites) were destroyed or otherwise appropriated, with 595 (30.4 percent or nearly one-third of the total) listed as having been abandoned, closed, or torn down. Moreover, when we consider the fate of those temples for which we have data on their exact location, some rather striking trends emerge. The largest numbers of temples razed to the ground were located in the city center (414 of 568 in Shanghai County, 72.9 percent), with only a few ending up being used as schools (76 of 568; 13.3 percent). Urban temples that survived Shanghai's temple destruction campaigns tended to be located in or near its old city, including state cult sites like the Guandi and City God temples, as well as sites managed by Buddhist and Daoist clerics. Another key aspect of temple location was the relative abundance of land in Shanghai's suburban areas, which meant that more temples were built there (in late Qing and Republican times) than in the city itself. These temples seem to have been more likely to be converted into schools and thereby better placed to avoid total destruction since, in principle at least, "build schools with temple property" campaigns allowed for at least a portion of the original edifice to remain standing and some property preserved. This suggests that, while temples throughout the Shanghai area suffered grievously under CCP rule, those located outside urban centers had a greater chance of surviving at least partially untouched.[7] While Shanghai (and the entire Jiangnan region) should not necessarily be viewed as representative of China as a whole, the data presented above do point to the importance of spatial gradients as one means of measuring the effectiveness of modern Chinese religious policies.

With the advent of the reform era, China began to experience a religious revival, which in turn brought new wrinkles to the interplay between religion and the state. Temple cults and the ritual events they organize now flourish as hotbeds of cultural innovation and negotiation, with local elites working to expand the space of religious activities while also legitimizing them.[8] Overall, the data coming out of China make it clear that modernization has not led to the decline of religiosity, which is in fact booming.[9] Such a revival represents a huge challenge to the state, which is trying to adapt by formulating new categories such as intangible cultural heritage. In addition, the term *minjian xinyang* 民間信仰 for temple cults is now gradually becoming established in state discourse as a legitimate category. Another new concept is that of religious ecology (*zongjiao shengtai* 宗教生態), more scholarly but still linked to actual policy proposals,[10] which is seen as a key factor in achieving the goal of a harmonious society (*hexie shehui* 和諧社會), especially to counter the influence of Christianity. In effect, the state seems to be pushing a hidden agenda, which is not so hidden now, to encourage the revival of indigenous religious traditions to prevent Christianity from filling the gap that in Republican times had largely been occupied by redemptive societies. However, this hardly means that things will spin out of control. It's quite clear that if a new temple arises featuring some sort of animal deity and an ecstatic medium, the state will generally shut it down unless it has very strong elite support or remolds itself into something more palatable by asking the medium to practice at home and not on its premises.

Another fascinating problem is whether religion might end up providing a means for the Chinese state to legitimize itself because this was one of the essential ways the imperial authorities did so in the past (consider, e.g., the Mandate of Heaven). Now that Communism's luster has faded, getting rich quick is no longer satisfying, and nationalism can turn into a powder keg, what will China's new leaders rely on to enhance their legitimacy? As the Chinese state continues to evolve, will it try to revive religion to legitimize its rule and will it be along the lines of the Christian ideals that Sun Yat-sen, Chiang Kai-shek, and so many Republican era elites advocated? The answer is as yet unknown, but it is interesting to note that China is also experiencing a "Confucian revival," especially in the realm of ritual. Confucian ceremonies are now performed throughout China, not just in the north but also places like Quzhou 衢州 (Zhejiang). One striking aspect of these ceremonies is that students, who used to be at the vanguard of temple destruction campaigns, are now drafted to help carry offerings to Confucius, suggesting that we have come full circle. There's also the use of Confucius Institutes (Kongzi xueyuan 孔子學院) and tolerance of classes in reading Confucian scriptures (*dujingban* 讀經班), which suggests that the state is trying to at least indirectly promote Confucianism, perhaps along the lines of the Singapore model.[11]

Other contemporary catalysts of China's religious revival come in the form of tourism. Recent research has identified tourism as a crucial arena for understanding the state's attempts to effectively manage and standardize the local forces shaping China's religious revival, with the impact of cultural tourism prompting some officials and elites to restore temples to increase revenue.[12] Another noteworthy phenomenon involves the impact of tourism on non-Han communities. In many parts of Southwest China, relative flexibility in state policies toward non-Han religious traditions has resulted in beliefs and practices once been labeled "superstition" gaining protection under the rubric of "ethnic customs" (*minzu fengsu* 民族風俗) or "intangible cultural heritage," which has in turn prompted some ritual specialists to try to rebrand their traditions according to these new criteria.[13]

In the case of modern Taiwan, since the end of martial law in 1987 temple cults have been more than passive observers of changing state policies; they now play active roles in political life. One particularly striking facet of religion in modern Taiwan is that political progress has not resulted in the decline of popular beliefs and practices; on the contrary, many men and women who participate in political affairs feel no qualms about publicly joining religious movements. Some scholars maintain that state-society interactions have contributed to the formation of a "civil religion" that has links to western ideas of modern democracy without fully conforming to secularization models.[14]

One example of the vibrancy of Taiwan's religious traditions is its cults dedicated to the goddess Mazu 媽祖, which are intimately tied to both the state and local society via intangible heritage programs. Mazu cults and their rituals often serve as arenas where local religious traditions strive to gain acceptance, following which (often in highly modified forms) they come to be promoted as symbols of cultural identity. Such processes involve negotiations between the deemphasis of some rituals and the accommodation of new practices and symbols, as well as the exploitation of new commercial opportunities. Moreover, while local residents may not always support state-sponsored heritage activities, they can take advantage of such occasions to demonstrate community empowerment and promote local identities.[15]

The importance of Taiwan's Mazu cults may also be seen in their pilgrimage networks. In particular, Cross-Strait pilgrimages feature different interest groups striving to promote diverse goals and identities, which include not only Taiwan versus China but also various local forms (Zhangzhou 漳州 vs. Quanzhou 泉州, Ta-chia 大甲 vs. Pei-kang 北港, etc.), many of which are linked to intersecting networks and alliances.[16] D. J W. Hatfield's monograph on Cross-Strait pilgrimages (especially those featuring Mazu worship) makes an important contribution to our knowledge of these phenomena by proposing the concept of "complicity," defined as recognizing a common project despite seemingly inextricable differences, with pilgrims from Taiwan and Fujian providing legitimacy to each other's agendas. Hatfield also calls our attention to the roles of state and parastate institutions trying to manage Cross-Strait pilgrimages (including how scholars can get caught up in these projects), noting that while such events are usually viewed in a positive light, there is also the need to avoid any appearance of "superstition." In addition, increasing skepticism and a growing sense of local identity among Taiwanese pilgrims have led to a questioning of Chinese attempts to promote Mazu as a symbol of Cross-Strait cultural homogeneity, with pro-unification narratives rubbing up against attempts by Taiwanese temples to assert local forms of "incense power." One result has been a declining interest in Cross-Strait pilgrimages since the late 2000s.[17]

In the arena of religion and the mass media—our second realm of religious change—modern technologies continue to mold the development of Chinese religious movements. In Taiwan the ability of Dharma Master Hsing Yun (星雲 法師; b. 1927) to utilize slide projectors to illustrate his lectures and broadcast his messages via radio and TV may have been influenced by some of the practices described in chapters 3 and 4. Similarly, since the 1960s, Taiwanese spirit-writing organizations such as the Hall of Sages and Worthies (Shengxian Tang 聖賢堂) in Taizhong have come to resemble the Republican-era bookstores in publishing religious books and periodicals with the help of a full-time staff.[18] However, few religious websites have utilized the full communicative potential of the internet to stimulate new forms of religious action, in part due to traditional notions of authentic religious experience plus the tendency to quantify merit based on the numbers of printed books that one sponsors.[19] Throughout China new forms of media are assuming increasing importance in its religious revival, with temples and religious bookstores selling or giving away DVDs and CDs that can be used for sutra chanting or listening to liturgical music. Moreover, many temples use computers on a regular basis for tasks such as printing stele inscriptions, temple histories, ritual texts, and even menus for vegetarian meals. Computers also provide some religious specialists with a means of resisting government policies, as can be seen in the case of the Dai 傣 monks of Xishuangbanna 西雙版納 (in southern Yunnan), who utilized computers brought in by compatriots in Thailand to reintroduce the traditional script in monastic education and sutra publication enterprises.[20] In both China and Taiwan, the growing availability of religious texts in both print and online is reshaping relationships between clerical elites and lay devotees in new and unexpected ways, particularly in terms of decreasing laypeople's dependence on religious leaders for face-to-face interaction in the quest for religious knowledge and enlightenment.[21]

When we turn our attention to our third realm of change, religious elites and individual forms of religious life in contemporary China, we discover similar patterns of change and continuity. One of the most noteworthy aspects of Wang Yiting's religious life, as described in chapter 6, was that all the groups he participated in were voluntary associations, not ascriptive communities. Moreover, while Wang Yiting may have resembled late imperial elites in that he took refuge in religion following personal crises, the voluntary associations he participated in were very different from their imperial era counterparts in terms of being consciously modeled on Christianity. In China today, while there is an effervescence of both ascriptive and voluntary forms of religious life, the latter now seem increasingly important. This is especially true in urban areas, where rapacious realtors and dynamo developers have effectively given the coup de grace to most of the sacred sites that survived the temple destruction campaigns of the twentieth century. Beliefs and practices do survive but in a more diversified fashion, especially in forms of healing and body cultivation that center on small-scale shrines, bookstores, and vegetarian restaurants.[22]

New forms of urban religion are prevalent in Taiwan as well, with many cities witnessing the rapid growth of "divine altars" (shentan 神壇) located in stores and apartments, especially those run by spirit-mediums.[23] Such sites often serve the needs of people who migrate to Taiwan's major cities and encounter difficulties adjusting to their new lives. If they feel that the altar's medium is trustworthy and the gods have responded to their concerns, these worshippers may persuade friends or relatives to accompany them on future visits. As a result, the rituals performed at these urban sacred sites contribute to a sense of community, though one that is not limited to any particular group or geographic boundary, and ascriptive links are being superseded by voluntary relationships. In addition, many urban worshippers rely on the internet (including Facebook) to publicize shrine rituals and other events.[24] We have shown that entrepreneurial urban shrines and spirit possession cults were already common in Shanghai in late Qing and Republican times. Often disparaged as "Buddha shops" (Fodian 佛店), they were the butt of official and elite criticism. Yet they have endured, and their contemporary heirs are more visible and well established than ever.

Religious life today also features a growing emphasis on individualism, with people increasingly pursuing their own forms of spiritual practice, especially those who live far away from their native places.[25] Many of these individuals are women. Elderly women have been vital players in preserving and transmitting traditional concepts and cosmologies, especially within the family, while a new generation of younger women practitioners are taking the lead in many religious groups and using their status in the fight against gender inequality. As Kang Xiaofei eloquently observes, in today's China "women are neither victims of superstition or obstacles of modernity. They ingeniously construct female religiosity with both traditional and modern resources at their own disposal."[26]

Another major force transforming Chinese religious life today is globalization, with thriving transnational religious networks (including spirit-medium cults) effectively challenging conventional wisdom on the insularity of Chinese society.[27] The role of transnational networks was clearly important in Jiangnan during the 1898–1948 period studied in this book (as can be seen in the way Shanghai intellectuals such as Wang Yiting established connections with Japan, overseas communities, and the West) and was even more obvious farther south in Fujian and Guangdong, where connections to Chinese communities in Southeast Asia were a major element shaping local religious life. These networks have grown by several orders of magnitude in contemporary times, with religious publications, temple building, and rituals in Shanghai and elsewhere in Jiangnan now literally followed in real time across the globe, and conversely. Transnational links have also influenced religion's role in environmental resistance movements, with trends in postwar Taiwan now beginning to have an impact in China.[28] Globalization, burgeoning religiosity, and the assertive nature of many religious associations pose unprecedented challenges for China's new leaders, as can be seen in the role of Falungong among overseas Chinese, the impact of global Christian movements (based in either North America or East Asia) on China's underground churches, the influence of Islam in Xinjiang, and the crisis of Tibetan Buddhism in China.[29]

Analysis of social scientific data is now endeavoring to get a grip on these trends. One example is *Religious Experience in Contemporary Taiwan and China*, a collection of studies edited by Tsai Yen-zen 蔡彥仁 based on a survey project conducted from 2008 to 2012 with funding provided by Taiwan's National Science Council.[30] This book's greatest strength lies in its comparative approach, with most chapters engaging in explicit comparisons to a similar survey undertaken in China by Yao Xinzhong 姚新中 and Paul Badham from 2004 to 2006.[31] The comparative perspective poses its share of risks, though, particularly when it comes to issues of terminology. According to Tsai's introduction, the percentage of Taiwan's population considered to be "religious" is high (86.1 percent), exceeding that of Britain (76.8 percent) and in sharp contrast to data from China (8.7 percent), but what it means to be religious is not fully explained. According to the criteria used to measure Taiwanese religious affiliation, percentages for respondents were folk religion 38.3 percent, Buddhism 18.6 percent, Daoism 13.2 percent, Buddho-Daoism [Fo-Dao shuangxiu 佛道雙修] 5.1 percent, Christianity 5 percent, I-Kuan Tao [Yiguandao 一貫道] 2.4 percent, no religion 15.4 percent, and other 2 percent. These results are based on responses to question 99 in the survey, which reads "Nin muqian de zongjiao xinyang shi 您目前的宗教信仰是?" (p. 332; the English version [translated as "What is your Religion"?] may be found on p. 302). The main problem with such questions is that many respondents tend to have only a nebulous understanding of the term *zongjiao* while also engaging in a wide range of practices without feeling the need to be initiated into any religious organization. As Vincent Goossaert and David Palmer observed in their analysis of the Yao and Badham survey, while claims of formal religious affiliation in China remained low (albeit more than doubling between 1995 and 2005 from just 2 to 5 percent) and roughly one-third of respondents claimed to be atheists, most engaged in practices such as burning incense and more than three-quarters believed in the presence of divine retribution. In addition, a total of 15 percent worshipped deity statues in their homes.[32]

Apart from survey data, an increasing number of scholars have begun to utilize the Geographic Information System (GIS) and other digital technologies in the study of Chinese religious life. One example may be found in Kenneth Dean and Zheng Zhenman's 鄭振滿 analysis of the historical development of temple cults in Putian 莆田 (Fujian).[33] More recent projects include Lai Chi-tim's 黎志添 Daoist Digital Museum at the Chinese University of Hong Kong's Center for Studies of Daoist Culture—http://dao.crs.cuhk.edu.hk/digitalmuseum/CH and the Online Spiritual Atlas of China (OSAC)—https://www.globaleast.org/osage/map. In the field of Taiwanese popular religion, one highly promising development is the mapping of temples and other forms of sacred space by Hung Ying-fa 洪瑩發 and his colleagues for Academia Sinica's Cultural Resources Geographic Information System (CRGIS; see http://crgis.rchss.sinica.edu.tw/). Based on the innovative use of GIS technology, including cooperative projects involving both scholars and local experts, CRGIS is now used as a platform for analyzing different forms of Taiwanese religious life, including temples, sacred trees, and images of the Wind Lion Deity (Fengshiye 風獅爺).

In terms of future research, one possibility involves the study of regions not covered by this volume. In Western Hunan, for example, the fifty years covered by this study witnessed almost no instances of temple destruction, in stark contrast to our case study of Shanghai and Zhejiang, while the suppression of ritual specialists and their practices was largely limited to sloganeering. It was not until the 1950s and 1960s that the CCP state was able to effectively exert its authority over beliefs and practices at the local level. This began with data collection efforts such as the "brethren nationalities visiting research groups" (xiongdi minzu fangwentuan 兄弟民族訪問團) and "ethnic identification" (minzu shibie 民族識別) projects, followed by systematic destruction of temples and the suppression of elites who supported them during the Land Reform and Great Leap Forward campaigns, and culminating with attacks on specialists and their ritual traditions during the Cultural Revolution.[34] Other examples include places that during this time period were colonies, including Hong Kong and Taiwan, where, with the exception of wartime, temple destruction seems to have been relatively limited (see chapter 1). Yet another illuminating comparison is with Chinese communities elsewhere in the world, including Europe and America, where deterritorialization occurred to an even greater extent than in cities such as Shanghai.[35] In all these places, religious change took place at different times and resulted in different reconfigurations. But in all cases the three realms we have identified (community, knowledge, and religiosity) have been at the crux of these changes.

NOTES

Introduction

1. Vincent Goossaert, "1898: The Beginning of the End for Chinese Religion?" *Journal of Asian Studies* 65.2 (2006): 307–36.

2. See, for example, Peter Zarrow, *China in War and Revolution, 1895–1949* (London: Routledge, 2005); Peter Zarrow, *After Empire: The Conceptual Transformation of the Chinese State, 1885–1924* (Stanford, CA: Stanford University Press, 2012); Lydia H. Liu, *Translingual Practice: Literature, National Culture, and Translated Modernity—China, 1900–1937* (Stanford, CA: Stanford University Press, 1995).

3. Among the most important works are Mayfair Mei-hui Yang, ed., *Chinese Religiosities: Afflictions of Modernity and State Formation* (Berkeley: University of California Press, 2008); Yoshiko Ashiwa and David Wank, eds., *Making Religion, Making the State: The Politics of Religion in Contemporary China* (Stanford, CA: Stanford University Press, 2009); Adam Yuet Chau, ed., *Religion in Contemporary China: Revitalization and Innovation* (London: Routledge, 2011); David A. Palmer, Glenn Shive, and Philip L. Wickeri, eds., *Chinese Religious Life* (Oxford: Oxford University Press, 2011); David Ownby, Vincent Goossaert and Ji Zhe, eds., *Making Saints in Modern China* (New York: Oxford University Press, 2017).

4. Rebecca A. Nedostup, *Superstitious Regimes: Religion and the Politics of Chinese Modernity* (Cambridge, MA: Harvard University Asia Center, 2009). Poon Shuk-wah, *Negotiating Religion in Modern China: State and Common People in Guangzhou, 1900–1937* (Hong Kong: Chinese University Press, 2010).

5. Vincent Goossaert and David A. Palmer, *The Religious Question in Modern China* (Chicago: University of Chicago Press, 2011).

6. Vincent Goossaert, Jan Kiely, and John Lagerwey, eds., *Modern Chinese Religion*, Vol. 2: *1850–2015* (Leiden: Brill, 2016).

7. Holmes Welch, *The Buddhist Revival in China* (Cambridge, MA: Harvard University Press, 1968).

8. See especially Jan Kiely and J. Brooks Jessup, eds., *Recovering Buddhism in Modern China* (New York: Columbia University Press, 2016).

9. Prasenjit Duara, *Sovereignty and Authenticity: Manchukuo and the East Asian Modern* (Lanham, MD: Rowman and Littlefield, 2003).

10. The use of the term redemptive societies is not without its pitfalls, as discussed in Nikolas Broy, "Syncretic Sects and Redemptive Societies: Toward a New Understanding of 'Sectarianism' in the Study of Chinese Religions," *Review of Religion and Chinese Society* 2 (2015): 145–85. Definitions vary between the very encompassing (see, e.g., Goossaert and Palmer, *Religious Question*, 292–97) and the more specific. In addition, it may lead one to overlook the fact that many other religious groups, such as lay Buddhist associations, also stressed a discourse of redemption, including the expression *jiushi* 救世. For these reasons, we use it as an ideal type without emphasizing a sharp difference in worldviews and ideas between redemptive societies and other religious groups.

11. For more on these phenomena, see David A. Palmer, Paul R. Katz, and Wang Chien-ch'uan, eds., *Redemptive Societies and New Religious Movements in Modern China,* special issue, *Minsu quyi* 民俗曲藝 [Journal of Chinese Ritual, Theatre, and Folklore] 172–73 (June–September 2011). See also Goossaert and Palmer, *Religious Question*, 135–37; David Ownby, "Redemptive Societies in the Twentieth Century," in *Modern Chinese Religion,* Vol. 2: *1850–2015*, Vincent Goossaert, Jan Kiely and John Lagerwey, eds. (Leiden: Brill, 2016), 685–727; David Ownby, *Falun Gong and the Future of China* (New York: Oxford University Press, 2008). A useful overview of Chinese-language works may be found in David Ownby, "Recent Chinese Scholarship on the History of 'Redemptive Societies': Guest Editor's Introduction," *Chinese Studies in History* 44.1–2 (Fall 2010–Winter 2011): 3–9.

12. Huang Ko-wu 黃克武, "Minguo chunian Shanghai Lingxue yanjiu: Yi 'Shanghai Lingxuehui' wei li" 民國初年上海的靈學研究：以「上海靈學會」為例, *Bulletin of the Institute of Modern History, Academia Sinica* 55 (2007): 99–136; Sakai Tadao 酒井忠夫, "Minguo chuqi zhi xinxing zongjiao yundong yu xinshidai chaoliu" 民國初期之新興宗教運動與新時代潮流, Chang Shu-e 張淑娥, trans., *Minjian zongjiao* 民間宗教 1 (1995): 1–36; Sun Jiang 孫江, *Kindai Chūgoku no kakumei to himitsu kessha: Chūgoku kakumei no shakaishi kenkyū (1895–1955)* 近代中國の革命と秘密結社：中國革命の社會史的研究 (一八九五-一九五五) (Tokyo: Kyūko sho-in, 2007).

13. The project was entitled "1898–1948: 50 Years that Changed Chinese Religion." The project's final conference was held on November 21–22, 2013. See http://www.mh.sinica.edu.tw/PGGroupStudyPlan_Page.aspx?groupStudyPlanID=8.

14. Kang Bao 康豹 (Paul R. Katz) and Gao Wansang 高萬桑 (Vincent Goossaert), eds., *Gaibian Zhongguo zongjiao de wushinian, 1898–1948* 改變中國宗教的五十年，1898–1948 (Nankang: Institute of Modern History, Academia Sinica, 2015). Some preliminary results were presented in Paul R. Katz, *Religion in China and Its Modern Fate* (Waltham, MA: Brandeis University Press, 2014).

15. For more on these phenomena, see Thomas David DuBois, *The Sacred Village: Social Change and Religious Life in Rural North China* (Honolulu: University of Hawai'i Press, 2005); James Flath, "Temple Fairs and the Republican State in North China," *Twentieth-Century China* 30.1 (2004): 39–63; David G. Johnson, *Spectacle and Sacrifice: The Ritual Foundations of Village Life in North China* (Cambridge, MA: Harvard University Press,

2009); Daniel L. Overmyer, *Local Religion in North China in the Twentieth Century: The Structure and Organization of Community Rituals and Beliefs* (Leiden: Brill, 2009); Stephen Jones, *In Search of the Daoists of North China* (Aldershot: Ashgate, 2010). See also Vincent Goossaert, "Is There a North China Religion? A Review Essay," *Journal of Chinese Religions* 39 (2011): 83–93.

16. See, for example, Megan Bryson, *Goddess on the Frontier: Religion, Ethnicity, and Gender in Southwest China* (Stanford, CA: Stanford University Press, 2016); David C. Graham, *Folk Religion in Southwest China* (Washington, DC: Smithsonian Institution, 1961); Kang Xiaofei and Donald S. Sutton, *Contesting the Yellow Dragon: Ethnicity, Religion, and the State in the Sino-Tibetan Borderland* (Leiden: Brill, 2016); Paul R. Katz, "Religious Life in Western Hunan during the Modern Era: Some Preliminary Observations," *Cahiers d'Extrême Asie*, 25 (December 2017): 181–218; Wang Chien-ch'uan, "Popular Groups Promoting 'The Religion of Confucius' in the Chinese Southwest and Their Activities since the Nineteenth Century (1840–2013): An Observation Centered on Yunnan's Eryuan County and Environs," in Sébastien Billioud, ed., *Contemporary Confucian Movements*, 90–121 (Leiden: Brill, 2018).

17. Excellent overviews of Christianity in modern China may be found in Daniel H. Bays, ed., *Christianity in China: From the Eighteenth Century to the Present* (Stanford, CA: Stanford University Press, 1996); Daniel H. Bays, *A New History of Christianity in China* (West Sussex: Wiley-Blackwell, 2012). See also Joseph Tse-Hei Lee, *The Bible and the Gun: Christianity in South China, 1860–1900* (New York: Routledge, 2003); Henrietta Harrison, "Rethinking Missionaries and Medicine in China: The Miracles of Assunta Pallotta, 1905–2005," *Journal of Asian Studies* 71.1 (2012): 127–48.

18. Goossaert and Palmer, *Religious Question*, 73–83; Ashiwa and Wank, *Making Religion, Making the State*, 44–55, 66–67, 137–46.

19. For more on the Japanese experience, see Jason Ānanda Josephson, *The Invention of Religion in Japan* Chicago: University of Chicago Press, 2012). See also articles by Elisabetta Porcu, John K. Nelson, Mark R. Mullins, and Ian Reader in the *Journal of Religion in Japan* 1.1 (2012): 3–106.

20. Christian Meyer, "How the 'Science of Religion' (*zongjiaoxue* 宗教學) as a Discipline Globalized 'Religion' in Republican China, 1890–1949: Global Concepts, Knowledge Transfer, and Local Discourses," in Thomas Jansen, Thoralf Klein, and Christian Meyer, eds., *Chinese Religions in the Age of Globalization, 1800–Present* (Leiden: Brill, 2014), 297–341.

21. Thought-provoking studies of this concept and its implications include Karel Dobbelaere, *Secularization: An Analysis at Three Levels* (Brussels: PIE–Peter Lang, 2002); Talal Asad, *Formations of the Secular: Christianity, Islam, Modernity* (Stanford, CA: Stanford University Press, 2003); José Casanova, "Secularization Revisited: A Reply to Talal Asad," in David Scott and Charles Hirschkind, eds., *Powers of the Secular Modern: Talal Asad and His Interlocutors* (Stanford, CA: Stanford University Press, 2006), 12–30; Roy Wallis and Steve Bruce, "Secularization: The Orthodox Model," in Steve Bruce, ed., *Religion and Modernization: Sociologists and Historians Debate the Secularization Thesis* (Oxford: Oxford University Press, 1992), 8–22. For Chinese debates on this concept, see Ji

Zhe 汲喆, "Ruhe chaoyue jingdian shisuhua lilun? Ping zongjiao shehuixue de sanzhong houshisuhua lunshu 如何超越經典世俗化理論？—評宗教社會學的三種後世俗化論述," *Shehuixue yanjiu* 社會學研究 136 (2008): 55–75.

22. Michael Szonyi, "Secularization Theories and the Study of Chinese Religions," *Social Compass* 56.3 (2009): 312–27.

23. Dobbelaere, *Secularization*.

24. Yang Fenggang, *Religion in China: Survival and Revival under Communist Rule* (New York: Oxford University Press, 2012).

25. Vincent Goossaert, "Daoists in the Modern Chinese Self-Cultivation Market: The Case of Beijing, 1850–1949," in David A. Palmer and Liu Xun, eds., *Daoism in the Twentieth Century: Between Eternity and Modernity* (Berkeley: University of California Press, 2012), 123–53.

26. Vincent Goossaert, "A Question of Control: Licensing Local Ritual Specialists in Jiangnan, 1850–1950," in Paul R. Katz and Liu Shufen 劉淑芬, eds., *Belief, Practice, and Cultural Adaptation: Papers from the Religion Section of the Fourth International Conference on Sinology* (Nankang: Academia Sinica, 2013), 569–604.

27. Peter Van der Veer, *The Modern Spirit of Asia: The Spiritual and the Secular in China and India* (Princeton, NJ: Princeton University Press, 2013).

28. Robert P. Weller, "Asia and the Global Economies of Charisma," in Pattana Kitiarsa, ed., *Religious Commodifications in Asia: Marketing Gods* (London: Routledge, 2008), 15–30.

29. Goossaert and Palmer, *Religious Question*, 68, 73–75, 83, 89.

30. Nedostup, *Superstitious Regimes*, 11–16, 39–43, 143–145; Kuo Ya-pei [郭亞珮], "Redeploying Confucius: The Imperial State Dreams of the Nation, 1902–1911," in Mayfair Mei-hui Yang, ed., *Chinese Religiosities: Afflictions of Modernity and State Formation* (Berkeley: University of California Press, 2008), 65–84; David Ownby, "The Politics of Redemption: Redemptive Societies and the Chinese State in Modern and Contemporary Chinese History," in Paul R. Katz and Liu Shufen 劉淑芬, eds., *Belief, Practice, and Cultural Adaptation: Papers from the Religion Section of the Fourth International Conference on Sinology* (Nankang: Academia Sinica, 2013), 677–735. For more on the way the term *superstition* was initially adopted by Chinese Christian elites, see Zhu Pingyi 祝平一, "Biwang xingmi: Ming Qing zhiji de Tianzhujiao yu *mixin* de jiangou 闢妄醒迷：明清之際的天主教與「迷信」的建構," *Bulletin of the Institute of History and Philology, Academia Sinica* 84.4 (2013): 695–752.

31. Robert P. Weller, "Taiwan and Global Religious Trends," *Taiwan zongjiao yanjiu* 臺灣宗教研究 12.1–2 (2013): 7–30.

32. For more on the role of modern religious organizations during this era, see Vincent Goossaert, "Republican Church Engineering: The National Religious Associations in 1912 China," in Mayfair Mei-hui Yang, ed., *Chinese Religiosities: Afflictions of Modernity and State Formation* (Berkeley: University of California Press, 2008), 209–32. See also, in the same volume, Ji Zhe 汲喆, "Secularization as Religious Restructuring: Statist Institutionalization of Chinese Buddhism and Its Paradoxes," 233–60.

33. Goossaert and Palmer, *Religious Question*, 393–404.

Chapter 1

1. Earlier versions of this chapter appeared in Paul R. Katz, "'Superstition' and Its Discontents: On the Impact of Temple Destruction Campaigns in China, 1898–1948," in Paul R. Katz and Liu Shufen 劉淑芬, eds., *Belief, Practice, and Cultural Adaptation: Papers from the Religion Section of the Fourth International Conference on Sinology* (Nankang: Academia Sinica, 2013), 605–82; and Katz, *Religion in China and Its Modern Fate*, 17–67.

2. Useful overviews of the historical phenomena discussed in this chapter may be found in Prasenjit Duara, "Knowledge and Power in the Discourse of Modernity: The Campaigns against Popular Religion in Early Twentieth-Century China," *Journal of Asian Studies* 50 (1991): 67–83; Prasenjit Duara, *Rescuing History from the Nation: Questioning Narratives of Modern China* (Chicago: University of Chicago Press, 1995). See also Nedostup, *Superstitious Regimes*; Poon, *Negotiating Religion*; Goossaert and Palmer, *Religious Question*.

3. Thomas David DuBois, "Local Religion and Festivals," in Vincent Goossaert, Jan Kiely, and John Lagerwey, eds., *Modern Chinese Religion*, Vol 2: *1850–2015* (Leiden: Brill, 2016), 371–400.

4. For more on these issues, see Nedostup, *Superstitious Regimes*, 103, 126, 142. See also Joseph W. Esherick, "Modernity and Nation in the Chinese City," in ed., *Remaking the Chinese City: Modernity and National Identity, 1900–1950* (Honolulu: University of Hawai'i Press, 2000), 1–16; Li Guannan, "Reviving China: Urban Reconstruction in Nanchang and the Guomindang National Revival Movement, 1932–1937," *Frontiers of History in China* 7.1 (2012): 106–13; Kristin Stapleton, *Civilizing Chengdu: Chinese Urban Reform, 1895–1937* (Cambridge, MA: Harvard University Press, 2000).

5. Poon Shuk-wah, "Thriving under an Anti-superstition Regime: The Cult of Dragon Mother in Yuecheng, Guangdong, during the 1930s," *Journal of Chinese Religions* 43.1 (May 2015): 34–58. See also Poon, *Negotiating Religion*, 59.

6. Anthony C. Yu, *State and Religion in China* (Chicago: Open Court Press, 2005); John Lagerwey, *China: A Religious State* (Hong Kong: Hong Kong University Press, 2010).

7. Hsiao Kung-ch'üan, *Rural China: Imperial Control in the Nineteenth Century* (Seattle: University of Washington Press, 1960); Daniel L. Overmyer, "Attitudes toward Popular Religion in the Ritual Texts of the Chinese State: The Collected Statutes of the Great Ming," *Cahiers d'Extrême Asie* 5 (1989–90): 191–221.

8. Vincent Goossaert, "Counting the Monks: The 1736–1739 Census of the Chinese Clergy," *Late Imperial China* 21.2 (2000): 40–85.

9. Barend ter Haar, *The White Lotus Teachings in Chinese Religious History* (Leiden: Brill, 1992); Barend ter Haar, *Ritual and Mythology of the Chinese Triads: Creating an Identity* (Leiden: Brill, 1998).

10. See, for example, Bays, *New History of Christianity*; Lian Xi, *Redeemed by Fire: The Rise of Popular Christianity in Modern China* (New Haven, CT: Yale University Press, 2010).

11. The term *yin* 淫 has been variously translated as "excessive," "licentious," "illicit," "improper," "perverse," "profane," and "profligate," depending on its context. For more

on this problem, see Paul R. Katz, "Daoism and Local Cults: A Case Study of the Cult of Marshal Wen," in Kwang-ching Liu and Richard Shek, eds., *Heterodoxy in Late Imperial China* (Honolulu: University of Hawai'i Press, 2004), 172–208; Vincent Goossaert, "The Destruction of Immoral Temples in Qing China," in *ICS Visiting Professor Lectures Series*, special issue, *Journal of Chinese Studies* 2 (2009): 131–53.

12. Prasenjit Duara, *Culture, Power, and the State: Rural North China, 1900–1942* (Stanford: Stanford University Press, 1988); James L. Watson, "Standardizing the Gods: The Promotion of Tien Hou ('Empress of Heaven') along the South China Coast, 960–1960," in David G. Johnson, Andrew J. Nathan, and Evelyn S. Rawski, eds., *Popular Culture in Late Imperial China* (Berkeley: University of California Press, 1985), 292–324. See also Terry Kleeman, "Licentious Cults and Bloody Victuals: Sacrifice, Reciprocity, and Violence in Traditional China," *Asia Major* 7.1 (1997): 185–211.

13. Timothy Brook, "The Policies of Religion: Late-Imperial Origins of the Regulatory State," in Yoshiko Ashiwa and David Wank, eds., *Making Religion, Making the State: The Politics of Religion in Contemporary China* (Stanford, CA: Stanford University Press, 2009), 22–42.

14. Goossaert and Palmer, *Religious Question*, 62–63, 125. See also Adam Y. Chau, "Superstition Specialist Households? The Household Idiom in Chinese Religious Practices," *Minsu quyi* 民俗曲藝 153 (2006): 157–202.

15. Chen Jinlong 陳金龍, *Nanjing Guomin zhengfu shiqi de zhengjiao guanxi: Yi Fojiao wei zhongxin de kaocha* 南京國民政府時期的政教關係：以佛教為中心的考察 (Beijing: Zhongguo shehui kexue chubanshe, 2011). See also the essays by Vincent Goossaert, Lo Shih-chieh 羅士傑, Qi Gang 祁剛, Yau Chi On 游子安, and Paul R. Katz in Kang Bao and Gao Wansang, eds., *Gaibian Zhongguo zongjiao de wushinian, 1898–1948* (Nankang: Institute of Modern History, Academia Sinica, 2015).

16. Nedostup, *Superstitious Regimes*, 39–43, 79–97, 108, 295–300; Poon, *Negotiating Religion*, 49, 73, 118. See also Rebecca Nedostup, "Ritual Competition and the Modernizing Nation-State," in Mayfair Mei-hui Yang, ed., *Chinese Religiosities: Afflictions of Modernity and State Formation* (Berkeley: University of California Press, 2008), 87–112.

17. The "ancient deities" category encompassed a wide range of local cults, especially those devoted to nature deities and heroes.

18. Many of these documents may be found in Chiu Hei-yuan 瞿海源, "Zhonghua minguo youguan zongjiao faling ji falü cao'an huibian" 中華民國有關宗教法令及法律草案彙編, *Zhongyang yanjiuyuan Minzuxue yanjiusuo ziliao huibian* 中央研究院民族學研究所資料彙編 2 (1990): 113–39. See also *Zhonghua minguoshi dang'an ziliao huibian, Diwuji, Diyibian*, series 5, pt. 1: *Wenhua* (1) 中華民國史檔案資料彙編，第5輯，第一編，文化(1) (Nanjing: Jiangsu guji chubanshe, 1994), 490–513, 1017–29, 1075–82.

19. Zhongxuan 中宣, "Pochu mixian zhi yiyi he banfa" 破除迷信之意義和辦法, *Shidai* 時代 1.3 (1929): 13–17. Zhongxuan was the pseudonym used by a Nationalist elite deeply concerned with religious affairs. See also Hu Qiaomu 胡喬木, "Fan mixin tigang 反迷信提綱," *Zhongguo qingnian* 中國青年 2.11 (1940), reprinted in *Zhonggong dangshi yanjiu* 中共黨史研究 1.5 (1999): 1–4.

20. "Shishi xinwen: Gailiang menshen: Pochu mixin: Minshengfu bandao sanxiang faban" 時事新聞：改良門神：破除迷信，閩省府頒到三項辦法, *Gongjiao zhoukan* 公教周刊 7.1 (1935): 9.

21. Zheng Guo 鄭國, "Minguo qianqi mixin wenti yanjiu (1912–1928)" 民國前期迷 信問題研究 (1912–1928), (MA thesis, Shandong University, 2003), 11. See also Wan Jianzhong 萬建中, "Minchu de fengsu bianqe yu bianqe fengsu" 民國的風俗變革與變革 風俗, *Liaoxibei minzu yanjiu* 遼西北民族研究 33 (2002): 119–28; Li Xuechang 李學昌 and Dong Jianbo 董建波, "20 shiji shangbanye Hangxian yingshen saihui shuailuo yinsu qianxi" 20 世紀上半葉杭縣迎神賽會衰落因素淺析, *Huadong shifan daxue xuabao (Zhexue shehui kexue ban)* 華東師範大學學報(哲學社會科學版) 39.5 (2007): 49–53.

22. We are grateful to Fu Haiyan 付海晏, Qi Gang 祁剛, and Liu Wenxing 劉文星 for sharing their views on this topic.

23. For historical background, see Parks M. Coble, *Facing Japan: Chinese Politics and Japanese Imperialism, 1931–1937* (Cambridge, MA: Harvard University Press, 1991); Diana Lary, *The Chinese People at War: Human Suffering and Social Transformation, 1937–1945* (New York: Cambridge University Press, 2010).

24. For more on the intellectual ideals of that era, see John Fitzgerald, *Awakening China: Politics, Culture, and Class in the Nationalist Revolution* (Stanford, CA: Stanford University Press, 1996); Henrietta Harrison, *The Making of the Republic Citizen: Political Ceremonies and Symbols in China, 1911–1929* (Oxford: Oxford University Press, 2000); Kuo Ya-pei, *Debating "Culture" in Interwar China*, Leiden Series in Modern East Asian Politics and History (London: Routledge, 2010). See also Paul A. Cohen, *History in Three Keys: The Boxers as Event, Experience, and Myth* (New York: Columbia University Press, 1997), 223–37.

25. Liu Chengyou 劉成有, "Luelun miaochan xingxue ji qi dui Daojiao de yingxiang— Cong 1928 nian de yiduan difangzhi ziliao tongji shuoqi" 略論廟產興學及其對道 教的影響—從1928年的一段地方志資料統計說起, *Zhongguo Daojiao* 中國道教 1 (2004): 50–52; Zheng Guo, "Minguo qianqi mixin wenti yanjiu (1912–1928)"; Nedostup, *Superstitious Regimes*, 11–16.

26. Nedostup, *Superstitious Regimes*, 79–87. See also Xu Xiaozheng 許效正, "Qingmo Minchu miaochan wenti yanjiu (1895–1916)" 清末民初廟產問題研究 (1895–1916) (PhD diss., Shaanxi Normal University, 2010), 120–37; Zhao Mingjuan 趙明娟, "20 shiji shangbanye Zhejiang Daojiaoshi yanjiu" 20世紀上半葉浙江道教史研究 (MA thesis, Zhejiang University, 2011), 5–6.

27. Poon, *Negotiating Religion*, 42–49. For more on Guangzhou's history during this era, see Michael Tsin, *Nation, Governance, and Modernity in China: Canton, 1900–1927* (Stanford, CA: Stanford University Press, 1999); Lai Chi-tim 黎志添, "Qingdai Daoguang nianjian Guangzhou chengqu cimiao de kongjian fenbu yanjiu: Yi Daoguang shiwunian 'Guangzhou shengcheng quantu' wei kaocha zhongxin" 清代道光年間廣州城區祠廟的 空間分佈及其意涵：以道光十五年「廣州省城全圖」為考察中心, *Journal of Chinese Studies* 63 (2016): 151–99.

28. Ai Ping 艾萍, "Minguo jinzhi yingshen saihui lunxi—Yi Shanghai wei ge'an 民國禁止迎神賽會論析—以上海為個案," *Jingsu shehui kexue* 江蘇社會科學 5 (2010): 216–21.

29. *Zhonghua minguoshi dang'an ziliao huibian, Diwuji, Diyibian*, 492–95.

30. Van der Veer, *Modern Spirit of Asia*. Van der Veer's focus is on comparing China and India, but other Asian countries should also be brought into the picture. For India, see David Smith, *Hinduism and Modernity* (Malden, MA: Blackwell, 2003); Yüksel Sezgin and Mirjam Künkler, "Regulation of 'Religion' and the 'Religious': The Politics of Judicialization and Bureaucratization in India and Indonesia," *Comparative Studies in Society and History* 56.2 (April 2014): 448–78.

31. Helen Hardacre, *Shintō and the State, 1868–1988* (Princeton, NJ: Princeton University Press, 1989).

32. Chiara Formichi, *Islam and the Making of the Nation: Kartosuwiryo and Political Islam in 20th-Century Indonesia* (Leiden: Brill, 2012); Raymond L. M. Lee and Susan E. Ackerman, *Sacred Tensions: Modernity and Religious Transformation in Malaysia* (Columbia: University of South Carolina Press, 1997).

33. Goossaert and Palmer, *Religious Question*, 54–56. For a stimulating comparison between religious change in China and Japan, see Thomas David DuBois, *Religion and the Making of Modern East Asia* (Cambridge: Cambridge University Press, 2011).

34. Pham Quynh Phuong, *Hero and Deity: Tran Hung Dao and the Resurgence of Popular Religion in Vietnam* (Chiang Mai: Mekong Press, 2009).

35. Laurel Kendall, *Shamans, Nostalgias, and the IMF: South Korean Popular Religion in Motion* (Honolulu: University of Hawai'i Press, 2009), 1–11.

36. Goossaert and Palmer, *Religious Question*, 44–49.

37. Yu Zhejun, 郁喆隽, *Shenming yu shimin: Minguo shiqi Shanghai diqu yingshen saihui yanjiu* 神明與市民：民國時期上海地區迎神賽會研究 (Shanghai: Shanghai Sanlian shudian, 2014), esp. 132–134. This is a Chinese improved version of Yu Zhejun, "Volksreligion im Spiegel der Zivilgesellschaftstheorie: Gottbegrüssungsprozession in Shanghai während der Republikzeit" (PhD diss., Leipzig University, 2010). See also Xu Xiaozheng, "Qingmo Minchu miaochan wenti yanjiu," 120–23. One notable exception is the late Qing political novel *The Broom to Sweep Away Superstition* (*Saomizhou* 掃迷帚), which was published in 1905. See Goossaert, "1898."

38. Li Ganchen 李幹忱, ed. and comp., *Pochu mixin quanshu* 破除迷信全書, in *Zhongguo minjian xinyang ziliao huibian* 中國民間信仰資料彙編, series 1, vol. 30 (Taipei: Xuesheng shuju, 1989). For more on the use of such labels, see David. A. Palmer, "Heretical Doctrines, Reactionary Secret Societies, Evil Cults: Labeling Heterodoxy in Twentieth-Century China," in Mayfair Mei-hui Yang, ed., *Chinese Religiosities: Afflictions of Modernity and State Formation* (Berkeley: University of California Press, 2008), 113–34. Examples of anti-superstition stories may be found in part 3 of Sherman Cochran, Andrew C. K. Hsieh, and Janis Cochran, eds. and trans., *One Day in China: May 21, 1936* (New Haven, CT: Yale University Press, 1983).

39. Hung Chang-tai 洪長泰, *Going to the People: Chinese Intellectuals and Folk Literature, 1918-1937* (Cambridge, MA: Harvard University Press, 1985). See also Poon, *Negotiating*, 74, 86; Zheng Guo, "Mingui qianqi mixin wenti yanjiu."

40. Nedostup, *Superstitious Regimes*, 105, 123-33. See also Peter Carroll, *Between Heaven and Modernity: Reconstructing Suzhou, 1895-1937* (Stanford, CA: Stanford University Press, 2006).

41. See the nearly 150 pages of data in *Zhonghua minguoshi dang'an ziliao huibian, Diwuji, Diyibian*, 580-726.

42. "Zhonghua minguo miaochan xingxue cujinhui xuanyan" 中華民國廟產興學促進會宣言, *Jiaoyu jikan* 教育季刊 1.2 (1930): 156-59.

43. Vincent Goossaert, "Détruire les temples pour construire les écoles: Reconstitution d'un objet historique," *Extrême-Orient Extrême-Occident* 33 (2011): 35-51.

44. Sarah Schneewind, *Community Schools and the State in Ming China* (Stanford, CA: Stanford University Press, 2006), 73-86, 146-50; Goossaert, "Destruction of Immoral Temples."

45. *Zhonghua minguoshi dang'an ziliao huibian, Diwuji, Diyibian*, 496-97, 504-13; Nedostup, *Superstitious Regimes*, 84-85.

46. Goossaert, "Question of Control." For more on police roles in enforcing temple destruction campaigns, see Yu Zhejun, *Shenming yu shimin*, 210-49.

47. Nedostup, *Superstitious Regimes*, 104; Poon, *Negotiating Religion*, 81-83.

48. Nedostup, "Ritual Competition and the Modernizing Nation-State," 96-97.

49. Chen Jinlong 陳金龍, "Minguo 'Simiao guanli tiaoli' de banbu yu feizhi" 民國《寺廟管理條例》的頒布與廢止, *Fayin* 法音 4 (2008): 54-59.

50. See especially Nedostup, *Superstitious Regimes*, 79-87, 103, 113, 148-49; Poon, *Negotiating Religion*, 45-47.

51. Xu Xiaozheng, "Qingmo Minchu miaochan wenti yanjiu," 101-14, 137. See also Shen Jie 沈潔, "Xiandaihua jianzhi dui xinyang kongjian de zhengyong – Yi ershi shiji chunian de miaochan xingxue yundong wei li" 現代化建制對信仰空間的徵用—以二十世紀初年的廟產興學運動為例, *Lishi jiaoxue wenti* 歷史教學問題 2 (2008): 56-59; Goossaert and Palmer, *Religious Question*, 49; Nedostup, *Superstitious Regimes*, 103-20. For more on late Qing local resistance, see Roxann Prazniak, *Of Camel Kings and Other Things: Rural Rebels against Modernity in Late Imperial China* (New York: Rowman and Littlefield, 1999).

52. Goossaert and Palmer, *Religious Question*, 46-47; Nedostup, *Superstitious Regimes*, 76-77. See also Vera Schwarcz, *The Chinese Enlightenment: Intellectuals and the Legacy of the May Fourth Movement of 1919* (Berkeley: University of California Press, 1986).

53. Tai Shuangqiu 邰爽秋, *Miaochan xingxue wenti* 廟產興學問題 (Shanghai: Zhonghua shubao liutongchu, 1929), 11-15.

54. "Pochu mixin: Xiaoshan xuesheng daohui Chenghuang" 破除迷信 — 蕭山學生搗毀城隍, *Zhenguang zazhi* 真光雜誌 28.2 (1929): 85-86.

55. Eric Reinders, "Shattered on the Rock of Ages: Western Iconoclasm and Chinese Modernity," in Fabio Rambelli and Eric Reinders, eds., *Buddhism and Iconoclasm in East Asia: A History* (London: Bloomsbury Academic, 2012), 89–133. See also Nedostup, *Superstitious Regimes*, 68. For more on how Christianity (and especially Catholicism) interacted with communal religious traditions, see Lee, *Bible and the Gun*; Eugenio Menegon, *Ancestors, Virgins, and Friars: Christianity as a Local Religion in Late Imperial China* (Cambridge, MA: Harvard University Press, 2009); Harrison, "Rethinking Missionaries and Medicine."

56. Feng Yuxiang 馮玉祥, "Mixin shi minzu luohou de xiangzheng, mixin shi wangguo miezhong de genyuan, geming de minzhong yao pochu mixin" 迷信是民族落後的象徵，迷信是亡國滅種的根源，革命的民眾要破除迷信, *Xinghua* 興華 25.16 (1928): 10–17.

57. Yan Yutang 嚴玉堂, "Zhengfu pochu mixin yu Zhongguo jidujiao de qiantu" 政府破除迷信與中國基督教的前途," *Xinghua* 興華 25.35 (1928): 13–14.

58. Important historical background may be found in Ryan Dunch, *Fuzhou Protestants and the Making of Modern China, 1857–1927* (New Haven, CT: Yale University Press, 2001).

59. *Haichaoyin* 海潮音 10.1 (1929): 80–82.

60. Vincent Goossaert, "Irrepressible Female Piety: Late Imperial Bans on Women Visiting Temples," *Nan Nü: Men, Women, and Gender in China* 10.2 (2008): 212–41. See also Julia C. Huang, Elena Valussi, and David A. Palmer, "Gender and Sexuality," in David A. Palmer, Glenn Shive, and Philip L. Wickeri, eds., *Chinese Religious Life* (Oxford: Oxford University Press, 2011), 107–23.

61. Kang Xiaofei, "Women and the Religious Question in Modern China," in Vincent Goossaert, Jan Kiely and John Lagerwey, eds., *Modern Chinese Religion, Vol. 2: 1850–2015* (Leiden: Brill, 2016), vol. 1, 491–559. See also Nedostup, *Superstitious Regimes*, 112; Poon, *Negotiating Religion*, 53, 63, 139–40.

62. Vincent Goossaert, "The Shifting Balance of Power in the City God Temples, Late Qing to 1937," *Journal of Chinese Religions* 43.1 (2015): 5–33; Yu Zhejun, *Shenming yu shimin*, 244–48. See also *Zhonghua minguoshi dang'an ziliao huibian, Diwuji, Diyibian*, 490–91; "Pochu mixin: Baoying xian feichu ouxiang yundong" 破除迷信—寶應縣廢除偶像運動, *Zhenguang zazhi* 真光雜誌 28.2 (1929): 84.

63. He Zhiming 何志明, "Minguo qi'an: Cong 'Da Chenghuang' dao 'Da dangbu'" 民國奇案：從「打城隍」到「打黨部」, *Wenshi tiandi* 文史天地 11 (2010): 41–45.

64. Sha Qingqing 沙青青, "Xinyang yu quanzheng: 1931 nian Gaoyou 'Da Chenghuang' fengchao zhi yanjiu" 信仰與權爭:1931年高郵「打城隍」風潮之研究, *Jindaishi yanjiu* 近代史研究 1 (2010): 115–27.

65. He Zhiming, "Minguo qi'an."

66. We are especially grateful to Ma Jun 馬軍 for providing a list of articles published in the *China Buddhist Association News* (*Zhongguo Fojiaohui bao* 中國佛教會報) from 1931 to 1933, which document the work by Wang Yiting in protecting Buddhist monastic properties (*huchi sichan* 護持寺產).

67. *Zhonghua minguoshi dang'an ziliao huibian, Diwuji, Diyibian,* 15–16. See also Beverly Foulks McGuire, "Bringing Buddhism into the Classroom: Jiang Qian's 江謙 (1876–1942) Vision for Education in Republican China," *Journal of Chinese Religions* 39 (2011): 33–54.

68. *Haichaoyin* 海潮音 10.1 (1929): 77–78; "Gedi miaochan zhi chuli" 各地廟產之處理, *Shenbao* 申報, February 19, 1929. The daily newspaper *Shenbao* was published in Shanghai from 1872 to 1949. Dates for *Shenbao* articles are given according to the western Gregorian calendar.

69. Fu Haiyan 付海晏, "Geming, falü yu miaochan: Minguo Beiping Tieshansi an yanjiu 革命, 法律與廟產—民國北平鐵山寺案研究, *Lishi yanjiu* 歷史研究 3 (2003): 105–20. See also Tai Shuangqiu, *Miaochan xingxue wenti*.

70. Ownby, "Redemptive Societies." For the histories of specific groups, see Duara, *Sovereignty and Authenticity*, 103–22, 139–40, 154–62; DuBois, *Sacred Village,* 107–85.

71. Yau Chi-on 游子安, "DaDao nanxing: 1920 zhi 1930 niandai Gang, Xing Tianqing caotang yu Daoyuan zhi daomai yinyuan" 大道南行：1920至1930年代港、星天清草堂與道院之道脈因緣, in Kang Bao and Gao Wansang, eds., *Gaibian Zhongguo zongjiao de wushinian, 1898–1948* (Nankang: Institute of Modern History, Academia Sinica, 2015), 141–67.

72. Goossaert and Palmer, *Religious Question*, 44–45.

73. Fu Haiyan, "Geming, falü yu miaochan."

74. Xu Xiaozheng, "Qingmo Minchu miaochan wenti yanjiu," 117.

75. Poon, *Negotiating Religion,* 48.

76. Goossaert and Palmer, *Religious Question*, 126–27.

77. *Zhonghua minguoshi dang'an ziliao huibian, Diwuji, Diyibian,* 509–13.

78. Zhongxuan, "Pochu mixin zhi yiyi he banfa."

79. Xu Xiaozheng, "Qingmo Minchu miaochan wenti yanjiu," 92–101. One notable exception may be found in Shen Jie 沈潔, "Fanmixin yu shequ xinyang kongjian de xiandai licheng—Yi 1934 nian Suzhou de qiuyu yishi wei li" 反迷信與社區信仰空間的現代歷程—以1934 年蘇州的求雨儀式為例, *Shilin* 史林 2 (2007): 44–63.

80. Lai Chi-tim 黎志添, "Minguo shiqi Guangzhou shi Zhengyipai huoju daoshi yingye daoguan fenbu de kongjian fenxi—Miaoyu, renkou yu Daojiao yishi" 民國時期廣州市正一派火居道士營業道館分布的空間分析—廟宇、人口與道教儀式, *Hanxue yanjiu* 漢學研究 32.4 (2014): 293–330. See also Goossaert, "Question of Control." The historical development of Daoism in modern China is examined in Vincent Goossaert, *The Taoists of Peking, 1800–1949: A Social History of Urban Clerics,* Harvard East Asian Monographs, no. 284 (Cambridge, MA: Harvard University Press, 2007); David A. Palmer and Liu Xun, eds., *Daoism in the Twentieth Century: Between Eternity and Modernity* (Berkeley: University of California Press, 2012). See also Liu Xun's pioneering study of Daoism in Shanghai, *Daoist Modern: Innovation, Lay Practice, and the Community of Inner Alchemy in Republican Shanghai* (Cambridge, MA: Harvard University Asia Center, 2009).

81. Goossaert and Palmer, *Religious Question*, 126; Liu Chengyou, "Luelun miaochan xingcu ji qi dui Daojiao de yingxiang," 51; Xu Xiaozheng, "Qingmo Minchu miaochan wenti yanjiu," 92–117.

82. Liu Xun, "Daoism from the Late Qing to Early Republican Periods," in Vincent Goossaert, Jan Kiely, and John Lagerwey, eds., *Modern Chinese Religion*, Vol. 2: *1850–2015* (Leiden: Brill, 2016), 806–40.

83. Willem A. Grootaers, *The Sanctuaries in a North-China City: A Complete Survey of the Cultic Buildings in the City of Hsuan-hua (Chahar)* (Brussels: Institut Belge des Hautes Études Chinoises, 1995); Sidney D. Gamble, *North China Villages: Social, Political, and Economic Activities before 1933* (Berkeley: University of California Press, 1963), 119; DuBois, *Sacred Village*, 30–33, 49–51, 56–59.

84. Goossaert and Palmer, *Religious Question*, 125, 128, 130.

85. See Lo Shih-chieh, "The Order of Local Things: Popular Politics and Religion in Modern Wenzhou (1840–1940)" (PhD diss., Brown University, 2010). See also his "Investiture and Local Politics: Yang fujun 楊府君 (Lord Yang) in Late Qing Wenzhou (1840–1867)," *Late Imperial China* 33.1 (June 2012): 89–121.

86. For more on the founding of Western-style schools in Wenzhou, see Hu Zhusheng 胡珠生, *Wenzhou jindaishi* 溫州近代史 (Shenyang: Liaoning renmin chubanshe, 2000), 203–10; Li Shizhong 李世眾, *WanQing shishen yu difang zhengzhi: Yi Wenzhou wei zhongxin de kaocha* 晚清士紳與地方政治：以溫州為中心的考察 (Shanghai: Shanghai renmin chubanshe, 2006).

87. *Ruian wenshi ziliao* 瑞安文史資料 5 (1987): 16.

88. See Zhang Gang 張棡 (1860–1942), *Zhang Gang riji* 張棡日記, ed. Yu Xiong 俞雄 (Shanghai: Shanghai shehui kexue chubanshe, 2003), 112.

89. Ibid., 386.

90. Qi Gang 祁剛, "Qingji Wenzhou diqu de miaochan banxue" 清季溫州地區的廟產辦學, in Kang Bao and Gao Wansang, eds., *Gaibian Zhongguo zongjiao de wushinian, 1898–1948* (Nankang: Institute of Modern History, Academia Sinica, 2015), 39–73.

91. Lo Shih-chieh 羅士傑, "Chenghuangshen yu jindai Wenzhou difang zhengzhi: Yi 1949 nian Huang Shisu dang Chenghuang wei taolun zhongxin" 城隍神與近代溫州地方政治—以1949 年黃式蘇當城隍為討論中心, in Kang Bao and Gao Wansang, eds., *Gaibian Zhongguo zongjiao de wushinian, 1898–1948* (Nankang: Institute of Modern History, Academia Sinica, 2015), 101–39.

92. Zhang Gang, *Zhang Gang riji*, 411–12.

93. Lo Shih-chieh, "Order of Local Things." See also Fang Zongbao 方宗苞, "Yuecheng daoshentuan" 樂成搗神團, *Yueqing wenshi ziliao* 樂清文史資料 1 (1984): 116. These events are also mentioned in *Haichaoyin* 10.1 (1929): 76.

94. Lo Shih-chieh, "Order of Local Things"; Zhang Gang, *Zhang Gang riji*, 550.

95. Xu Yao 徐躍, "Qingmo Sichuan miaochan xingxue ji you ci chansheng de sengsu jiufen" 清末四川廟產興學及由此產生的僧俗糾紛, *Jindaishi yanjiu* 近代史研究 5

(2008): 73–88. See also Liang Yong 梁勇, "Qingmo 'Miaochan xingxue' yu xiangcun quanshi de zhuanyi—Yi Baxian wei zhongxin" 清末'廟產興學'與鄉村權勢的轉移—以巴縣為中心, *Shehuixue yanjiu* 社會學研究 1 (2008): 102–19, 244; Xu Xiaozheng, "Qingmo Minchu miaochan wenti yanjiu," 92–117.

96. Xu Xiaoming 許曉明, "Zongjiao wenhua da shiyi: Qingmo Minchu Guangxi 'Miaochan xingxue' yundong" 宗教文化大失憶：清末民初廣西「廟產興學」運動, *Nanfang luntan* 南方論壇 12 (2007): 94–95.

97. Fu Haiyan 付海晏, "1940 niandai Edong simiao caichanquan chutan" 1940年代鄂東寺廟財產權初探, *Guizhou shifan daxue xuebao (Shehui kexueban)* 貴州師范大學學報(社會科學版) 5 (2005): 6–10.

98. Chen Jiaju 陳家駒, "Qingdai zhongqi yihuan Baojing Tanyi simiao de shanbian yu shiwei" 清代中期以還保靖壇遺寺廟的嬗變與式微, in Kang Bao 康豹 (Paul R. Katz), Long Haiqing 龍海清, and Luo Kanglong 羅康隆, eds., *Xiangxi zongjiao wenhua diaocha yu yanjiu* 湘西宗教文化調查與研究 (Beijing: Zhongyang minzu chubanshe), 361–78 (forthcoming); Chen Qigui 陳啟貴, "Fenghuang simiao de xingqi fada yu shuailuo xiaomie yuanyin diaocha baogao" 鳳凰寺廟的興起發達與衰落消滅原因調查報告, in *Xiangxi zongjiao wenhua diaocha yu yanjiu*, 379–414 (forthcoming); Katz, "Religious Life in Western Hunan."

99. Wen Guoliang 溫國良, ed. and trans., *Taiwan zongdufu gongwen leicuan zongjiao shiliao huibian (Mingzhi 28 nian 10 yue zhi Mingzhi 35 nian 4 yue)* 臺灣總督府公文類纂宗教史料彙編(明治二十八年十月至明治三十五年四月) (Nantou: Taiwan sheng wenxian weiyuanhui, 1999), 205–470. See also Tsai Chin-tang 蔡錦堂, *Nihon teikoku shugi ka Taiwan no shūkyō seisaku* 日本帝国主義下台湾の宗教政策 (Tokyo: Dōseisha, 1994).

100. Wan Jianzhong, "Minguo de fengsu biange yu biange fengsu."

101. Goossaert and Palmer, *Religious Question*, 62–63.

102. Susan Naquin, *Peking: Temples and City Life, 1400–1900* (Berkeley: University of California Press, 2000); Goossaert, *Taoists of Peking*. See also the journal *Sanjiao wenxian* 三教文獻: *Matériaux pour l'étude de la religion chinoise* for the years 1997, 1998, 1999, and 2005; as well as Dong Xiaoping 董曉萍 and Lü Min 呂敏 (Marianne Bujard), eds., *Beijing neicheng simiao beikezhi* 北京內城寺廟碑刻志, 4 vols. (Beijing: Guojia tushuguan chubanshe, 2011–17).

103. Poon, *Negotiating Religion*, 42–49.

104. Yau Chi-on, "DaDao nanxing."

105. Chen Jinlong 陳金龍, "Cong Miaochan xingxue fengbo kan Minguo shiqi de zhengjiao guanxi—Yi 1927 dao 1937 nian wei zhongxin de kaocha" 從廟產興學風波看民國時期的政教關係—以 1927 至 1937 年為中心的考察, *Guangdong shehui kexue* 廣東社會科學, 1 (2006): 114–121.

106. Zhao Mingjuan, "20 shiji shangbanye Zhejiang Daojiaoshi yanjiu," 5, 10–12.

107. Goossaert and Palmer, *Religious Question*, p. 131; Fu Haiyan, "1940 niandai Edong simiao caichanquan chutan". For more on the wartime era, see Lary, *Chinese People at*

War, as well as Stephen R. MacKinnon, Diana Lary, and Ezra F. Vogel, eds., *China at War: Regions of China, 1937–1945* (Stanford, CA: Stanford University Press, 2007); Hans J. van de Ven, *War and Nationalism in China, 1925–1945* (London: RoutledgeCurzon, 2003).

108. Xue Yu, *Buddhism, War, and Nationalism: Chinese Monks in the Struggle against Japanese Aggression, 1931–1945* (New York: Routledge, 2005), J. Brooks Jessup, "The Householder Elite: Buddhist Activism in Shanghai, 1920–1956" (PhD diss., University of California, Berkeley, 2010).

109. See, for example, Duara, *Culture, Power, and the State*; Naquin, *Peking*.

110. Xiao Tian 小田, "Jindai Jiangnan miaohui yu nongjia jingji shenghuo" 近代江南廟會與農家經濟生活, *Zhongguo nongshi* 中國農史 21.2 (2002): 79–86. See also Shen Jie, "Fanmixin yu shequ xinyang kongjian de xiandai licheng."

111. Poon, *Negotiating Religion*, 43–44, 48–60, 85; Goossaert and Palmer, *Religious Question*, 128–30.

112. Goossaert, "Local Politics," *Daoism: Religion, History and Society* 5 (2013): 57–80.

113. See especially Tobie S. Meyer-Fong, *What Remains: Coming to Terms with Civil War in 19th Century China* (Stanford, CA: Stanford University Press, 2013), as well as Nedostup, *Superstitious Regimes*, 118–19, 142.

114. Song Zuanyou 宋鑽友, *Guangdongren zai Shanghai* 廣東人在上海 (Shanghai: Shanghai renmin chubanshe, 2007); Gao Hongxia 高紅霞, *Shanghai Fujianren yanjiu* 上海福建人研究 (Shanghai: Shanghai renmin chubanshe, 2007). See also Bryna Goodman, *Native Place, City, and Nation: Regional Networks and Identities in Shanghai, 1853–1937* (Berkeley: University of California Press, 1995).

115. Studies of Shanghai's religious life include Ruan Renze 阮仁澤 and Gao Zhennong 高振農, eds., *Shanghai zongjiaoshi* 上海宗教史 (Shanghai: Shanghai renmin chubanshe, 1992); Ge Zhuang 葛壯, *Zongjiao yu jindai Shanghai shehui de bianqian* 宗教與近代上海社會的變遷 (Shanghai: Shanghai shudian chubanshe, 1999).

116. Paul R. Katz, "Jindai Zhongguo simiao pohuai yundong de kongjian tezheng—Yi Jiangnan dushi wei zhongxin" 近代中國寺廟破壞運動的空間特徵—以江南都市為重心, *Bulletin of the Institute of Modern History, Academia Sinica* 95 (2017): 1–37. We are deeply grateful to Wu Cheng-che 吳政哲 for his help in collecting and analyzing these data.

117. Zhang Hua 張化 et al., ed. and comp., *Shanghai zongjiao tonglan* 上海宗教通覽 (Shanghai: Shanghai guji chubanshe, 2004), 11–12, 223–24. The *Overview* was used by Vincent Goossaert in his article "Détruire les temples pour construire les écoles."

118. Only 23 of the supposedly 1,135 Buddhist temples housed resident monks (*seng* 僧), while just 27 had nuns (*ni* 尼). A total of 72 had lay Buddhist householders (*jushi* 居士) in residence.

119. Zhang Hua et al., *Shanghai zongjiao tonglan*, 6–183, 217–330; Goossaert, "Détruire les temples pour construire les écoles."

120. Figure 1.1 is adapted from the French original published in Goossaert, "Détruire les temples pour construire les écoles." There were also five instances of such sites being converted into charitable schools (*yishu* 義塾), as well as one case of a temple being turned into a community school (*shexue* 社學) in 1537 but later rebuilt as a temple. The latter case might best be considered in light of Sarah Schneewind's research discussed above.

121. Liu Wenxing 劉文星, "Jindai Hushe yu siyuan de hudong: Yi Shanghai Shousheng An shijian wei zhongxin" 近代湖社與寺院的互動：以上海壽聖庵事件為中心, in Kang Bao and Gao Wansang, eds., *Gaibian Zhongguo zongjiao de wushinian, 1898–1948* (Nankang: Institute of Modern History, Academia Sinica, 2015), 427–93. See also Huzhou Archives, ed. and comp., *Shenbao Huzhou lüHu tongxiang tuanti shiliao* 申報湖州旅滬同鄉團體史料 (Huzhou: Huzhou Archives, 2011), 119–20, 133–34, 137, 140–41, 150–51, 152–54.

122. *Zhonghua minguoshi dang'an ziliao huibian, Diwuji, Diyibian,* 509–13.

123. Ai Ping, "Minguo jinzhi yingshen saihui lunxi."

124. "Pochu mixin—Shanghaixian Gong'anju chajin Chenghuang quqie" 破除迷信―上海縣公安局查禁城隍娶妾. *Zhenguang zazhi* 真光雜誌 28.2 (1929): 84.

125. Haichaoyin 海潮音 10.1 (1929): 78, 80.

126. Wang Liping, "Tourism and Spatial Changes in Hangzhou, 1900–1927," in Joseph W. Esherick, ed., *Remaking the Chinese City: Modernity and National Identity, 1900–1950* (Honolulu: University of Hawai'i Press, 2000), 107–20; He Wangfang 何王芳, "Minguo shiqi Hangzhou chengshi shehui shenghuo yanjiu" 民國時期杭州城市社會生活研究 (PhD diss., Zhejiang University, 2006), 167–96. See also Goossaert, "Local Politics"; and Zhao Mingjuan, "20 shiji shangbanye Zhejiang Daojiaoshi yanjiu," 43–47.

127. Li Xuechang and Dong Jianpo, "20 shiji shangbanye Hangxian yingshen saihui shuailuo yinsu qianxi."

128. *Haichaoyin* 10.1 (1929): 81; "Pochu mixin" — Shaoxing juban miaochan xingxue" 破除迷信 — 紹興舉辦廟產興學, *Zhenguang zazhi* 28.2 (1929): 86.

129. "Ni'an gaizuo xuexiao zhi bozhe" 尼庵改作學校之波折, *Shenbao*, October 27, 1922.

130. "Pochu mixin - Huishen zaji Shaoxing juban miaochan xingxue" 破除迷信 — 毀神雜記, *Zhenguang zazhi* 28.2 (1929): 84–85; Yang Dehui 楊德惠, "Ningbo daohui ouxiang ji" 寧波搗毀偶像記, *Shenbao*, January 20, 1929.

131. *Haichaoyin* 10.1 (1929): 78–79.

132. Zhang Weijing 張韋靜, "Dui pochu mixin yundong de shangque" 對破除迷信運動的商榷, *Ningbo Minguo ribao she* 寧波民國日報社, ed., *Ningbo Minguo ribao liu zhounian jinian ji ershi nian guoqing jinian hekan* 寧波民國日報六周年紀念暨二十年國慶紀念合刊 (1931): 90–92.

133. Huang Shiling 黃式陵, "Pochu mixin wenti: Cong Yuyao daohui Minjiaoguan an shuoqi" 破除迷信問題：從餘姚搗毀民教館案說起, *Chenguang zhoukan* 晨光周刊 5.47 (1936): 6–10.

134. See the following local gazetteer: Zhang Chuanbao 張傳保, et al., ed. & comp., *Yinxian tongzhi* 鄞縣通志 (1935–1951), pp. 725–93, in *Zhongguo difangzhi jicheng, Zhejiang fuxianzhi ji* 中國地方志集成, 浙江府縣志輯, volumes 16-18 (Shanghai: Shanghai shudian chubanshe, 1993). The historical significance of this work is discussed in Barend ter Haar, "Local Society and the Organization of Cults in Early Modern China: A Preliminary Study," *Studies in Central and East Asian Religions* 8 (1995): 1–43.

Chapter 2

1. We thank Wu Cheng-che 吳政哲 for his help in obtaining Republican era documents and Wu Jen-shu 巫仁恕 for extremely valuable comments on a draft. This chapter expands on data and arguments presented in Goossaert, "Local Politics"; Gao Wansang 高萬桑 (Vincent Goossaert), "Wanqing ji Minguo shiqi Jiangnan diqu de yingshen saihui" 晚清及民國時期江南地區的迎神賽會, in Kang Bao and Gao Wansang, eds., *Gaibian Zhongguo zongjiao de wushinian, 1898–1948* (Nankang: Institute of Modern History, Academia Sinica, 2015), pp. 75–99; Goossaert, "Shifting Balance."

2. Among recent work on the history of festivals, see Paul R. Katz, ed., *Festivals and Local Society"* special issue, *Minsu quyi* 民俗曲藝 147 (2005).

3. On regulation of the New Year celebrations, see Chen Hsi-yuan 陳熙遠, "Zhongguo ye weimian – Ming Qing shiqi de yuanxiao, yejin yu kuanghuan" 中國夜未眠—明清時期的元宵、夜禁與狂歡, *Bulletin of the Institute of History and Philology, Academia Sinica* 75.2 (2004): 283–329.

4. A pioneering (though very outdated) work is Wu Cheng-han, "The Temple Fairs in Late Imperial China" (PhD diss., Princeton University, 1988). More recent works include Jiang Bin 姜彬, ed., *Wu Yue minjian xinyang minsu: Wu Yue diqu minjian xinyang yu minjian wenyi guanxi de kaocha he yanjiu* 吳越民間信仰民俗: 吳越地區民間信仰與民間文藝關係的考察和研究 (Shanghai: Shanghai wenyi chubanshe, 1992); Wang Jian 王健, *Lihai xiangguan: Ming Qing yilai Jiangnan Susong diqu minjian xinyang yanjiu* 利害相關: 明清以來江南蘇松地區民間信仰研究 (Shanghai: Shanghai renmin chubanshe, 2010). On festivals in Republican period Hangzhou, see He Shanmeng 何善蒙, *Minguo Hangzhou minjian xinyang* 民國杭州民間信仰 (Hangzhou: Hangzhou chubanshe, 2012), chapter 4.

5. Fan Zushu 范祖述, *Hangsu yifeng* 杭俗遺風 (Shanghai: Shanghai wenyi chubanshe, 1989). See the prefaces for 1863 and 1864, with additional notes by Hong Yueru 洪岳如 added in the 1920s.

6. On *Shenbao*'s reporting on religion, see Vincent Goossaert, "Anatomie d'un discours anticlérical: Le *Shenbao*, 1872–1878," *Extrême-Orient Extrême-Occident* 24 (2002): 113–31.

7. This typology builds and expands on the case study of Hangzhou found in Goossaert, "Local Politics."

8. See, notably, Wang Jian, *Lihai xiangguan*, chap. 2.

9. Vincent Goossaert, "Bureaucratie, taxation, et justice: Taoïsme et construction de l'État au Jiangnan (Chine), XVIIᵉ-XIXᵉ siècles," *Annales HSS* 4 (2010): 999–1027; Vincent Goossaert, "The Heavenly Master, Canonization, and the Daoist Construction of Local Religion in Late Imperial Jiangnan," *Cahiers d'Extrême-Asie* 20 (2011): 229–45; Gao

Wansang (Vincent Goossaert), "Qingdai Jiangnan diqu de Chenghuangmiao, Zhang Tianshi ji Daojiao guanliao tixi" 清代江南地區的城隍廟、張天師及道教官僚體系, *Qingshi yanjiu* 清史研究 1 (2010): 1–11.

10. "Saihui xiansheng" 賽會先聲, *Shenbao*, July 4, 1896.

11. "Jinhua shenghui" 金華盛會, *Shenbao*, July 23, 1890. On state and Daoist canonizations in late imperial Jiangnan (and how they were entwined), see Goossaert, "Heavenly Master."

12. Dates in the traditional calendar are provided as month/day.

13. Wu Jen-shu 巫仁恕, "Jieqing, xinyang yu kangzheng – Ming Qing chenghuang xinyang yu chengshi qunzhong de jiti kangyi xingwei" 節慶信仰與抗爭-明清城隍信仰與城市群眾的集體抗議行為, *Bulletin of the Institute of Modern History, Academia Sinica* (2000): 145–210, esp. 169; "Jiehui jianse" 節會減色, *Shenbao*, April 14, 1880; "Jiehui jisheng" 節會紀盛, *Shenbao*, April 9, 1882. See also Chen Hsi-yuan 陳熙遠, "Liji yu guijie: Shilun youyi zai tan yu miao, guan yu min zhijian de Shanghai sanxunhui" 厲祭與鬼節—試論游移在壇與廟、官與民之間的上海三巡會, Paper presented at the conference The Modern History of Urban Daoism, Tainan, November 13–14, 2010.

14. Hamashima Atsutoshi 濱島敦俊, *Sōkan shinkō: kinsei Kōnan nōson shakai to minkan shinkō* 總管信仰: 近世江南農村社會と民間信仰 (Tokyo: Kenbun Shuppan, 2001), 205–19; Wu Jen-shu 巫仁恕, "Ming Qing Jiangnan Dongyue shen xinyang yu chengshi qunzhong de jiti kangyi – Yi Suzhou minbian wei taolun zhongxin" 明清江南東嶽神信仰與城市群眾的集體抗議-以蘇州民變為討論中心, in Li Hsiao-t'i 李孝悌, ed., *Zhongguo de chengshi shenghuo* 中國的城市生活 (Taipei: Lianjing, 2005), 149–206.

15. "Jiaohui leijian" 醮會纍見, *Shenbao*, August 16, 1879.

16. Tao Jin 陶金 and Vincent Goossaert, "Daojiao yu Suzhou difang shehui" 道教與蘇州地方社會, in Fan Lizhu and Robert Weller, eds., *Jiangnan diqu de zongjiao yu gonggong shenghuo* 江南地區的宗教與公共生活 (Shanghai: Shanghai renmin chubanshe, 2015), 86–112. On Qionglongshan, see also Vincent Goossaert, "Daoism and Local Cults in Modern Suzhou: A Case Study of Qionglongshan 穹窿山," in Philip Clart, ed., *Chinese and European Perspectives on the Study of Chinese Popular Religions* (Taipei: BoyYoung, 2012), 199–228.

17. Vincent Goossaert, "Managing Chinese Religious Pluralism in the Nineteenth-Century City Gods Temples," in Thomas Jansen, Thoralf Klein, and Christian Meyer, eds., *Globalization and the Making of Religious Modernity in China* (Boston: Brill, 2014), 29–51.

18. Fang Ling 方玲, "Hangzhou Laodongyuemiao de bianqian" 杭州老東嶽廟的變遷, *Xianggang zhongwen daxue Daojiao wenhua yanjiu zhongxin tongxun* 香港中文大學道教文化研究中心通訊 12 (2008): 3–4; Fang Ling, "The Old Eastern Peak Temple in Hangzhou," in Liu Xun and Vincent Goossaert, eds., *Daoism in Modern China: Clerics and Temples in Urban Transformations, 1860–Present* (London: Routledge, 2021).

19. Paul R. Katz, *Demon Hordes and Burning Boats: The Cult of Marshal Wen in Late Imperial Chekiang* (Albany: State University of New York Press, 1995). The Hangzhou festival is discussed on pages 159–66. On Marshal Wen's festival in Ningbo, see "Jinzhi shenhui" 禁止神會, *Shenbao*, April 30, 1895.

20. "Hang yan" 杭諺, *Shenbao*, April 27, 1894.

21. "Chijin chuhui" 弛禁出會, *Shenbao*, July 7, 1882; "Saihui xiansheng," *Shenbao*, July 4, 1896. The detailed description of the Marshal Wan Festival in Fan Zushu, *Hangsu yifeng*, (14–17) is translated in Katz, *Demon Hordes*, 163–64, 209–13.

22. Fan Zushu, *Hangsu yifeng*, 10–11.

23. For more on Dutian, see Fan Chun-wu 范純武, "Ming Qing Jiangnan Dutian xinyang de fazhan jiqi yishuo" 明清江南都天信仰的發展及其異說, in Gao Zhihua 高致華, ed., *Tanxun minjian zhushen yu xinyang wenhua* 探尋民間諸神與信仰文化 (Hefei: Huangshan shushe, 2006), 87–115.

24. On penitents in temple festivals, see Paul R. Katz, *Divine Justice: Religion and the Development of Chinese Legal Culture* (London: Routledge, 2009), 107–115.

25. "Qingbo zazhi" 清波雜志, *Shenbao*, November 17, 1885. On associations of registered servants of the gods, see Goossaert, "Bureaucratie," 1022–23.

26. "Yingsai mishen" 迎賽米神, *Shenbao*, August 9, 1887.

27. Fan Zushu, *Hangsu yifeng*, 23–24.

28. "Xiling rangyi" 西泠禳疫, *Shenbao*, September 14, 1895.

29. The second Guanyin birthday is on the 19th day of the 6th lunar month. The third, on the 19th day of the 9th lunar month, drew fewer out-of-town pilgrims.

30. Yü Chün-fang, *Kuan-yin: The Chinese Transformation of Avalokiteśvara* (New York: Columbia University Press, 2001), 360–69; Wang Jian 王健, "Ming Qing yilai Hangzhou jinxiang shi chutan" 明清以來杭州進香史初探, *Shilin* 史林 4 (2012): 89–97.

31. Rostislav Berezkin and Vincent Goossaert, "The Three Mao Lords in Modern Jiangnan: Cult and Pilgrimage between Daoism and *Baojuan* Recitation," *Bulletin de l'EFEO* 99 (2012–13): 295–326.

32. On the impact of the Taiping War, see Goossaert, "Shifting Balance"; Meyer-Fong, *What Remains*.

33. "Saihui jisheng" 賽會紀盛, *Shenbao*, April 12, 876.

34. "Hangcheng saihui" 杭城賽會, *Shenbao*, September 6, 1887.

35. On the Dushenhui 都神會 in Zhenjiang, see "Jingkou saihui" 京口賽會, *Shenbao*, June 6, 1879.

36. Wu Jen-shu, "Jieqing, xinyang yu kangzheng."

37. Wei Wenjing 魏文靜, "Ming Qing yingshen saihui lüjin buzhi yu shangyehua—Yi Jiangnan yingshen saihui jingji gongneng wei zhongxin de tantao" 明清迎神賽會屢禁不止與商業化—以江南迎神賽會經濟功能為中心的探討, *Lishi jiaoxue* 歷史教學 14 (2009): 27–34. Wang Liqi 王利器, *Yuan Ming Qing sandai jinhui xiaoshuo xiqu shiliao* 元明清三代禁毀小說戲曲史料 (Shanghai: Shanghai guji chubanshe, 1981), collected a large amount of material on bans against festivals.

38. Goossaert, "Destruction of Immoral Temples."

39. "Fohui yijin" 佛會宜禁, *Shenbao*, February 8, 1878.

40. "Hangzhou dengshi" 杭州燈市, *Shenbao*, February 23, 1897.

41. See, for example, "Liupu naliang ji" 柳浦納涼記, *Shenbao*, July 8, 1896.

42. Goossaert, "Managing Chinese Religious Pluralism."

43. For instance, see "Xunqing kaijin" 徇情開禁, *Shenbao*, May 21, 1905 (in Nanjing, the yamen staff pleaded for and obtained the lifting of a ban); "Reng ni saihui" 仍擬賽會, *Shenbao*, April 21, 1906 (in Songjiang, local gentry entreated the prefect to lift a ban); "Xiangmin qingxing Dutian saihui" 鄉民請行都天賽會, *Shenbao*, May 23, 1907 (in Zhenjiang, local gentry negotiated a scaled-down Dutian procession).

44. Goossaert, "Irrepressible Female Piety."

45) See "Shijin saihui" 示禁賽會, *Shenbao*, May 7, 1900, about the City God procession in Anqing, where the money-collecting practices of the associations was the main point of contention.

46. "Yongjin Dushenhui gaoshi" 永禁都神會告示, *Shenbao*, May 14, 1883. This follows a pattern in which festivals were banned after the Taiping War but reactivated when an epidemic caused the public to cry out for the procession to take place and officials gave in.

47. "Saihui zhisheng" 賽會志盛, *Shenbao*, June 20, 1888.

48. "Saihui jiancong" 賽會減從, *Shenbao*, November 8, 1877.

49. "Jiehui jianse," *Shenbao*, 14 April 1880; "Caijin jiehui" 裁禁節會, *Shenbao*, August 11, 1881; "Jinzhi saihui" 禁止賽會, *Shenbao*, April 10, 1889. On other bans on penitents in the City God processions in Suzhou, see Wang Liqi, *Yuan Ming Qing sandai jinhui xiaoshuo xiqu shiliao*, 169 (quoting the *Huizuan gongguoge* 匯纂功過格). On Tan Junpei, see Goossaert, "Irrepressible Female Piety," 232.

50. Wang Liqi, *Yuan Ming Qing sandai jinhui xiaoshuo xiqu shiliao*, 97–98, quoting the *Sanyutang waiji* 三魚堂外集.

51. *Wujun suihua jili* 吳郡歲華紀麗, by Yuan Jinglan 袁景瀾, fl. 1820–1873 (Nanjing: Jiangsu guji chubanshe, 1998), 3.115.

52. See, for instance, "Xunli shijin" 循例示禁, *Shenbao*, November 13, 1887, "Lingjie yingshen" 令節迎神, *Shenbao*, 12 November 1890; "Jiehui lizhi" 節會例志, *Shenbao*, 29 August 1890. Similar bans in Beijing are described in Wang Liqi, *Yuan Ming Qing sandai jinhui xiaoshuo xiqu shiliao*, 86 (quoting the *Yanjing suishi ji* 燕京歲時記).

53. Most descriptions suggest that the processions actually ended in the morning hours, and reports of other overt violations abound. In "Saihui zhilue" 賽會志略, *Shenbao*, November 9, 1893, the journalist wonders if officials are going to do anything about the open violations.

54. "Qingming saihui" 清明賽會, *Shenbao*, April 6, 1894, notes that among more than a hundred penitents there were three or four women in spite of the ban.

55. Goossaert, "Irrepressible Female Piety."

56. See, for instance, "Xiangshi shengse" 香市生色, *Shenbao*, April 20, 1882.

57. Fan Zushu, *Hangsu yifeng*, 8.

58. This story is told in detail in Goossaert, "Local Politics," 69–72.

59. "Taixi chijin" 臺戲弛禁, *Shenbao*, June 6, 1878.

60. "Nanping xiaozhong" 南屏曉鐘, *Shenbao*, July 23, 1896.

61. "Nanping wanzhong" 南屏晚鐘, *Shenbao*, September 1, 1896.

62. "Lingyin songtao" 靈隱松濤, *Shenbao*, June 16, 1891.

63. "Yongjin Dushenhui gaoshi" 永禁都神會告示, *Shenbao*, September 14, 1883, reported that a Ningbo prefect allowed a procession (otherwise banned) during an epidemic; and "Huaiyang shenghui" 淮揚盛會, *Shenbao*, September 14, 1883, reported that local gentry in Yangzhou twisted officials' arms and obtain the right to hold a pestilence-expelling procession.

64. Between 1872 and 1906, *Shenbao* reports on the Hangzhou City God processions indicate that sometimes "ancillary associations" could join and at other times were barred from joining, resulting in alternating "successful" and "dull" processions.

65. Soldiers in the Hangzhou garrison organized their Ziwei shangdi 紫微上帝 procession on a large scale but without ancillary associations; it was said to be very well controlled. "Nanping xiaozhong," *Shenbao*, February 21, 1897.

66. "Jinhui rucheng" 禁會入城, *Shenbao*, November 5, 1882, reported on a festival in Ningbo during which soldiers blocked the city gates, creating much tension in the city.

67. See for instance "Gechu saihui louxi banfa" 革除賽會陋習辦法, *Shenbao*, July 7, 1909 about the policy of confiscating *saihui* resources in Changshu.

68. Chen Zhongping, *Modern China's Network Revolution: Chambers of Commerce and Sociopolitical Change in the Early Twentieth Century* (Stanford, CA: Stanford University Press, 2011).

69. See "Bing bo saihui jukuan xingxue" 禀撥賽會鉅款興學, *Shenbao*, May 2, 1909, on guilds in Zhenjiang 鎮江, where the Daotai approved a proposal to convert the guilds' festival funds into educational funds (各業會厘即改為學厘).

70. The best documented case is that of Beijing. See Niida Noboru 仁井田陞, *Pekin kōshō girudo shiryō shū* 北京工商ギルド資料集, 6 vols. (Tokyo: Tōyō bunka, 1975–83); Sidney D. Gamble, *Peking: A Social Survey* (New York: George H. Doran, 1921).

71. "Xi-Jin mixin shenquan zhi jixi" 錫金迷信神權之積習, *Shenbao*, May 24, 1909.

72. This section draws on Goossaert, "Shifting Balance."

73. "Changzhou dada Chenghuang" 常州大打城隍, *Shenbao*, February 25, 1912. Several cases are mentioned in Zheng Guo 鄭國, "Jindai geming yundong yu pochu mixin – Yi Xuzhou Chenghuangmiao weizhu de kaocha" 近代革命運動與破除迷信—以徐州城隍廟為主的考察, *Hefei shifan xueyuan xuebao* 合肥師範學院學報 26.2 (2008): 54–57.

74. Nedostup, *Superstitious Regimes*, 68–74, 84, 96, 99, 106–7, 111–14, 125–26; Sha Qingqing, "Xinyang yu quanzheng."

75. Kang Youwei 康有為 himself, in his "apocryphal" 1898 memorial on instituting a Confucian state religion (請尊孔聖為國教立教部教會以孔子紀年而廢淫祠摺),

specifically targeted the City God temples for destruction. Jian Bozan 翦伯贊 et al., comps., *Wuxu bianfa* 戊戌變法 (Shanghai: Shenzhou guoguangshe, 1953), 231.

76. See, for instance, the descriptions in Lin Shuimei 林水梅 and Xie Jizhong 謝濟 中, "Lianchengxian chengguan de Chenghuang miaohui" 連城縣城關的城隍廟會, in Yang Yanjie 楊彥杰, ed., *Minxi de chengxiang miaohui yu cunluo wenhua* 閩西的城鄉 廟會與村落文化. 傳統客家社會叢書, *Chuantong Kejia shehui congshu*, vol 4 (Hong Kong: International Hakka Studies Association, 1997), 18–33. For Liancheng, Fujian, where the temple was managed by seven lineages, see Zeng Cun 曾材, "Huiyi Ningdu Chenghuangmiao" 回憶寧都城隍廟, in Luo Yong 羅勇 and Lin Shaoping 林曉平, eds., *Gannan miaohui yu minsu* 贛南廟會與民俗. Vol. 7: *Chuantong Kejia shehui congshu* 傳統 客家社會叢書(Hong Kong: International Hakka Studies Association, 1998), 230–40. In Ningdu, Jiangxi, the temple was managed by eighteen guilds.

77. Yu Zhejun, *Shenming yu shimin*.

78. Chen Hsi-yuan, "Liji yu guijie."

79. Yu Zhejun, *Shenming yu shimin*, 222–25; Ai Ping, "Minguo jinzhi yingshen saihui lunxi"; Fu Haiyan, "Geming, falü, yumiaochan," 117.

80. "Suzhou: Lumu Zhen zhi yingshen saihui" 蘇州—陸墓鎮之迎神賽會, *Shenbao*, August 23, 1919, reports on Suzhou police officers participating as penitents in a procession.

81. Zhou Zhenhe 周振鶴, *Suzhou fengsu* 蘇州風俗 (1928, reprint Shanghai: Wenyi chubanshe, 1989), 80.

82. Poon Shuk-wah, "Thriving under an Anti-superstition Regime."

83. Xiao Tian 小田, "Shequ chuantong de jindai mingyun—Yi Suzhou 'Qionglong laohui' wei duixiang de li'an yanjiu" 社區傳統的近代命運—以蘇州穹窿老會為對象的例案 研究, *Jiangsu shehui kexue* 江蘇社會科學 6 (2002): 141–47. Early on, Sun Yat-sen and his associates, together with YMCA activists, tried to persuade the village leaders to stop organizing processions.

84. Shen Jie, "Fan mixin yu shequ xinyang kongjian de xiandai licheng." See also Nedostup, *Superstitious Regimes*, 136–37, on the massive rain-making *jiao* at the Xuanmiaoguan.

85. Li Xuechang and Dong Jianbo, "Ershi shiji shangbanye Hangxian yingshen saihui shuailuo yinsu jianxi."

86. He Shanmeng 何善蒙, "Yingshen saihui haishi putong shaoxiang?" 迎神賽會還是普 通燒香?, in Wang Gang 王崗 (Richard Wang) and Li Tiangang 李天綱, eds., *Zhongguo jinshi difang shehuizhong de zongjiao yu guojia* 中國近世地方社會中的宗教與國家 (Shanghai: Fudan daxue chubanshe, 2014), 69–103. See also *Minguo Hangzhou minjian xinyang*, 91–97, on a *chaoshen* organized at a downtown Dongyue temple after 1945 that was banned but actually continued when temple leaders obtained authorization to hold the festival not as a *saihui* but as "ordinary worship." This is one instance among many of negotiations to mitigate a ban through skillful rhetoric.

87. See the descriptions for 1947 in "Hangzhou xiangfan nongbao lei: Shi'er ri Hangzhou xun" 杭州香汎農胞淚—十二日杭州訊, *Shenbao*, March 17, 1947.

88. Fan Zushu, *Hangsu yifeng*, 13–14.

89. Ibid., 18–19.

90. Vincent Goossaert, "Territorial Cults and the Urbanization of the Chinese World: A Case Study of Suzhou," in Peter van der Veer, ed., *Handbook of Religion and the Asian City* (Berkeley: University of California Press, 2015), 52–68.

91. Xiao Tian 小田, "Lun Jiangnan xiangcun nüwu de jindai jingyu" 論江南鄉村女巫的近代境遇, *Jindaishi yanjiu* 近代史研究 5 (2014): 39–55.

92. Vincent Goossaert, "Question of Control."

93. Rostislav Berezkin and Vincent Goossaert, "Shangfangshan and the Wutong Cult in Modern and Contemporary Jiangnan," *Journal of Chinese Studies* 中國文化研究所學報, 70, 2020, p. 153-202. Goossaert, "Daoism and Local Cults in Modern Suzhou."

94. See, for example, "Nüwu pianqian zhi panhuan" 女巫騙錢之判還, *Shenbao*, June 11, 1924 (where a Daoist collaborates with the medium); "Zhang xunguan hetui Santaitai" 張巡官喝退三太太, *Shenbao*, December 24, 1933.

95. "Cuhai yupo – Tu coushe heren" 醋海餘波—途甌撮合人, *Shenbao*, July 4, 1935; "Li Suzhen suqing yufu lihun" 李素貞訴請與夫離婚, *Shenbao*, December 24, 1934.

96. "Xiaohai huanbing xianghui zhiliao" 小孩患病香灰治療, *Shenbao*, September 7, 1936.

97. "Kunshan: Chengqu nüwu jiying qudi" 崑山- 城區女巫虺應取締, *Shenbao*, August 24, 1929.

98. "Zhuyi shenyi" 注意神醫, *Shenbao*, February 16, 1927.

99. "Shenfo muou luolie yitang" 神佛木偶羅列一堂, *Shenbao*, December 26, 1935.

100. "Huahua xuxu shuo Lengqie" 花花絮絮說楞伽, *Shenbao*, September 18, 1927; "Bayue shibari zhi Shihu" 八月十八日之石湖, *Shenbao*, September 14, 1935. The last article reports that some mediums dressed up as gods.

101. "Bayue shibari zhi Shihu," *Shenbao*, September 14, 1935.

102. "Yu Xiaolian bing Sufu qing hui yinci gao" 余孝廉稟蘇撫請毀淫祠稿, *Shenbao*, June 4, 1905.

103. "Daohui yinci shouru" 搗毀淫詞受辱, *Shenbao*, May 29, 1905.

104. "Suzhou" 蘇州, *Shenbao*, October 12, 1928. On the anti-Muhuajing campaign, see "Suzhou" 蘇州, *Shenbao*, March 5, 1929; "Xiangshan dangbu fenhui guiyao Muhuajing jixiang" 香山黨部焚燬鬼妖木化精記詳, *Shenbao*, March 8, 1929.

105. "Xingchunqiao benyue ji" 行春橋奔月記, *Shenbao*, September 20, 1927.

106. "Maoyuan xinliang" 茂苑新凉, *Shenbao*, August 6, 1890.

107. "Wuyi jie: Huodong wuwei zhongzhi daxian" 巫醫刼—活動五位終止大仙, *Shenbao*, December 12, 1947.

108. Long Feijun 龍飛俊, "Shanghai Longwangmiao de taitaimen" 上海龍王廟的太太們, in Wang Gang and Li Tiangang, eds., *Zhongguo jinshi difang shehuizhong de zongjiao yu guojia* (Shanghai: Fudan daxue chubanshe, 2014), 119–38.

109. Xiao Tian, in "Lun Jiangnan xiangcun nüwu de jindai jingyu," 47–49, discusses two cases (dated 1919 and 1937) of dead women enshrined as wives of Pudong City Gods and the elite reactions to such practices.

110. "Shehui du" 社會蠹, *Shenbao*, June 8, 1909.

111. "Wangnü jia Wutong" 亡女嫁五通, *Shenbao*, October 24, 1946.

112. Goossaert, "Local Politics."

113. Wang Liping, "Tourism and Spatial Changes."

114. Fan Zushu, *Hangsu yifeng*, 16–17.

115. Poon Shuk-Wah, in "Thriving under an Anti-superstition Regime," discusses a similar phenomenon for Guangzhou.

116. Ibid.

117. Poon Shuk-wah, *Negotiating Religion*; Wang Di, *Street Culture in Chengdu: Public Space, Urban Commoners, and Local Politics, 1870–1930* (Stanford, CA: Stanford University Press, 2003).

118. The Republican period saw the rise of public theaters in all Chinese cities, but this does not seem to have dampened the popular taste for performances at festivals.

119. Joseph Bosco, "Urban Processions: Colonial Decline and Revival as Heritage in Postcolonial Hong Kong," in Peter van der Veer, ed., *Handbook of Religion and the Asian City* (Berkeley: University of California Press, 2015), 110–30. See also the articles on processions in Mumbai and other Asian cities in the same volume.

120. Joseph Ramonéda, "Une tentative d'enfermement de l'Église: Les arrêtés municipaux d'interdiction des processions extérieures sous la République concordataire (1870–1905)," *Clio@Thémis* 4 (2011): 1–24.

121. Trent E. Maxey, *The "Greatest Problem": Religion and State Formation in Meiji Japan* (Cambridge, MA: Harvard University Asia Center, 2014). We are very grateful to Trent Maxey for discussing these issues with Vincent in March 2016.

122. Wilbur M. Fridell, *Japanese Shrine Mergers, 1906–12: State Shinto Moves to the Grassroots* (Tokyo: Sophia University, 1973), 48.

123. Ibid., 84–86.

124. Sarah Thal, *Rearranging the Landscape of the Gods: The Politics of a Pilgrimage Site in Japan, 1573–1912* (Chicago: University of Chicago Press, 2005), offers a rich and fascinating history of one pilgrimage site (Mount Zozu 象頭山 in Shikoku) during the modern period and the way the shrines, their priests, and their various devotees and sponsors adapted throughout the many turns of politics.

Chapter 3

1. See, for example, Barbara Mittler, *A Newspaper for China? Power, Identity, and Change in Shanghai's News Media, 1872-1912* (Cambridge, MA: Harvard University Asia Center, 2004); Tsai Weipin, *Reading Shenbao: Nationalism, Consumerism, and Individuality in China, 1919-37* (Basingstoke: Palgrave Macmillan, 2010); Rudolf G. Wagner, ed., *Word, Image, and City in Early Chinese Newspapers, 1870-1910* (Albany: State University of New York Press, 2007). For more on the impact of new printing technologies, see Christopher Reed, *Gutenberg in Shanghai: Chinese Print Capitalism, 1876-1937* (Vancouver: University of British Columbia Press, 2004); Cynthia Brokaw and Christopher Reed, eds., *From Woodblocks to the Internet: Chinese Publishing and Print Culture in Transition, circa 1800 to 2008* (Leiden: Brill, 2010).

2. See especially the following recent studies: Philip Clart and Gregory Adam Scott, eds., *Religious Publishing and Print Culture in Modern China, 1800-2012* (Boston: De Gruyter, 2014); Philip Clart, "New Technologies and the Production of Religious Texts in China, 19th-21st Century," in Vincent Goossaert, Jan Kiely, and John Lagerwey, eds., *Modern Chinese Religion,* Vol. 2: *1850-2015* (Leiden: Brill, 2016), 560-78.

3. For more on these issues, see James Robson, "Brushes with Some 'Dirty Truths': Handwritten Manuscripts and Religion in China," *History of Religions* 51.4 (2012): 317-43; Glen Dudbridge, *The Legend of Miaoshan*, rev. ed. (Oxford: Oxford University Press, 2004); Paul R. Katz, *Images of the Immortal: The Cult of Lü Dongbin at the Palace of Eternal Joy* (Honolulu: University of Hawai'i Press, 1999).

4. See T. H. Barrett, *The Woman Who Invented Printing* (New Haven, CT: Yale University Press, 2008); Frances Wood and Mark Barnard, *The Diamond Sutra: The Story of the World's Earliest Dated Printed Book* (London: British Library, 2010).

5. Excellent overviews of these trends may be found in Cynthia Brokaw and Kai-wing Chow, eds., *Printing and Book Culture in Late Imperial China* (Berkeley: University of California Press, 2005); Lucille Chia and Hilde de Weerdt, eds., *Knowledge and Text Production in an Age of Print* (Leiden: Brill, 2011).

6. Li Shiyu 李世瑜, "Baojuan xinyan" 寶卷新研, *Wenxue yichan zengkan* 文學遺產增刊 4 (1957): 165-81, reprinted in Li, *Baojuan lunji* 寶卷論集, *Zongjiao yu shehui congshu* 宗教與社會叢書, vol. 2, pp. 2-19 (Taipei: Lantai chubanshe, 2007).

7. Susan Naquin, "The Transmission of White Lotus Sectarianism in Late Imperial China," in David G. Johnson, Andrew J. Nathan, and Evelyn S. Rawski, eds., *Popular Culture in Late Imperial China* (Berkeley: University of California Press, 1985), 255-91; Daniel L. Overmyer, "Values in Chinese Sectarian Literature: Ming and Ch'ing *pao-chüan*," in David G. Johnson, Andrew J. Nathan, and Evelyn S. Rawski, eds., *Popular Culture in Late Imperial China* (Berkeley: University of California Press, 1985), 219-54; David L. Overmyer, *Precious Volumes: An Introduction to Chinese Sectarian Scriptures from the Sixteenth and Seventeenth Centuries* (Cambridge, MA: Harvard University Press, 1999). See also Ma Xisha 馬西沙 and Han Bingfang 韓秉方, *Zhongguo minjian zongjiaoshi* 中國民間宗教史 (Shanghai: Shanghai renmin chubanshe, 1992), 173-87; Yau Chi-on (You Zi'an) 游子安, *Shan yu ren tong: Ming Qing yilai de cishan yu jiaohua* 善與人同：明清以來的慈善與教化 (Beijing: Zhonghua shuju, 2005).

8. Clart, "New Technologies."

9. Gregory Adam Scott and Philip Clart, "Introduction: Print Culture and Religion in Chinese History," in Philip Clart and Gregory Adam Scott, eds., *Religious Publishing and Print Culture in Modern China, 1800–2012* (Boston: De Gruyter, 2014), 1–16.

10. Adrian A. Bennett, *Missionary Journalist in China: Young J. Allen and His Magazines, 1860–1883* (Athens: University of Georgia Press, 1983).

11. Zhang Xiantao, *The Origins of the Modern Chinese Press: The Influence of the Protestant Missionary Press in Late Qing China* (London: Routledge, 2007), 34–50, 105–11.

12. George Kam Wah Mak, "The Colportage of the Protestant Bible in Late Qing China: The Example of the British and Foreign Bible Society," in Philip Clart and Gregory Adam Scott, eds., *Religious Publishing and Print Culture in Modern China, 1800–2012* (Boston: De Gruyter, 2014), 17–50; Joseph Tse-Hei Lee and Christie Chui-Shan Chow, "Publishing Prophecy: A Century of Adventist Print Culture in China," in Philip Clart and Gregory Adam Scott, eds., *Religious Publishing and Print Culture in Modern China, 1800–2012* (Boston: De Gruyter, 2014), 51–90. See also Goossaert and Palmer, *Religious Question*, 68–83.

13. On Islam, see Zhang Zhihua 張志華, *Zhongguo Isilan wenhua yaolue* 中國伊斯蘭文化要略 (Yinchuan: Ningxia renmin chubanshe, 2010). See also Stephane A. Dudoignon, Komatsu Hisao, and Kosugi Yasushi, eds., *Intellectuals in the Modern Islamic World: Transmission, Transformation, and Communication* (London: Routledge, 2009). On Judaism, see M. Avrum Ehrlich, ed., *The Jewish-Chinese Nexus: A Meeting of Civilizations* (London: Routledge, 2008).

14. Shawn Frederick McHale, *Print and Power: Confucianism, Communism, and Buddhism in the Making of Modern Vietnam* (Honolulu: University of Hawai'i Press, 2004); Anne Ruth Hansen, *How to Behave: Buddhism and Modernity in Colonial Cambodia, 1860–1930* (Honolulu: University of Hawai'i Press, 2007); J. B. P. More, *Muslim Identity, Print Culture, and the Dravidian Factor in Tamil Nadu* (New Delhi: Orient Longman, 2004); Ulrike Stark, *An Empire of Books: The Naval Kishore Press and the Diffusion of the Printed Word in Colonial India* (Ranikhet: Permanent Black, 2008).

15. Nancy Stalker, "Showing Faith: Exhibiting Ōmoto to Consumers in Early-Twentieth-Century Japan," in Thomas David DuBois, ed., *Casting Faiths: Imperialism and the Transformation of Religion in East and Southeast Asia* (New York: Palgrave Macmillan, 2009), 239–56.

16. Wu Yakui 吳亞魁, "Qingmo Minguo shiqi Shanghai de zongjiao chuban gaiguan: Yi Fo–Daojiao wei zhongxi" 清末民國時期上海的宗教出版概觀：以佛道教為中心, in Kang Bao and Gao Wansang, eds., *Gaibian Zhongguo zongjiao de wushinian, 1898–1948* (Nankang: Institute of Modern History, Academia Sinica, 2015), 261–336. See also Wang Chien-Chuan, "Morality Book Publishing and Popular Religion in Modern China: A Discussion Centered on Morality Book Publishers in Shanghai," Gregory Adam Scott trans., in Philip Clart and Gregory Adam Scott, eds., *Religious Publishing and Print Culture in Modern China, 1800–2012* (Boston: De Gruyter, 2014), 233–64.

17. "Digital Bibliography of Modern Chinese Buddhism," accessed August 5, 2016, http://bib.buddhiststudies.net/

18. Jessup, "Householder Elite"; Gregory Adam Scott, "Conversion by the Book: Buddhist Print Culture in Early Republican China" (PhD diss., Columbia University, 2013).

19. Jan Kiely, "Spreading the Dharma with the Mechanized Press: New Buddhist Print Cultures in the Modern Chinese Print Revolution, 1865–1949," in Cynthia Brokaw and Christopher Reed, eds., *From Woodblocks to the Internet: Chinese Publishing and Print Culture in Transition, circa 1800 to 2008.* (Leiden: Brill, 2010), 185–210.

20. Clart, "New Technologies," 569.

21. Gregory Adam Scott, "Navigating the Sea of Scriptures: The Buddhist Studies Collectanea, 1918–1923," in Philip Clart and Gregory Adam Scott, eds., *Religious Publishing and Print Culture in Modern China, 1800–2012* (Boston: De Gruyter, 2014), 91–138. See also Jan Kiely, "Shanghai Public Moralist Nie Qijie and Morality Book Publication Projects in Republican China," *Twentieth-Century China* 36.1 (January 2011): 4–22; Jessup, "Householder Elite"; Scott and Clart, "Introduction."

22. For more on this phenomenon, see Fan Chun-wu 范純武, "Jinxiandai Zhongguo Fojiao yu fuji" 近現代中國佛教與扶乩, *Yuanguang Foxue xuebao* 圓光佛學學報 3 (1999): 261–92. See also Wang Chien-ch'uan 王見川, "Jindai Zhongguo de fuji, cishan yu 'mixin' – Yi *Yinguang wenchao* wei kaocha xiansuo" 近代中國的扶乩、慈善與「迷信」—以印光文鈔為考查線索, in Paul R. Katz and Liu Shufen 劉淑芬, eds., *Belief, Practice, and Cultural Adaptation: Papers from the Religion Section of the Fourth International Conference on Sinology* (Nankang: Academia Sinica, 2013), 531–568.

23. Francesca Tarocco, *The Cultural Practices of Modern Chinese Buddhism: Attuning the Dharma* (New York: Routledge, 2007), 16–20, 30, 46–49, 59–63. See also Wu Ping 吳平, "Jindai Shanghai de Fojiao chuban jigou" 近代上海的佛教出版機構, *Huaxia wenhua* 華夏文化 1 (2000): 37, 41–42.

24. Daniela Campo, "Chan Master Xuyun: The Embodiment of an Ideal, the Transmission of a Model," in David Ownby, Vincent Goossaert, and Ji Zhe, eds., *Making Saints in Modern China* (Oxford: Oxford University Press, 2017), 99–136; Jan Kiely, "The Charismatic Monk and the Chanting Masses: Master Yinguang and His Pure Land Revival Movement," in David Ownby, Vincent Goossaert, and Ji Zhe, eds., *Making Saints in Modern China* (New York: Oxford University Press, 2017), 30–77.

25. Gregory Adam Scott, "A Revolution of Ink: Chinese Buddhist Periodicals in the Early Republic," in Jan Kiely and J. Brooks Jessup, eds., *Recovering Buddhism in Modern China* (New York: Columbia University Press, 2016), 111–40.

26. J. Brooks Jessup, "Beyond Ideological Conflict: Political Incorporation of Buddhist Youth in the Early PRC," *Frontiers of History in China* 7.4 (2012): 551–81.

27. Chiara Betta, "Silas Aaron Hardoon (1851–1931): Marginality and Adaptation in Shanghai" (PhD diss., University of London, 1997).

28. Data on Buddhist radio stations and their programming may be found in Meng Lingbing 孟令兵, *Lao Shanghai wenhua qipa* 老上海文化奇葩 (Shanghai: Shanghai

renmin chubanshe, 2003), 83–85; Gao Zhennong 高振農, "Minguo nianjian de Shanghai Foxue shuju" 民國年間的上海佛學書局, http://read.goodweb.cn/news/news_view. asp?newsid=79749. See also Tarocco, *Cultural Practices*, 30, 33–34. For a comparative perspective, see Lee Tong Soon, "Technology and the Production of Islamic Space: The Call to Prayer in Singapore," *Ethnomusicology* 43.1 (1999): 86–100.

29. Meng Lingbing, *Lao Shanghai wenhua qipa*, 85–86; Huang Weichu 黃維楚, *Huayan zimu ji qi changfa* 華嚴字母及其唱法 (Shanghai: Foxue shuju, 2009). See also Ge Tao 葛濤, *Changpian yu jindai Shanghai shehui shenghuo* 唱片與近代上海社會生活 (Shanghai: Shanghai cishu chubanshe, 2009); Yung Sai-shing (Rong Shicheng) 容世誠, *Yueyun liusheng: Changpian gongye yu Guangdong quyi (1903–1953)* 粵韻留聲：唱片工業與廣東曲藝 (1903–1953) (Hong Kong: Tiandi tushu, 2006); Jessup, "Householder Elite," 56–58.

30. The following discussion is based mainly on the following sources: Francesca Tarocco, "Buddhist Music," in S. Sadie and J. Tyrrell, eds., *The New Grove Dictionary of Music and Musicians* (Online version, 2004) Oxford University Press: https://global. oup.com/academic/product/the-new-grove-dictionary-of-music-and-musicians-9780195170672?cc=tw&lang=en&; Chen Pi-yen, "Buddhist Chant, Devotional Song, and Commercial Popular Music: From Ritual to Rock Mantra," *Ethnomusicology* 49.2 (2005): 266–86; Larry Tse-Hsiung Lin, "The Development and Conceptual Transformation of Chinese Buddhist Songs in the Twentieth Century" (PhD diss., University of California, San Diego, 2012); Larry Tse-Hsiung Lin, "Li Shutong's Buddhist-Themed School Songs of the Early Twentieth Century and Their Japanese Influences," paper presented at the conference 2013 e-CASE and e-Tech, Japan, April 3–5, 2013. We are profoundly grateful to Raoul Birnbaum for his helpful comments and source materials provided during a series of email exchanges in July and August 2016.

31. Peter Micic, "School Songs and Modernity in Late Qing and Early Republican China" (PhD diss., Monash University, 1999), esp. 40–48, 54–76, 148–64. See also Liu Ching-chih, *A Critical History of New Music in China* (Hong Kong: Chinese University Press, 2010).

32. Pioneering work on Hongyi's life and career has been done by Raoul Birnbaum. See his "Master Hongyi Looks Back: A 'Modern Man' Becomes a Monk in Twentieth-Century China," in Steven Heine and Charles S. Prebish, eds., *Buddhism in the Modern World: Adaptations of an Ancient Tradition* (New York: Oxford University Press, 2003), 75–124; "The Deathbed Image of Master Hongyi," in Jacqueline Stone and Bryan Cuevas, eds., *The Buddhist Dead: Practices, Discourses, Representations* (Honolulu: University of Hawai'i Press, 2007), 175–207; "Two Turns in the Life of Master Hongyi, a Buddhist Monk in Twentieth-Century China," in David Ownby, Vincent Goossaert, and Ji Zhe, eds., *Making Saints in Modern China* (New York: Oxford University Press, 2017), 161–208.

33. Hongyi's ideas about music may also be related to the goal of preserving China's "national essence" (*guocui* 國粹). On the religious aspects of this issue, see Goossaert and Palmer, *Religious Question*, 108–21. On aesthetics, see Wang Cheng-hua, "The Qing Imperial Collection circa 1905–25: National Humiliation Heritage Preservation and Exhibition Culture," in Wu Hung, ed., *Reinventing the Past: Archaism and Antiquarianism in Chinese Art and Visual Culture* (Chicago: Center for the Art of East Asia, University of Chicago, 2010), 320–41.

34. Lin, "Development and Conceptual Transformation," 80. The Chinese original reads 人天長夜，宇宙黮暗，誰啟以光明？三界火宅，眾苦煎迫，誰濟以安寧？大悲大智大雄力，南無佛陀耶！ This song may also be found on YouTube (see, e.g., https://www.youtube.com/watch?v=OM9WyA_gyN0).

35. For more on Feng, see Geremie R. Barmé, *An Artistic Exile: A Life of Feng Zikai (1898–1975)* (Berkeley: University of California Press, 2002).

36. We have used the edition Chen Hailiang 陳海量, *Zaijia xueFo yaodian* 在家學佛要典 (Taipei: Fojiao chubanshe, 1982), 243–46, 257–58, 292–96, 321–57.

37. Lin, "Development and Conceptual Transformation", 89, 95.

38. Wu Haoran 吳浩然, ed., *Minguo manhua fengfan* 民國漫畫風範 (Jinan: Qilu shushe, 2011); Li Zhongqing 李忠清 and Yang Xiaomin 楊小民, eds., *Jiushi baitai: 1912–1949 laomanhua · Manhua shehui* 舊世百態：1912-1949老漫畫·漫畫社會 (Beijing: Xiandai chubanshe, 1999).

39. Cheung Chi-Wai 張志偉, "Tuxiang yishu yu Zhongguo jidujiaoshi yanjiu: *Shanghai qingnian* (1914–1927) zhong de manhua yingyong" 圖像藝術與中國基督教史研究：《上海青年》（1914-1927）中的漫畫應用, in Peter Tze Ming Ng (Wu Ziming 吳梓明) and Wu Xiaoxin 吳小新, eds., *Jidu yu Zhongguo shehui: Dierjie Guoji nianqing xuezhe yantaohui lunwenji* 基督與中國社會：第二屆國際年青學者研討會論文集 (Hong Kong: Centre for the Study of Religion and Chinese Society, Chung Chi College, 2006), 331–72. See also Cheung Chi-Wai, *Jiduhua yu shisuhua de zhengzha: Shanghai Jidujiao qingnianhui yanjiu (1900–1922)* 基督化與世俗化的掙扎：上海基督教青年會研究 (1900–1922) (Taipei: National Taiwan University Press, 2010).

40. Poon Shuk-wah 潘淑華, "'Husheng' yu 'Jintu': 1930 niandai Shanghai de dongwu baohu yu Fojiao yundong" 「護生」與「禁屠」：1930年代上海的動物保護與佛教運動, in Kang Bao and Gao Wansang, eds., *Gaibian Zhongguo zongjiao de wushinian, 1898–1948* (Nankang: Institute of Modern History, Academia Sinica, 2015), 399–426. See also Chen Xing 陳星, *Feng Zikai manhua yanjiu* 豐子愷漫畫研究 (Hangzhou: Xileng yinshe, 2004), 58–115.

41. Liu Xun, *Daoist Modern*, esp. 231–71; Liu Xun, "Daoism from the Late Qing to Early Republican Periods". See also Goossaert, *Taoists of Peking*, 308–19.

42. Liu Xun, *Daoist Modern*, 174, 186, 209–16, 240–60, 275; Liu Xun, "Daoism from the Late Qing to Early Republican Periods." See also Wu Yakui 吳亞魁, *Jiangnan Quanzhen Daojiao* 江南全真道教 (Hong Kong: Zhonghua shuju, 2006).

43. For more on these associations and their activities, see David K. Jordan and Daniel L. Overmyer, *The Flying Phoenix: Aspects of Chinese Sectarianism in Taiwan* (Princeton, NJ: Princeton University Press, 1986). See also Philip A. Clart, "Chinese Tradition and Taiwanese Modernity: Morality Books as Social Commentary and Critique," in Philip A. Clart and Charles B. Jones, eds., *Religion in Modern Taiwan: Tradition and Innovation in a Changing Society* (Honolulu: University of Hawai'i Press, 2003), 84–97; Vincent Goossaert, "Spirit Writing, Canonization, and the Rise of Divine Saviors: Wenchang, Lüzu, and Guandi, 1700–1858," *Late Imperial China* 36.2 (2015): 82–125, esp. 104–5; Paul R. Katz, "Spirit-Writing and the Dynamics of Elite Religious Life in Republican Era Shanghai," in

Ting Jen-chieh 丁仁傑 et al., eds., *Jindai Zhongguo de zongjiao fazhan lunwenji* 近代中國的宗教發展論文集 (Taipei: Academia Historica, 2015), 275–350. See also Palmer, Katz, and Wang, *Redemptive Societies and New Religious Movements*.

44. Yau Chi-on, "The Xiantiandao and Publishing in the Guangzhou-Hong Kong Area from the Late Qing to the 1930s: The Case of the Morality Book Publisher Wenzaizi," Philip Clart trans., in Philip Clart and Gregory Adam Scott, eds., *Religious Publishing and Print Culture in Modern China, 1800–2012* (Boston: De Gruyter, 2014), 187–232; Wang Chien-ch'uan, "Morality Book Publishing"; Fan Chun-wu 范純武, "Feiluan, xiuzhen yu banshan: Zheng Guanying yu Shanghai zongjiao shijie" 飛鸞、修真與辦善：鄭觀應與上海的宗教世界, in Wu Jen-shu 巫仁恕, Lin May-li 林美莉, and Kang Bao 康豹 (Paul R. Katz), eds., *Cong chengshi kan Zhongguo de xiandaixing* 從城市看中國的現代性 (Nankang: Institute of Modern History, Academia Sinica, 2010), 247–74.

45. *Minguo shiqi chuban shumu huibian* 民國時期出版書目彙編 (Beijing: Guojia tushuguan chubanshe, 2010), 20:227. See also Paul R. Katz, "Illuminating Goodness: Some Preliminary Considerations of Religious Publishing in Modern China," in Philip Clart and Gregory Adam Scott, eds., *Religious Publishing and Print Culture in Modern China, 1800–2012* (Boston: De Gruyter, 2014), 265–94.

46. *Minguo shiqi chuban shumu huibian*, 20:237–76, 318–22.

47. Erik Hammerstrom, *The Science of Chinese Buddhism: Early Twentieth-Century Engagements* (New York: Columbia University Press, 2015); David A. Palmer, *Qigong Fever: Body, Science, and Utopia in China* (New York: Columbia University Press, 2007).

48. Huang Ko-wu 黃克武, "Minguo chunian Shanghai de Lingxue yanjiu."

49. Jheng Ya-Yin 鄭雅尹, "Qingmo Minchu de 'gui' yu 'zhaoxiangshu' – Di Baoxian Pingdengge biji zhong de xiandaixing meiying" 清末民初的「鬼」與「照相術」—狄葆賢《平等閣筆記》中的現代性魅影, *Qinghua zhongwen xuebao* 清華中文學報 13 (2015): 229–81.

50. Fan Chun-wu, "Duan Zhengyuan and the Moral Studies Society: 'Religionized Confucianism' during the Republican Period," in David Ownby, Vincent Goossaert, and Ji Zhe, eds., *Making Saints in Modern China* (New York: Oxford University Press, 2017), 137–60. See also Catherine Despeux, "The "New Clothes" of Sainthood in China: The Case of Nan Huaijin (1918–2012)," in David Ownby, Vincent Goossaert, and Ji Zhe, eds., *Making Saints in Modern China* (New York: Oxford University Press, 2017), 349–93.

51. Rudolf Löwenthal, *The Religious Periodical Press in China* (Peking: Synodal Commission in China, 1940), 139–92, 282–92 (reprinted by the Chinese Materials Center in San Francisco in 1978).

52. Thomas David DuBois, "Japanese Print Media and Manchurian Cultural Community: Religion in the Pages of the *Shengjing Times*, 1906–1944," in Thomas David DuBois, ed., *Casting Faiths: Imperialism and the Transformation of Religion in East and Southeast Asia* (New York: Palgrave Macmillan, 2009), 217–38.

53. Löwenthal, *Religious Periodical Press*, 177–78.

54. Rostislav Berezkin, "Printing and Circulating 'Precious Scrolls' in Early Twentieth-Century Shanghai and Its Vicinity: Toward an Assessment of Multifunctionality of the Genre," in Philip Clart and Gregory Adam Scott, eds., *Religious Publishing and Print Culture in Modern China, 1800-2012* (Boston: De Gruyter, 2014), 139–86; Rostislav Berezkin, "Lithographic Printing and the Development of the Baojuan 寶卷 Genre in Shanghai in the 1900–1920s: On the Question of the Interaction between Print Technology and Popular Literature in China (Preliminary Observations)," *Zhongzheng daxue Zhongwen xueshu niankan* 中正大學中文學術年刊 17 (2011): 337–68; Bai Ruosi 白若思 (Rostislav Berezkin), "You 1900–1937 nianjian *Huaming baojuan* de kanke kan Zhongguo ershi shiji chu chuban wenhua yu minjian xinyang ji suwenxue zhi guanxi" 由 1900–1937年間《花名寶卷》的刊刻看中國二十世紀初出版文化與民間信仰及俗文學之關係, in Kang Bao and Gao Wansang, eds., *Gaibian Zhongguo zongjiao de wushinian, 1898-1948* (Nankang: Institute of Modern History, Academia Sinica, 2015), 169–92.

55. "Jixian lin Shanghai Jiyunxuan jiyu erze" 濟仙臨上海集雲軒乩諭二則, *Daode zazhi* 道德雜誌 1.2 (1921): 87–95.

56. Clart, "New Technologies."

57. Jessup, "Householder Elite," 49–59; Clart, "New Technologies."

58. See, for example, Sawada Mizuho 澤田瑞穗, *Zōho hōkan no kenkyū* 增補寶卷の研究 (Tokyo: Dōkyō kankōkai, 1975), 70–75.

59. Berezkin, "Lithographic Printing."

60. Berezkin, "Printing and Circulating 'Precious Scrolls'"; Berezkin, "Lithographic Printing."

61. Patricia Ebrey, ed., *Women and the Family in Chinese History* (London: Routledge, 2003); Dorothy Ko, *Teachers of the Inner Chambers: Women and Culture in Seventeenth-Century China* (Stanford, CA: Stanford University Press, 1995); Susan Mann, *Precious Records: Women in China's Long Eighteenth Century* (Stanford, CA: Stanford University Press, 1997).

62. Paul J. Bailey, *Gender and Education in China: Gender Discourses and Women's Schooling in the Early Twentieth Century* (London: Routledge, 2007).

63. Zhou Zuoren 周作人, "Gua dou ji" 瓜豆集, in *Zhou Zuoren quanji* 周作人全集, vol. 4 (Taipei: Landeng wenhua shiye, 1992), 25.

64. Hu Shih 胡適, *Sishi zishu* 四十自述 (Taipei: Yuandong tushu gongsi, 1992), 39–41.

65. Qijun 琦君, *San geng you meng shu dang zhen* 三更有夢書當枕 (Taipei: Erya chubanshe, 1975), 42–43.

66. Löwenthal, *Religious Periodical Press*, 287.

67. Paul R. Katz, "An Unbreakable Thread? Preliminary Observations on the Interaction between Chinese and Taiwanese Religious Traditions under Japanese Colonial Rule," *Taiwan zongjiao yanjiu* 臺灣宗教研究 11.2 (2012): 39–70. See also Lai Ch'ung-jen 賴崇仁, "Taizhong Ruicheng shuju ji qi gezaice yanjiu" 台中瑞成書局及其歌仔冊研究 (MA thesis, Feng-chia University, 2004).

68. Information on Huang's life and activities may be found in Wang Chien-ch'uan 王見川, "Guomin zhengfu lai Tai (1949) qian liang'an de zongjiao wanglai yu cishan huodong chutan: Jian tan Lanji shuju Huang Maosheng de jiaose" 國民政府來台 (1949) 前兩岸的宗教往來與慈善活動初探：兼談蘭記書局黃茂盛的角色, *Mazu yu minjian xinyang: Yanjiu tongxun* 媽祖與民間信仰: 研究通訊 1 (2012): 57–69; Wang Chien-ch'uan 王見川 and Li Shih-wei 李世偉, *Taiwan de minjian zongjiao yu xinyang* 台灣的民間宗教與信仰 (Luzhou: BoyYoung, 2000), 130–31.

69. See Wang Chien-ch'uan "Guomin zhengfu lai Tai."

70. *Jiayi shizhi* 嘉義市志, *juan* 卷 *10 (Zongjiao lisu zhi* 宗教禮俗志) (Jiayi: Jiayi City Government, 2005).

71. Kiely, "Shanghai Public Moralist."

72. Ownby, "Politics of Redemption," 683–741.

73. Wang Chien-Chuan, "Morality Book Publishing"; Paul R. Katz, "Illuminating Goodness."

Chapter 4

1. Kiely, "Shanghai Public Moralist."

2. Yau Chi-on (You Zi'an) 游子安, *Quanhua jinzhen: Qingdai shanshu yanjiu* 勸化金箴：清代善書研究 (Tianjin: Tianjin renmin chubanshe, 1999), 240–95, reprinted the 1935 *Gujin shanshu dacidian* 古今善書大辭典, an important synthesis of the morality literature. Since then Yau has published a number of important pieces exploring the development of morality books and presses since the late Qing, especially in the Cantonese world. See, notably, his *Shan yu ren tong* and "Xiantiandao and Publishing."

3. D. T Suzuki. and Paul Carus, *Treatise on Response and Retribution* (1906, reprint La Salle, IL: Open Court, 1973), 3. http://www.terebess.hu/english/taishang.html.

4. Fan Chun-wu 范純武, "Bade: Jindai Zhongguo jiushi tuanti de daode leimu yu shijian 八德:近代中國救世團體的道德類目與實踐." In Kang Bao and Gao Wansang, eds. *Gaibian Zhongguo zongjiao de wushinian, 1898–1948* (Nankang: Institute of Modern History, Academia Sinica, 2015), 225–259.

5. On Yinguang, see Kiely, "Charismatic Monk." Zhang Xuesong 張雪松, *Fayu lingyan: Zhongguo Fojiaoxiandaihua lishi jinchengzhong de Yinguang fashi yanjiu* 法雨靈岩: 中國佛教現代化歷史進程中的印光法師研究 (Taipei: Fagu wenhua, 2011).

6. Wang Chien-ch'uan, "Jindai Zhongguo de fuji, cishan yu 'mixin.'"

7. On Jingkong, see Sun Yanfei, "Jingkong: From Universal Saint to Sectarian Saint," in David Ownby, Vincent Goossaert and Ji Zhe, eds., *Making Saints in Modern China* (New York: Oxford University Press, 2017), 394–418.

8. Yau Chi-on, *Shan yu ren tong*, 164–82.

9. Kiely, "Shanghai Public Moralist."

10. Goossaert, "Spirit Writing."

11. Scott, "Navigating the Sea of Scriptures."

12. Nie's *Ganying leichao* was included in Wang's canon, *Fushou baozang*, vol. 63.

13. The only scholars who have seen and/or mentioned this canon, to our knowledge, are Yau Chi-on, in his *Shan yu ren tong*, 160–64 (where Yau provides the entire table of contents), 332–33, and Sakai Tadao 酒井忠夫, "Jinxiandai Zhongguo de shanshu yu Xinshenghuo yundong" 近現代中國的善書與新生活運動, Lai Hsu-chen 賴旭貞, trans., *Minjian zongjiao* 2 (1996), 93–103, esp. 101. On its importance, see Katz, "Illuminating Goodness," 282.

14. These four persons are not well documented in historical sources and we have not been able to find their birth and death dates.

15. By then the reigning Heavenly Master was the sixty-third, Zhang Enpu 張恩溥 (1904–69), on whom see Li Liliang 李麗涼, *Yidai tianshi: Zhang Enpu yu Taiwan Daojiao* 弌代天師: 張恩溥與台灣道教 (Taipei: Guoshiguan, 2012). Wang Yiting had been close to (and coorganized the funeral of) the sixty-second Heavenly Master, Zhang Yuanxu 張元旭 (1862–1925). See Vincent Goossaert, "Zhang Yuanxu: The Making and Unmaking of a Daoist Saint," in David Ownby, Vincent Goossaert, and Ji Zhe, eds., *Making Saints in Modern China* (New York: Oxford University Press, 2017), 78–98.

16. See, for instance, the discussion of the classifications used by the Mingshan shuju press in Katz, "Illuminating Goodness," 279–82.

17. The inner alchemical section is mostly devoted to texts of the early-nineteenth-century master (by 1936 a classic author) Liu Yiming 劉一明 (1734–1821).

18. The Fushou baozang comprises one Jingaishan text: the *Jingshi gongguoge* 警世功過格 (vol. 62).

19. On the Eight Virtues, see Fan Chun-wu, "Bade."

20. *Fushou baozang*, vol. 80.

21. *Fushou baozang*, vol. 45.

22. On this text, see Catherine M. Bell, "'A Precious Raft to Save the World': The Interaction of Scriptural Traditions and Printing in a Chinese Morality Book," *Late Imperial China* 17.1 (1996): 158–200. Note, however, that these three classics are all present in the canon.

23. *Fushou baozang*, vols. 69–72.

24. On this theme, see Vincent Goossaert, *Bureaucratie et salut. Devenir un dieu en Chine* (Genève: Labor and Fides, 2017).

25. The next two books of the *Fushou baozang* contain Republican period stories: *Xingren zhong* 醒人鐘 (vol. 73, spirit-written stories revealed in Hubei province); and *Dongmingji* 洞冥記 (vols. 74–75), discussed below.

26. Vincent Goossaert, "Guerre, violence, et eschatologie: Interprétations religieuses de la guerre des Taiping (1851–1864)," in Jean Baechler, ed., *Guerre et Religion*, (Paris: Hermann, 2016), 81–94.

27. See, for instance, *Xingguibian* 醒閨編 (vol. 59 of the *Fushou baozang*), which includes very detailed revelations by the sectarian goddess Yaochi jinmu 瑤池金母, dated 1861 and supposedly related in Yunnan Province, detailing war actions (in that case, involving the Panthay Rebellion rather than the Taiping War) and the intervention of the gods on the side of the faithful.

28. Vincent Goossaert, "Modern Daoist Eschatology: Spirit-Writing and Elite Soteriology in Late Imperial China." *Daoism: Religion, History, and Society* 6 (2014): 219–46.

29. This genre and style invented in the *Dongmingji* proved influential and was revived in 1980s Taiwan, where the spirit-writing text *Diyu youji* 地獄遊記 was widely disseminated and met with impressive success.

30. Wang Chien-ch'uan, "Popular Groups."

31. On the eschatological theme of Guandi as the new Jade Emperor in this and related texts, see Wang Chien-ch'uan 王見川, "Taiwan 'Guandi dang Yuhuang' chuanshuo de youlai" 臺灣「關帝當玉皇」傳說的由來, in *Hanren zongjiao, minjian xinyang yu yuyanshu de tansuo: Wang Chien-ch'uan zixuanji* 漢人宗教、民間信仰與預言書的探索：王見川自選集 (Taipei: BoyYoung, 2008), 411–30.

32. *Fushou baozang*, vol. 65. Scholarly opinions on the date of the *Yuli baochao* differ; we tend to consider it a product of of the early nineteenth century. See Vincent Goossaert, ed. and trans., *Livres de morale révélés par les dieux* (Paris: Belles-Lettres, 2012).

33. As the *Yuding jinke jiyao* runs to thousands of pages, the *Fushou baozang* (vol. 60) only includes its section on women's morality.

34. The *Xunnü baozhen* is discussed in Clart, "Chinese Tradition and Taiwanese Modernity."

35. Kiely, "Shanghai Public Moralist," 22.

36. Wang Chien-ch'uan, "Spirit Writing Groups in Modern China (1840–1937): Textual Production, Public Teachings, and Charity," Vincent Goossaert, trans., in Vincent Goossaert, Jan Kiely, and John Lagerwey, eds., *Modern Chinese Religion,* Vol. 2: *1850–2015* (Leiden: Brill, 2016), 651–84.

37. Wang Chien-ch'uan, "Morality Book Publishing." Wang notes that several large religious Shanghai presses not affiliated with Xiantiandao or Tongshanshe published material such as the *Dongmingji*.

38. Vincent Goossaert, "La sexualité dans les livres de morale chinois," in Florence Rochefort and Maria Eleonora Sanna, eds., *Normes religieuses et genre: Mutations, résistances, et reconfiguration, xixe–xxie siècle* (Paris: Armand Colin, 2013), 37–46.

39. Philip C. C. Huang, *Code, Custom, and Legal Practice in China: The Qing and the Republic Compared* (Stanford, CA: Stanford University Press, 2001).

40. For a masterful survey of the evolution of discourses on women and superstition during this period, see Kang Xiaofei, "Women and the Religious Question."

41. Clart, "Chinese Tradition."

42. Ibid., 91.

43. These are the *Wanshan xianzi ji* 萬善先資集, by Zhou Mengyan (vol. 76); *Aiwupian* 愛物篇 (preface 1860, vol. 77); *Leshengji* 樂生集 (preface 1795, vol. 78); and *Husheng huaji* (vol. 78).

44. Vincent Goossaert, "Animals and Eschatology in the Nineteenth-Century Discourse," in Martina Siebert and Roel Sterckx, and Dagmar Schäfer, eds., *Animals Through Chinese History. Earliest Times to 1911* (Cambridge: Cambridge University Press, 2019), 181–198.

45. *Fushou baozang*, vol. 19.

46. Poon Shuk-wah, "'Husheng' yu Jintu."

Chapter 5

1. Goossaert, "1898." This chapter is a much-expanded version of Vincent Goossaert, "Diversity and Elite Religiosity in Modern China: A Model," *Approaching Religion* 7.1 (2017): 10–20.

2. William T. Rowe, *Saving the World: Chen Hongmou and Elite Consciousness in Eighteenth-Century China* (Stanford, CA: Stanford University Press, 2001), 436.

3. Donald Sutton, "From Credulity to Scorn: Confucians Confront the Spirit Mediums in Late Imperial China." *Late Imperial China* 21.2 (2000): 1–39, esp. 23–24.

4. A handy synthesis of the historiography of late imperial elites is Chen Shih-jung 陳世榮, "Guojia yu difang shehui de hudong: Jindai shehui jingying de yanjiu dianfan yu weilai de yanjiu qushi" 國家與地方社會的互動：近代社會菁英的研究典範與未來的研究趨勢, *Bulletin of the Institute of Modern History, Academia Sinica* 54 (2006): 129–68.

5. Goossaert, "Managing Chinese Religious Pluralism."

6. See chapter 2.

7. Susan L. Glosser, *Chinese Visions of Family and State, 1915–1953* (Berkeley: University of California Press, 2003).

8. Goossaert and Palmer, *Religious Question*, 54–55, 124–25, 131.

9. Nedostup, *Superstitious Regimes*, 104, 144–47.

10. Adam Y. Chau, "Modalities of Doing Religion." in David A. Palmer, Glenn Shive, and Philip L. Wickeri, eds., *Chinese Religious Life* (Oxford: Oxford University Press, 2011), 67–84.

11. Goossaert used the term *culture religieuse* in an earlier French publication, "Yu Yue (1821-1906) explore l'au-delà: La culture religieuse des élites chinoises à la veille des revolutions," in Roberte Hamayon, Denise Aigle, Isabelle Charleux, and Vincent Goossaert, eds., *Miscellanea Asiatica* (Sankt Augustin: Monumenta Serica, 2011), 623–56.

12. Henrietta Harrison, *The Man Awakened from Dreams: One Man's Life in a North China Village, 1857–1942* (Stanford, CA: Stanford University Press, 2005). See also Goossaert, *Taoists of Peking*, 152, 173, 242, 244 (discussing the famous Weng Tonghe diary); Wang Chien-ch'uan 王見川, "Qingmo de guanshen yu fuji: Jiantan qishi liuxing de chenyan" 清末的官紳與扶乩：兼談其時流行的讖言, *Mazu yu minjian xinyang: Yanjiu tongxun* 媽祖與民間信仰：研究通訊 2 (2012): 34–47 (on Zeng Guofan).

13. Naquin, *Peking*; David Faure, *Emperor and Ancestor: State and Lineage in South China* (Stanford, CA: Stanford University Press, 2007); and Michael Szonyi, *Practicing Kinship: Lineage and Descent in Late Imperial China* (Stanford, CA: Stanford University Press, 2002) have all documented how local elites invested massively in certain institutions (lineages, charities) in late imperial times, often, though not always, at the detriment of local temples. There are, however, counterexemples in which local elites did reinforce their involvement in community temples during the nineteenth and early twentieth centuries. Paul R. Katz, "Local Elites and Sacred Sites in Hsin-Chuang: The Growth of the Ti-tsang An during the Japanese Occupation," in Lin Mei-rong 林美容, ed., *Belief, Ritual, and Society: Papers from the Third International Conference on Sinology, Anthropology Section* (Nankang: Institute of Ethnology, Academia Sinica, 2003), 179–227. On the case of the City God temples, especially in the context of the post-Taiping reconstruction of communal institutions, see Goossaert, "Shifting Balance."

14. On a continuation of elite involvement in describing local religious culture, see Paul R. Katz, "Writing a Place for Rites: The Value of 'Old Customs' in Modern Wenzhou," *Journal of Chinese Religions* 43.1 (2015): 59–88.

15. On the religious culture of the prestigious Suzhou Peng family, see Daniel Burton-Rose, "Terrestrial Reward as Divine Recompense: The Self-Fashioned Piety of the Peng Lineage of Suzhou, 1650s–1870s" (PhD diss., Princeton University, 2016).

16. Goossaert, *Taoists of Peking*, 283–297.

17. On Zheng Guanying's involvement with Daoist self-cultivation and spirit-writing, see Fan Chun-wu "Xiuzhen, feiluan yu banshan"; Goossaert, *Taoists of Peking*, 174, 328; Liu Xun, *Daoist Modern*, 22–23.

18. Vincent Goossaert, "Spiritual Techniques among Late Imperial Chinese Elites," in Angela Hobart, Thierry Zarcone and Jean-Pierre Brach, eds., *Spiritual Techniques* (Canon Pyon: Sean Kingston, forthcoming).

19. On modern spirit-writing groups, see Katz, "Spirit-writing"; Fan Chun-wu 范純武, *Qingmo minjian cishan shiye yu luantang yundong* 清末民間慈善事業與鸞堂運動 (Taipei: BoyYoung, 2015).

20. Yau Chi-on, *Shan yu ren tong*; Wang Chien-ch'uan, "Spirit-Writing Groups," 651–84; Fan Chun-wu, "Bade."

21. Philip Clart, "Confucius and the Mediums: Is There a 'Popular Confucianism'?" *T'oung Pao* 89, 1–3 (2003): 1–38, Jordan and Overmyer, *Flying Phoenix*.

22. See, for example, "Jinwushuo" 禁巫說, *Shenbao*, June 8, 1899; "Weishengbu zhuyi fangyi" 衛生部注意防疫, *Shenbao*, April 14, 1929; "Qudi shenfang zhibing" 取締神方治病, *Shenbao*, April 26, 1929; "Tongling yanjin shenfang zhibing" 通令嚴禁神方治病, *Shenbao*, May 5, 1929. See also "Fuji shanhuo" 扶乩煽惑, *Xiangbao* 湘報 78 (1898): 310; "Yishi zaping: Fuji zhibing" 醫事雜評：扶乩治病, *Shaoxing yiyao xuebao* 紹興醫藥學報 12.6 (1922): 13.

23. "Jishi" 乩詩, *Shenbao*, February 25, 1913; "Jitan xinyu" 乩壇新語, *Shenbao*, October 26, 1926. See also "Fuji yu xinli" 扶乩與心理, *Hongmeigui* 紅玫瑰 2.13 (1925): 1–2; "Fuji kaoyuan" 扶乩考源, *Hongmeigui* 紅玫瑰 2.14 (1925): 1–2.

24. "Kexue lingjitu" 科學靈乩圖, *Shenbao*, May 14, 1934; "Kexue lingji" 科學靈乩, *Shenbao*, May 22, 1934. See also "Fulu: Fuji de xueli shuoming" 附錄：扶乩的學理說明, *Daode zazhi* 道德雜誌 1.1 (1921): 117–20; "Kexue changshi: Fuji zhi kexue de jieshi" 科學常識：扶乩之科學的解釋, *Nongmin* 農民 3.2 (1927): 6–7.

25. "Wu Peifu zhi fuji yu yiqi" 吳佩孚之扶乩與奕棋, *Shenbao*, July 22, 1926; Mao Dun 茅盾 "1927 nian da geming: Huiylu(9)" 一九二七年大革命：回憶錄[九], *Xin wenxue shiliao* 新文學史料 4 (1980): 1–15. See also Liu Bingrong 劉秉榮, *Junfa yu mixin* 軍閥與迷信 (Beijing: Huawen chubanshe, 1993).

26. "Yinyangfeng: Chen Jitang fuji" 陰陽風：陳濟棠扶乩, *Yijing* 逸經 16 (1936): 52.

27. Liu Xun, "Immortals and Patriarchs: The Daoist World of a Manchu Official and His Family in Nineteenth Century China," *Asia Major*, 3rd ser., 17.2 (2004): 161–218.

28. Harrison, *Man Awakened*.

29. Vincent Goossaert, "Anatomie d'un discours anticlerical"; Vincent Goossaert, "Starved of Resources: Clerical Hunger and Enclosures in Nineteenth-Century China," *Harvard Journal of Asiatic Studies* 62.1 (2002): 77–133.

30. Goossaert, "Yu Yue explore l'au-delà."

31. Goossaert and Palmer, *Religious Question*, chap. 4.

32. Meyer-Fong, *What Remains*, chap. 2.

33. Goossaert and Palmer, *Religious Question*, 70.

34. "Lunshuo: Jizu pochu mixin bian" 論說：濟祖破除迷信辯, *Daode zazhi* 道德雜誌 2.8 (1922): 48. For more on the historical development of Jigong's cult, see Meir Shahar, *Crazy Ji: Chinese Religion and Popular Literature* (Cambridge, MA: Harvard University Press, 1998).

35. Sakai Tadao, "Minguo chuqi zhi xinxing zongjiao yundong yu xinshidai chaoliu," 23, 28.

36. On *lisheng* 禮生, see Liu Yonghua, *Confucian Rituals and Chinese Villagers: Ritual Change and Social Transformation in a Southeastern Chinese Community, 1368–1949* (Leiden: Brill, 2013).

37. Goossaert and Palmer, *Religious Question*, 78; Daniel H. Bays and Ellen Widmer, eds., *China's Christian Colleges: Cross-Cultural Connections, 1900–1950* (Stanford, CA: Stanford University Press, 2009).

38. On the question of levels of urbanization and their effect on religious life, see Poon, "Thriving under an Anti-superstition Regime"; Lo, "Chenhuangshen yu jindai Wenzhou difang zhengzhi"; Qi Gang, "Qingji Wenzhou diqu de miaochan banxue."

39. Goossaert, "Question of Control."

40. Liu Wenxing, "Jindai Hushe yu siyuan de hudong."

41. Liu Xun, "Of Poems, Gods, and Spirit-Writing Altars: The Daoist Beliefs and Practice of Wang Duan (1793–1839)," *Late Imperial China* 36.2 (2015): 23–81.

42. See Elena Valussi, "Men Built Religion, and Women Made It Superstitious: Gender and Superstition in Republican China," *Journal of Chinese Religions* 48:1 (2020): 87–125; Kang,

"Women and the Religious Question." Some spirit-writing groups maintained gender segregation during the Republican period to show their high "moral" standards, but this practice became ever more marginal.

43. Liu Xun, *Daoist Modern*, provides many examples.

44. Timothy Brook, "Buddhism in the Chinese Constitution: Recording Monasteries in North Zhili," in *The Chinese State in Ming Society* (London: RoutledgeCurzon, 2005), 158–81; Vincent Goossaert, "Quanzhen, What Quanzhen? Late Imperial Daoist Clerical Identities in Lay Perspective," in Vincent Goossaert and Liu Xun, eds., *Quanzhen Daoists in Chinese Society and Culture, 1500–2010* (Berkeley: Institute of East Asian Studies, 2013), 19–43.

45. Katz, "Writing a Place for Rites."

46. See, for example, Jay Taylor, *The Generalissimo: Chiang Kai-shek and the Struggle for Modern China* (Cambridge, MA: Belknap Press of Harvard University Press, 2009); Hollington Kong Tong, *Chiang Kai-shek, Soldier and Statesman: Authorized Biography by Hollington K. Tong*, (London: Hurst and Blackett, 1938).

47. Further evidence of Chiang's Christian faith may also be found in a volume of translations of comments appended to his own copy of the Bible, which contains a long postscript by Chin Hsiao-yi 秦孝儀 (1921–2007) on Chiang's Christianity. See *Jiang Zhongzheng xiansheng shougai Shengjing shengyong yigao* 蔣中正先生手改聖經聖詠譯稿, Wu Ching-hsiung 吳經熊, trans., 6 vols. (Taipei: Chung-kuo Kuomintang tang-shih wei-yuan-hui, 1986).

48. Huang Ko-wu 黃克武, "Xiushen yu zhiguo—Jiang Jieshi de xingke shenghuo 修身與治國—蔣介石的省克生活, *Bulletin of Academia Historica* 34 (2012): 45–68. A more extended discussion of Chiang's religious life can be found in Katz, *Religion in China*, 113–14.

49. See Taylor, *Generalissimo*, 27–28, 73–76, 91–92, 108–9, 259–60, 456; Tong, *Chiang Kai-shek*, 595–99. See also Cynthia J. Brokaw, *The Ledgers of Merit and Demerit: Social Change and Moral Order in Late Imperial China* (Princeton, NJ: Princeton University Press, 1991).

50. Grace Yen Shen, "Scientism in the Twentieth Century," in Vincent Goossaert, Jan Kiely, and John Lagerwey, eds., *Modern Chinese Religion*, Vol. 2: *1850–2015* (Leiden: Brill, 2015), vol. 1, 91–137; Hammerstrom, *Science of Chinese Buddhism*.

51. Jiang Jianming 江建明 (Brooks J. Jessup), "Dazao xiandai dushi de Fojiao shenfen rentong – Yi 1920 niandai Shanghai de Shijie fojiao jushilin weili" 打造現代都市的佛教身分認同–1920年代上海的世界佛教居士林為例, in Kang Bao and Gao Wansang, eds., *Gaibian Zhongguo zongjiao de wushinian, 1898–1948* (Nankang: Institute of Modern History, Academia Sinica, 2015), 337–61.

52. Yang Kaili 楊凱里 (Jan Kiely), "Zai jingying dizi yu nianfo dazhong zhijian – Minguo shiqi Yinguang fashi jingtu yundong de shehui jianzhang" 在精英弟子與念佛大眾之間-民國時期印光法師淨土運動的社會緊張, in Kang Bao and Gao Wansang, *Gaibian Zhongguo zongjiao de wushinian, 1898–1948* (Nankang: Institute of Modern History, Academia Sinica, 2015), 363–97.

53. Katz, "Spirit-Writing."

54. David Ownby, "Sainthood, Science, and Politics: The Life of Li Yujie, Founder of the Tiandijiao," in David Ownby, Vincent Goossaert and Ji Zhe, eds., *Making Saints in Modern China* (New York: Oxford University Press, 2017), 241–71; David Palmer, "Dao and Nation: Li Yujie, May Fourth Activist, Daoist Cultivator, and Redemptive Society Patriarch in Mainland China and Taiwan," in David A. Palmer and Liu Xun, eds., *Daoism in the Twentieth Century: Between Eternity and Modernity* (Berkeley: University of California Press, 2012), 173–95.

55. Goossaert and Palmer, *Religious Question*, 177–79.

Chapter 6

1. Some of the data presented below also appear in chapter 3 of Katz, *Religion in China*.

2. This work is preserved in the Shanghai Municipal Archives. Qin's account was edited by Ye Erkai 葉爾愷 (1864–1942), an artist, calligrapher, and former Qing education commissioner (*duxue* 督學) from Renhe 仁和 County (Hangzhou 杭州, Zhejiang), who was also a prominent lay Buddhist.

3. Tang Wenzhi 唐文治, *Rujing tang wenji* 茹經堂文集 (1935), in *Minguo congshu* 民國叢書, 5th series, vols. 94–95 (Shanghai: Shanghai shuju, 1996), 11–12.

4. Wang Zhongxiu 王中秀, ed. and comp., *Wang Yiting nianpu changbian* 王一亭年譜長編 (Shanghai: Shanghai shuhua chubanshe, 2010).

5. Shen Wenquan 沈文泉, *Haishang qiren Wang Yiting* 海上奇人王一亭 (Beijing: Zhongguo shehui kexue chubanshe, 2011); Chen Zuen 陳祖恩 and Li Huaxing 李華興, *Wang Yiting zhuan* 王一亭傳 (Shanghai: Shanghai cishu chubanshe, 2007); Zhang Jia 張佳, "Shanghai shenshang jushi de zongjiao shenghuo yu Fojiao xiandaihua zhuanxing: Yi Wang Yiting (1867–1938) wei ge'an" 上海紳商居士的宗教生活與佛教現代化轉型：以王一亭（1867–1938）為個案 (PhD diss., Chinese University of Hong Kong, 2014); Xiao Fenqi 蕭芬琪 (Siu Fun-kee), *Wang Yiting* 王一亭 (Shijiazhuang: Hebei jiaoyu chubanshe, 2002); Shen Kuiyi, "Wang Yiting in the Social Networks of 1910s–1930s Shanghai," in Nara Dillon and Jean C. Oi, eds., *At the Crossroads of Empires: Middlemen, Social Networks, and State-Building in Republican China* (Stanford, CA: Stanford University Press, 2008), 45–64.

6. Regrettably, the mountain was leveled in the course of local industrialization efforts. See Shen Wenquan, *Haishang qiren Wang Yiting*, 1–2.

7. Ibid., 14–22. We are also grateful to Liu Wenxing 劉文星 for his kind assistance.

8. For more on this point, see the biography of Wang in Yu Lingbo 于凌波, *Zhongguo jinxiandai Fojiao renwu zhi* 中國近現代佛教人物志 (Beijing: Zongjiao wenwu chubanshe, 1995), 346–49.

9. For more on Ren, see Roberta May-hwa Wue, "Making the Artist: Ren Bonian (1840–1895) and Portraits of the Shanghai Art World" (PhD diss., New York University, 2001); Lai Yu-chih, "Remapping Borders: Ren Bonian's Frontier Paintings and Urban Life in 1880s Shanghai," *Art Bulletin* 86.3 (September 2004): 550–72.

10. Shen Wenquan, *Haishang qiren Wang Yiting*, 83–110. A virtuoso in both literati painting and calligraphy, Li Weizhuang was also a lay Buddhist, and Wang may have acquired some of his skills in painting Buddhist deities from him.

11. Siu Fun-kee (Xiao Fenqi 蕭芬琪), "The Case of Wang Yiting (1867-1938): A Unique Figure in Early Twentieth Century Chinese Art History" (M.Phil. thesis, University of Hong Kong, 2000). See also Knight Biggerstaff, *The Earliest Modern Government Schools in China* (Ithaca, NY: Cornell University Press, 1961).

12. "Wang Yiting xiansheng jiaxun" 王一亭先生家訓, *Xinghua* 興華 28.48 (1931): 24.

13. For more on Wang's artistic career, see Tsao Hsing-yuan, "A Forgotten Celebrity: Wang Zhen (1867-1933), Businessman, Philanthropist, and Artist," in Chou Ju-hsi, ed., *Art at the Close of China's Empire*, Phoebus Occasional Papers in Art History, no. 8 (Tempe: Arizona State University Press, 1998), 94–109; Xiao Fenqi, *Wang Yiting*, 29–31; Siu, "Case of Wang Yiting," 44–46.

14. Chen Zuen 陳祖恩 & Li Huaxing 李華興, *Wang Yiting zhuan* 王一亭傳 (Shanghai: Shanghai cishu chubanshe, 2007).

15. Christian Henriot, *Shanghai Ladies of the Night: Prostitution and Society in 19th and 20th Century Shanghai* (Cambridge: Cambridge University Press, 1997); Bryna Goodman, "What Is in a Network? Local, Personal, and Public Loyalties in the Context of Changing Conceptions of the State and Social Welfare," in Dillon and Oi, eds., *At the Crossroads of Empires*, 155–78.

16. Hu Danian, *China and Albert Einstein: The Reception of the Physicist and His Theory in China, 1917-1979* (Cambridge, MA: Harvard University Press, 2005), 71–72. See also Chen Zuen and Li Huaxing, *Bailong shanren*, 187–91.

17. Joanna Handlin Smith, *The Art of Doing Good: Charity in Late Ming China* (Berkeley: University of California Press, 2009); Kathryn Edgerton-Tarpley, *Tears from Iron: Cultural Responses to Famine in Nineteenth-Century China* (Berkeley: University of California Press, 2008); Fuma Susumu 夫馬進, *Chūgoku zenkai zendōshi kenkyū* 中國善會善堂史研究 (Tokyo: Dōbōsha shuppan, 1997); Angela Ki Che Leung (Liang Qizi 梁其姿), *Shishan yu jiaohua: Ming Qing de cishan zuzhi* 施善與教化：明清的慈善組織 (Taipei: Lien-ching Publishing, 1997).

18. Shen, "Wang Yiting in the Social Networks," 53.

19. Paul R. Katz, "'It Is Difficult to be Indifferent to One's Roots': Taizhou Sojourners and Flood Relief during the 1920s," *Bulletin of the Institute of Modern History, Academia Sinica* 54 (2006): 1–58; Tao Shuimu 陶水木, "Beiyang zhengfu shiqi lüHu Zheshang de cishan huodong" 北洋政府時期旅滬浙商的慈善活動, *Zhejiang shehui kexue* 浙江社會科學 6 (2005): 177–83. See also He Kongjiao 何孔蛟, "Minguo Shanghai zui da de liuyanglei cishan jihou: Xin Puyutang" 民國上海最大的留養類慈善機構：新普育堂, *Wenshi yuekan* 文史月刊 8 (2006): 52–56; Chang Chien-Chiu 張建俅, "Jindai Zhongguo zhengfu yu shehui tuanti de tantao—Yi Zhongguo hongshizihui wei li (1919-1949)" 近代中國政府與社會團體的探討—以中國紅十字會為例 (1912-1949), *Bulletin of the Institute of Modern History, Academia Sinica* 47 (2004): 101–64.

20. See *Reports of Shanghai's Associations for Planning Rapid Relief for Those Provinces Stricken by Flood* (*Shanghai choumu gesheng shuizai jizhenhui gongzuo baogao* 上海籌募各省水災急賑會工作報告), Shanghai choumu gesheng shuizai jizhenhui 上海籌募各省水災急振會, ed. & comp., 1935. Preserved in the Library of the Institute of History, Shanghai Academy of Social Sciences (Shanghai shekeyuan Lishisuo tushuguan 上海社科院歷史所圖書館). We are deeply grateful to Ma Jun 馬軍 and the library staff for their assistance during a visit there in October 2006.

21. Along with Shi Xingzhi 施省之 (1865–1945), these four renowned Buddhist laymen were known as "Three Zhi's and One Ting" (*sanzhi yiting* 三之一亭). See Shen Kuiyi, "Art in Shanghai Capitalist Networks: a Case Study of Wang Yiting," *Chungguksa yongu* 中國史研究, 35 (2005): 281–322. For more on Guan, see Daniela Campo, "Guan Jiongzhi 關絅之 (1879–1942 and Elite Buddhist Networks in Republican Shanghai: Revolutionary Ideals and Traditional Values of Chinese Religious Modernity," manuscript.

22. See Wang Zongxiu 王中秀 et. al., eds., *Jinxiandai jinshi shuhuajia runli* 近現代金石書畫家潤例 (Shanghai: Shanghai shuhua chubanshe, 2004), 41; Wang Zhongxiu, *Wang Yiting nianpu changbian*, 12–13; Shen Wenquan, *Haishang qiren Wang Yiting*, 83–110, esp. 103–6.

23. Walter B. Davis, "For Fate, Faith, and Charity: Wang Yiting's Paintings of Street People," paper presented at the symposium The Challenge of Modernity: Chinese Painting in the Late Nineteenth and Early Twentieth Centuries, Guggenheim Museum, New York, May 22, 1998. We are profoundly grateful to Walter Davis for providing guidance and generously sharing valuable source materials. He has also prepared a pioneering monograph about Wang Yiting, including aspects of his religious life, entitled *Culture in Common: Wang Yiting's Art of Exchange with Japan* (Leiden: Brill, 2020).

24. "Wushuhui huanying xin huizhang" 武術會歡迎新會長, *Shibao*, August 28, 1920. For more on the importance of the concept of national essence in modern Chinese discourse on physical education, see Andrew D. Morris, *Marrow of the Nation: A History of Sport and Physical Culture in Republican China* (Berkeley: University of California Press, 2004); Yu Chien-ming 游鑑明, *Yundongchang neiwai: Jindai Huazhong nüzi tiyu (1895–1937)* 運動場內外：近代華東地區的女子體育 (1895–1937) (Taipei: Institute of Modern History, Academia Sinica, 2009).

25. *Taiji dawen* 太極答問 (Shanghai: Zhonghua shuju, 1929), 77. An outside instructor is someone formally recognized as a qualified teacher of Taiji boxing who is also allowed to teach these techniques and take on disciples of his own. We are very grateful to Liu Xun 劉迅 for sharing this information.

26. *Taiji quanshu* 太極拳術 (Shanghai: Zhonghua shuju, 1925), 1.

27. *Taiji dawen*, 39–40, 45–47.

28. Liu Xun, *Daoist Modern*.

29. Chen Zuen and Li Huaxing, *Bailong shanren*, 233–51.

30. Don Alvin Pittman, *Toward a Modern Chinese Buddhism: Taixu's Reforms* (Honolulu: University of Hawai'i Press, 2001); Gabriele Goldfuss, *Vers un bouddhisme du xxe siècle:*

Yang Wenhui (1837–1911), réformateur laïque et imprimeur (Paris: Collège de France, Institut des Hautes Études Chinoises, 2001); Tarocco, *Cultural Practices*; Chen Bing 陳兵 and Deng Zimei 鄧子美, *Ershi shiji Zhongguo Fojiao* 二十世紀中國佛教 (2000, reprint Taipei: Xiandai Chan chubanshe, 2003); Li Xiangping 李向平, *Jiushi yu jiuxin: Zhongguo jindai Fojiao fuxing sichao yanjiu* 救世與救心：中國近代佛教復興思潮研究 (Shanghai: Shanghai renmin chubanshe, 1993).

31. Chen Yongge 陳永革, *Fojiao honghua de xiandai zhuanxing: Minguo Zhejiang Fojiao yanjiu (1912–1949)* 佛教弘化的現代轉型: 民國浙江佛教研究 (1912–1949) (Beijing: Zongjiao wenhua chubanshe, 2003); Gao Zhennong 高振農, "Shanghai Fojiaoshi" 上海佛教史, in Ruan Renze 阮仁澤 and Gao Zhennong 高振農, eds., *Shanghai zongjiaoshi* 上海宗教史 (Shanghai: Shanghai renmin chubanshe, 1992), 27–349, esp. 170–88; You Youwei 游有維, *Shanghai jindai Fojiao jianshi* 上海近代佛教簡史 (Shanghai: Huadong shifan daxue chubanshe, 1988), 80–84, 96–105; Ge Zhuang, *Zongjiao yu jindai Shanghai shehui de bianqian*, 197.

32. Chen Zuen and Li Huaxing, *Bailong shanren*, 143–67.

33. Zhong Qiongning 鍾瓊寧, "Minchu Shanghai jushi Fojiao de fazhan (1912–1937)" 民初上海居士佛教的發展 (1912–1937), *Yuanguang Foxue xuebao* 圓光佛學學報 3 (1999): 155–90, esp. 183–84. See also Jessup, "Householder Elite"; Tarocco, *Cultural Practices*, 27–31.

34. Gao Zhennong, "Shanghai Fojiaoshi," 188–206; You Youwei, *Shanghai jindai Fojiao jianshi*, 87–94.

35. Gao Zhennong, "Minguo nianjian Shanghai Fojiaojie zhenzai huodong ziliao diandi" 民國年間上海佛教界賑災活動資料點滴, *Fayin* 法音 10 (1998): 28–31.

36. Chang Yen-ching 張晏菁, "Hongyang Jingtu: Lü Bicheng (1883–1943) nüjushi xueFo licheng de mengjing shuxie" 弘揚淨土：呂碧城（1883–1943）女居士學佛歷程的夢境書寫, *Xinshiji zongjiao yanjiu* 新世紀宗教研究 15.2 (2016): 123–52. See also Jia Jinhua, Kang Xiaofei, and Yao Ping, eds., *Gendering Chinese Religion: Subject, Identity, and Body* (Albany: State University of New York Press, 2014).

37. Scott, "Navigating the Sea of Scriptures"; Kiely, "Spreading the Dharma"; Tarocco, *Cultural Practices*, 16–20, 30, 46–49, 59–63.

38. Wu Ping, "Jindai Shanghai de Fojiao chuban jigou."

39. Qin Xitian 秦錫田 (1861-1940), "Wuxing Wang jun shilue" 吳興王君事略, in *Wang Yiting jushi shilue* 王一亭居士事略 (1938). This work is preserved in the Shanghai Municipal Archives. See also Wang Zhongxiu, *Wang Yiting nianpu changbian*, 660.

40. Zhang Jia, "Shanghai shenshang jushi de zongjiao shenghuo yu Fojiao xiandaihua zhuanxing," 19.

41. Mark Elvin, "The Gentry Democracy in Shanghai" (PhD diss., Cambridge University, 1969), 230–56.

42. For more on these events, see Taixu 太虛, "Zhuinian Wang Yiting zhangzhe" 追念王一亭長者, *Haichaoyin* 海潮音 19.11 (1938): 4–5. Wang's obituary may be found on page 57 of the same issue. See also Yu Lingbo, *Zhongguo jinxiandai Fojiao renwuzhi*, 346; Chen

Zuen and Li Huaxing, *Bailong shanren*, 143–67. For the cult of Guanyin, as well as her sacred site at Mount Putuo, see Yü Chün-fang, *Kuan-yin*.

43. The Three Refuges are the Buddha (*fo* 佛), the dharma (*fa* 法), and the *sangha* (*seng* 僧).

44. You Youwei, *Shanghai jindai Fojiao jianshi*, 85–87; Chen Bing and Deng Zimei, *Ershi shiji Zhongguo Fojiao*, 63, 155–56.

45. "Zuori Ailiyuan zhi zhenji shuizai hui" 昨日愛儷園之賑濟水災會, *Shibao*, September 6, 1917; "Shuhua choujuanhui dingqi kaicai" 書畫籌捐會訂期開彩, *Shibao*, April 23, 1918.

46. Betta, "Silas Aaron Hardoon." See also Tarocco, *Cultural Practices*, 30, 33–34; You Youwei, *Shanghai jindai Fojiao jianshi*, 84–85.

47. Xiao Fenqi, *Wang Yiting*, 135–40, 164, 166. See also Bailong shanren 白龍山人 (Wang Yiting), *Bailong shanren huace* 白龍山人畫冊 (Taipei: Taiwan Zhonghua shuju, 1968); Wang Zhen 王震 (Wang Yiting) and Wu Changshuo 吳昌碩, *Foxiang tishi* 佛像題詩, copy located in the Fu Sinian Library of the Institute of History and Philology, Academia Sinica.

48. Yü Chün-fang, *The Renewal of Buddhism in China: Chu-hung and the Late Ming Synthesis* (New York: Columbia University Press, 1981).

49. See especially the work of Raoul Birnbaum, including "Master Hongyi Looks Back" and "The Deathbed Image of Master Hongyi." See also Chen Xing 陳星, *Li Shutong shenbian de wenhua mingren* 李叔同身邊的文化名人 (Beijing: Zhonghua shuju, 2005), 204–6; Tarocco, *Cultural Practices*, 16–20, 71–75, 99–105.

50. Wang's participation in and leadership of the World Buddhist Householder Association are clearly documented in the *Reports of the Achievements of the World Buddhist Householder Association* (*Shijie Fojiao jushilin chengji baogaoshu* 世界佛教居士林成績報告書, Shanghai, 1933), which contains records of his writings and also his photograph. Reprinted in Huang Xianian 黃夏年, ed., *Minguo Fojiao qikan wenxian jicheng chubian* 民國佛教期刊文獻集成補編, volume 47 (Beijing: Zhongguo shudian, 2008). The drawback of such fame can be seen in a notice published by Wang in the January 16, 1931 issue of the *Foxue banyuekan* 佛學半月刊, which warns fellow Buddhists to beware of fraudulent individuals who had been impersonating him and using his name card (*mingpian* 名片).

51. Shi Yinshun 釋印順 (1906–2005), *Taixu dashi nianpu* 太虛大師年譜 (Taipei: Zhengwen chubanshe, 1988), 257–65, esp. 265; "Jiang zongsiling dui Wang Yiting de tanhua" 蔣總司令對王一亭居士的談話, *Haichaoyin* 10 (1928): 1; Shen Wenquan, *Haishang qiren Wang Yiting*, 126.

52. The Huzhou Native Place Association (Huzhou tongxianghui 湖州同鄉會) was subsequently established in 1906 with Wang as one of its founding members.

53. Liu Wenxing, "Jindai Hushe yu siyuan de hudong."

54. Taixu's views on the strengths and weaknesses of Chinese and Japanese Buddhist specialists are discussed in Tarocco, *Cultural Practices*, 37.

55. For more on these events, see Welch, *Buddhist Revival*, 40–45, 166–67; Pittman, *Toward a Modern Chinese Buddhism*, 109–10, 130–33; Chen Bing and Deng Zimei, *Ershi shiji Zhongguo Fojiao*, 59–69.

56. Zhong Qiongning, "Minchu Shanghai jushi Fojiao de fazhan."

57. See the photograph of Wang reciting the name of the Buddha in Xiao Fenqi, *Wang Yiting*, 132.

58. Wang's pursuit of meditation may also have resulted from business failures he and his sons suffered. See Liu Wenxing 劉文星, *Li Yujie xiansheng nianpu changbian* 李玉階先生年譜長編 (Nantou: Tiandijiao chubanshe, 2001), 85–88.

59. Wang Zhongxiu, *Wang Yiting nianpu changbian*, 714–15; Shen Wenquan, *Haishang qiren Wang Yiting*, 119.

60. *Shanxi Fojiao zazhi* 山西佛教雜誌, October 15, 1934, 515–16; *Hongfakan* 弘法刊 27 (1935): 351–52; *Hushengbao* 護生報 July 1, 1935, 213.

61. We are grateful to Lo Shih-chieh 羅士傑 for sharing this information with us.

62. For more on vegetarianism in Shanghai's urban life, see Tarocco, *Cultural Practices*, 31–39.

63. This is clearly documented in Siu, "Case of Wang Yiting," 68–82.

64. These events were reported in *Shenbao*. See "Guanyu Riben Dadizhen zhi zuoxun" 關於日本地震大災之昨訊, *Shenbao*, June 6, 1923; "Jiuji Riben dizhen dazai xiaoxi zhongzhong (fu tupian)" 救濟日本地震大災消息種種 (附圖片), *Shenbao*, September 7, 1923; "Zuori zhi jiuji Rizai xiaoxi" 昨日之救濟日災消息, *Shenbao*, September 8, 1923.

65. Wang Zhongxiu, *Wang Yiting nianpu changbian*, 289–300; Shen Wenquan, *Haishang qiren Wang Yiting*, 219–234; Chen Zuen and Li Huaxing, *Bailong shanren*, 211–29.

66. Wang Yiting houren chongqiao Zong-Ri 'Youhao zhi zhong' "王一亭後人重敲中日友好之鐘," *Zhongwen daobao* 中文導報 (September 2, 2012). See http://www.chubun.com/modules/article/view.article.php/142914/c127; http://blog.ifeng.com/article/29982396.html (accessed September 19, 2018).

67. *Kantō daishinsai* 関東大震災 (Tokyo: Zaidan hōjin Tōkyōto ireidō kyōkai, 2005), 9–13.

68. *Shibusawa Eiichi denki shiryō* 澀澤榮一傳記資料, 68 vols. (Tokyo: Shibusawa Eiichi Memorial Museum, 1955–71), 40:101. For more information, see also the Shibusawa Eiichi Memorial Museum website http://www.shibusawa.or.jp/english/index.html.

69. Chen Zuen and Li Huaxing, *Bailong shanren*, 235–42.

70. See especially Gregory Adam Scott, "The Buddhist Nationalism of Dai Jitao" 戴季陶, *Journal of Chinese Religions* 39 (2011): 55–81.

71. Katz, "Spirit-Writing," 282–304.

72. Fan Chun-wu, "Feiluan, xiuzhen yu banshan."

73. Chen Yingning 陳攖寧, "Tianxian Bicheng nüshi jiangtan jilu" 天仙碧城女史降壇紀錄, *Yangshan banyuekan* 揚善半月刊 1.3 (1933): 48–50. See also Liu Xun, *Daoist Modern*, 70–76, 300.

74. "Fuji de yuanli: Wu Tingfang boshi yi xinjiu xueshuo zhengming" 扶乩的原理：伍廷芳博士以新舊學說證明, *Xinminsheng* 新民聲 1.13 (1944): 27–28; Bao Tianxiao 包天笑, "Fuji zhi shu" 扶乩之術, in *Chuanyinglou huiyilu* 釧影樓回憶錄 (Taiyuan: Shanxi guji chubanshe, 1999), p. 84.

75. Xu Dishan 許地山, *Fuji mixin di yanjiu* 扶箕迷信底研究 (Changsha: Shangwu yinshuguan, 1941). A Christian, Xu was born in Tainan but fled with his family to the mainland after the Japanese assumed control of Taiwan in 1895.

76. "Fuji yu diexian" 扶乩與碟仙, *Taipingyang zhoubao* 太平洋周報 1.23 (1942): 299–301.

77. "Sun Zhongshan jiangjiji" 孫中山降乩記, *Shenbao*, October 2, 1926. See also "Yizhou: Xuexiao dashi•Geren xinwen: Fuji yishi—Mou yaoren qing shenxian zhan guojia dashi" 一周:學校大事•個人新聞：扶乩異事—某要人請神仙占家國大事, *Qinghua shuqi zhoukan* 清華暑期週刊 5 (1934): 287–88.

78. "Yu Jinhe fuji ji" 余晉龢扶乩記, *Dadi zhoubao* 大地週報 15 (1946): 9.

79. Chen Weiming 陳微明, "Wang'er Banwu xingshu" 亡兒邦武行述, *Jueyouqing* 覺有情 123–24 (1944): 10–11; Chen Weiming, "Bangwu jiyu" 邦武乩語, *Jueyouqing* 133–34 (1945): 2.

80. Zhou Yumin 周育民, "Minguo shiqi yige wentan juzi jibixia de lingjie" 民國時期一個文壇巨子乩筆下的靈界, *Minjian zongjiao* 民間宗教 1 (1995): 37–55.

81. "Huang Yanpei mixin fuluan" 黃炎培迷信扶鸞, *Shishi xinwen* 時事新聞 8 (1948): 10. See also "Siren hui shuohua ma? Fuji Taishang guiling suo xie de zi" 死人會說話嗎?扶乩臺上鬼靈所寫的字, *Shizhao yuebao* 時兆月報 23.3 (1928): 11.

82. "Dashijie dachang Fojiao" 大世界大昌佛教, *Shenbao*, May 25, 1926; "Jigong Tang zhengqiu huiyuan xiaoxi" 濟公堂徵求會員消息, *Shenbao*, June 10, 1926. See also "Fuluan zatan" 扶鸞雜談, *Shehui zhi hua* 社會之花 1.13 (1924): 1–5.

83. Goossaert and Palmer, *Religious Question*, 93, 98, 212, 215; DuBois, *Sacred Village*, 106–26.

84. Katz, "Spirit-Writing", 304–15.

85. Tao Shuimu, "Beiyang zhengfu shiqi lüHu Zheshang de cishan huodong."

86. For more on the history of Jigong and his cult, see Shahar, *Crazy Ji.*

87. Wang Chien-ch'uan 王見川, "Qingmo Minchu Zhongguo de Jigong xinyang yu fuji tuanti: Jian tan Zhongguo Jishenghui de youlai" 清末民初中國的濟公信仰與扶乩團體：兼談中國濟生會的由來, *Minsu quyi* 162 (2008): 139–69; Wang Chien-ch'uan, "Jindai Zhongguo de fuji, cishan yu 'mixin.'" See also Zhang Jia, "Shanghai shenshang jushi de zongjiao shenghuo yu Fojiao xiandaihua zhuanxing," 179–95; Zhang Jia 張佳, "Zhongguo Jishenghui suojian jindai shenshang jushi zhi Jigong xinyang" 中國濟生會所見近代紳商居士之濟公信仰," *Zongjiaoxue yanjiu* 宗教學研究 1 (2015): 105–14. Additional material on Wang Yiting's involvement in the association may be found in Wang Zhongxiu, *Wang Yiting nianpu changbian*, 190, 198, 204; Fan Chun-wu, "Jinxiandai Zhongguo Fojiao yu mixin," 290; Yu Lingbo, *Zhongguo jinxiandai Fojiao renwuzhi*, 347–49; Yau Chi-on. *Shan yu ren tong*, 155–60.

88. See, for example, "Faqi yanju zhuzhen" 發起演劇助賑, *Shenbao*, October 27, 1917; "Jishenghui yu fangzhenyuan wanglai diangao" 濟生會與放賑員往來電稿, *Shenbao*, May 22, 1918; "Jishenghui huikuan zhenji Taian shuizai" 濟生會匯款賑濟泰安水災, *Shenbao*, April 5, 1919; "Jishenghui zuzhi jiuhudui" 濟生會組織救護隊, *Shenbao*, May 19, 1919; "Taishu shuizai qizhen wanglaidian" 台屬水災乞賑往來電, *Shenbao*, July 27, 1920; "Jishenghui chouban Taizhen xiaoxi" 濟生會籌辦台賑消息, *Shenbao*, August 24, 1920; "Jishenghui fashou pingjia mantou yuwen" 濟生會發售平價饅頭餘聞, *Shenbao*, September 3, 1920; "Zhongguo Jishenghui zhenzai shoujiang" 中國濟生會賑災受獎, *Shenbao*, November 9, 1922; "Jishenghui yi gong dai zhen jianzhu Anhui shuiti" 濟生會以工代賑建築安徽水堤, *Shenbao*, February 2, 1928. See also Zhang Jia, "Shanghai shenshang jushi de zongjiao shenghuo yu Fojiao xiandaihua zhuanxing", 195–213.

89. Hupao cuanzhichu 虎跑纂志處, ed., *Hupao Fozu zangdianzhi* 虎跑佛祖藏殿志 (1921), in Bai Huawen 白化文 et al., eds., *Zhongguo Fosizhi congkan* 中國佛寺志叢刊, ser. 1, vol. 72 (Yangzhou: Jiangsu guji chubanshe, 1996), 15–16, 81–84, 341–42; Shi Anren 釋安仁, *Huyin chanyuan jishi* 湖隱禪院記事 (1921), in Bai Huawen et al., eds., *Zhongguo Fosizhi congkan xubian*, vol. 7 (Yangzhou: Jiangsu guji chubanshe, 2001), 5, 41–44. See also "Jiyunxuan zashi" 集雲軒雜詩, *Shenbao*, October 20, 1922; "Jigong Foyuan zhi jixu choujian" 濟公佛院之繼續籌建, *Shenbao*, June 1, 1923; "Zuori huanying Banchan" 昨日歡迎班禪, *Shenbao*, May 28, 1934.

90. Wang Chien-ch'uan, "Qingmo Minchu Zhongguo de Jigong xinyang yu fuji tuanti," 155–59.

91. Thomas David DuBois, "The Salvation of Religion? Public Charity and the New Religions of the Early Republic," *Minsu quyi* 172 (2011): 73–126; Wang Chien-ch'uan, "Minguo shiqi Daoyuan Hongwanzihui zhenzai jilu" 民國時期道院紅卍字會賑災記錄, *Minjian zongjiao* 民間宗教 1 (1995): 217–24.

92. *Taiwan Nichi-nichi shimpō* 臺灣日日新報, May 25, 1918.

93. Wang Chien-ch'uan, "Qingmo Minchu Zhongguo de Jigong xinyang yu fuji tuanti," 159. The character *jue* 覺 in Jueqi derives from the association's lineage poem.

94. Chen Boxi 陳伯熙, ed. and comp., *Shanghai yishi daguan* 上海軼事大觀 (1924), reprint Shanghai: Shanghai shudian chubanshe, 2000), 371. See also Hupao cuanzhichu, *Hupao Fozu zangdianzhi*, 318–19; Wang Chien-ch'uan, "Qingmo Minchu Zhongguo de Jigong xinyang yu fuji tuanti," 160–61.

95. Wang Chien-ch'uan, "Jindai Zhongguo de fuji, cishan yu 'mixin.'"

96. Shanghai Jiyunxuan 上海集雲軒, ed., *Jishi tayuanzhi* 濟師塔院志 (1939), in Bai Huawen 白化文 et al., eds., *Zhongguo Fosizhi congkan xubian* 中國佛寺志叢刊續編, vol. 6 (Yangzhou: Jiangsu guji chubanshe, 2001), 9, 11–12, 15–18, 45–47.

97. Shi Anren, *Huyin chanyuan jishi*, 71.

98. The text in question may be found in Xu Shangshu 許尚樞, *Tiantaishan Jigong huofo* 天台山濟公活佛 (Beijing: Guoji wenhua chuban gongsi, 1997). Although it was destroyed during the Cultural Revolution, this temple was rebuilt during the late 1980s, with construction completed in 1990.

99. Meihua guanzhu 梅花館主 (Wang Yiting), "Xin Wutai paiyan Jigong huofo zhi qianyin houguo" 新舞台排演濟公活佛之前因後果, *Xiju yuekan* 戲劇月刊 2.5 (1929): 4–5. We are deeply grateful to Vincent Durand-Dastès for telling us about these sources during personal communications on October 3–6, 2011.

100. This painting is reproduced in Bailong shanren, *Bailong shanren huace*.

101. This was also the case with another prominent member of the Rescuing Life Association, Xu Qianlin 徐乾麟 (b. 1863). Data in the Shanghai Municipal Archives indicate that he was involved in a wide range of religious organizations, including redemptive societies.

102. Another important leader was Li Yujie 李玉階 (1900–1994). Also a Perfected Sovereign of the Tiandejiao 天德教, he later founded the Tiandijiao 天帝教 in 1979 in Taiwan. See Ownby, "Politics of Redemption," as well as the discussion of Li in chapter 5.

103. Liu Wenxing, *Li Yujie xiansheng nianpu*, 85.

104. For more on this group's activities in Shanghai during the Sino-Japanese War, which expanded to include both Christians and Communists, see Nara Dillon, "The Politics of Philanthropy: The Balance between Public and Private Refugee Relief in Shanghai, 1932–1949," in Nara Dillon and Jean C. Oi, eds., *At the Crossroads of Empires: Middlemen, Social Networks, and State-Building in Republican China* (Stanford, CA: Stanford University Press, 2008), 179–205.

105. Duara, *Sovereignty and Authenticity*, 112; Sun Yusheng 孫語聖, "Shijie Hongwanzihui Zhonghua zonghui yu Minguo shiqi de shehui jiuji" 世界紅卍字會中華總會與民國時期的社會救濟, *Anda shixue* 安大史學 2 (2004): 192–200; Wang Chien-ch'uan, "Minguo shiqi Daoyuan Hongwanzihui zhenzai jilu."

106. Goossaert, *Taoists of Peking*, 308–19. See also Mori Yuria, "Identity and Lineage: The *Taiyi jinhua zongzhi* and the Spirit-Writing Cult to Patriarch Lü in Qing China," in Livia Kohn and Harold D. Roth, eds., *Daoist Identity: History, Lineage, and Ritual* (Honolulu: University of Hawai'i Press, 2002), 165–84.

107. Shiga Ichiko, "The Manifestations of Lüzu in Modern Guangdong and Hong Kong: The Rise of Spirit-Writing Cults," in Livia Kohn and Harold D. Roth, eds., *Daoist Identity: History, Lineage, and Ritual* (Honolulu: University of Hawai'i Press, 2002), 185–209; Lai Chi-tim [黎志添], "Hong Kong Daoism: A Study of Daoist Altars and Lü Dongbin Cults," *Social Compass* 50.4 (2003): 459–70. See also Graeme Lang and Lars Ragvald, *The Rise of a Refugee God: Hong Kong's Wong Tai Sin* (Hong Kong: Oxford University Press, 1993).

108. Vincent Goossaert, "The Quanzhen Clergy, 1700–1950," in John Lagerwey, ed., *Religion and Chinese Society: The Transformation of a Field* (Paris: École Française d'Extrême Orient, 2004), 699–771. See also Qing Xitai 卿希泰, ed., *Zhongguo Daojiaoshi* 中國道教史, vol. 4 (Chengdu: Sichuan renmin chubanshe, 1995), 298–304.

109. Monica Esposito, "Daoism in the Qing," in Livia Kohn, ed., *Daoism Handbook* (Leiden: Brill, 2000), 623–58, esp. 645–50; Monica Esposito, "Longmen 龍門 Taoism in Qing China: Doctrinal Ideal and Local Reality," *Journal of Chinese Religions* 29 (2001): 191–231; Monica Esposito, "The Discovery of Jiang Yuanting's *Daozang jiyao* in Jiangnan: A Presentation of the Daoist Canon of the Qing Dynasty," in Mugitani Kunio 麥谷邦夫,

ed., *Kōnan dōkyō no kenkyū* 江南道教の研究 (Kyoto: Jinbun Kagaku Kenkyūjo, 2007), 79–110; Cao Benye 曹本冶 and Xu Hongtu 徐宏圖, *Wenzhou Pingyang Dongyueguan Daojiao yinyue yanjiu* 溫州平陽東嶽觀道教音樂研究 (Taipei: Xinwenfeng, 2000), 18–20, 31–34, 42; Chen Yaoting 陳耀庭, "Shanghai Daojiaoshi" 上海道教史, in Ruan Renze 阮仁澤 and Gao Zhennong 高振農, eds., *Shanghai zongjiaoshi* 上海宗教史 (Shanghai: Shanghai renmin chubanshe, 1992), 353–438, esp. 400, 413–28.

110. *Longmen zhengzong Jueyun benzhi daotong xinchuan* 龍門正宗覺雲本支道統薪傳, in *Zangwai Daoshu* 藏外道書 (Chengdu: Bashu shushe, 1994), volume 31, 438–45. See also Wu Yakui, *Jiangnan Quanzhen Daojiao*, 256–58.

111. Gao Wansang 高萬桑 (Vincent Goossaert), "Jingaishan wangluo: Jinxiandai Jiangnan de Quanzhen jushi zuzhi" 金蓋山網絡：近現代江南的全真居士組織," in Zhao Weidong 趙衞東, ed., *Quanzhendao yanjiu* 全真道研究, vol. 1 (Jinan: Qilu shushe, 2011), 319–39; Vincent Goossaert, "The Jingaishan Network in Modern Jiangnan," in Liu Xun and Goossaert, eds., *Daoism in Modern China: Clerics and Temples in Urban Transformations, 1860–Present* (London: Routledge, 2021); Wang Zongyao 王宗耀, *Huzhou Jin'gaishan Gu Meihuaguan zhi* 湖州金蓋山古梅花觀志 (Huzhou: Huzhou Daojiao xilie neibu congshu, 2003); Wang Zongyu 王宗昱, "Wuxing Quanzhendao shiliao" 吳興全真道史料, in Poul Andersen and Florian Reiter, eds., *Scriptures, Schools, and Forms of Practice in Daoism: A Berlin Symposium* (Wiesbaden: Harrassowitz, 2005), 215–32; Zhang Jia, "Shanghai shenshang jushi de zongjiao shenghuo yu Fojiao xiandaihua zhuanxing," 214, 225–27.

112. *Daotong yuanliuzhi* 道統源流志, Yan Heyi 嚴合怡, ed., 2 vols. (Wuxi: Zhonghua yinshuaju, 1929), 2:30.

113. Wang Lianyou 王蓮友, ed., *Chongjian Jinling Yuxuguan jishi zhengxinlu* 重建金陵玉虛觀紀事徵信錄 (1936), in *Zhongguo Daoguanzhi congkan xubian* 中國道觀志叢刊續編, vol. 15 (Yangzhou: Guangling shushe, 2004), 3–4, 17.

114. Katz, "Illuminating Goodness."

115. Yau Chi-on, *Shan yu ren tong*, 160–64, 332–33.

116. Chen Chuanxi 陳傳席, "Ping xiandai mingjia yu dajia. Xu—Wang Yiting" 評現代名家與大家・續 — 王一亭, *Guohuajia* 國畫家 3 (2006): 7–9, esp. 9.

117. Tarocco, *Cultural Practices*, 34–35.

118. Zhang Jia, "Shanghai shenshang jushi de zongjiao shenghuo yu Fojiao xiandaihua zhuanxing", 28–29.

119. Tsou Mingteh, "Christian Missionary as Confucian Intellectual: Gilbert Reid (1857–1927) and the Reform Movement in the Late Qing," in Daniel H. Bays, ed., *Christianity in China: From the Eighteenth Century to the Present* (Stanford, CA: Stanford University Press, 1996), 73–90; Hu Suping 胡素萍, "Li Jiabai yu Shangxian Tang—Qingmo Minchu zai Hua chuanjiaoshi huodong ge'an yanjiu" 李佳白與尚賢堂—清末民初在華傳教士活動個案研究, *Shixue yuekan* 史學月刊 9 (2005): 57–63; David A. Palmer, "Chinese Redemptive Societies: Historical Phenomenon or Sociological Category?" *Minsu quyi*, 172 (2011): 21–72.

120. Sun Guangyong 孫廣勇, "Rongru yu chuanbo—Jianlun Li Jiabai ji qi Shangxian Tang de wenhua jiaoliu huodong" 融入與傳播—簡論李佳白及其尚賢堂的文化交流活動, *Shehui kexue zhanxian* 社會科學戰線 6 (2005): 299–301; Yao Minquan 姚民權 and Zhang Letian 張樂天, "Shanghai Jidujiao shi" 上海基督教史, in Ruan Renze and Gao Zhennong, eds., *Shanghai zongjiaoshi* (Shanghai: Shanghai renmin chubanshe, 1992), 787–1019, esp. 847–50; Tarocco, *Cultural Practices*, 38.

121. Our heartfelt thanks go to Professor Shiba Yoshinobu 斯波義信 and the library staff for their help, as well as Huang Tzu-chin 黄自進, Matsushige Mitsuhiro 松重充浩, and Tatara Keisuke 多多良圭介 for making the arrangements for us to visit.

122. This couplet has been preserved in the Shanghai History Museum. The Chinese original reads as follows: 卅載訂深交，聯宗教為大同，欽諛道，不偏守墨。一朝感永訣，留典成陳跡，憾登堂，空想尚賢.

123. Cohen, *History in Three Keys*, xii–xiii, 59–68.

124. Michael Saler, "Modernity and Enchantment: A Historiographic Review," *American Historical Review* 111.3 (June 2006): 692–716.

Conclusion

1. James Flath and Norman Smith, eds., *Beyond Suffering: Recounting War in Modern China* (Vancouver: University of British Columbia Press, 2011); Christian Henriot and Wen-hsin Yeh, eds., *In the Shadow of the Rising Sun: Shanghai under Japanese Occupation* (Cambridge: Cambridge University Press, 2004).

2. Thomas David DuBois, *Empire and the Meaning of Religion in Northeast Asia: Manchuria, 1900–1945* (Cambridge: Cambridge University Press, 2016).

3. Xue Yu. *Buddhism, War, and Nationalism.*

4. On "sectarian" groups in Jiangnan during this period, see Shao Yong 邵雍, *Jindai Jiangnan mimi shehui* 近代江南秘密社會 (Shanghai: Shanghai renmin chubanshe, 2013).

5. Steve A. Smith, "Local Cadres Confront the Supernatural: The Politics of Holy Water (*Shenshui* 神水) in the PRC, 1949–1966," in Julia Strauss, ed., *The History of the PRC (1949–1976)* (Cambridge: Cambridge University Press, 2007), 145–68.

6. Goossaert and Palmer, *Religious Question*, 140–65. See also Steve A. Smith, "Talking Toads and Chinless Ghosts: The Politics of 'Superstitious' Rumors in the People's Republic of China," *American Historical Review* 111.2 (2006): 405–27.

7. Kang Bao 康豹, "Jindai Zhongguo simiao yundong de kongjian tezheng — Yi Jiangnan dushi wei zhongxin 近代中國寺廟破壞運動的空間特徵 — 以江南都市為重心, *Bulletin of the Institute of Modern History, Academia Sinica*, 95 (2017): 1–37.

8. Adam Chau, "Expanding the Space of Popular Religion: Local Temple Activism and the Politics of Legitimation in Contemporary Rural China," in Ashiwa and Wank, *Making Religion, Making the State*, 211–40; Kenneth Dean, "Further Partings of the Way: The Chinese State and Daoist Ritual Traditions in Contemporary China," in Ashiwa and Wank, *Making Religion, Making the State*, 179–210; Mayfair Mei-hui Yang, "Shamanism

and Spirit Possession in Chinese Modernity: Some Preliminary Reflections on a Gendered Religiosity of the Body," *Review of Religion and Chinese Society* 2.1 (2015): 51–86.

9. Ian Johnson, *The Souls of China: The Return of Religion after Mao* (London: Penguin, 2017).

10. Philip Clart, "Conceptualizations of 'Popular Religion' in Recent Research in the People's Republic of China," in Wang Chien-chuan 王見川, Li Shih-wei 李世偉, and Hung Ying-fa 洪瑩發, eds., *Yanjiu xinshiye: Mazu yu Huaren minjian xinyang guoji yantaohui lunwenji* 研究新視界：媽祖與華人民間信仰國際研討會論文集 (Taipei: BoyYoung, 2014), 391–412. See also Sun Yanfei, "Religions in Sociopolitical Context: The Reconfiguration of Religious Ecology in Post-Mao China" (PhD diss., University of Chicago, 2010).

11. Sébastien Billioud and Joël Thoraval, *The Sage and the People: The Confucian Revival in China* (Oxford: Oxford University Press, 2015); Sébastien Billioud, "The Hidden Tradition: Confucianism and Its Metamorphoses in Modern and Contemporary China," in Vincent Goossaert, Jan Kiely and John Lagerwey, eds., *Modern Chinese Religion*, Vol. 2: *1850–2015* (Leiden: Brill, 2016), 767–805. See also Sébastien Billioud, "Confucian Revival and the Emergence of *Jiaohua* Organizations: A Case Study of the Yidan Xuetang," *Modern China* 37.3 (2011): 286–314; Anna Sun, "The Revival of Confucian Rites in Contemporary China," in Yang Fenggang and Joseph Tamney, eds., *Confucianism and Spiritual Traditions in Modern China and Beyond* (Leiden: Brill, 2012), 309–28.

12. For more on this phenomenon, see Tim Oakes and Donald S. Sutton, eds., *Faiths on Display: Religion, Tourism, and the Chinese State* (Lanham, MD: Rowman and Littlefield, 2010).

13. Louisa Schein, *Minority Rules: The Miao and the Feminine in China's Cultural Politics* (Durham, NC: Duke University Press, 2000); Sylvie Beaud, "Masques en parade: Étude d'une identité à la jonction du politique et du rituel—l'exemple du Théâtre de Guan Suo 關索 (Yunnan, Chine)" (PhD diss., Université de Paris-Ouest, Nanterre, 2012); Sylvie Beaud, "Being Han in a Multi-ethnic Region of the People's Republic of China," *Asian Ethnicity* 15.4 (2014): 535–51; Kao Ya-ning, "Religious Revival among the Zhuang People in China: Practicing 'Superstition' and Standardizing a Zhuang Religion," *Journal of Current Chinese Affairs* 43.2 (2014): 107–44.

14. Paul R. Katz, "Religion and the State in Postwar Taiwan," *China Quarterly* 174 (2003): 395–412; Shih Fang-Long, "From Regulation and Rationalisation to Production: Government Policy on Religion in Taiwan," in Dafydd Fell, Henning Klöter, and Chang Bi-Yu, eds., *What Has Changed? Taiwan before and after the Change in Ruling Parties* (Wiesbaden: Harrassowitz, 2006), 265–83. Richard Madsen, *Democracy's Dharma: Religious Renaissance and Political Development in Taiwan* (Berkeley: University of California Press, 2007); Kuo Cheng-tian, *Religion and Democracy in Taiwan* (Albany: State University of New York Press, 2008).

15. See, for example, Lu Mei-huan 呂玫鍰, "Yichanhua guocheng zhong de Mazu jinxiang: Yishi bianqian yu difang fuquan kaocha" 遺產化過程中的媽祖進香：儀式變遷與地方賦權的考察, *Minsu quyi* 192 (2016): 47–96; Hsu Yu-tsuen 徐雨村, "Minsu ji

youguan wenwu' denglu zhiding yu difang shijian: Yi 'Yunlin Liufangma guolu' wei li" 「民俗及有關文物」登錄指定與地方實踐：以「雲林六房媽過爐」為例, *Minsu quyi* 192 (2016): 221–65. See also Lin Wei-Ping 林瑋嬪, "Weihe yao jianmiao? Cong miaoyu Xingjian de wuzhihua guocheng tantao Mazu shequn zaizao" 為何要建廟？從廟宇興建的物質化過程探討馬祖社群再造, *Taiwan shehui jikan* 台灣社會研究季刊 92 (2013): 1–33; Chang Hsun 張珣, "Cong minjian xinyang yu difang chanye kan guojia yu difang de guanxi: Yi Xingang Fengtian Gong wei li" 從民間信仰與地方產業看國家與地方的關係：以新港奉天宮為例, in Chang Hsun, ed., *Hanren minzhong zongjiao yanjiu: Tianye yu lilun de jiehe* 漢人民眾宗教研究：田野與理論的結合 (Nankang: Academia Sinica, 2013), 115–60.

16. Paul R. Katz and Murray Rubinstein, eds., *Religion and the Formation of Taiwanese Identities* (New York: Palgrave Macmillan, 2003).

17. D. J W. Hatfield, *Taiwanese Pilgrimage to China: Ritual, Complicity, Community* (New York: Palgrave Macmillan, 2010).

18. Gareth Fisher, "Morality Books and the Revival of Lay Buddhism in China," in Adam Yuet Chau, ed., *Religion in Contemporary China: Revitalization and Innovation* (London: Routledge, 2011), 53–80; Stuart Chandler, *Establishing a Pure Land on Earth* (Honolulu: University of Hawaiʻi Press, 2004); Philip Clart, "Merit beyond Measure: Notes on the Moral (and Real) Economy of Religious Publishing in Taiwan," in Philip Clart and Paul Crowe, eds., *The People and the Dao: New Studies of Chinese Religions in Honour of Prof. Daniel L. Overmyer* (Sankt Augustin: Institut Monumenta Serica, 2009), 127–42. See also Clart, "New Technologies and the Production of Religious Texts in China, 19th–21st Century."

19. Philip Clart, "Mediums and the New Media: The Impact of Electronic Publishing on Temple and Moral Economies in Taiwanese Popular Religion," *Journal of Sinological Studies* 3 (2012): 127–41; Franceca Tarocco, "Pluralism and Its Discontents: Buddhism and Proselytizing in Modern China," in Juliana Finucane and R. Michael Feener, eds., *Proselytizing and the Limits of Religious Pluralism in Contemporary Asia* (Singapore: Springer, 2014), 237–54. See also Stephen D. O'Leary, "Utopian and Dystopian Possibilities of Networked Religion in the New Millennium," in Morten T. Højsgarard and Margit Warburg, eds., *Religion and Cyberspace* (London: Routledge, 2009), 38–49; Lorne L. Dawson, "The Mediation of Religious Experience in Cyberspace," in Morten T. Højsgarard and Margit Warburg, eds., *Religion and Cyberspace* (London: Routledge, 2009), 15–37.

20. Chau, *Religion in Contemporary China*, 19–20. See also Thomas Borchert, "Worry for the Dai Nation: Sipsongpannā, Chinese Modernity, and the Problems of Buddhist Modernism," *Journal of Asian Studies* 67.1 (2008): 107–42; Sara L. M. Davis, *Song and Silence: Ethnic Revival on China's Southwest Borders* (New York: Columbia University Press, 2005).

21. Chandler, *Establishing a Pure Land*; Clart, "Sacred Texts."

22. Goossaert and Palmer, *Religious Question*, 275–77.

23. Julian Pas, "Religious Life in Present Day Taiwan: A Field Observation Report, 1994–1995," *Journal of Chinese Religions* 24 (1996): 131–58; Sung Kuang-yu 宋光宇, "Shentan de xingcheng: Gaoxiongshi shentan diaocha ziliao de chubu fenxi" 神壇的形成：高雄市神壇調查資料的初步分析, in *Simiao yi minjian wenhua yantaohui lunwenji* 寺廟與民間文化研討會論文集 (Taipei: Committee for Cultural Construction, 1995), 97–128; Dai Sike 戴思客 (Lawrence Scott Davis), "Yu yu nü: Shitan jitong xiucixue" 語與女：試探乩童修辭學, *Si yu yan* 思與言 35.2 (1994): 267–312; Tsai Pei-ju 蔡佩如, *Chuansuo tianren zhi ji de nüren: Nüjitong de xingbie tezhi yu shenti yihan* 穿梭天人之際的女人：女童乩的性別特質與身體意涵 (Taipei: Tangshan Publishing, 2001).

24. Chao Shin-yi, "A *Danggi* [童乩] Temple in Taipei: Spirit-Mediums in Modern Urban Taiwan," *Asia Major, 3rd ser.,* 15.2 (2002): 129–56; Lin Wei-Ping, *Materializing Magic Power: Chinese Popular Religion in Villages and Cities* (Cambridge, MA: Harvard University Press, 2015). Similar phenomena have contributed to Christianity's growing popularity in urban China. See Cao Nanlai, *Constructing China's Jerusalem: Christians, Power, and Place in Contemporary Wenzhou* (Stanford, CA: Stanford University Press, 2011).

25. Goossaert and Palmer, *Religious Question*, 281–86.

26. Kang Xiaofei, "Women and the Religious Question," 548. See also Kang Xiaofei, "Rural Women, Old Age, and Temple Work: A Case from Northwestern Sichuan," *China Perspectives* 4 (2009): 42–53; Ellen Cline, "Female Spirit Mediums and Religious Authority in Contemporary Southeastern China," *Modern China* 36.5 (2010): 520–55; Maria Jaschok and Shui Jingjun, *Women, Religion, and Space in China: Islamic Mosques and Daoist Temples, Catholic Convents and Chinese Virgins* (New York: Routledge, 2011); Lee Anru, "Women of the Sisters' Hall: Religion and the Making of Women's Alternative Space in Taiwan's Economic Restructuring," *Gender, Place, and Culture: A Journal of Feminist Geography* 15.4 (2008): 373–93; Jessie G. Lutz, ed., *Pioneering Chinese Christian Women: Gender, Christianity, and Social Mobility* (Bethlehem, PA: Lehigh University Press, 2010).

27. Kenneth Dean, "The Return Visits of Overseas Chinese to Ancestral Villages in Putian, Fujian," in Tim Oakes and Donald S. Sutton, eds., *Faiths on Display: Religion, Tourism, and the Chinese State,* 235–63 (Lanham, MD: Rowman and Littlefield, 2010). See also the work of Robert P. Weller, including "Global Religious Changes and Civil Life in Two Chinese Societies: A Comparison of Jiangsu and Taiwan," *Review of Faith and International Affairs* 13.2 (2015): 13–24; Weller, "Taiwan and Global Religious Trends."

28. Robert P. Weller, "Chinese Cosmology and the Environment," in David A. Palmer, Glenn Shive, and Philip L. Wickeri, eds., *Chinese Religious Life* (Oxford: Oxford University Press, 2011), 124–38.

29. Goossaert and Palmer, *Religious Question*, 403.

30. Tsai Yen-zen, ed., *Religious Experience in Contemporary Taiwan and China* (Taipei: Chengchi University Press, 2013).

31. Yao Xinzhong and Paul Badham, *Religious Experience in Contemporary China* (Cardiff: University of Wales Press, 2007).

32. Goossaert and Palmer, *Religious Question*, 274.

33. Kenneth Dean and Zheng Zhenman [鄭振滿], *Ritual Alliances of the Putian Plain*, vol. 1: *Historical Introduction to the Return of the Gods*; vol. 2: *A Survey of the Village Temples and Ritual Activities* (Leiden: Brill, 2010).

34. Katz, "Religious Life."

35. See, for example, Ji Zhe, "Territoires migratoires et lieux religieux: Cartes des religions des Chinois en Île-de-France," in Lucine Endelstein, Sébastien Fath, and Séverine Mathieu, eds., *Dieu change en ville: Religion, espace, immigration* (Paris: L'Harmattan, 2010), 137–55; Pan Junliang, "L'évolution de l'organisation des Églises Wenzhou à Paris: Renégocier le pouvoir et l'autorité," in Yannick Fer and Gwendoline Malogne-Fer, eds., *Le protestantisme à Paris: Diversité et recompositions contemporaines* (Geneva: Labor and Fides, 2017), 283–304.

BIBLIOGRAPHY

Ai Ping 艾萍. "Minguo jinzhi yingshen saihui lunxi—Yi Shanghai wei ge'an" 民
國禁止迎神賽會論析—以上海為個案. *Jingsu shehui kexue* 江蘇社會科學
5 (2010): 216–21.

Asad, Talal. *Formations of the Secular: Christianity, Islam, Modernity*. Stanford,
CA: Stanford University Press, 2003.

Ashiwa Yoshiko and David Wank, eds. *Making Religion, Making the State: The
Politics of Religion in Contemporary China*. Stanford, CA: Stanford University
Press, 2009.

Bai Ruosi 白若思 (Rostislav Berezkin). "You 1900–1937 nianjian *Huaming
baojuan* de kanke kan Zhongguo ershi shiji chu chuban wenhua yu minjian
xinyang ji suwenxue zhi guanxi" 由1900–1937年間《花名寶卷》的刊刻看
中國二十世紀初出版文化與民間信仰及俗文學之關係. In Kang Bao and
Gao Wansang, *Gaibian Zhongguo zongjiao de wushinian*, 169–92.

Bailey, Paul J. *Gender and Education in China: Gender Discourses and Women's
Schooling in the Early Twentieth Century*. London: Routledge, 2007.

Bailong shanren 白龍山人 (Wang Yiting). *Bailong shanren huace* 白龍山人畫冊.
Taipei: Taiwan Zhonghua shuju, 1968.

Bao Tianxiao 包天笑. "Fuji zhi shu" 扶乩之術. In *Chuanyinglou huiyilu* 釧影樓
回憶錄, 84. Taiyuan: Shanxi guji chubanshe, 1999.

Barmé, Geremie R. *An Artistic Exile: A Life of Feng Zikai (1898–1975)*. Berkeley:
University of California Press, 2002.

Barrett, T. H. *The Woman Who Invented Printing*. New Haven, CT: Yale
University Press, 2008.

Bays, Daniel H., ed. *Christianity in China: From the Eighteenth Century to the
Present*. Stanford, CA: Stanford University Press, 1996.

Bays, Daniel H. *A New History of Christianity in China*. West Sussex: Wiley-
Blackwell, 2012.

Bays, Daniel H., and Ellen Widmer, eds. *China's Christian Colleges: Cross-Cultural Connections, 1900–1950*. Stanford, CA: Stanford University Press, 2009.

Beaud, Sylvie. "Being Han in a Multi-ethnic Region of the People's Republic of China." *Asian Ethnicity* 15.4 (2014): 535–51.

Beaud, Sylvie. "Masques en parade: Étude d'une identité à la jonction du politique et du rituel—l'exemple du Théâtre de Guan Suo 關索 (Yunnan, Chine)." PhD diss., Université de Paris-Ouest, Nanterre, 2012.

Bell, Catherine M. "'A Precious Raft to Save the World': The Interaction of Scriptural Traditions and Printing in a Chinese Morality Book." *Late Imperial China* 17.1 (1996): 158–200.

Bennett, Adrian A. *Missionary Journalist in China: Young J. Allen and His Magazines, 1860–1883*. Athens: University of Georgia Press, 1983.

Berezkin, Rostislav. "Lithographic Printing and the Development of the *Baojuan* 寶卷 Genre in Shanghai in the 1900–1920s: On the Question of the Interaction between Print Technology and Popular Literature in China (Preliminary Observations)." *Zhongzheng daxue Zhongwen xueshu niankan* 中正大學中文學術年刊 17 (2011): 337–68.

Berezkin, Rostislav. "Printing and Circulating 'Precious Scrolls' in Early Twentieth-Century Shanghai and Its Vicinity: Toward an Assessment of Multifunctionality of the Genre." In Clart and Scott, *Religious Publishing*, 139–86.

Berezkin, Rostislav, and Vincent Goossaert. "The Wutong Cult in the Suzhou Area from the Late 19th Century to the Present," *Journal of Chinese Studies* 中國文化研究所學報 70 (2020): 153–202.

Berezkin, Rostislav, and Vincent Goossaert. "The Three Mao Lords in Modern Jiangnan: Cult and Pilgrimage between Daoism and *Baojuan* Recitation." *Bulletin de l'EFEO* 99 (2012–13): 295–326.

Betta, Chiara. "Silas Aaron Hardoon (1851–1931): Marginality and Adaptation in Shanghai." PhD diss., University of London, 1997.

Biggerstaff, Knight. *The Earliest Modern Government Schools in China*. Ithaca, NY: Cornell University Press, 1961.

Billioud, Sébastien. "Confucian Revival and the Emergence of *Jiaohua* Organizations: A Case Study of the Yidan Xuetang." *Modern China* 37.3 (2011): 286–314.

Billioud, Sébastien. "The Hidden Tradition: Confucianism and Its Metamorphoses in Modern and Contemporary China." In Goossaert, Kiely, and Lagerwey, *Modern Chinese Religion*. Vol. 2: *1850–2015*, 767–805.

Billioud, Sébastien, and Joël Thoraval. *The Sage and the People: The Confucian Revival in China.* Oxford: Oxford University Press, 2015.

Birnbaum, Raoul. "The Deathbed Image of Master Hongyi." In Jacqueline Stone and Bryan Cuevas, eds., *The Buddhist Dead: Practices, Discourses, Representations,* 175–207. Honolulu: University of Hawai'i Press, 2007.

Birnbaum, Raoul. "Master Hongyi Looks Back: A 'Modern Man' Becomes a Monk in Twentieth-Century China." In Steven Heine and Charles S. Prebish, eds., *Buddhism in the Modern World: Adaptations of an Ancient Tradition,* 75–124. New York: Oxford University Press, 2003.

Birnbaum, Raoul. "Two Turns in the Life of Master Hongyi, a Buddhist Monk in Twentieth-Century China." In Ownby, Goossaert and Ji, *Making Saints,* 161–208.

Borchert, Thomas. "Worry for the Dai Nation: Sipsongpannā, Chinese Modernity, and the Problems of Buddhist Modernism." *Journal of Asian Studies* 67.1 (2008): 107–42.

Bosco, Joseph. "Urban Processions: Colonial Decline and Revival as Heritage in Postcolonial Hong Kong." In van der Veer, *Handbook of Religion and the Asian City,* 110–30.

Brokaw, Cynthia J. *The Ledgers of Merit and Demerit: Social Change and Moral Order in Late Imperial China.* Princeton, NJ: Princeton University Press, 1991.

Brokaw, Cynthia, and Kai-wing Chow, eds. *Printing and Book Culture in Late Imperial China.* Berkeley: University of California Press, 2005.

Brokaw, Cynthia, and Christopher Reed, eds. *From Woodblocks to the Internet: Chinese Publishing and Print Culture in Transition, circa 1800 to 2008.* Leiden: Brill, 2010.

Brook, Timothy. "Buddhism in the Chinese Constitution: Recording Monasteries in North Zhili." In *The Chinese State in Ming Society,* 158–81. London: RoutledgeCurzon, 2005.

Brook, Timothy. "The Policies of Religion: Late-Imperial Origins of the Regulatory State." In Ashiwa and Wank, *Making Religion, Making the State,* 22–42.

Broy, Nikolas. "Syncretic Sects and Redemptive Societies: Toward a New Understanding of 'Sectarianism' in the Study of Chinese Religions." *Review of Religion and Chinese Society* 2 (2015): 145–85.

Bryson, Megan. *Goddess on the Frontier: Religion, Ethnicity, and Gender in Southwest China.* Stanford, CA: Stanford University Press, 2016.

Burton-Rose, Daniel. "Terrestrial Reward as Divine Recompense: The Self-Fashioned Piety of the Peng Lineage of Suzhou, 1650s–1870s." PhD diss., Princeton University, 2016.

Campo, Daniela. "Chan Master Xuyun: The Embodiment of an Ideal, the Transmission of a Model." In Ownby, Goossaert and Ji, *Making Saints*, 99–136.

Campo, Daniela. "Guan Jiongzhi 關絅之 (1879–1942) and Elite Buddhist Networks in Republican Shanghai: Revolutionary Ideals and Traditional Values of Chinese Religious Modernity." Manuscript.

Cao Benye 曹本冶 and Xu Hongtu 徐宏圖. *Wenzhou Pingyang Dongyueguan Daojiao yinyue yanjiu* 溫州平陽東嶽觀道教音樂研究. Taipei: Xinwenfeng, 2000.

Cao Nanlai. *Constructing China's Jerusalem: Christians, Power, and Place in Contemporary Wenzhou*. Stanford, CA: Stanford University Press, 2011.

Carroll, Peter. *Between Heaven and Modernity: Reconstructing Suzhou, 1895–1937*. Stanford, CA: Stanford University Press, 2006.

Casanova, José. "Secularization Revisited: A Reply to Talal Asad." In David Scott and Charles Hirschkind, eds., *Powers of the Secular Modern: Talal Asad and His Interlocutors*, 12–30. Stanford, CA: Stanford University Press, 2006.

Chandler, Stuart. *Establishing a Pure Land on Earth*. Honolulu: University of Hawai'i Press, 2004.

Chang Chien-Chiu 張建俅. "Jindai Zhongguo zhengfu yu shehui tuanti de tantao: Yi Zhongguo hongshizihui wei li (1919–1949)" 近代中國政府與社會團體的探討—以中國紅十字會為例 (1912–1949). *Bulletin of the Institute of Modern History, Academia Sinica* 47 (2004): 101–64.

Chang Hsun 張珣. "Cong minjian xinyang yu difang chanye kan guojia yu difang de guanxi: Yi Xingang Fengtian Gong wei li" 從民間信仰與地方產業看國家與地方的關係：以新港奉天宮為例. In Chang Hsun, ed., *Hanren minzhong zongjiao yanjiu: Tianye yu lilun de jiehe* 漢人民眾宗教研究：田野與理論的結合, 115–60. Nankang: Academia Sinica, 2013.

Chang Yen-ching 張晏菁. "Hongyang Jingtu: Lü Bicheng (1883–1943) nüjushi xue Fo licheng de mengjing shuxie" 弘揚淨土：呂碧城（1883–1943）女居士學佛歷程的夢境書寫. *Xinshiji zongjiao yanjiu* 新世紀宗教研究 15.2 (2016): 123–52.

Chao Shin-yi. "A *Danggi* [童乩] Temple in Taipei: Spirit-Mediums in Modern Urban Taiwan." *Asia Major, 3rd ser.*, 15.2 (2002): 129–56.

Chau, Adam Y. "Expanding the Space of Popular Religion: Local Temple Activism and the Politics of Legitimation in Contemporary Rural China." In Ashiwa and Wank, *Making Religion, Making the State*, 211–40.

Chau, Adam Y. "Modalities of Doing Religion." In Palmer, Shive, and Wickeri, *Chinese Religious Life*, 67–84.

Chau, Adam Y., ed. *Religion in Contemporary China: Revitalization and Innovation*. London: Routledge, 2011.

Chau, Adam Y. "Superstition Specialist Households? The Household Idiom in Chinese Religious Practices." *Minsu quyi* 民俗曲藝 153 (2006): 157–202.

Chen Bing 陳兵 and Deng Zimei 鄧子美. *Ershi shiji Zhongguo Fojiao* 二十世紀中國佛教. 2000, reprint Taipei: Xiandai Chan chubanshe, 2003.

Chen Boxi 陳伯熙, ed. and comp. *Shanghai yishi daguan* 上海軼事大觀. 1924, reprint, Shanghai: Shanghai shudian chubanshe, 2000.

Chen Chuanxi 陳傳席. "Ping xiandai mingjia yu dajia. Xu: Wang Yiting" 評現代名家與大家‧續—王一亭. *Guohuajia* 國畫家 3 (2006): 7–9.

Chen Hailiang 陳海量. *Zaijia xueFo yaodian* 在家學佛要典. Taipei: Fojiao chubanshe, 1982.

Chen Hsi-yuan 陳熙遠. "Liji yu guijie—Shilun youyi zai tan yu miao, guan yu min zhijian de Shanghai sanxunhui" 厲祭與鬼節—試論游移在壇與廟、官與民之間的上海三巡會. Paper presented at the conference The Modern History of Urban Daoism, Tainan, November 13–14, 2010.

Chen Hsi-yuan 陳熙遠. "Zhongguo ye weimian – Ming Qing shiqi de yuanxiao, yejin yu kuanghuan" 中國夜未眠—明清時期的元宵、夜禁與狂歡. *Bulletin of the Institute of History and Philology, Academia Sinica* 75.2 (2004): 283–329.

Chen Jiaju 陳家駒. "Qingdai zhongqi yihuan Baojing Tanyi simiao de shanbian yu shiwei" 清代中期以還保靖壇遺寺廟的嬗變與式微. In Kang Bao, Long Haiqing, and Luo Kanglong, *Xiangxi zongjiao wenhua diaocha yu yanjiu*, 361–78.

Chen Jinlong 陳金龍. "Minguo 'Simiao guanli tiaoli' de banbu yu feizhi" 民國《寺廟管理條例》的頒布與廢止. *Fayin* 法音 4 (2008): 54–59.

Chen Jinlong 陳金龍. *Nanjing Guomin zhengfu shiqi de zhengjiao guanxi: Yi Fojiao wei zhongxin de kaocha* 南京國民政府時期的政教關係：以佛教為中心的考察. Beijing: Zhongguo shehui kexue chubanshe, 2011.

Chen Pi-yen. "Buddhist Chant, Devotional Song, and Commercial Popular Music: From Ritual to Rock Mantra." *Ethnomusicology* 49.2 (2005): 266–86.

Chen Qigui 陳啟貴. "Fenghuang simiao de xingqi fada yu shuailuo xiaomie yuanyin diaocha baogao" 鳳凰寺廟的興起發達與衰落消滅原因調查報告. In Kang Bao, Long Haiqing, and Luo Kanglong, *Xiangxi zongjiao wenhua diaocha yu yanjiu*, 379–414.

Chen Shih-jung 陳世榮. "Guojia yu difang shehui de hudong: jindai shehui jingying de yanjiu dianfan yu weilai de yanjiu qushi" 國家與地方社會的互動：近代社會菁英的研究典範與未來的研究趨勢. *Bulletin of the Institute of Modern History, Academia Sinica* 54 (2006): 129–68.

Chen Weiming 陳微明. "Bangwu jiyu" 邦武乩語. *Jueyouqing* 覺有情 133–34 (1945): 2.

Chen Weiming 陳微明. "Wang'er Banwu xingshu" 亡兒邦武行述. *Jueyouqing* 覺有情 123–24 (1944): 10–11.

Chen Xing 陳星. *Feng Zikai manhua yanjiu* 豐子愷漫畫研究. Hangzhou: Xileng yinshe, 2004.

Chen Xing 陳星. *Li Shutong shenbian de wenhua mingren* 李叔同身邊的文化名人. Beijing: Zhonghua shuju, 2005.

Chen Yaoting 陳耀庭. "Shanghai Daojiaoshi" 上海道教史. In Ruan Renze and Gao Zhennong, *Shanghai zongjiaoshi*, 353–438.

Chen Yingning 陳攖寧. "Tianxian Bicheng nüshi jiangtan jilu" 天仙碧城女史降壇紀錄. *Yangshan banyuekan* 揚善半月刊 1.3 (1933): 48–50.

Chen Yongge 陳永革. *Fojiao honghua de xiandai zhuanxing: Minguo Zhejiang Fojiao yanjiu (1912–1949)* 佛教弘化的現代轉型: 民國浙江佛教研究 (1912–1949). Beijing: Zongjiao wenhua chubanshe, 2003.

Chen Zhongping. *Modern China's Network Revolution: Chambers of Commerce and Sociopolitical Change in the Early Twentieth Century.* Stanford, CA: Stanford University Press, 2011.

Chen Zuen 陳祖恩 and Li Huaxing 李華興. *Wang Yiting zhuan* 王一亭傳. Shanghai: Shanghai cishu chubanshe, 2007.

Cheung Chi-Wai 張志偉. *Jiduhua yu shisuhua de zhengzha: Shanghai Jidujiao qingnianhui yanjiu (1900–1922)* 基督化與世俗化的掙扎：上海基督教青年會研究（1900–1922). Taipei: National Taiwan University Press, 2010.

Cheung Chi-Wai 張志偉. "Tuxiang yishu yu Zhongguo jidujiaoshi yanjiu: *Shanghai qingnian* (1914–1927) zhong de manhua yingyong" 圖像藝術與中國基督教史研究：《上海青年》（1914–1927）中的漫畫應用. In Peter Tze Ming Ng (Wu Ziming 吳梓明) and Wu Xiaoxin 吳小新, eds., *Jidu yu Zhongguo shehui: Dierjie Guoji nianqing xuezhe yantaohui lunwenji* 基督與中國社會：第二屆國際年青學者研討會論文集, 331–72. Hong Kong:

Centre for the Study of Religion and Chinese Society, Chung Chi College, 2006.

Chia, Lucille, and Hilde de Weerdt, eds. *Knowledge and Text Production in an Age of Print*. Leiden: Brill, 2011.

Chiu Hei-yuan 瞿海源. "Zhonghua minguo youguan zongjiao faling ji falü cao'an huibian" 中華民國有關宗教法令及法律草案彙編. *Zhongyang yanjiuyuan Minzuxue yanjiusuo ziliao huibian* 中央研究院民族學研究所資料彙編 2 (1990): 113–39.

Clart, Philip. "Chinese Tradition and Taiwanese Modernity: Morality Books as Social Commentary and Critique." In Philip Clart and Charles B. Jones, eds, *Religion in Modern Taiwan*, 84–97. Honolulu: University of Hawai'i Press, 2003.

Clart, Philip. "Conceptualizations of 'Popular Religion' in Recent Research in the People's Republic of China." In Wang Chien-chuan 王見川, Li Shih-wei 李世偉, and Hung Ying-fa 洪瑩發, eds., *Yanjiu xinshiye: Mazu yu Huaren minjian xinyang guoji yantaohui lunwenji* 研究新視界：媽祖與華人民間信仰國際研討會論文集, 391–412. Taipei: BoyYoung, 2014.

Clart, Philip. "Confucius and the Mediums: Is there a 'Popular Confucianism'?" *T'oung Pao* 89.1–3 (2003): 1–38.

Clart, Philip. "Mediums and the New Media: The Impact of Electronic Publishing on Temple and Moral Economies in Taiwanese Popular Religion." *Journal of Sinological Studies* 3 (2012): 127–41.

Clart, Philip. "Merit beyond Measure: Notes on the Moral (and Real) Economy of Religious Publishing in Taiwan." In Philip Clart and Paul Crowe, eds., *The People and the Dao: New Studies of Chinese Religions in Honour of Prof. Daniel L. Overmyer*, 127–42. Sankt Augustin: Institut Monumenta Serica, 2009.

Clart, Philip. "New Technologies and the Production of Religious Texts in China, 19th–21st Century." In Goossaert, Kiely and Lagerwey, *Modern Chinese Religion*: Vol. 2: *1850–2015*, 560–78.

Clart, Philip, and Gregory Adam Scott, eds. *Religious Publishing and Print Culture in Modern China, 1800–2012*. Boston: De Gruyter, 2014.

Cline, Ellen. "Female Spirit Mediums and Religious Authority in Contemporary Southeastern China." *Modern China* 36.5 (2010): 520–55.

Coble, Parks M. *Facing Japan: Chinese Politics and Japanese Imperialism, 1931–1937*. Cambridge, MA: Harvard University Press, 1991.

Cochran, Sherman, Andrew C. K. Hsieh, and Janis Cochran, eds. and trans. *One Day in China: May 21, 1936*. New Haven, CT: Yale University Press, 1983.

Cohen, Paul A. *History in Three Keys: The Boxers as Event, Experience, and Myth*. New York: Columbia University Press, 1997.

Dai Sike 戴思客 (Lawrence Scott Davis). "Yu yu nü: Shitan jitong xiucixue" 語與女：試探乩童修辭學. *Si yu yan* 思與言 35.2 (1994): 267–312.

Daotong yuanliuzhi 道統源流志. Yan Heyi 嚴合怡, ed. 2 vols. Wuxi: Zhonghua yinshuaju, 1929.

Davis, Sara L. M. *Song and Silence: Ethnic Revival on China's Southwest Borders*. New York: Columbia University Press, 2005.

Davis, Walter B. *Culture in Common: Wang Yiting's Art of Exchange with Japan*. Leiden: Brill, 2020.

Davis, Walter B. "For Fate, Faith, and Charity: Wang Yiting's Paintings of Street People." Paper presented at the symposium The Challenge of Modernity: Chinese Painting in the Late Nineteenth and Early Twentieth Centuries. Guggenheim Museum, New York, May 22, 1998.

Dawson, Lorne L. "The Mediation of Religious Experience in Cyberspace." In Højsgarard and Warburg, *Religion and Cyberspace*, 15–37.

Dean, Kenneth. "Further Partings of the Way: The Chinese State and Daoist Ritual Traditions in Contemporary China." In Ashiwa and Wank, *Making Religion, Making the State*, 179–210.

Dean, Kenneth. "The Return Visits of Overseas Chinese to Ancestral Villages in Putian, Fujian." In Oakes and Sutton, *Faiths on Display*, 235–63.

Dean, Kenneth, and Zheng Zhenman [鄭振滿]. *Ritual Alliances of the Putian Plain*. Vol. 1: *Historical Introduction to the Return of the Gods*; vol. 2: *A Survey of the Village Temples and Ritual Activities*. Leiden: Brill, 2010.

Despeux, Catherine. "The 'New Clothes' of Sainthood in China: The Case of Nan Huaijin (1918–2012)." In Ownby, Goossaert and Ji, *Making Saints*, 349–93.

"Digital Bibliography of Modern Chinese Buddhism." Accessed August 5, 2016. http://bib.buddhiststudies.net.

Dillon, Nara and Jean C. Oi, eds. *At the Crossroads of Empires: Middlemen, Social Networks, and State-Building in Republican China*. Stanford, CA: Stanford University Press, 2008.

Dillon, Nara. "The Politics of Philanthropy: The Balance between Public and Private Refugee Relief in Shanghai, 1932–1949." In Dillon and Oi, *At the Crossroads of Empires: Middlemen, Social Networks, and State-Building in Republican China*, 179–205.

Dobbelaere, Karel. *Secularization: An Analysis at Three Levels*. Brussels: PIE–Peter Lang, 2002.

Dong Xiaoping 董曉萍 and Lü Min 呂敏 (Marianne Bujard), eds. *Beijing neicheng simiao beikezhi* 北京內城寺廟碑刻志, 4 vols. Beijing: Guojia tushuguan chubanshe, 2011–17. A total of twelve volumes are planned.

Duara, Prasenjit. *Culture, Power, and the State: Rural North China, 1900–1942*. Stanford, CA: Stanford University Press, 1988.

Duara, Prasenjit. "Knowledge and Power in the Discourse of Modernity: The Campaigns against Popular Religion in Early Twentieth-Century China." *Journal of Asian Studies* 50.1 (1991): 67–83.

Duara, Prasenjit. *Rescuing History from the Nation: Questioning Narratives of Modern China*. Chicago: University of Chicago Press, 1995.

Duara, Prasenjit. *Sovereignty and Authenticity: Manchukuo and the East Asian Modern*. Lanham, MD: Rowman and Littlefield, 2003.

DuBois, Thomas D., ed. *Casting Faiths: Imperialism and the Transformation of Religion in East and Southeast Asia*. New York: Palgrave Macmillan, 2009.

DuBois, Thomas David. *Empire and the Meaning of Religion in Northeast Asia: Manchuria, 1900–1945*. Cambridge: Cambridge University Press, 2016.

DuBois, Thomas David. "Japanese Print Media and Manchurian Cultural Community: Religion in the Pages of the *Shengjing Times*, 1906–1944." In DuBois, *Casting Faiths*, 217–38.

DuBois, Thomas David. "Local Religion and Festivals." In Goossaert, Kiely, and Lagerwey, *Modern Chinese Religion*. Vol. 2: *1850–2015*, 371–400.

DuBois, Thomas David. *Religion and the Making of Modern East Asia*. Cambridge: Cambridge University Press, 2011.

DuBois, Thomas David. *The Sacred Village: Social Change and Religious Life in Rural North China*. Honolulu: University of Hawai'i Press, 2005.

DuBois, Thomas David. "The Salvation of Religion? Public Charity and the New Religions of the Early Republic." *Minsu quyi* 民俗曲藝 172 (2011): 73–126.

Dudbridge, Glen. *The Legend of Miaoshan*. Rev. ed. Oxford: Oxford University Press, 2004. Originally published in 1978.

Dudoignon, Stephane A., Komatsu Hisao, and Kosugi Yasushi, eds. *Intellectuals in the Modern Islamic World: Transmission, Transformation, and Communication*. London: Routledge, 2009.

Dunch, Ryan. *Fuzhou Protestants and the Making of Modern China, 1857–1927*. New Haven. CT: Yale University Press, 2001.

Ebrey, Patricia, ed. *Women and the Family in Chinese History*. London: Routledge, 2003.

Edgerton-Tarpley, Kathryn. *Tears from Iron: Cultural Responses to Famine in Nineteenth-Century China*. Berkeley: University of California Press, 2008.

Ehrlich, M. Avrum, ed. *The Jewish-Chinese Nexus: A Meeting of Civilizations*. London: Routledge, 2008.

Elvin, Mark. "The Gentry Democracy in Shanghai." PhD diss., Cambridge University, 1969.

Esherick, Joseph W. "Modernity and Nation in the Chinese City." In Esherick, *Remaking the Chinese City: Modernity and National Identity, 1900–1950*, 1–16.

Esherick, Joseph W., ed. *Remaking the Chinese City: Modernity and National Identity, 1900–1950*. Honolulu: University of Hawai'i Press, 2000.

Esposito, Monica. "Daoism in the Qing." In Livia Kohn, ed., *Daoism Handbook*, 623–58. Leiden: Brill, 2000.

Esposito, Monica. "The Discovery of Jiang Yuanting's *Daozang jiyao* in Jiangnan: A Presentation of the Daoist Canon of the Qing Dynasty." In Mugitani Kunio 麥谷邦夫, ed., *Kōnan dōkyō no kenkyū* 江南道教の研究, 79–110. Kyoto: Jinbun Kagaku Kenkyūjo, 2007.

Esposito, Monica. "Longmen 龍門 Taoism in Qing China: Doctrinal Ideal and Local Reality." *Journal of Chinese Religions* 29 (2001): 191–231.

Fan Chun-wu 范純武. "Bade: Jindai Zhongguo jiushi tuanti de daode leimu yu shijian" 八德:近代中國救世團體的道德類目與實踐. In Kang Bao and Gao Wansang, *Gaibian Zhongguo zongjiao de wushinian*, 225–59.

Fan Chun-wu 范純武. "Duan Zhengyuan and the Moral Studies Society: 'Religionized Confucianism' during the Republican Period." In Ownby, Goossaert and Ji, *Making Saints*, 137–60.

Fan Chun-wu 范純武. "Feiluan, xiuzhen yu banshan: Zheng Guanying yu Shanghai zongjiao shijie" 飛鸞、修真與辦善：鄭觀應與上海的宗教世界. In Wu Jen-shu 巫仁恕, Lin May-li 林美莉, and Kang Bao 康豹 (Paul R. Katz), eds., *Cong chengshi kan Zhongguo de xiandaixing* 從城市看中國的現代性, 247–74. Nankang: Institute of Modern History, Academia Sinica, 2010.

Fan Chun-wu 范純武. "Jinxiandai Zhongguo Fojiao yu fuji" 近現代中國佛教與扶乩. *Yuanguang Foxue xuebao* 圓光佛學學報 3 (1999): 261–92.

Fan Chun-wu 范純武. "Ming Qing Jiangnan Dutian xinyang de fazhan jiqi yishuo" 明清江南都天信仰的發展及其異說. In Gao Zhihua 高致華, ed., *Tanxun minjian zhushen yu xinyang wenhua* 探尋民間諸神與信仰文化, 87–115. Hefei: Huangshan shushe, 2006.

Fan Chun-wu 范純武. *Qingmo minjian cishan shiye yu luantang yundong* 清末民間慈善事業與鸞堂運動. Taipei: BoyYoung, 2015.

Fan Zushu 范祖述. *Hangsu yifeng* 杭俗遺風. Shanghai: Shanghai wenyi chubanshe, 1989.

Fang Ling 方玲. "Hangzhou Laodongyuemiao de bianqian" 杭州老東嶽廟的變遷. *Xianggang zhongwen daxue Daojiao wenhua yanjiu zhongxin tongxun* 香港中文大學道教文化研究中心通訊 12 (2008): 3–4.

Fang Ling 方玲. "The Old Eastern Peak Temple in Hangzhou." In Liu Xun and Vincent Goossaert, eds., *Daoism in Modern China: Clerics and Temples in Urban Transformations, 1860–Present*. London: Routledge, 2021.

Fang Zongbao 方宗苞. "Yuecheng daoshentuan" 樂成搗神團. *Yueqing wenshi ziliao* 樂清文史資料 1 (1984): 116.

Faure, David. *Emperor and Ancestor: State and Lineage in South China*. Stanford, CA: Stanford University Press, 2007.

Feng Yuxiang 馮玉祥. "Mixin shi minzu luohou de xiangzheng, mixin shi wangguo miezhong de genyuan, geming de minzhong yao pochu mixin" 迷信是民族落後的象徵，迷信是亡國滅種的根源，革命的民眾要破除迷信. *Xinghua* 興華 25.16 (1928): 10–17.

Fisher, Gareth. "Morality Books and the Revival of Lay Buddhism in China." In Chau, *Religion in Contemporary China*, 53–80.

Fitzgerald, John. *Awakening China: Politics, Culture, and Class in the Nationalist Revolution*. Stanford, CA: Stanford University Press, 1996.

Flath, James. "Temple Fairs and the Republican State in North China." *Twentieth-Century China* 30. (2004): 39–63.

Flath, James, and Norman Smith, eds. *Beyond Suffering: Recounting War in Modern China*. Vancouver: University of British Columbia Press, 2011.

Formichi, Chiara. *Islam and the Making of the Nation: Kartosuwiryo and Political Islam in 20th-Century Indonesia*. Leiden: Brill, 2012.

Fridell, Wilbur M. *Japanese Shrine Mergers, 1906–12: State Shinto Moves to the Grassroots*. Tokyo: Sophia University, 1973.

Fu Haiyan 付海晏. "Geming, falü yu miaochan: Minguo Beiping Tieshansi an yanjiu" 革命, 法律與廟產—民國北平鐵山寺案研究. *Lishi yanjiu* 歷史研究 3 (2003): 105–20.

Fu Haiyan 付海晏. "1940 niandai Edong simiao caichanquan chutan" 1940 年代鄂東寺廟財產權初探. *Guizhou shifan daxue xuebao (Shehui kexueban)* 貴州師范大學學報(社會科學版) 5 (2005): 6–10.

"Fuji de yuanli: Wu Tingfang boshi yi xinjiu xueshuo zhengming" 扶乩的原理：伍廷芳博士以新舊學說證明. *Xinminsheng* 新民聲 1.13 (1944): 27–28.

"Fuji kaoyuan" 扶乩考源. *Hongmeigui* 紅玫瑰 2.14 (1925): 1–2.

"Fuji shanhuo" 扶乩煽惑. *Xiangbao* 湘報 78 (1898): 310.

"Fuji yu diexian" 扶乩與碟仙. *Taipingyang zhoubao* 太平洋週報 1.23 (1942): 299–301.

"Fuji yu xinli" 扶乩與心理. *Hongmeigui* 紅玫瑰 2.13 (1925): 1–2.

"Fulu: Fuji de xueli shuoming" 附錄：扶乩的學理說明. *Daode zazhi* 道德雜誌 1.1 (1921): 117–20.

"Fuluan zatan" 扶鸞雜談. *Shehui zhi hua* 社會之花 1.13 (1924): 1–5.

Fuma Susumu 夫馬進. *Chūgoku zenkai zendōshi kenkyū* 中國善會善堂史研究. Tokyo: Dōbōsha shuppan, 1997.

Gamble, Sidney D. *North China Villages: Social, Political, and Economic Activities before 1933.* Berkeley: University of California Press, 1963.

Gamble, Sidney D. *Peking: A Social Survey.* New York: George H. Doran, 1921.

Gao Hongxia 高紅霞. *Shanghai Fujianren yanjiu* 上海福建人研究. Shanghai: Shanghai renmin chubanshe, 2007.

Gao Wansang 高萬桑 (Vincent Goossaert). "Jingaishan wangluo: Jinxiandai Jiangnan de Quanzhen jushi zuzhi" 金蓋山網絡：近現代江南的全真居士組織. In Zhao Weidong 趙衛東, ed., *Quanzhendao yanjiu* 全真道研究. 1:319–39. Jinan: Qilu shushe, 2011.

Gao Wansang 高萬桑 (Vincent Goossaert). "Qingdai Jiangnan diqu de Chenghuangmiao, Zhang Tianshi ji Daojiao guanliao tixi" 清代江南地區的城隍廟、張天師及道教官僚體系. *Qingshi yanjiu* 清史研究 1 (2010): 1–11.

Gao Wansang 高萬桑 (Vincent Goossaert). "Wanqing ji Minguo shiqi Jiangnan diqu de yingshen saihui" 晚清及民國時期江南地區的迎神賽會. In Kang Bao and Gao Wansang, *Gaibian Zhongguo zongjiao de wushinian*, 75–99.

Gao Zhennong 高振農. "Minguo nianjian Shanghai Fojiaojie zhenzai huodong ziliao diandi" 民國年間上海佛教界賑災活動資料點滴. *Fayin* 法音 10 (1998): 28–31.

Gao Zhennong 高振農. "Minguo nianjian de Shanghai Foxue shuju" 民國年間的上海佛學書局. http://read.goodweb.cn/news/news_view.asp?newsid=79749.

Gao Zhennong 高振農. "Shanghai fojiaoshi" 上海佛教史. In Ruan Renze and Gao Zhennong, *Shanghai zongjiaoshi*, 27–349.

Ge Tao 葛濤. *Changpian yu jindai Shanghai shehui shenghuo* 唱片與近代上海社會生活. Shanghai: Shanghai cishu chubanshe, 2009.

Ge Zhuang 葛壯. *Zongjiao yu jindai Shanghai shehui de bianqian* 宗教與近代上海社會的變遷. Shanghai: Shanghai shudian chubanshe, 1999.

Glosser, Susan L. *Chinese Visions of Family and State, 1915–1953*. Berkeley: University of California Press, 2003.

Goldfuss, Gabriele. *Vers un bouddhisme du xxᵉ siècle: Yang Wenhui (1837–1911), réformateur laïque et imprimeur*. Paris: Collège de France. Institut des Hautes Études Chinoises, 2001.

Goodman, Bryna. *Native Place, City, and Nation: Regional Networks and Identities in Shanghai, 1853–1937*. Berkeley: University of California Press, 1995.

Goodman, Bryna. "What Is in a Network? Local, Personal, and Public Loyalties in the Context of Changing Conceptions of the State and Social Welfare." In Dillon and Oi, *At the Crossroads of Empires: Middlemen, Social Networks, and State-Building in Republican China*, 155–78.

Goossaert, Vincent. "Anatomie d'un discours anticlérical: Le *Shenbao*, 1872–1878." *Extrême-Orient Extrême-Occident* 24 (2002): 113–31.

Goossaert, Vincent. "Animals and Eschatology in the Nineteenth-Century Discourse." In Roel Sterckx, Martina Siebert and Dagmar Schäfer, eds., *Animals Through Chinese History. Earliest Times to 1911*, 181–98. Cambridge: Cambridge University Press, 2019.

Goossaert, Vincent. "1898: The Beginning of the End for Chinese Religion?" *Journal of Asian Studies* 65.2 (2006): 307–36.

Goossaert, Vincent. *Bureaucratie et salut: Devenir un dieu en Chine*. Geneva: Labor et Fides, 2017.

Goossaert, Vincent. "Bureaucratie, taxation, et justice: Taoïsme et construction de l'État au Jiangnan (Chine), xviiᵉ–xixᵉ siècles." *Annales HSS* 4 (2010): 999–1027.

Goossaert, Vincent. "Counting the Monks: The 1736–1739 Census of the Chinese Clergy." *Late Imperial China* 21.2 (2000): 40–85.

Goossaert, Vincent. "Daoism and Local Cults in Modern Suzhou: A Case Study of Qionglongshan 穹窿山." In Philip Clart, ed., *Chinese and European Perspectives on the Study of Chinese Popular Religions*, 199–228. Taipei: BoyYoung, 2012.

Goossaert, Vincent. "Daoists in the Modern Chinese Self-Cultivation Market: The Case of Beijing, 1850–1949." In Palmer and Liu, *Daoism in the Twentieth Century*, 123–53.

Goossaert, Vincent. "The Destruction of Immoral Temples in Qing China." In *ICS Visiting Professor Lectures Series*. Special issue, *Journal of Chinese Studies* 2 (2009): 131–53.

Goossaert, Vincent. "Détruire les temples pour construire les écoles: Reconstitution d'un objet historique." *Extrême-Orient Extrême-Occident* 33 (2011): 35–51.

Goossaert, Vincent. "Diversity and Elite Religiosity in Modern China: A Model." *Approaching Religion* 7.1 (2017): 10–20.

Goossaert, Vincent. "Guerre, violence, et eschatologie: Interprétations religieuses de la guerre des Taiping (1851–1864)." In Jean Baechler, ed., *Guerre et Religion*, 81–94. Paris: Hermann, 2016.

Goossaert, Vincent. "The Heavenly Master, Canonization, and the Daoist Construction of Local Religion in late Imperial Jiangnan." *Cahiers d'Extrême-Asie* 20 (2011): 229–45.

Goossaert, Vincent. "Irrepressible Female Piety: Late Imperial Bans on Women Visiting Temples." *Nan Nü: Men, Women, and Gender in China* 10.2 (2008): 212–41.

Goossaert, Vincent. "Is There a North China Religion? A Review Essay." *Journal of Chinese Religions* 39 (2011): 83–93.

Goossaert, Vincent. "The Jingaishan Network in Modern Jiangnan." In Liu Xun and Vincent Goossaert, eds., *Daoism in Modern China: Clerics and Temples in Urban Transformations, 1860–Present*. London: Routledge, 2021.

Goossaert, Vincent. "La sexualité dans les livres de morale chinois." In Florence Rochefort and Maria Eleonora Sanna, eds., *Normes religieuses et genre: Mutations, résistances, et reconfiguration, xix–xxi*e *siècle*, 37–46. Paris: Armand Colin, 2013.

Goossaert, Vincent, ed. and trans. *Livres de morale révélés par les dieux*. Paris: Belles-Lettres, 2012.

Goossaert, Vincent. "The Local Politics of Festivals: Hangzhou, 1850–1950." *Daoism: Religion, History and Society* 5 (2013): 57–80.

Goossaert, Vincent. "Managing Chinese Religious Pluralism in the Nineteenth-Century City Gods Temples." In Jansen, Klein, and Meyer, *Globalization and the Making of Religious Modernity in China*, 29–51.

Goossaert, Vincent. "Modern Daoist Eschatology: Spirit-Writing and Elite Soteriology in Late Imperial China." *Daoism: Religion, History, and Society* 6 (2014): 219–46.

Goossaert, Vincent. "The Quanzhen Clergy, 1700–1950." In John Lagerwey, ed., *Religion and Chinese Society: The Transformation of a Field*, 699–771. Paris: École Française d'Extrême Orient, 2004.

Goossaert, Vincent. "Quanzhen, What Quanzhen? Late Imperial Daoist Clerical Identities in Lay Perspective." In Vincent Goossaert and Liu Xun, eds., *Quanzhen Daoists in Chinese Society and Culture, 1500–2010*, 19–43. Berkeley: Institute of East Asian Studies, 2013.

Goossaert, Vincent. "A Question of Control: Licensing Local Ritual Specialists in Jiangnan, 1850–1950." In Katz and Liu Shufen, *Belief, Practice, and Cultural Adaptation*, 569–604.

Goossaert, Vincent. "Republican Church Engineering: The National Religious Associations in 1912 China." In Yang, *Chinese Religiosities*, 209–32.

Goossaert, Vincent. "The Shifting Balance of Power in the City God Temples, Late Qing to 1937." *Journal of Chinese Religions* 43.1 (2015): 5–33.

Goossaert, Vincent. "Spirit Writing, Canonization, and the Rise of Divine Saviors: Wenchang, Lüzu, and Guandi, 1700–1858." *Late Imperial China* 36.2 (2015): 82–125.

Goossaert, Vincent. "Spiritual Techniques among Late Imperial Chinese Elites." In Angela Hobart, Thierry Zarcone & Jean-Pierre Brach, eds., *Spiritual Techniques*. Canon Pyon: Sean Kingston, forthcoming.

Goossaert, Vincent. "Starved of Resources: Clerical Hunger and Enclosures in Nineteenth-Century China." *Harvard Journal of Asiatic Studies* 62.1 (2002): 77–133.

Goossaert, Vincent. *The Taoists of Peking, 1800–1949: A Social History of Urban Clerics*. Harvard East Asian Monographs, no. 284. Cambridge, MA: Harvard University Asia Center, 2007.

Goossaert, Vincent. "Territorial Cults and the Urbanization of the Chinese World: A Case Study of Suzhou." In van der Veer, *Handbook of Religion and the Asian City*, 52–68.

Goossaert, Vincent. "Yu Yue (1821–1906) explore l'au-delà: La culture religieuse des élites chinoises à la veille des revolutions." In Roberte Hamayon, Denise Aigle, Isabelle Charleux, and Vincent Goossaert, eds., *Miscellanea Asiatica*, 623–56. Sankt Augustin: Monumenta Serica, 2011.

Goossaert, Vincent. "Zhang Yuanxu: The Making and Unmaking of a Daoist Saint." In Ownby, Goossaert and Ji, *Making Saints*, 78–98.

Goossaert, Vincent, Jan Kiely, and John Lagerwey, eds. *Modern Chinese Religion*. Vol. 2: *1850–2015*. Leiden: Brill, 2016.

Goossaert, Vincent, and David Palmer. *The Religious Question in Modern China*. Chicago: University of Chicago Press, 2011.

Graham, David C. *Folk Religion in Southwest China*. Washington, DC: Smithsonian Institution, 1961.

Grootaers, Willem A. *The Sanctuaries in a North-China City: A Complete Survey of the Cultic Buildings in the City of Hsuan-hua (Chahar)*. Brussels: Institut Belge des Hautes Études Chinoises, 1995.

Hamashima Atsutoshi 濱島敦俊. *Sōkan shinkō: kinsei Kōnan nōson shakai to minkan shinkō* 總管信仰: 近世江南農村社会と民間信仰. Tokyo: Kenbun Shuppan, 2001.

Hammerstrom, Erik J. *The Science of Chinese Buddhism: Early Twentieth-Century Engagements*. New York: Columbia University Press, 2015.

Hansen, Anne Ruth. *How to Behave: Buddhism and Modernity in Colonial Cambodia, 1860–1930*. Honolulu: University of Hawai'i Press, 2007.

Hardacre, Helen. *Shintō and the State, 1868–1988*. Princeton, NJ: Princeton University Press, 1989.

Harrison, Henrietta. "Rethinking Missionaries and Medicine in China: The Miracles of Assunta Pallotta, 1905–2005." *Journal of Asian Studies* 71.1 (2012): 127–48.

Harrison, Henrietta. *The Making of the Republic Citizen: Political Ceremonies and Symbols in China, 1911–1929*. Oxford: Oxford University Press, 2000.

Harrison, Henrietta. *The Man Awakened from Dreams: One Man's Life in a North China Village, 1857–1942*. Stanford, CA: Stanford University Press, 2005.

Hatfield, D. J W. *Taiwanese Pilgrimage to China: Ritual, Complicity, Community*. New York: Palgrave Macmillan, 2010.

He Kongjiao 何孔蛟. "Minguo Shanghai zui da de liuyanglei cishan jihou: Xin Puyutang" 民國上海最大的留養類慈善機構 : 新普育堂. *Wenshi yuekan* 文史月刊 8 (2006): 52–56.

He Shanmeng 何善蒙. *Minguo Hangzhou minjian xinyang* 民國杭州民間信仰. Hangzhou: Hangzhou chubanshe, 2012.

He Shanmeng 何善蒙. "Yingshen saihui haishi putong shaoxiang?" 迎神賽會 還是普通燒香? In Wang Gang and Li Tiangang, *Zhongguo jinshi difang shehuizhong de zongjiao yu guojia*, 69–103.

He Wangfang 何王芳. "Minguo shiqi Hangzhou chengshi shehui shenghuo yanjiu" 民國時期杭州城市社會生活研究. PhD diss., Zhejiang University, 2006.

He Zhiming 何志明. "Minguo qi'an: Cong 'Da Chenghuang' dao 'Da dangbu'" 民 國奇案：從「打城隍」到「打黨部」. *Wenshi tiandi* 文史天地 11 (2010): 41–45.

Henriot, Christian. *Shanghai Ladies of the Night: Prostitution and Society in 19th and 20th Century Shanghai.* Cambridge: Cambridge University Press, 1997.

Henriot, Christian, and Wen-hsin Yeh, eds. *In the Shadow of the Rising Sun: Shanghai under Japanese Occupation.* Cambridge: Cambridge University Press, 2004.

Hojsgarard, Morten T. and Margit Warburg, eds. *Religion and Cyberspace.* London: Routledge, 2009.

Hsiao Kung-ch'üan. *Rural China: Imperial Control in the Nineteenth Century.* Seattle: University of Washington Press, 1960.

Hsu Yu-tsuen 徐雨村. "'Minsu ji youguan wenwu' denglu zhiding yu difang shijian: Yi 'Yunlin Liufangma guolu' wei li" 「民俗及有關文物」登錄指 定與地方實踐：以「雲林六房媽過爐」為例. *Minsu quyi* 民俗曲藝 192 (2016): 221–65.

Hu Danian. *China and Albert Einstein: The Reception of the Physicist and His Theory in China, 1917–1979.* Cambridge, MA: Harvard University Press, 2005.

Hu Qiaomu 胡喬木. "Fan mixin tigang" 反迷信提綱. *Zhongguo qingnian* 中國 青年 2.11 (1940), reprinted in *Zhonggong dangshi yanjiu* 中共黨史研究 1.5 (1999): 1–4.

Hu Shih 胡適. *Sishi zishu* 四十自述. Taipei: Yuandong tushu gongsi, 1992.

Hu Suping 胡素萍. "Li Jiabai yu Shangxian Tang—Qingmo Minchu zai Hua chuanjiaoshi huodong ge'an yanjiu" 李佳白與尚賢堂—清末民初在華傳教 士活動個案研究. *Shixue yuekan* 史學月刊 9 (2005): 57–63.

Hu Zhusheng 胡珠生. *Wenzhou jindaishi* 溫州近代史. Shenyang: Liaoning renmin chubanshe, 2000.

Huang, Julia C., Elena Valussi, and David A. Palmer. "Gender and Sexuality." In Palmer, Shive, and Wickeri, *Chinese Religious Life*, 107–23.

Huang Ko-wu 黃克武. "Minguo chunian Shanghai Lingxue yanjiu: Yi 'Shanghai Lingxuehui' wei li" 民國初年上海的靈學研究：以「上海靈學會」為例. *Bulletin of the Institute of Modern History, Academia Sinica* 55 (2007): 99–136.

Huang Ko-wu 黃克武. "Xiushen yu zhiguo—Jiang Jieshi de xingke shenghuo" 修身與治國—蔣介石的省克生活. *Bulletin of Academia Historica* 34 (2012): 45–68.

Huang, Philip C. C. *Code, Custom, and Legal Practice in China: The Qing and the Republic Compared*. Stanford, CA: Stanford University Press, 2001.

Huang Shiling 黃式陵. "Pochu mixin wenti: Cong Yuyao daohui Minjiaoguan an shuoqi" 破除迷信問題：從餘姚搗毀民教館案說起. *Chenguang zhoukan* 晨光周刊 5.47 (1936): 6–10.

Huang Weichu 黃維楚. *Huayan zimu ji qi changfa* 華嚴字母及其唱法. Shanghai: Foxue shuju, 2009.

"Huang Yanpei mixin fuluan" 黃炎培迷信扶鸞. *Shishi xinwen* 時事新聞 8 (1948): 10.

Hung Chang-tai 洪長泰. *Going to the People: Chinese Intellectuals and Folk Literature, 1918–1937*. Cambridge, MA: Harvard University Press, 1985.

Hupao cuanzhichu 虎跑纂志處, ed. *Hupao Fozu zangdianzhi* 虎跑佛祖藏殿志 (1921). In Bai Huawen 白化文 et al., eds., *Zhongguo Fosizhi congkan* 中國佛寺志叢刊, ser. 1, vol. 72. Yangzhou: Jiangsu guji chubanshe, 1996.

Huzhou Archives, ed. and comp. *Shenbao Huzhou lüHu tongxiang tuanti shiliao* 申報湖州旅滬同鄉團體史料. Huzhou: Huzhou Archives, 2011.

Jansen, Thomas, Thoralf Klein, and Christian Meyer, eds. *Chinese Religions in the Age of Globalization, 1800–Present*. Leiden: Brill, 2014.

Jaschok, Maria, and Shui Jingjun. *Women, Religion, and Space in China: Islamic Mosques and Daoist Temples, Catholic Convents and Chinese Virgins*. New York: Routledge, 2011.

Jessup, J. Brooks. "Beyond Ideological Conflict: Political Incorporation of Buddhist Youth in the Early PRC." *Frontiers of History in China* 7.4 (2012): 551–81.

Jessup, J. Brooks. "The Householder Elite: Buddhist Activism in Shanghai, 1920–1956." PhD diss., University of California, Berkeley, 2010.

Jheng Ya-Yin 鄭雅尹. "Qingmo Minchu de 'gui' yu 'zhaoxiangshu' – Di Baoxian *Pingdengge biji* zhong de xiandaixing meiying" 清末民初的「鬼」與「照相術」—狄葆賢《平等閣筆記》中的現代性魅影. *Qinghua zhongwen xuebao* 清華中文學報 13 (2015): 229–81.

Ji Zhe 汲喆. "Ruhe chaoyue jingdian shisuhua lilun? Ping zongjiao shehuixue de sanzhong houshisuhua lunshu" 如何超越經典世俗化理論？—評宗教社會學的三種後世俗化論述. *Shehuixue yanjiu* 社會學研究 136 (2008): 55–75.

Ji Zhe. "Secularization as Religious Restructuring: Statist Institutionalization of Chinese Buddhism and its Paradoxes." In Yang, *Chinese Religiosities*, 233–60.

Ji Zhe. "Territoires migratoires et lieux religieux: Cartes des religions des Chinois en Île-de-France." In Lucine Endelstein, Sébastien Fath, and Séverine Mathieu, eds., *Dieu change en ville: Religion, espace, immigration*, 137–55. Paris: L'Harmattan, 2010.

Jia Jinhua, Kang Xiaofei, and Yao Ping, eds. *Gendering Chinese Religion: Subject, Identity, and Body*. Albany: State University of New York Press, 2014.

Jian Bozan 翦伯贊 et al., comps. *Wuxu bianfa* 戊戌變法. Shanghai: Shenzhou guoguangshe, 1953.

Jiang Bin 姜彬, ed. *Wu Yue minjian xinyang minsu: Wu Yue diqu minjian xinyang yu minjian wenyi guanxi de kaocha he yanjiu* 吳越民間信仰民俗: 吳越地區民間信仰與民間文藝關係的考察和研究. Shanghai: Shanghai wenyi chubanshe, 1992.

Jiang Jianming 江建明 (J. Brooks Jessup). "Dazao xiandai dushi de Fojiao shenfen rentong – Yi 1920 niandai Shanghai de Shijie fojiao jushilin weili" 打造現代都市的佛教身分認同–1920年代上海的世界佛教居士林為例. In Kang Bao and Gao Wansang, *Gaibian Zhongguo zongjiao de wushinian*, 337–61.

Jiang Zhongzheng xiansheng shougai shengjing shengyong yigao 蔣中正先生手改聖經聖詠譯稿. Wu Ching-hsiung 吳經熊, trans. 6 vols. Taipei: Chung-kuo Kuomintang tang-shih wei-yuan-hui, 1986.

"Jiang zongsiling dui Wang Yiting de tanhua" 蔣總司令對王一亭居士的談話. *Haichaoyin* 10 (1928): 1.

Jiayi shizhi 嘉義市志. Jiayi: Jiayi City Government, 2005.

"Jixian lin Shanghai Jiyunxuan jiyu erze" 濟仙臨上海集雲軒乩諭二則. *Daode zazhi* 道德雜誌 1.2 (1921): 87–95.

Johnson, David G., Andrew J. Nathan, and Evelyn S. Rawski, eds. *Popular Culture in Late Imperial China*. Berkeley: University of California Press, 1985.

Johnson, David G. *Spectacle and Sacrifice: The Ritual Foundations of Village Life in North China*. Cambridge, MA: Harvard University Press, 2009.

Johnson, Ian. *The Souls of China: The Return of Religion after Mao*. London: Penguin, 2017.

Jones, Stephen. *In Search of the Daoists of North China*. Aldershot: Ashgate, 2010.

Jordan, David K., and Daniel L. Overmyer. *The Flying Phoenix: Aspects of Chinese Sectarianism in Taiwan*. Princeton, NJ: Princeton University Press, 1986.

Josephson, Jason Ānanda. *The Invention of Religion in Japan*. Chicago: University of Chicago Press, 2012.

Kang Bao 康豹 (Paul R. Katz) and Gao Wansang 高萬桑 (Vincent Goossaert), eds. *Gaibian Zhongguo zongjiao de wushinian, 1898–1948* 改變中國宗教的五十年，1898–1948. Nankang: Institute of Modern History, Academia Sinica, 2015.

Kang Bao 康豹 (Paul R. Katz), Long Haiqing 龍海清, and Luo Kanglong 羅康隆, eds. *Xiangxi zongjiao wenhua diaocha yu yanjiu* 湘西宗教文化調查與研究. Beijing: Zhongyang minzu chubanshe, forthcoming.

Kang Xiaofei. "Rural Women, Old Age, and Temple Work: A Case from Northwestern Sichuan." *China Perspectives* 4 (2009): 42–53.

Kang Xiaofei. "Women and the Religious Question in Modern China." In Goossaert, Kiely, and Lagerwey, *Modern Chinese Religion*. Vol. 2: *1850–2015*, 491–559.

Kang Xiaofei and Donald S. Sutton. *Contesting the Yellow Dragon: Ethnicity, Religion, and the State in the Sino-Tibetan Borderland*. Leiden: Brill, 2016.

Kantō daishinsai 関東大震災. Tokyo: Zaidan hōjin Tōkyōto ireidō kyōkai, 2005.

Kao Ya-ning. "Religious Revival among the Zhuang People in China: Practicing 'Superstition' and Standardizing a Zhuang Religion." *Journal of Current Chinese Affairs* 43.2 (2014): 107–44.

Katz, Paul R. "Daoism and Local Cults: A Case Study of the Cult of Marshal Wen." In Kwang-ching Liu and Richard Shek, eds., *Heterodoxy in Late Imperial China*, 172–208. Honolulu: University of Hawai'i Press, 2004.

Katz, Paul R. *Demon Hordes and Burning Boats: The Cult of Marshal Wen in Late Imperial Chekiang*. Albany: State University of New York Press, 1995.

Katz, Paul R. *Divine Justice: Religion and the Development of Chinese Legal Culture*. London: Routledge, 2009.

Katz, Paul R., ed. *Festivals and Local Society*. Special issue, *Minsu quyi* 民俗曲藝 147 (2005).

Katz, Paul R. "Illuminating Goodness: Some Preliminary Considerations of Religious Publishing in Modern China." In Clart and Scott, *Religious Publishing*, 265–94.

Katz, Paul R. *Images of the Immortal: The Cult of Lü Dongbin at the Palace of Eternal Joy*. Honolulu: University of Hawai'i Press, 1999.

Katz, Paul R. "'It Is Difficult to Be Indifferent to One's Roots': Taizhou Sojourners and Flood Relief during the 1920s." *Bulletin of the Institute of Modern History, Academia Sinica* 54 (2006): 1–58.

Katz, Paul R. "Jindai Zhongguo simiao pohuai yundong de kongjian tezheng – Yi Jiangnan dushi wei zhongxin" 近代中國寺廟破壞運動的空間特徵—以江南都市為重心. *Bulletin of the Institute of Modern History, Academia Sinica* 95 (2017): 1–37.

Katz, Paul R. "Local Elites and Sacred Sites in Hsin-Chuang—The Growth of the Ti-tsang An during the Japanese Occupation." In Lin Mei-rong, ed., *Belief, Ritual, and Society: Papers from the Third International Conference on Sinology, Anthropology Section*, 179–227. Nankang: Institute of Ethnology, Academia Sinica, 2003.

Katz, Paul R. *Religion in China and Its Modern Fate*. Waltham, MA: Brandeis University Press, 2014.

Katz, Paul R. "Religion and the State in Postwar Taiwan." *China Quarterly* 174 (2003): 395–412.

Katz, Paul R. "Religious Life in Western Hunan during the Modern Era: Some Preliminary Observations," *Cahiers d'Extrême Asie* 25 (2016): 181–218.

Katz, Paul R. "Spirit-Writing and the Dynamics of Elite Religious Life in Republican Era Shanghai." In Ting Jen-chieh 丁仁傑, ed., *Jindai Zhongguo de zongjiao fazhan lunwenji* 近代中國的宗教發展論文集, 275–350. Taipei: Academia Historica, 2015.

Katz, Paul R. "'Superstition' and Its Discontents: On the Impact of Temple Destruction Campaigns in China, 1898–1948." In Katz and Liu Shufen, *Belief, Practice, and Cultural Adaptation*, 605–82.

Katz, Paul R. "An Unbreakable Thread? Preliminary Observations on the Interaction between Chinese and Taiwanese Religious Traditions under Japanese Colonial Rule." *Taiwan zongjiao yanjiu* 臺灣宗教研究 11.2 (2012): 39–70.

Katz, Paul R. "Writing a Place for Rites: The Value of 'Old Customs' in Modern Wenzhou." *Journal of Chinese Religions* 43.1 (2015): 59–88.

Katz, Paul R., and Liu Shufen 劉淑芬, eds. *Belief, Practice, and Cultural Adaptation: Papers from the Religion Section of the Fourth International Conference on Sinology*. Nankang: Academia Sinica, 2013.

Katz, Paul R., and Murray Rubinstein, eds. *Religion and the Formation of Taiwanese Identities*. New York: Palgrave Macmillan, 2003.

Kendall, Laurel. *Shamans, Nostalgias, and the IMF: South Korean Popular Religion in Motion*. Honolulu: University of Hawai'i Press, 2009.

"Kexue changshi: Fuji zhi kexue de jieshi" 科學常識：扶乩之科學的解釋 *Nongmin* 農民 3.2 (1927): 6–7.

Kiely, Jan. "The Charismatic Monk and the Chanting Masses: Master Yinguang and His Pure Land Revival Movement." In Ownby, Goossaert and Ji, *Making Saints*, 30–77.

Kiely, Jan. "Shanghai Public Moralist Nie Qijie and Morality Book Publication Projects in Republican China." *Twentieth-Century China* 36.1 (2011): 4–22.

Kiely, Jan. "Spreading the Dharma with the Mechanized Press: New Buddhist Print Cultures in the Modern Chinese Print Revolution, 1865–1949." In Brokaw and Reed, *From Woodblocks to the Internet*, 185–210.

Kiely, Jan, and J. Brooks Jessup, eds. *Recovering Buddhism in Modern China*. New York: Columbia University Press, 2016.

Kleeman, Terry. "Licentious Cults and Bloody Victuals: Sacrifice, Reciprocity, and Violence in Traditional China." *Asia Major* 7.1 (1997): 185–211.

Ko, Dorothy. *Teachers of the Inner Chambers: Women and Culture in Seventeenth-Century China*. Stanford, CA: Stanford University Press, 1995.

Kohn, Livia, and Harold D. Roth, eds. *Daoist Identity: History, Lineage, and Ritual*. Honolulu: University of Hawai'i Press, 2002.

Kuo Cheng-tian. *Religion and Democracy in Taiwan*. Albany: State University of New York Press, 2008.

Kuo Ya-pei [郭亞珮]. *Debating "Culture" in Interwar China*. Leiden Series in Modern East Asian Politics and History. London: Routledge, 2010.

Kuo Ya-pei. "Redeploying Confucius: The Imperial State Dreams of the Nation, 1902–1911." In Yang, *Chinese Religiosities*, 65–84.

Lagerwey, John. *China: A Religious State*. Hong Kong: Hong Kong University Press, 2010.

Lai Chi-tim [黎志添]. "Hong Kong Daoism: A Study of Daoist Altars and Lü Dongbin Cults." *Social Compass* 50.4 (2003): 459–70.

Lai Chi-tim 黎志添. "Minguo shiqi Guangzhou shi Zhengyipai huoju daoshi yingye daoguan fenbu de kongjian fenxi—Miaoyu, renkou yu Daojiao yishi" 民國時期廣州市正一派火居道士營業道館分布的空間分析—廟宇、人口與道教儀式. *Hanxue yanjiu* 漢學研究 32.4 (2014): 293–330.

Lai Chi-tim 黎志添. "Qingdai Daoguang nianjian Guangzhou chengqu cimiao de kongjian fenbu yanjiu: Yi Daoguang shiwunian 'Guangzhou shengcheng quantu' wei kaocha zhongxin" 清代道光年間廣州城區祠廟的空間分佈及其意涵：以道光十五年「廣州省城全圖」為考察中心. *Journal of Chinese Studies* 63 (2016): 151–99.

Lai Ch'ung-jen 賴崇仁. "Taizhong Ruicheng shuju ji qi gezaice yanjiu" 台中瑞成書局及其歌仔冊研究. MA thesis, Feng-chia University, 2004.

Lai Yu-chih. "Remapping Borders: Ren Bonian's Frontier Paintings and Urban Life in 1880s Shanghai." *Art Bulletin* 86.3 (September 2004): 550–72.

Lang, Graeme and Lars Ragvald. *The Rise of a Refugee God: Hong Kong's Wong Tai Sin*. Hong Kong: Oxford University Press, 1993.

Lary, Diana. *The Chinese People at War: Human Suffering and Social Transformation, 1937–1945*. New York: Cambridge University Press, 2010.

Lee Anru. "Women of the Sisters' Hall: Religion and the Making of Women's Alternative Space in Taiwan's Economic Restructuring." *Gender, Place and Culture: A Journal of Feminist Geography* 15.4 (2008): 373–93.

Lee, Joseph Tse-Hei. *The Bible and the Gun: Christianity in South China, 1860–1900*. New York: Routledge, 2003.

Lee, Joseph Tse-Hei, and Christie Chui-Shan Chow. "Publishing Prophecy: A Century of Adventist Print Culture in China." In Clart and Scott, *Religious Publishing*, 51–90.

Lee, Raymond L. M., and Susan E. Ackerman. *Sacred Tensions: Modernity and Religious Transformation in Malaysia*. Columbia: University of South Carolina Press, 1997.

Lee Tong Soon. "Technology and the Production of Islamic Space: The Call to Prayer in Singapore." *Ethnomusicology* 43.1 (1999): 86–100.

Leung, Angela Ki Che (Liang Qizi 梁其姿). *Shishan yu jiaohua: Ming Qing de cishan zuzhi* 施善與教化：明清的慈善組織. Taipei: Lien-ching Publishing, 1997.

Li Ganchen 李幹忱, ed. and comp. *Pochu mixin quanshu* 破除迷信全書. In *Zhongguo minjian xinyang ziliao huibian* 中國民間信仰資料彙編, series 1, vol. 30. Taipei: Xuesheng shuju, 1989.

Li Guannan. "Reviving China: Urban Reconstruction in Nanchang and the Guomindang National Revival Movement, 1932–1937." *Frontiers of History in China* 7.1 (2012): 106–13.

Li Liliang 李麗涼. *Yidai tianshi: Zhang Enpu yu Taiwan Daojiao* 弌代天師：張恩溥與台灣道教. Taipei: Guoshiguan, 2012.

Li Shiyu 李世瑜. "Baojuan xinyan" 寶卷新研. *Wenxue yichan zengkan* 文學遺產增刊 4 (1957): 165–81. Reprinted in Li Shiyu, *Baojuan lunji* 寶卷論集. *Zongjiao yu shehui congshu* 宗教與社會叢書, vol. 1: 2–19. Taipei: Lantai chubanshe, 2007.

Li Shizhong 李世眾. *WanQing shishen yu difang zhengzhi: Yi Wenzhou wei zhongxin de kaocha* 晚清士紳與地方政治：以溫州為中心的考察. Shanghai: Shanghai renmin chubanshe, 2006.

Li Xiangping 李向平. *Jiushi yu jiuxin: Zhongguo jindai Fojiao fuxing sichao yanjiu* 救世與救心：中國近代佛教復興思潮研究. Shanghai: Shanghai renmin chubanshe, 1993.

Li Xuechang 李學昌 and Dong Jianbo 董建波. "20 shiji shangbanye Hangxian yingshen saihui shuailuo yinsu qianxi" 20 世紀上半葉杭縣迎神賽會衰落因素淺析. *Huadong shifan daxue xuabao (Zhexue shehui kexue ban)* 華東師範大學學報(哲學社會科學版) 39.5 (2007): 49–53.

Li Zhongqing 李忠清 and Yang Xiaomin 楊小民, eds. *Jiushi baitai: 1912–1949 laomanhua · Manhua shehui* 舊世百態：1912–1949老漫畫·漫畫社會. Beijing: Xiandai chubanshe, 1999.

Lian Xi. *Redeemed by Fire: The Rise of Popular Christianity in Modern China*. New Haven, CT: Yale University Press, 2010.

Liang Yong 梁勇. "Qingmo 'Miaochan xingxue' yu xiangcun quanshi de zhuanyi—Yi Baxian wei zhongxin" 清末'廟產興學'與鄉村權勢的轉移—以巴縣為中心. *Shehuixue yanjiu* 社會學研究 1 (2008): 102–19.

Lin, Larry Tse-Hsiung. "The Development and Conceptual Transformation of Chinese Buddhist Songs in the Twentieth Century." PhD diss., University of California, San Diego, 2012.

Lin, Larry Tse-Hsiung. "Li Shutong's Buddhist-Themed School Songs of the Early Twentieth Century and Their Japanese Influences." Paper presented at the conference 2013 e-CASE and e-Tech International Conference, Kitakyushu, Japan, April 3–5, 2013.

Lin Shuimei 林水梅 and Xie Jizhong 謝濟中. "Lianchengxian chengguan de Chenghuang miaohui" 連城縣城關的城隍廟會. In Yang Yanjie 楊彥杰, ed., *Minxi de chengxiang miaohui yu cunluo wenhua* 閩西的城鄉廟會與村落文化, 18–33. Hong Kong: International Hakka Studies Association, 1997.

Lin Wei-Ping. *Materializing Magic Power: Chinese Popular Religion in Villages and Cities*. Cambridge, MA: Harvard University Press, 2015.

Lin Wei-Ping 林瑋嬪. "Weihe yao jianmiao? Cong miaoyu Xingjian de wuzhihua guocheng tantao Mazu shequn zaizao" 為何要建廟？從廟宇興建的物質化過程探討馬祖社群再造. *Taiwan shehui jikan* 台灣社會研究季刊 92 (2013): 1–33.

Liu Bingrong 劉秉榮. *Junfa yu mixin* 軍閥與迷信. Beijing: Huawen chubanshe, 1993.

Liu Chengyou 劉成有. "Luelun miaochan xingxue ji qi dui Daojiao de yingxiang—Cong 1928 nian de yiduan difangzhi ziliao tongji shuoqi" 略論廟產興學及其對道教的影響—從1928年的一段地方志資料統計說起. *Zhongguo Daojiao* 中國道教 1 (2004): 50–52.

Liu Ching-chih. *A Critical History of New Music in China*. Hong Kong: Chinese University Press, 2010.

Liu, Lydia H. *Translingual Practice: Literature, National Culture, and Translated Modernity—China, 1900–1937*. Stanford, CA: Stanford University Press, 1995.

Liu Wenxing 劉文星. "Jindai Hushe yu siyuan de hudong: yi Shanghai Shousheng An shijian wei zhongxin" 近代湖社與寺院的互動:以上海壽聖庵事件為中心. In Kang Bao and Gao Wansang, *Gaibian Zhongguo zongjiao de wushinian*, 427–93.

Liu Wenxing 劉文星. *Li Yujie xiansheng nianpu changbian* 李玉階先生年譜長編. Nantou: Tiandijiao chubanshe, 2001.

Liu Xun. "Daoism from the Late Qing to Early Republican Periods." In Goossaert, Kiely, and Lagerwey, *Modern Chinese Religion*. Vol. 2: *1850–2015*, 806–37.

Liu Xun and Vincent Goossaert, eds. *Daoism in Modern China: Clerics and Temples in Urban Transformations, 1860–Present*. London: Routledge, 2021.

Liu Xun. *Daoist Modern: Innovation, Lay Practice, and the Community of Inner Alchemy in Republican Shanghai*. Cambridge, MA: Harvard University Asia Center, 2009.

Liu Xun. "Immortals and Patriarchs: The Daoist World of a Manchu Official and His Family in Nineteenth Century China." *Asia Major,* 3rd ser., 17.2 (2004): 161–218.

Liu Xun. "Of Poems, Gods, and Spirit-Writing Altars: The Daoist Beliefs and Practice of Wang Duan (1793–1839)." *Late Imperial China* 36.2 (2015): 23–81.

Liu Yonghua. *Confucian Rituals and Chinese Villagers: Ritual Change and Social Transformation in a Southeastern Chinese Community, 1368–1949*. Leiden: Brill, 2013.

Lo Shih-chieh 羅士傑. "Chenhuangshen yu jindai Wenzhou difang zhengzhi – yi 1949 nian Huang Shisu dang Chenghuang wei taolun zhongxin 城隍神與近代溫州地方政治-以1949年黃式蘇當城隍為討論中心." In Kang Bao and Gao Wansang, *Gaibian Zhongguo zongjiao de wushinian*, 101–39.

Lo Shih-chieh. "Investiture and Local Politics: Yang fujun 楊府君 (Lord Yang) in Late Qing Wenzhou (1840–1867)." *Late Imperial China* 33.1 (2012): 89–121.

Lo Shih-chieh. "The Order of Local Things: Popular Politics and Religion in Modern Wenzhou (1840–1940)." Ph.D. diss., Brown University, 2010.

Long Feijun 龍飛俊. "Shanghai Longwangmiao de taitaimen" 上海龍王廟的太太們. In Wang Gang and Li Tiangang, *Zhongguo jinshi difang shehuizhong de zongjiao yu guojia*, 119–38.

Longmen zhengzong Jueyun benzhi daotong xinchuan 龍門正宗覺雲本支道統薪傳. In *Zangwai Daoshu* 藏外道書, vol. 31. Chengdu: Bashu shushe, 1994.

Löwenthal, Rudolf. *The Religious Periodical Press in China*. Peking: Synodal Commission in China, 1940. Reprinted by the Chinese Materials Center in San Francisco in 1978.

Lu Mei-huan 呂玫鍰. "Yichanhua guocheng zhong de Mazu jinxiang: Yishi bianqian yu difang fuquan kaocha" 遺產化過程中的媽祖進香：儀式變遷與地方賦權的考察. *Minsu quyi* 民俗曲藝 192 (2016): 47–96.

Lu Zhongwei. "Huidaomen in the Republican Period." David Ownby, trans. *Chinese Studies in History* 44. 1–2 (Fall 2010–Winter 2011): 10–37.

"Lunshuo: Jizu pochu mixin bian" 論說：濟祖破除迷信辯. *Daode zazhi* 道德雜誌 2.8 (1922): 48.

Lutz, Jessie G., ed. *Pioneering Chinese Christian Women: Gender, Christianity, and Social Mobility*. Bethlehem, PA: Lehigh University Press, 2010.

Ma Xisha 馬西沙 and Han Bingfang 韓秉方. *Zhongguo minjian zongjiaoshi* 中國民間宗教史. Shanghai: Shanghai renmin chubanshe, 1992.

MacKinnon, Stephen R., Diana Lary and Ezra F. Vogel, eds. *China at War: Regions of China, 1937–1945*. Stanford, CA: Stanford University Press, 2007.

Madsen, Richard. *Democracy's Dharma: Religious Renaissance and Political Development in Taiwan*. Berkeley: University of California Press, 2007.

Mak, George Kam Wah. "The Colportage of the Protestant Bible in Late Qing China: The Example of the British and Foreign Bible Society." In Clart and Scott, *Religious Publishing*, 17–50.

Mann, Susan. *Precious Records: Women in China's Long Eighteenth Century*. Stanford, CA: Stanford University Press, 1997.

Mao Dun 茅盾. "1927 nian da geming: Huiyilu (9)" 一九二七年大革命：回憶錄[九]. *Xin wenxue shiliao* 新文學史料 4 (1980): 1–15.

Maxey, Trent E. *The "Greatest Problem": Religion and State Formation in Meiji Japan*. Cambridge, MA: Harvard University Asia Center, 2014.

McGuire, Beverly Foulks. "Bringing Buddhism into the Classroom: Jiang Qian's 江謙 (1876–1942) Vision for Education in Republican China." *Journal of Chinese Religions* 39 (2011): 33–54.

McHale, Shawn Frederick. *Print and Power: Confucianism, Communism, and Buddhism in the Making of Modern Vietnam*. Honolulu: University of Hawai'i Press, 2004.

Meihua guanzhu 梅花館主 (Wang Yiting). "Xin Wutai paiyan Jigong huofo zhi qianyin houguo" 新舞台排演濟公活佛之前因後果, *Xiju yuekan* 戲劇月刊 2.5 (1929): 4–5.

Menegon, Eugenio. *Ancestors, Virgins, and Friars: Christianity as a Local Religion in Late Imperial China*. Cambridge, MA: Harvard University Press, 2009.

Meng Lingbing 孟令兵. *Lao Shanghai wenhua qipa* 老上海文化奇葩. Shanghai: Shanghai renmin chubanshe, 2003.

Meyer, Christian. "How the 'Science of Religion' (*zongjiaoxue* 宗教學) as a Discipline Globalized 'Religion' in Republican China, 1890–1949: Global Concepts, Knowledge Transfer, and Local Discourses." In Jansen, Klein, and Meyer, *Chinese Religions in the Age of Globalization, 1800–Present*, 297–341.

Meyer-Fong, Tobie. *What Remains: Coming to Terms with Civil War in 19th Century China*. Stanford, CA: Stanford University Press, 2013.

Micic, Peter. "School Songs and Modernity in Late Qing and Early Republican China." PhD diss., Monash University, 1999.

Minguo shiqi chuban shumu huibian 民國時期出版書目彙編. Beijing: Guojia tushuguan chubanshe, 2010

Mittler, Barbara. *A Newspaper for China? Power, Identity, and Change in Shanghai's News Media, 1872–1912*. Cambridge, MA: Harvard University Asia Center, 2004.

More, J. B .P. *Muslim Identity, Print Culture, and the Dravidian Factor in Tamil Nadu*. New Delhi: Orient Longman, 2004.

Mori Yuria. "Identity and Lineage: The *Taiyi jinhua zongzhi* and the Spirit-Writing Cult to Patriarch Lü in Qing China." In Kohn and Roth, *Daoist Identity: History, Lineage, and Ritual*, 165–84.

Morris, Andrew D. *Marrow of the Nation: A History of Sport and Physical Culture in Republican China*. Berkeley: University of California Press, 2004.

Naquin, Susan. *Peking: Temples and City Life, 1400–1900*. Berkeley: University of California Press, 2000.

Naquin, Susan. "The Transmission of White Lotus Sectarianism in Late Imperial China." In Johnson, Nathan, and Rawski, *Popular Culture in Late Imperial China*, 255–91.

Nedostup, Rebecca. "Ritual Competition and the Modernizing Nation-State." In Yang, *Chinese Religiosities*, 87–112.

Nedostup, Rebecca. *Superstitious Regimes: Religion and the Politics of Chinese Modernity*. Cambridge, MA: Harvard University Asia Center, 2009.

Niida Noboru 仁井田陞. *Pekin kōshō girudo shiryō shū* 北京工商ギルド資料集. 6 vols. Tokyo: Tōyō bunka, 1975–83.

Oakes, Tim, and Donald S. Sutton, eds. *Faiths on Display: Religion, Tourism, and the Chinese State*. Lanham, MD: Rowman and Littlefield, 2010.

O'Leary, Stephen D. "Utopian and Dystopian Possibilities of Networked Religion in the New Millennium." In Højsgarard and Warburg, *Religion and Cyberspace*, 38–49.

Overmyer, Daniel L. "Attitudes toward Popular Religion in the Ritual Texts of the Chinese State: The Collected Statutes of the Great Ming." *Cahiers d'Extrême Asie* 5 (1989–90): 191–221.

Overmyer, Daniel L. *Local Religion in North China in the Twentieth Century: The Structure and Organization of Community Rituals and Beliefs*. Leiden: Brill, 2009.

Overmyer, Daniel L. *Precious Volumes: An Introduction to Chinese Sectarian Scriptures from the Sixteenth and Seventeenth Centuries*. Cambridge, MA: Harvard University Press, 1999.

Overmyer, Daniel L. "Values in Chinese Sectarian Literature: Ming and Ch'ing *pao-chüan*." In Johnson, Nathan, and Rawski, *Popular Culture in Late Imperial China*, 219–54.

Ownby, David. *Falun Gong and the Future of China*. New York: Oxford University Press, 2008.

Ownby, David. "The Politics of Redemption: Redemptive Societies and the Chinese State in Modern and Contemporary Chinese History." In Katz and Liu Shufen, eds., *Belief, Practice, and Cultural Adaptation*, 683–741.

Ownby, David. "Recent Chinese Scholarship on the History of 'Redemptive Societies': Guest Editor's Introduction." *Chinese Studies in History* 44.1–2 (Fall 2010–Winter 2011): 3–9.

Ownby, David A. "Redemptive Societies in the Twentieth Century." In Goossaert, Kiely, and Lagerwey, *Modern Chinese Religion*. Vol. 2: *1850–2015*, 685–727.

Ownby, David A. "Sainthood, Science, and Politics: The Life of Li Yujie, Founder of the Tiandijiao." In Ownby, Goossaert, and Ji, *Making Saints*, 241–71.

Ownby, David A., Vincent Goossaert, and Ji Zhe, *Making Saints in Modern China*. New York: Oxford University Press, 2017.

Palmer, David A. "Dao and Nation: Li Yujie, May Fourth Activist, Daoist Cultivator, and Redemptive Society Patriarch in Mainland China and Taiwan." In Palmer and Liu, *Daoism in the Twentieth Century*, 173–95.

Palmer, David A. "Heretical Doctrines, Reactionary Secret Societies, Evil Cults: Labeling Heterodoxy in Twentieth-Century China." In Yang, *Chinese Religiosities*, 113–34.

Palmer, David A. *Qigong Fever: Body, Science, and Utopia in China*. New York: Columbia University Press, 2007.

Palmer, David A., Paul R. Katz and Wang Chien-ch'uan, eds. *Redemptive Societies and New Religious Movements in Modern China*. Special issue. *Minsu quyi* 民俗曲藝 172–73 (June–September 2011).

Palmer, David A., and Liu Xun, eds. *Daoism in the Twentieth Century: Between Eternity and Modernity*. Berkeley: University of California Press, 2012.

Palmer, David A., Glenn Shive, and Philip L. Wickeri, eds. *Chinese Religious Life*. Oxford: Oxford University Press, 2011.

Pan Junliang. "L'évolution de l'organisation des Églises Wenzhou à Paris: Renégocier le pouvoir et l'autorité." In Yannick Fer and Gwendoline Malogne-Fer, eds., *Le protestantisme à Paris: Diversité et recompositions contemporaines*, 283–304. Geneva: Labor et Fides, 2017.

Pas, Julian. "Religious Life in Present Day Taiwan: A Field Observation Report, 1994–1995." *Journal of Chinese Religions* 24 (1996): 131–58.

Pham Quynh Phuong. *Hero and Deity: Tran Hung Dao and the Resurgence of Popular Religion in Vietnam*. Chiang Mai: Mekong Press, 2009.

Pittman, Don Alvin. *Toward a Modern Chinese Buddhism: Taixu's Reforms*. Honolulu: University of Hawai'i Press, 2001.

"Pochu mixin: Xiaoshan xuesheng daohui Chenghuang" 破除迷信 — 蕭山學生搗毀城隍. *Zhenguang zazhi* 真光雜誌 28.2 (1929): 84–85.

Poon Shuk-wah 潘淑華. "'Husheng' yu 'Jintu': 1930 niandai Shanghai de dongwu baohu yu Fojiao yundong" 「護生」與「禁屠」: 1930 年代上海的動物保護與佛教運動. In Kang Bao and Gao Wansang, *Gaibian Zhongguo zongjiao de wushinian*, 399–426.

Poon Shuk-wah. *Negotiating Religion in Modern China: State and Common People in Guangzhou, 1900–1937*. Hong Kong: Chinese University Press, 2010.

Poon Shuk-wah. "Thriving under an Anti-superstition Regime: The Dragon Mother Cult in Yuecheng, Guangdong, during the 1930s." *Journal of Chinese Religions* 43.1 (2015): 34–58.

Prazniak, Roxann. *Of Camel Kings and Other Things: Rural Rebels against Modernity in Late Imperial China*. New York: Rowman and Littlefield, 1999.

Qi Gang 祈剛. "Qingji Wenzhou diqu de miaochan banxue 清季溫州地區的廟產辦學." In Kang Bao and Gao Wansang, *Gaibian Zhongguo zongjiao de wushinian*, 39–73.

Qijun 琦君. *San geng you meng shu dang zhen* 三更有夢書當枕. Taipei: Erya chubanshe, 1975.

Qing Xitai 卿希泰, ed. *Zhongguo Daojiaoshi* 中國道教史, vol. 4. Chengdu: Sichuan renmin chubanshe, 1995.

Ramonéda, Joseph. "Une tentative d'enfermement de l'Église: Les arrêtés municipaux d'interdiction des processions extérieures sous la République concordataire (1870–1905)." *Clio@Thémis* 4 (2011): 1–24.

Reed, Christopher. *Gutenberg in Shanghai: Chinese Print Capitalism, 1876–1937*. Vancouver: University of British Columbia Press, 2004.

Reinders, Eric. "Shattered on the Rock of Ages: Western Iconoclasm and Chinese Modernity." In Fabio Rambelli and Eric Reinders, eds., *Buddhism and Iconoclasm in East Asia: A History*, 89–133. London: Bloomsbury Academic, 2012.

Reports of the Achievements of the World Buddhist Householder Association (*Shijie Fojiao jushilin chengji baogaoshu* 世界佛教居士林成績報告書), 1933. In Huang Xianian 黃夏年, ed. *Minguo Fojiao qikan wenxian jicheng chubian* 民國佛教期刊文獻集成補編, volume 47. Beijing: Zhongguo shudian, 2008.

Reports of Shanghai's Associations for Planning Rapid Relief for Those Provinces Stricken by Flood (*Shanghai choumu gesheng shuizai jizhenhui gongzuo baogao* 上海籌募各省水災急賑會工作報告), 1935. Shanghai choumu gesheng shuizai jizhenhui 上海籌募各省水災急振會, ed. & comp. Preserved in the Library of the Institute of History, Shanghai Academy of Social Sciences (Shanghai shekeyuan Lishisuo tushuguan 上海社科院歷史所圖書館).

Robson, James. "Brushes with Some 'Dirty Truths': Handwritten Manuscripts and Religion in China." *History of Religions* 51.4 (2012): 317–43.

Rowe, William T. *Saving the World.: Chen Hongmou and Elite Consciousness in Eighteenth-Century China.* Stanford, CA: Stanford University Press, 2001.

Ruan Renze 阮仁澤 and Gao Zhennong 高振農, eds. *Shanghai zongjiaoshi* 上海宗教史. Shanghai: Shanghai renmin chubanshe, 1992.

Sakai Tadao 酒井忠夫. "Jinxiandai Zhongguo de shanshu yu xinshenghuo yundong" 近現代中國的善書與新生活運動. Lai Xuzhen 賴旭貞, trans. *Minjian zongjiao* 民間宗教 2 (1996): 93–103.

Sakai Tadao 酒井忠夫. *Kingendai Chūgoku ni okeru shūkyō kessha no kenkyū* 近、現代中國における宗教結社の研究. Tokyo: Tokyo kabushiki kaishi kokusho kankōkai, 2002.

Sakai Tadao 酒井忠夫. "Minguo chuqi zhi xinxing zongjiao yundong yu xinshidai chaoliu" 民國初期之新興宗教運動與新時代潮流. Chang Shu-e 張淑娥 trans. *Minjian zongjiao* 民間宗教 1 (1995): 1–36.

Saler, Michael. "Modernity and Enchantment: A Historiographic Review." *American Historical Review* 111.3 (June 2006): 692–716.

Sawada Mizuho 澤田瑞穗. *Zōho hōkan no kenkyū* 增補寶卷の研究. Tokyo: Dōkyō kankōkai, 1975.

Schein, Louisa. *Minority Rules: The Miao and the Feminine in China's Cultural Politics.* Durham, NC: Duke University Press, 2000.

Schneewind, Sarah. *Community Schools and the State in Ming China.* Stanford, CA: Stanford University Press, 2006.

Schwarcz, Vera. *The Chinese Enlightenment: Intellectuals and the Legacy of the May Fourth Movement of 1919.* Berkeley: University of California Press, 1986.

Scott, Gregory Adam. "The Buddhist Nationalism of Dai Jitao 戴季陶." *Journal of Chinese Religions* 39 (2011): 55–81.

Scott, Gregory Adam. "Conversion by the Book: Buddhist Print Culture in Early Republican China." PhD diss., Columbia University, 2013.

Scott, Gregory Adam. "Navigating the Sea of Scriptures: The Buddhist Studies Collectanea, 1918–1923." In Clart and Scott, *Religious Publishing*, 91–138.

Scott Gregory Adam. "A Revolution of Ink: Chinese Buddhist Periodicals in the Early Republic." In Jan Kiely and J. Brooks Jessup, eds., *Recovering Buddhism in Modern China*, 111–40. New York: Columbia University Press, 2016.

Scott, Gregory Adam, and Philip Clart. "Introduction: Print Culture and Religion in Chinese History." In Clart and Scott, *Religious Publishing*, 1–16.

Sezgin, Yüksel, and Mirjam Künkler. "Regulation of 'Religion' and the 'Religious': The Politics of Judicialization and Bureaucratization in India and Indonesia." *Comparative Studies in Society and History* 56.2 (April 2014): 448–78.

Sha Qingging 沙青青. "Xinyang yu quanzheng: 1931 nian Gaoyou 'Da Chenghuang' fengchao zhi yanjiu" 信仰與權爭：1931年高郵「打城隍」風潮之研究. *Jindaishi yanjiu* 近代史研究 1 (2010): 115–27.

Shahar, Meir. *Crazy Ji: Chinese Religion and Popular Literature*. Cambridge, MA: Harvard University Press, 1998.

Shanghai Jiyunxuan 上海集雲軒, ed. *Jishi tayuanzhi* 濟師塔院志 (1939). In Bai Huawen 白化文 et al., eds., *Zhongguo Fosizhi congkan xubian* 中國佛寺志叢刊續編, vol. 6. Yangzhou: Jiangsu guji chubanshe, 2001.

Shao Yong 紹雍. *Jindai Jiangnan mimi shehui* 近代江南秘密社會. Shanghai: Shanghai renmin chubanshe, 2013.

Shao Yong 紹雍. *Zhongguo huidaomen* 中國會道門. Shanghai: Shanghai renmin chubanshe, 1997.

Shen, Grace Yen. "Scientism in the Twentieth Century." In Goossaert, Kiely, and Lagerwey, *Modern Chinese Religion*. Vol. 2: *1850-2015*, 91–137.

Shen Jie 沈潔. "Fanmixin yu shequ xinyang kongjian de xiandai licheng—Yi 1934 nian Suzhou de qiuyu yishi wei li" 反迷信與社區信仰空間的現代歷程—以1934年蘇州的求雨儀式為例. *Shilin* 史林 2 (2007): 44–63.

Shen Jie 沈潔. "Xiandaihua jianzhi dui xinyang kongjian de zhengyong – Yi ershi shiji chunian de miaochan xingxue yundong wei li" 現代化建制對信仰空間的徵用—以二十世紀初年的廟產興學運動為例. *Lishi jiaoxue wenti* 歷史教學問題 2 (2008): 56–59.

Shen Kuiyi. "Wang Yiting in the Social Networks of 1910s–1930s Shanghai." In Dillon and Oi, *At the Crossroads of Empires: Middlemen, Social Networks, and State-Building in Republican China*, 45–64.

Shen Wenquan 沈文泉. *Haishang qiren Wang Yiting* 海上奇人王一亭. Beijing: Zhongguo shehui kexue chubanshe, 2011.

Shenbao 申報. Shanghai: Shenbaoguan, daily, 1872–1949.

Shi Anren 釋安仁. *Huyin chanyuan jishi* 湖隱禪院記事 (1921). In Bai Huawen 白化文 et al., eds., *Zhongguo Fosizhi congkan xubian*, vol. 7. Yangzhou: Jiangsu guji chubanshe, 2001.

Shi Yinshun 釋印順. *Taixu dashi nianpu* 太虛大師年譜. Taipei: Zhengwen chubanshe, 1988.

Shibao 時報. Shanghai: Shibaoshe, daily, 1904–1939.

Shibusawa Eiichi denki shiryō 澀澤榮一傳記資料. 68 vols. Tokyo: Shibusawa Eiichi Memorial Museum, 1955–71.

Shiga Ichiko. "The Manifestations of Lüzu in Modern Guangdong and Hong Kong: The Rise of Spirit-writing Cults." In Kohn and Roth, *Daoist Identity: History, Lineage, and Ritual*, 185–209.

Shih Fang-Long. "From Regulation and Rationalisation to Production: Government Policy on Religion in Taiwan." In Dafydd Fell, Henning Klöter, and Chang Bi-Yu, eds., *What Has Changed? Taiwan before and after the Change in Ruling Parties*, 265–83. Wiesbaden: Harrassowitz, 2006.

"Siren hui shuohua ma? Fuji Taishang guiling suo xie de zi" 死人會說話嗎?:扶乩臺上鬼靈所寫的字. *Shizhao yuebao* 時兆月報 23.3 (1928): 11.

Smith, David. *Hinduism and Modernity*. Malden, MA: Blackwell, 2003.

Smith, Joanna Handlin. *The Art of Doing Good: Charity in Late Ming China*. Berkeley: University of California Press, 2009.

Smith, Steve A. "Local Cadres Confront the Supernatural: The Politics of Holy Water (*Shenshui* 神水) in the PRC, 1949–1966." In Julia Strauss, ed., *The History of the PRC (1949–1976)*, 145–68. Cambridge: Cambridge University Press, 2007.

Smith, Steve A. "Talking Toads and Chinless Ghosts: The Politics of 'Superstitious' Rumors in the People's Republic of China." *American Historical Review* 111.2 (2006): 405–27.

Song Zanyou 宋鑽友. *Guangdongren zai Shanghai* 廣東人在上海. Shanghai: Shanghai renmin chubanshe, 2007.

Stalker, Nancy. "Showing Faith: Exhibiting Ōmoto to Consumers in Early-Twentieth-Century Japan." In DuBois, *Casting Faiths*, 239–56.

Stapleton, Kristin. *Civilizing Chengdu: Chinese Urban Reform, 1895–1937*. Cambridge, MA: Harvard University Press, 2000.

Stark, Ulrike. *An Empire of Books: The Naval Kishore Press and the Diffusion of the Printed Word in Colonial India*. Ranikhet: Permanent Black, 2008.

Sun, Anna. "The Revival of Confucian Rites in Contemporary China." In Yang Fenggang and Joseph Tamney, eds., *Confucianism and Spiritual Traditions in Modern China and Beyond*, 309–28. Leiden: Brill, 2012.

Sun Guangyong 孫廣勇. "Rongru yu chuanbo—Jianlun Li Jiabai ji qi Shangxian Tang de wenhua jiaoliu huodong" 融入與傳播—簡論李佳白及其尚賢堂的文化交流活動. *Shehui kexue zhanxian* 社會科學戰線 6 (2005): 299–301.

Sun Jiang 孫江. *Kindai Chūgoku no kakumei to himitsu kessha: Chūgoku kakumei no shakaishi kenkyū (1895–1955)* 近代中國の革命と秘密結社：中國革命の社會史的研究 (一八九五-一九五五). Tokyo: Kyūko sho-in, 2007.

Sun Yanfei. "Jingkong: From Universal Saint to Sectarian Saint." In Ownby, Goossaert and Ji, *Making Saints*, 394–418.

Sun Yanfei. "Religions in Sociopolitical Context: The Reconfiguration of Religious Ecology in Post-Mao China." PhD diss., University of Chicago, 2010.

Sun Yusheng 孫語聖. "Shijie Hongwanzihui Zhonghua zonghui yu Minguo shiqi de shehui jiuji" 世界紅卍字會中華總會與民國時期的社會救濟. *Anda shixue* 安大史學 2 (2004): 192–200.

Sung Kuang-yu 宋光宇. "Shentan de xingcheng: Gaoxiongshi shentan diaocha ziliao de chubu fenxi" 神壇的形成：高雄市神壇調查資料的初步分析. In *Simiao yi minjian wenhua yantaohui lunwenji* 寺廟與民間文化研討會論文集, 97–128. Taipei: Committee for Cultural Construction, 1995.

Sutton, Donald. "From Credulity to Scorn: Confucians Confront the Spirit Mediums in Late Imperial China." *Late Imperial China* 21.2 (2000): 1–39.

Suzuki, D. T., and Paul Carus. *Treatise on Response and Retribution*. 1906, reprint La Salle, IL: Open Court, 1973. http://www.terebess.hu/english/taishang.html.

Szonyi, Michael. *Practicing Kinship: Lineage and Descent in Late Imperial China*. Stanford, CA: Stanford University Press, 2002.

Szonyi, Michael. "Secularization Theories and the Study of Chinese Religions." *Social Compass* 56.3 (2009): 312–27.

Tai Shuangqiu 邰爽秋. *Miaochan xingxue wenti* 廟產興學問題. Shanghai: Zhonghua shubao liutongchu, 1929.

Taiji dawen 太極答問. Shanghai: Zhonghua shuju, 1929.

Taiji quanshu 太極拳術. Shanghai: Zhonghua shuju, 1925.

Tang Wenzhi 唐文治. *Rujing tang wenji* 茹經堂文集 (1935). In *Minguo congshu* 民國叢書, 5th series, vols. 94–95. Shanghai: Shanghai shuju, 1996.

Tao Jin 陶金 and Vincent Goossaert. "Daojiao yu Suzhou difang shehui" 道教與蘇州地方社會. In Fan Lizhu and Robert Weller, eds., *Jiangnan diqu de zongjiao yu gonggong shenghuo* 江南地區的宗教與公共生活, 86–112. Shanghai: Shanghai renmin chubanshe, 2015.

Tao Shuimu 陶水木. "Beiyang zhengfu shiqi lüHu Zheshang de cishan huodong" 北洋政府時期旅滬浙商的慈善活動. *Zhejiang shehui kexue* 浙江社會科學 6 (2005): 177–83.

Tarocco, Francesca. "Buddhist Music." In S. Sadie and J. Tyrrell, eds., *The New Grove Dictionary of Music and Musicians*. Online version, 2004. Oxford University Press. https://global.oup.com/academic/product/grove-music-online-9780333913987?lang=en&cc=fr. (accessed October 4, 2018).

Tarocco, Francesca. *The Cultural Practices of Modern Chinese Buddhism: Attuning the Dharma*. New York: Routledge, 2007.

Tarocco, Francesca. "Pluralism and Its Discontents: Buddhism and Proselytizing in Modern China." In Juliana Finucane and R. Michael Feener, eds., *Proselytizing and the Limits of Religious Pluralism in Contemporary Asia*, 237–54. Singapore: Springer, 2014.

Taylor, Jay. *The Generalissimo: Chiang Kai-shek and the Struggle for Modern China*. Cambridge, MA: Belknap Press of Harvard University Press, 2009.

ter Haar, Barend. "Local Society and the Organization of Cults in Early Modern China: A Preliminary Study." *Studies in Central and East Asian Religions* 8 (1995): 1–43.

ter Haar, Barend. *Ritual and Mythology of the Chinese Triads: Creating an Identity*. Leiden: Brill, 1998.

ter Haar, Barend. *The White Lotus Teachings in Chinese Religious History*. Leiden: Brill, 1992.

Thal, Sarah. *Rearranging the Landscape of the Gods: The Politics of a Pilgrimage Site in Japan, 1573–1912*. Chicago: University of Chicago Press, 2005.

Tong, Hollington Kong. *Chiang Kai-shek, Soldier and Statesman: Authorized Biography by Hollington K. Tong*. London: Hurst and Blackett, 1938.

Tsai Chin-tang 蔡錦堂. *Nihon teikoku shugi ka Taiwan no shūkyō seisaku* 日本帝国主義下台湾の宗教政策. Tokyo: Dōseisha, 1994.

Tsai Pei-ju 蔡佩如. *Chuansuo tianren zhi ji de nüren: Nüjitong de xingbie tezhi yu shenti yihan* 穿梭天人之際的女人：女童乩的性別特質與身體意涵. Taipei: Tangshan Publishing, 2001.

Tsai Weipin. *Reading Shenbao: Nationalism, Consumerism, and Individuality in China, 1919–37*. Basingstoke: Palgrave Macmillan, 2010.

Tsai Yen-zen, ed. *Religious Experience in Contemporary Taiwan and China.* Taipei: Chengchi University Press, 2013.

Tsao Hsing-yuan. "A Forgotten Celebrity: Wang Zhen (1867–1933), Businessman, Philanthropist, and Artist." In Chou Ju-hsi, ed., *Art at the Close of China's Empire*, 94–109. Phoebus Occasional Papers in Art History, no. 8. Tempe: Arizona State University Press, 1998.

Tsin, Michael. *Nation, Governance, and Modernity in China: Canton, 1900–1927.* Stanford, CA: Stanford University Press, 1999.

Tsou Mingteh. "Christian Missionary as Confucian Intellectual: Gilbert Reid (1857–1927) and the Reform Movement in the Late Qing." In Bays, *Christianity in China*, 73–90.

Valussi, Elena. "Men Built Religion, and Women Made It Superstitious: Gender and Superstition in Republican China," *Journal of Chinese Religions* 48.1 (2020): 87–125.

van de Ven, Hans J. *War and Nationalism in China, 1925–1945.* London: RoutledgeCurzon, 2003.

van der Veer, Peter, ed. *Handbook of Religion and the Asian City.* Berkeley: University of California Press, 2015.

van der Veer, Peter. *The Modern Spirit of Asia: The Spiritual and the Secular in China and India.* Princeton, NJ: Princeton University Press, 2013.

Wagner, Rudolf G., ed. *Word, Image, and City in Early Chinese Newspapers, 1870–1910.* Albany: State University of New York Press, 2007.

Wallis, Roy, and Steve Bruce. "Secularization: The Orthodox Model." In Steve Bruce, ed., *Religion and Modernization: Sociologists and Historians Debate the Secularization Thesis.* Oxford: Oxford University Press, 1992.

Wan Jianzhong 萬建中. "Minchu de fengsu biange yu biange fengsu" 民國的風俗變革與變革風俗. *Liaoxibei minzu yanjiu* 遼西北民族研究 33 (2002): 119–28.

Wang Cheng-hua. "The Qing Imperial Collection circa 1905–25: National Humiliation Heritage Preservation and Exhibition Culture." In Wu Hung, ed., *Reinventing the Past: Archaism and Antiquarianism in Chinese Art and Visual Culture*, 320–41. Chicago: Center for the Art of East Asia, University of Chicago, 2010.

Wang Chien-ch'uan 王見川. "Guomin zhengfu lai Tai (1949) qian liang'an de zongjiao wanglai yu cishan huodong chutan: Jian tan Lanji shuju Huang Maosheng de jiaose" 國民政府來台（1949）前兩岸的宗教往來與慈善活動初探：兼談蘭記書局黃茂盛的角色. *Mazu yu minjian xinyang: Yanjiu tongxun* 媽祖與民間信仰: 研究通訊 1 (2012): 57–69.

Wang Chien-ch'uan 王見川. "Jindai Zhongguo de fuji, cishan yu 'mixin' – Yi *Yinguang wenchao* wei kaocha xiansuo" 近代中國的扶乩、慈善與「迷信」—以印光文鈔為考查線索. In Katz and Liu Shufen, *Belief, Practice, and Cultural Adaptation*, 531–68.

Wang Chien-ch'uan 王見川. "Minguo shiqi Daoyuan Hongwanzihui zhenzai jilu" 民國時期道院紅卍字會賑災記錄. *Minjian zongjiao* 民間宗教 1 (1995): 217–24.

Wang Chien-ch'uan 王見川. "Morality Book Publishing and Popular Religion in Modern China: A Discussion Centered on Morality Book Publishers in Shanghai," Gregory Adam Scott trans. In Clart and Scott, *Religious Publishing*, 233–64.

Wang Chien-ch'uan. "Popular Groups Promoting 'The Religion of Confucius' in the Chinese Southwest and Their Activities since the Nineteenth Century (1840–2013): An Observation Centered on Yunnan's Eryuan County and Environs." In Sébastien Billioud, ed., *The Varieties of Confucian Experience. Documenting a Grassroots Revival of Tradition*, 90-121. Leiden: Brill, 2018.

Wang Chien-ch'uan 王見川. "Qingmo de guanshen yu fuji: jiantan qishi liuxing de chenyan" 清末的官紳與扶乩 : 兼談其時流行的讖言. *Mazu yu minjian xinyang: Yanjiu tongxun* 媽祖與民間信仰：研究通訊 2 (2012): 34–47.

Wang Chien-ch'uan 王見川. "Qingmo Minchu Zhongguo de Jigong xinyang yu fuji tuanti: Jian tan Zhongguo Jishenghui de youlai" 清末民初中國的濟公信仰與扶乩團體：兼談中國濟生會的由來. *Minsu quyi* 民俗曲藝 162 (2008): 139–69.

Wang Chien-ch'uan. "Spirit-Writing Groups in Modern China (1840–1937): Textual Production, Public Teachings, and Charity." Vincent Goossaert, trans. In Goossaert, Kiely, and Lagerwey, *Modern Chinese Religion*. Vol. 2: *1850–2015*, 651–84.

Wang Chien-ch'uan 王見川. "Taiwan 'Guandi dang Yuhuang' chuanshuo de youlai" 臺灣「關帝當玉皇」傳說的由來. In *Hanren zongjiao, minjian xinyang yu yuyanshu de tansuo: Wang Chien-ch'uan zixuanji* 漢人宗教、民間信仰與預言書的探索：王見川自選集. Taipei: BoyYoung, 2008, 411–30.

Wang Chien-ch'uan 王見川 and Li Shih-wei 李世偉. *Taiwan de minjian zongjiao yu xinyang* 台灣的民間宗教與信仰. Luzhou: BoyYoung, 2000.

Wang Di. *Street Culture in Chengdu: Public Space, Urban Commoners, and Local Politics, 1870–1930*. Stanford, CA: Stanford University Press, 2003.

Wang Gang 王崗 (Richard Wang) and Li Tiangang 李天綱, eds. *Zhongguo jinshi difang shehuizhong de zongjiao yu guojia* 中國近世地方社會中的宗教與國家. Shanghai: Fudan daxue chubanshe, 2014.

Wang Jian 王健. *Lihai xiangguan: Ming Qing yilai Jiangnan Susong diqu minjian xinyang yanjiu* 利害相關：明清以來江南蘇松地區民間信仰研究. Shanghai: Shanghai renmin chubanshe, 2010.

Wang Jian 王健. "Ming Qing yilai Hangzhou jinxiang shi chutan" 明清以來杭州進香史初探. *Shilin* 史林 4 (2012): 89–97.

Wang Lianyou 王蓮友, ed. *Chongjian Jinling Yuxuguan jishi zhengxinlu* 重建金陵玉虛觀紀事徵信錄 (1936). In *Zhongguo Daoguanzhi congkan xubian* 中國道觀志叢刊續編, vol. 15. Yangzhou: Guangling shushe, 2004.

Wang Liping. "Tourism and Spatial Changes in Hangzhou, 1900–1927." In Esherick, *Remaking the Chinese City: Modernity and National Identity, 1900-1950*, 107–20.

Wang Liqi 王利器. *Yuan Ming Qing sandai jinhui xiaoshuo xiqu shiliao* 元明清三代禁毀小說戲曲史料. Shanghai: Shanghai guji chubanshe, 1981.

"Wang Yiting xiansheng jiaxun" 王一亭先生家訓. *Xinghua* 興華 28.48 (1931): 24.

Wang Zhen 王震 (Wang Yiting) and Wu Changshuo 吳昌碩. *Foxiang tishi* 佛像題詩. Copy located in the Fu Sinian Library of the Institute of History and Philology, Academia Sinica.

Wang Zhongxiu 王中秀, ed. and comp. *Wang Yiting nianpu changbian* 王一亭年譜長編. Shanghai: Shanghai shuhua chubanshe, 2010.

Wang Zhongxiu 王中秀 et al., eds. *Jinxiandai jinshi shuhuajia runli* 近現代金石書畫家潤例. Shanghai: Shanghai shuhua chubanshe, 2004.

Wang Zongyao 王宗耀. *Huzhou Jin'gaishan Gu Meihuaguan zhi* 湖州金蓋山古梅花觀志. Huzhou: Huzhou Daojiao xilie neibu congshu, 2003.

Wang Zongyu 王宗昱. "Wuxing Quanzhendao shiliao" 吳興全真道史料. In Poul Andersen and Florian Reiter, eds., *Scriptures, Schools, and Forms of Practice in Daoism: A Berlin Symposium*, 215–32. Wiesbaden: Harrassowitz, 2005.

Watson, James L. "Standardizing the Gods: The Promotion of Tien Hou ('Empress of Heaven') along the South China Coast, 960–1960." In Johnson, Nathan, and Rawski, *Popular Culture in Late Imperial China*, 292–324.

Wei Wenjing 魏文靜. "Ming Qing yingshen saihui lüjin buzhi yu shangyehua – Yi Jiangnan yingshen saihui jingji gongneng wei zhongxin de tantao" 明清迎神賽會屢禁不止與商業化—以江南迎神賽會經濟功能為中心的探討. *Lishi jiaoxue* 歷史教學 14 (2009): 27–34.

Welch, Holmes. *The Buddhist Revival in China*. Cambridge, MA: Harvard University Press, 1968.

Weller, Robert P. "Asia and the Global Economies of Charisma." In Pattana Kitiarsa, ed., *Religious Commodifications in Asia: Marketing Gods*, 15–30. London: Routledge, 2008.

Weller, Robert P. "Chinese Cosmology and the Environment." In Palmer, Shive, and Wickeri, *Chinese Religious Life*, 124–38.

Weller, Robert P. "Global Religious Changes and Civil Life in Two Chinese Societies: A Comparison of Jiangsu and Taiwan." *Review of Faith and International Affairs* 13.2 (2015): 13–24.

Weller, Robert P. "Taiwan and Global Religious Trends." *Taiwan zongjiao yanjiu* 臺灣宗教研究 12.1–2 (2013): 7–30.

Wen Guoliang 溫國良, ed. and trans. *Taiwan zongdufu gongwen leicuan zongjiao shiliao huibian (Mingzhi 28 nian 10 yue zhi Mingzhi 35 nian 4 yue)* 臺灣總督府公文類纂宗教史料彙編(明治二十八年十月至明治三十五年四月). Nantou: Taiwan sheng wenxian weiyuanhui, 1999.

Wood, Frances, and Mark Barnard. *The Diamond Sutra: The Story of the World's Earliest Dated Printed Book*. London: British Library, 2010.

Wu Cheng-han. "The Temple Fairs in Late Imperial China." PhD diss., Princeton University, 1988.

Wu Haoran 吳浩然, ed. *Minguo manhua fengfan* 民國漫畫風範. Jinan: Qilu shushe, 2011.

Wu Jen-shu 巫仁恕. "Jieqing, xinyang yu kangzheng – Ming Qing chenghuang xinyang yu chengshi qunzhong de jiti kangyi xingwei" 節慶信仰與抗爭-明清城隍信仰與城市群眾的集體抗議行為. *Bulletin of the Institute of Modern History, Academia Sinica* 34 (2000): 145–210.

Wu Jen-shu 巫仁恕. "Ming Qing Jiangnan Dongyue shen xinyang yu chengshi qunzhong de jiti kangyi – Yi Suzhou minbian wei taolun zhongxin" 明清江南東嶽神信仰與城市群眾的集體抗議-以蘇州民變為討論中心. In Li Hsiao-t'i 李孝悌, ed., *Zhongguo de chengshi shenghuo* 中國的城市生活, 149–206. Taipei: Lianjing, 2005.

Wu Ping 吳平. "Jindai Shanghai de Fojiao chuban jigou" 近代上海的佛教出版機構. *Huaxia wenhua* 華夏文化 1 (2000): 37, 41–42.

Wu Yakui 吳亞魁. *Jiangnan Quanzhen Daojiao* 江南全真道教. Hong Kong: Zhonghua shuju, 2006.

Wu Yakui 吳亞魁. "Qingmo Minguo shiqi Shanghai de zongjiao chuban gaiguan: Yi Fo–Daojiao wei zhongxin" 清末民國時期上海的宗教出版概觀：以佛道教為中心. In Kang Bao and Gao Wansang, *Gaibian Zhongguo zongjiao de wushinian*, 261–336.

Wue, Roberta May-hwa. "Making the Artist: Ren Bonian (1840–1895) and Portraits of the Shanghai Art World." PhD diss., New York University, 2001.

Wujun suihua jili 吳郡歲華紀麗, by Yuan Jinglan 袁景瀾 (fl. 1820–1873). Nanjing: Jiangsu guji chubanshe, 1998.

Xiao Fenqi 蕭芬琪 (Siu Fun-kee). *Wang Yiting* 王一亭. Shijiazhuang: Hebei jiaoyu chubanshe, 2002.

Xiao Tian 小田. "Jindai Jiangnan miaohui yu nongjia jingji shenghuo" 近代江南廟會與農家經濟生活. *Zhongguo nongshi* 中國農史 21.2 (2002): 79–86.

Xiao Tian 小田. "Lun Jiangnan xiangcun nüwu de jindai jingyu" 論江南鄉村女巫的近代境遇. *Jindaishi yanjiu* 近代史研究 5 (2014): 39–55.

Xiao Tian 小田. "Shequ chuantong de jindai mingyun—Yi Suzhou 'Qionglong laohui' wei duixiang de li'an yanjiu" 社區傳統的近代命運—以蘇州穹窿老會為對象的例案研究. *Jiangsu shehui kexue* 江蘇社會科學 6 (2002): 141–47.

Xu Dishan 許地山. *Fuji mixin di yanjiu* 扶箕迷信底研究. Changsha: Shangwu yinshuguan, 1941.

Xu Shangshu 許尚樞. *Tiantaishan Jigong huofo* 天台山濟公活佛. Beijing: Guoji wenhua chuban gongsi, 1997.

Xu Xiaoming 許曉明. "Zongjiao wenhua da shiyi: Qingmo Minchu Guangxi 'Miaochan xingxue' yundong" 宗教文化大失憶：清末民初廣西「廟產興學」運動. *Nanfang luntan* 南方論壇 12 (2007): 94–95.

Xu Xiaozheng 許效正. "Qingmo Minchu miaochan wenti yanjiu (1895–1916)" 清末民初廟產問題研究 (1895–1916). PhD diss., Shaanxi Normal University, 2010.

Xu Yao 徐躍. "Qingmo Sicuan miaochan xingxue ji you ci chansheng de sengsu jiufen" 清末四川廟產興學及由此產生的僧俗糾紛. *Jindaishi yanjiu* 近代史研究 5 (2008): 73–88.

Xue Yu. *Buddhism, War, and Nationalism: Chinese Monks in the Struggle against Japanese Aggression, 1931–1945*. New York: Routledge, 2005.

Yan Yutang 嚴玉堂. "Zhengfu pochu mixin yu Zhongguo jidujiao de qiantu" 政府破除迷信與中國基督教的前途. *Xinghua* 興華 25.35 (1928): 13–14.

Yang Fenggang. *Religion in China: Survival and Revival under Communist Rule*. New York: Oxford University Press, 2012.

Yang Kaili 楊凱里 (Jan Kiely). "Zai jingying dizi yu nianfo dazhong zhijian – Minguo shiqi Yinguang fashi jingtu yundong de shehui jianzhang" 在精英弟子與念佛大眾之間-民國時期印光法師淨土運動的社會緊張. In Kang Bao and Gao Wansang, *Gaibian Zhongguo zongjiao de wushinian*, 363–97.

Yang, Mayfair Mei-hui, ed. *Chinese Religiosities: Afflictions of Modernity and State Formation*. Berkeley: University of California Press, 2008.

Yang, Mayfair Mei-hui. "Shamanism and Spirit Possession in Chinese Modernity: Some Preliminary Reflections on a Gendered Religiosity of the Body." *Review of Religion and Chinese Society* 2.1 (2015): 51–86.

Yao Minquan 姚民權 and Zhang Letian 張樂天. "Shanghai Jidujiao shi" 上海基督教史. In Ruan Renze and Gao Zhennong, *Shanghai zongjiaoshi*, 787–1019.

Yao Xinzhong and Paul Badham. *Religious Experience in Contemporary China*. Cardiff: University of Wales Press, 2007.

Yau Chi-on (You Zi'an) 游子安. "DaDao nanxing: 1920 zhi 1930 niandai Gang, Xing Tianqing caotang yu Daoyuan zhi daomai yinyuan" 大道南行: 1920 至1930年代港、星天清草堂與道院之道脈因緣. In Kang Bao and Gao Wansang, *Gaibian Zhongguo zongjiao de wushinian*, 141–67.

Yau Chi-on (You Zi'an) 游子安. *Quanhua jinzhen: Qingdai shanshu yanjiu* 勸化金箴 : 清代善書研究. Tianjin: Tianjin renmin chubanshe, 1999.

Yau Chi-on (You Zi'an) 游子安. *Shan yu ren tong: Ming Qing yilai de cishan yu jiaohua* 善與人同 : 明清以來的慈善與教化. Beijing: Zhonghua shuju, 2005.

Yau Chi-on (You Zi'an) 游子安. "The Xiantiandao and Publishing in the Guangzhou-Hong Kong Area from the Late Qing to the 1930s: The Case of the Morality Book Publisher Wenzaizi," Philip Clart, trans. In Clart and Scott, *Religious Publishing*, 187–232.

Yinxian tongzhi 鄞縣通志 (1935–1951). Zhang Chuanbao 張傳保, et al., ed. & comp. In *Zhongguo difangzhi jicheng, Zhejiang fuxianzhi ji* 中國地方志集成, 浙江府縣志輯. Volumes 16–18. Shanghai: Shanghai shudian chubanshe, 1993.

"Yinyangfeng: Chen Jitang fuji" 陰陽風 : 陳濟棠扶乩. *Yijing* 逸經 16 (1936): 52.

"Yishi zaping: Fuji zhibing" 醫事雜評 : 扶乩治病. *Shaoxing yiyao xuebao* 紹興醫藥學報 12.6 (1922): 13.

"Yizhou: Xuexiao dashi•Geren xinwen: Fuji yishi—Mou yaoren qing shenxian zhan guojia dashi" 一周:學校大事•個人新聞:扶乩異事:某要人請神仙占家國大事. *Qinghua shuqi zhoukan* 清華暑期週刊 5 (1934): 287–88.

You Youwei 游有維. *Shanghai jindai Fojiao jianshi* 上海近代佛教簡史. Shanghai: Huadong shifan daxue chubanshe, 1988.

Youtai xianguan biji 右台仙館筆記. Yu Yue 俞樾 (1821–1906). Shanghai: Shanghai guji chubanshe, 1986.

Yu, Anthony C. *State and Religion in China*. Chicago: Open Court Press, 2005.

Yu Chien-ming 游鑑明. *Yundongchang neiwai: Jindai Huazhong nüzi tiyu (1895–1937)* 運動場內外：近代華東地區的女子體育 (1895–1937). Taipei: Institute of Modern History, Academia Sinica, 2009.

Yü Chün-fang. *Kuan-yin: The Chinese Transformation of Avalokiteśvara*. New York: Columbia University Press, 2001.

Yü Chün-fang. *The Renewal of Buddhism in China: Chu-hung and the Late Ming Synthesis*. New York: Columbia University Press, 1981.

"Yu Jinhe fuji ji" 余晉龢扶乩記. *Dadi zhoubao* 大地週報 15 (1946): 9.

Yu Lingbo 于凌波. *Zhongguo jinxiandai Fojiao renwu zhi* 中國近現代佛教人物志. Beijing: Zongjiao wenwu chubanshe, 1995.

Yu Zhejun 郁喆雋. *Shenming yu shimin: Minguo shiqi Shanghai diqu yingshen saihui yanjiu* 神明與市民：民國時期上海地區迎神賽會研究. Shanghai: Shanghai Sanlian shudian, 2014.

Yung Sai-shing (Rong Shicheng) 容世誠. *Yueyun liusheng: Changpian gongye yu Guangdong quyi (1903–1953)* 粵韻留聲：唱片工業與廣東曲藝 (1903–1953). Hong Kong: Tiandi tushu, 2006.

Zarrow, Peter. *After Empire: The Conceptual Transformation of the Chinese State, 1885–1924*. Stanford: Stanford University Press, 2012.

Zarrow, Peter. *China in War and Revolution, 1895–1949*. London: Routledge, 2005.

Zeng Cun 曾材. "Huiyi Ningdu Chenghuangmiao" 回憶寧都城隍廟. In Luo Yong 羅勇 and Lin Shaoping 林曉平, eds., *Gannan miaohui yu minsu* 贛南廟會與民俗, 230–40. Hong Kong: International Hakka Studies Association, 1998.

Zhang Gang 張棡 (1860–1942). *Zhang Gang riji* 張棡日記, ed. Yu Xiong 俞雄. Shanghai: Shanghai shehui kexue chubanshe, 2003.

Zhang Hua 張化 et al., ed. and comp. *Shanghai zongjiao tonglan* 上海宗教通覽. Shanghai: Shanghai guji chubanshe, 2004.

Zhang Jia 張佳. "Shanghai shenshang jushi de zongjiao shenghuo yu Fojiao xiandaihua zhuanxing: Yi Wang Yiting (1867–1938) wei ge'an" 上海紳商居士的宗教生活與佛教現代化轉型：以王一亭 (1867–1938) 為個案. PhD diss., Chinese University of Hong Kong, 2014.

Zhang Jia 張佳. "Zhongguo Jishenghui suojian jindai shenshang jushi zhi Jigong xinyang" 中國濟生會所見近代紳商居士之濟公信仰. *Zongjiaoxue yanjiu* 宗教學研究 1 (2015): 105–14.

Zhang Weijing 張韋靜. "Dui pochu mixin yundong de shangque" 對破除迷信運動的商榷, *Ningbo Minguo ribao liu zhounian jinian ji ershi nian guoqing jinian hekan* 寧波民國日報六周年紀念暨二十年國慶紀念合刊 (1931), 90–92.

Zhang Xiantao. *The Origins of the Modern Chinese Press: The Influence of the Protestant Missionary Press in Late Qing China.* London: Routledge, 2007.

Zhang Xuesong 張雪松. *Fayu lingyan: Zhongguo fojiao xiandaihua lishi jinchengzhong de Yinguang fashi yanjiu* 法雨靈岩：中國佛教現代化歷史進程中的印光法師研究. Taipei: Fagu wenhua, 2011.

Zhang Zhihua 張志華. *Zhongguo Isilan wenhua yaolüe* 中國伊斯蘭文化要略. Yinchuan: Ningxia renmin chubanshe, 2010.

Zhao Mingjuan 趙明娟. "20 shiji shangbanye Zhejiang Daojiaoshi yanjiu" 20世紀上半葉浙江道教史研究. MA thesis, Zhejiang University, 2011.

Zheng Guo 鄭國. "Jindai geming yundong yu pochu mixin – Yi Xuzhou Chenghuangmiao weizhu de kaocha" 近代革命運動與破除迷信—以徐州城隍廟為主的考察. *Hefei shifan xueyuan xuebao* 合肥師範學院學報 26.2 (2008): 54–57.

Zheng Guo 鄭國, "Minguo qianqi mixin wenti yanjiu (1912–1928)" 民國前期迷信問題研究 (1912–1928). MA thesis, Shandong University, 2003.

Zhong Qiongning 鍾瓊寧. "Minchu Shanghai jushi Fojiao de fazhan (1912–1937)" 民初上海居士佛教的發展 (1912–1937). *Yuanguang Foxue xuebao* 圓光佛學學報 3 (1999): 155–90.

"Zhonghua minguo miaochan xingxue cujinhui xuanyan" 中華民國廟產興學促進會宣言. *Jiaoyu jikan* 教育季刊 1.2 (1930): 156–59.

Zhonghua minguoshi dang'an ziliao huibian, Diwuji, Diyibian. Series 5, pt. 1: *Wenhua (1)* 中華民國史檔案資料彙編，第5輯，第一編，文化(1). Nanjing: Jiangsu guji chubanshe, 1994.

Zhongxuan 中宣. "Pochu mixian zhi yiyi he banfa" 破除迷信之意義和辦法. *Shidai* 時代 1.3 (1929): 13–17.

Zhou Yumin 周育民. "Minguo shiqi yige wentan juzi jibixia de lingjie" 民國時期一個文壇巨子乩筆下的靈界. *Minjian zongjiao* 民間宗教 1 (1995): 37–55.

Zhou Zhenhe 周振鶴. *Suzhou fengsu* 蘇州風俗. 1928, reprint Shanghai: Wenyi chubanshe, 1989.

Zhou Zuoren 周作人. "Gua dou ji" 瓜豆集. In *Zhou Zuoren quanji* 周作人全集, vol. 4. Taipei: Landeng wenhua shiye, 1992.

Zhu Pingyi 祝平一. "Biwang xingmi: Ming Qing zhiji de Tianzhujiao yu *mixin de jiangou*" 闢妄醒迷：明清之際的天主教與「迷信」的建構. *Bulletin of the Institute of History and Philology, Academia Sinica* 84.4 (2013): 695–752.

VINCENT GOOSSAERT obtained his PhD at EPHE, Paris (Ecole pratique des hautes études, 1997), was a research fellow at CNRS (1998–2012) and is now Professor of Daoism and Chinese religions at EPHE, PSL; he has served as dean of its graduate school (2014–2018). He has been Visiting Professor at the Chinese University of Hong Kong, Geneva University, and Renmin University. His research deals with the social history of Chinese religion in late imperial and modern times. He is co-editor of *T'oung Pao*, a leading journal in sinology established in 1890. His published monographs include *L'interdit du bœuf en Chine. Agriculture, éthique et sacrifice* (Paris: Collège de France, Institut des Hautes Études Chinoises, 2005); *The Taoists of*
Peking, 1800–1949. A Social History of Urban Clerics (Cambridge: Harvard University Asia Center, 2007); *The Religious Question in Modern China*, with David A. Palmer (Chicago: University of Chicago Press, 2011; Levenson Prize 2013); *Livres de morale révélés par les dieux* (Paris: Belles-Lettres, 2012); *Bureaucratie et salut. Devenir un dieu en Chine* (Genève: Labor et Fides, 2017); and *Heavenly Masters. Two Thousand Years of the Daoist State* (2021).

PAUL R. KATZ received his B.A. from Yale in 1984 and his Ph.D. from Princeton in 1990. After teaching at different universities in Taiwan from 1991 to 2002, he joined the Institute of Modern History in 2002 and was promoted to the rank of Research Fellow in 2005, becoming Program Director of the Chiang Ching-kuo Foundation for International Scholarly Exchange that same year. His research centers on modern Chinese religious life, with his most recent monograph (*Religion in China and its Modern Fate*) being published in early 2014. At present, he is working on the interaction between Han and non-Han religious traditions in Southwest China.

Milton Keynes UK
Ingram Content Group UK Ltd.
UKHW030339071224
452074UK00003B/86